D0842731

JUDITH

VOLUME 40

THE ANCHOR BIBLE is a fresh approach to the world's greatest classic. Its object is to make the Bible accessible to the modern reader; its method is to arrive at the meaning of biblical literature through exact translation and extended exposition, and to reconstruct the ancient setting of the biblical story, as well as the circumstances of its transcription and the characteristics of its transcribers.

THE ANCHOR BIBLE is a project of international and interfaith scope: Protestant, Catholic, and Jewish scholars from many countries contribute individual volumes. The project is not sponsored by any ecclesiastical organization and is not intended to reflect any particular theological doctrine. Prepared under our joint supervision, THE ANCHOR BIBLE is an effort to make available all the significant historical and linguistic knowledge which bears on the interpretation of the biblical record.

THE ANCHOR BIBLE is aimed at the general reader with no special formal training in biblical studies; yet, it is written with most exacting standards of scholarship, reflecting the highest technical accomplishment.

This project marks the beginning of a new era of cooperation among scholars in biblical research, thus forming a common body of knowledge to be shared by all.

William Foxwell Albright
David Noel Freedman
GENERAL EDITORS

THE ANCHOR BIBLE

JUDITH

A NEW TRANSLATION
WITH INTRODUCTION
AND COMMENTARY
BY

Carey A. Moore

DOUBLEDAY & COMPANY, INC.
GARDEN CITY, NEW YORK
1985

Text Acknowledgements for JUDITH

Grateful acknowledgement is made to the following for permission to quote from their copyrighted material:

The Books of Esther and Judith by George T. Montague, Pamphlet Bible Series, 21, Paulist Press. Reprinted by permission of Paulist Press.

from *The Forgotten Language* by Erich Fromm. Copyright 1951, © 1979 by Erich Fromm. Reprinted by permission of Holt, Rinehart and Winston, Publishers.

The Book of Judith by Morton S. Enslin, Jewish Apocryphal Literature, vol. VII. Reprinted by permission of E. J. Brill, Leiden, Netherlands.

Artistry and Faith in the Book of Judith by Toni Anne Craven, University Microfilms International. Reprinted by permission of the author.

Excerpts from Judith are taken from the New American Bible, copyright © 1970, by the Confraternity of Christian Doctrine, Washington, D. C., and are used by permission of copyright owner. All rights reserved.

"Narrative Structure in the Book of Judith," *Protocol Series of the Colloquies of the Center for Hermeneutical Studies in Hellenistic and Modern Culture,* XII/17 (March 1974) by Luis Alonso-Schökel et al. Reprinted by permission of the Center for Hermeneutical Studies in Hellenistic and Modern Culture, Berkeley, California.

Arnaldo Momigliana, "Biblical Studies and Classical Studies: Simple Reflections about Historical Method," BA 45 (1982). Reprinted by permission of the editor, *The Biblical Archaeologist.*

T. Craven, "Artistry and Faith in the Book of Judith," *Semeia* 8 (1977). Reprinted by permission of the editor, *Semeia Studies.*

Brian McNeil, "Reflections on the Book of Judith," *The Downside Review* 96 (1978). Reprinted by permission of the editor, *Downside Review.*

Library of Congress Cataloging in Publication Data
Bible O.T. Apocrypha. Judith. English. 1985.
Judith: a new translation with introduction and commentary.

(The Anchor Bible; 40B)
Bibliography: pp. 109–17
Includes index.
1. Bible. O.T. Apocrypha. Judith—Commentaries.
I. Moore, Carey A., 1930– . II. Title.
III. Series: Bible. English. Anchor Bible. 1964;
v. 40B.
BS192.2.A11964.G3 vol. 40B 220.7′7s [229′.24077]
[BS1733]
ISBN 0-385-14424-5

Library of Congress Catalog Card Number 83-11694
Copyright © 1985 by Doubleday & Company, Inc.
All Rights Reserved
Printed in the United States of America
First Edition

To Ed and Fritz,
pastors skillful in making the Bible
relevant to everyday living

THE APOCRYPHA

The term "Apocrypha" (or "deuterocanonical books" in Roman Catholic usage) is popularly understood to describe the fifteen books or parts of books from the pre-Christian period that the Roman Catholic, Orthodox, and Eastern churches accept, wholly or partially, as canonical Scripture but Protestants and Jews do not. The designation and the definition are inaccurate on many counts. An apocryphon is literally a "hidden writing," kept secret from all but the initiate, being too exalted for the general public; virtually none of these books makes such a claim. Roman Catholics do not accept all of them as canonical Scripture, for 1 and 2 Esdras and the Prayer of Manasseh are not included in the official Catholic canon drawn up at the Council of Trent (1545–63). Many Protestant churches have no official decision declaring these books to be noncanonical; in fact, up to the last century they were included in most English Protestant Bibles.

What is certain is that these books did not find their way into the final Jewish Palestinian canon of Scripture. Thus, despite their Jewish origins (though parts of 2 Esdras are Christian and Latin in origin), they were preserved for the most part in Greek by Christians as a heritage from the Alexandrian Jewish community and their basic text is found in the codices of the LXX. However, recent discoveries, especially that of the Dead Sea Scrolls, have brought to light the original Hebrew or Aramaic texts of some of these books. Leaving aside the question of canonicity, Christians and Jews now unite in recognizing the importance of these books for tracing the history of Judaism and Jewish thought in the centuries between the last of the Hebrew Scriptures and the advent of Christianity.

PREFACE

Many people know the story of Judith. The name itself may not have that "instant name-recognition" so highly prized by the advertising world, but certainly the story's central event does. Whenever people asked me what I was working on and I replied, "A commentary on Judith," I consistently got the same response, whether they were college students, colleagues in the arts and sciences, or friends and acquaintances: "She's the gal who cut off the general's head, isn't she?" To be sure, they would differ on the particular word they used to describe Judith—"gal," "woman," "Jewess," etc.—but they all had the essence of the plot: "She's the one who cut off the general's head." Moreover, they usually said it with a certain amusement and approval, all of which would have delighted the ancient author, who intended to entertain and himself had a strong sense of humor. However, being of an ironic cast of mind, he would probably have preferred a description like "She was the saint who cut off the general's head."

Western artists have also delighted in the story of Judith, especially during the Renaissance, when, freed from many of the Church's earlier restrictions on depicting an artistic subject, an artist could give free expression to painting a biblical story that featured two of the most basic and universal concerns of men and women in any time and place: sex and death.

But just having the right ingredients does not automatically make a great story any more than it makes a great pie or cake. *How* the ingredients are treated is the secret, and as the old saying goes, "The proof of the pudding is in the eating." Even though Judith is a well-told story, it obviously did not please everyone; although the book was ultimately included in the Christian canon of the West, it was excluded from the Jewish Bible. The present volume is intended to show how understandable and defensible both decisions were.

Although the writing of an Anchor Bible commentary is an exacting and time-consuming activity, it is a much easier one if the commentator has a fascinating biblical book to work on, one filled with action, color, and controversy. The book of Judith has all of those qualities. Moreover, writing this commentary has been made much easier and more pleasant because of the efforts of a number of people, only a few of whom I shall mention here.

A scholar could not ask for a better editor than Professor David Noel Freedman: learned, judicious, concise, and supportive. Only he and I know how very much this volume has been strengthened by his efforts. Nor could a writer ask for more help and support from professional editors than I have

received from Ms. Eve F. Roshevsky and her Anchor Bible staff at Doubleday. Ms. Anna Jane Moyer, the Readers' Services Librarian at Gettysburg
College, has succeeded in securing for me, promptly and inexpensively, books
and articles that other scholars have had great difficulty in procuring. Nor am
I unmindful of my indebtedness to my alma mater, Gettysburg College,
which over the years has provided me the library, the teaching schedule, and
the sabbatical that enabled me to do this volume. But most of all, I am
mindful of my indebtedness to scholars, living and dead, whose books and
articles have increased my understanding and appreciation of the book of
Judith. If there are any points in this commentary where I have seen further
or more clearly than some of them, then it is because I was standing on their
shoulders, profiting from their labors.

Finally, I must observe to the reader what I have more than once observed
to my wife about Judith as presented by the ancient author: "I wouldn't have
wanted to have been married to her, but she sure would have been somebody
to watch!"

C. A. MOORE

CONTENTS

List of Illustrations

PRINCIPAL ABBREVIATIONS

1. PUBLICATIONS

AB   The Anchor Bible. Garden City, N.Y.: Doubleday, 1964–

AB 7B   Moore, Carey A. *Esther,* AB, vol. 7B. Garden City, N.Y.: Doubleday, 1971

AB 44   Moore, Carey A. *Daniel, Esther, and Jeremiah: The Additions.* Garden City, N.Y.: Doubleday, 1977

AFBJ   *Artistry and Faith in the Book of Judith,* Toni Anne Craven, SBLDS 70. Chico, Calif.: Schólars Press, 1983

ANET²   *Ancient Near Eastern Texts Relating to the Old Testament,* ed. J. B. Pritchard. 2d ed. Princeton: Princeton University Press, 1955

APAT   *Die Apokryphen und Pseudepigraphen des Alten Testamentes,* ed. E. E. Kautzsch, I. Tübingen: Mohr, 1900

APOT   *The Apocrypha and Pseudepigrapha of the Old Testament,* ed. R. H. Charles. 2 vols. Oxford: Clarendon Press, 1913

BA   Biblical Archeologist

BAR   Biblical Archaeology Review

BASOR   Bulletin of the American Schools of Oriental Research

BiblOr   Bibliotheca Orientalis

BZAW   Beihefte zur Zeitschrift für die Alttestamentliche Wissenschaft

CBQ   Catholic Biblical Quarterly

CJ   Classical Journal

EAEHL   *Encyclopedia of Archaeological Excavations in the Holy Land,* ed. Michael Avi-Yonah and E. Stern. 4 vols. Englewood Cliffs, N.J.: Prentice-Hall, 1975–78

EncJud   *Encyclopaedia Judaica.* 16 vols. Jerusalem: Keter Publishing House Jerusalem, 1971

ExpTim   The Expository Times

HDB   *A Dictionary of the Bible,* ed. James Hastings. 5 vols. New York: Charles Scribner's Sons, 1901

IDB   *The Interpreter's Dictionary of the Bible,* ed. G. A. Buttrick et al. 4 vols. New York: Abingdon Press, 1962

IOTG   *An Introduction to the Old Testament in Greek,* ed. H. B. Swete. Revised by R. R. Ottley. Oxford: Oxford University Press, 1914

JAOS   Journal of the American Oriental Society

JBL   Journal of Biblical Literature

JQR   Jewish Quarterly Review

Klio   Klio Beiträge zur Alten Geschichte

LSJ	Henry G. Liddell and Robert Scott, ed., *Greek-English Lexicon*. 9th ed. Revised by Henry S. Jones. 2 vols. Oxford: Oxford University Press, 1940. Reprinted 1948 and after
OTTV	*The Old Testament Text and Versions: The Hebrew Text in Transmission and the History of the Ancient Versions,* B. J. Roberts. University of Wales Press, 1951
PSBA	Proceedings of the Society of Biblical Archaeology
RB	Revue biblique
RSR	Recherches de science religieuse
SEÅ	Svensk exegetisk årsbok
TRev	Theologische Revue
TQ	Theologische Quartalschrift
VT	Vetus Testamentum
ZAW	Zeitschrift für die Alttestamentliche Wissenschaft
ZDMG	Zeitschrift der deutschen morgenländischen Gesellschaft
ZDPV	Zeitschrift des deutschen Palästina-Vereins

2. VERSIONS

Copt	The Coptic
Eth	The Ethiopic
GNB	The Good News Bible, 1979
JB	The Jerusalem Bible, 1966
KJ	The King James, or Authorized Version, 1611
LXX	The Septuagint
LXXᴬ	Codex Alexandrinus, fifth century A.D.
LXXᴮ	Codex Vaticanus, fourth century A.D.
LXXᴺ	Codex Basiliano-Vaticanus, eighth–ninth century A.D.
LXXˢ	Codex Sinaiticus, fourth century A.D.
LXXᵇ⁻ʷ	Greek minuscules
b	19; Rome, Chigi R. vi. 38
b	108; Rome, Vat. Gr. 330
c	64; Paris; Bibl. Nat. Gr. 2
d	107; Ferrara, Bibl. Comun. Gr. 188.1
e	46; Paris, Bibl. Nat. Coisl. Gr. 4
f	583; Paris, Bibl. Nat. Gr. 1087
g	76; Paris, Bibl. Nat. Gr. 4
h	55; Rome, Vat. Regin. Gr. 1
j	243; Paris, Bibl. Nat. Coisl. Gr. 8
k	58; Rome, Vat. Regin. Gr. 10
l	534; Paris, Bibl. Nat. Coisl. Gr. 18
m	126; Moscow, Syn-Bibl. Gr. 19
p	106; Ferrara, Bibl. Comun. Gr. 187.1
r	311; Moscow, Syn-Bibl. Gr. 354
s	130; Vienna, Hofbibl. Theol. Gr. 23

u	542; Paris, Bibl. Nat. Gr. 10
v	249; Rome, Vat. Pii II. Gr. 1
w	248; Rome, Vat. Gr. 346
NEB	The New English Bible, 1961, 1970
OL	The *Vetus Latina* (or Old Latin), based on the LXX
OLᶜ	Corbeiensis 7
OLᵐ	Munich MS 6239
OLᵒ	Orator. B. vii
OLᵖ	Pechianus
OLˢ	Sabatier
RSV	The Revised Standard Version, 1946, 1952 (Unless otherwise identified, quotations from other books of the Bible or Apocrypha are from the RSV.)
SG	The Chicago Bible, ed. Smith and Goodspeed, 1960
Syr	The Syriac
Vg	The Vulgate of Jerome, based on the Hebrew text

3. OTHER ABBREVIATIONS

Akk	Akkadian
Ant.	The *Jewish Antiquities* of Josephus, ca. A.D. 93
Ar	Arabic
Aram	Aramaic
Arm	Armenian
Bab	Babylonian
Gk	Greek
Heb	Hebrew
lit.	literally
min/s.	minuscule/s
mod.	modern
MS/S	manuscript/s
MT	The Masoretic Text
NT	The New Testament
OT	The Old Testament
Pers	Persian
vers/s.	version/s

GLOSSARY OF TERMS

Aramaism A characteristic feature of Aramaic occurring in another language or dialect

Chiasmus The inversion of the order of syntactical elements in the second of two juxtaposed and syntactically parallel phrases, clauses, or even sections

Dittography The accidental repetition by a scribe, as he copies a manuscript, of a letter, word, or section of material

Gloss In textual criticism a term for an explanatory comment in the margin or between the lines which some later scribe incorporated into the text he was copying

Haplography The accidental omission by a scribe, as he copies a manuscript, of a letter, word, or section of material

Hapax legomenon A word or form occurring once and only once

Hebraism A characteristic feature of Hebrew occurring in another language or dialect, e.g., Gk *kai egeneto* is a Hebraism for Heb *wayĕhî*

Hendiadys A rhetorical figure using two nouns connected by "and" to express one idea, e.g., "to the north and east of" equals "to the northeast of"

Homeoteleuton A case of haplography induced by the eye of the copyist skipping from the first occurrence to the second such occurrence of the word or ending, with the omission of the intervening words or letters

Merismus A literary device in which two extremes of any series are given, but they are inclusive of any and everything in between

Minuscule Either as adjective or noun, pertaining to medieval Greek manuscripts copied in a script later and smaller than that of the uncial (see below)

Passim Latin for "at different places"

Recension A version brought about by the revision of a text based on a critical evaluation of other texts; here especially, the stages reached in a series of attempts to bring the Greek translation of the OT into line with a Hebrew text prevailing at each stage and in a given location

Semiticism Here a characteristic feature of either Hebrew or Aramaic occurring in a non-Semitic language

Terminus a quo Latin for "end from which," i.e., the earliest date

Terminus ad quem Latin for "end to which," i.e., the latest date

Uncial Either as adjective or noun, pertaining to early medieval Greek manuscripts copied in large, capital letters; uncials are conventionally designed with uppercase *sigla*, e.g., Codex Vaticanus is LXX[B]

Vorlage German for "prototype," i.e., the original or model after which anything is copied or patterned

TRANSCRIPTION EQUIVALENTS

Hebrew and Aramaic

' = aleph	k = kaph
' = ayin	q = qoph
h = he	s = samekh
ḥ = heth	ṣ = tsade
ṭ = teth	ś = sin
y = yodh	š = shin

The remaining Hebrew letters have natural English equivalents. Often in this commentary, especially where the vocalization of the Hebrew word is not in question, only the consonants have been written, as this was the way Hebrew was written in the pre-masoretic stage.

Where possible, personal names in the present translation are the familiar anglicized spellings of the OT rather than precise transliterations of the Greek text, that is, the Gk *Ozeias* in 6:15 is rendered "Uzziah."

Greek

e = epsilon	u = upsilon
z = zeta	ph = phi
ē = eta	ch = chi
th = theta	ps = psi
x = xi	ō = omega

The remaining Greek letters have natural English equivalents.

JUDITH
A Translation

I. Nebuchadnezzar's War with King Arphaxad (1:1–16 [Vg 1:1–12])

1 ¹ It was the twelfth year of the reign of Nebuchadnezzar, who ruled over the Assyrians from his capital, Nineveh, that Arphaxad was ruling over the Medes from Ecbatana. ² (Arphaxad had surrounded Ecbatana with walls of hewn stones four and a half feet thick and nine feet long, and the walls he had made one hundred and five feet high and seventy-five feet wide. ³ At its gates he had placed towers one hundred and fifty feet high, with foundations ninety feet thick. ⁴ He had designed its gates, which were one hundred and five feet high and sixty feet wide, to allow his army of mighty men to parade forth, with his infantry in full formation.) ⁵ In that year King Nebuchadnezzar went to war against King Arphaxad in the Great Plain (this plain is on the borders of Rages). ⁶ There rallied to him all the inhabitants of the highlands, all those living along the Euphrates, the Tigris, and the Hydaspes, and in the plains, King Arioch of the Elymaeans. Thus, many nations had mustered to join the forces of the Cheleoudites.

⁷ Nebuchadnezzar king of the Assyrians also contacted all the inhabitants of Persia and all those living in the West: those living in Cilicia and Damascus, Lebanon and Anti-Lebanon, all those living along the coast, ⁸ those among the peoples of Carmel and Gilead and those in Upper Galilee and the great valley of Esdraelon, ⁹ all those in Samaria and its towns, and beyond the Jordan as far as Jerusalem, Betane, Chelus, Kadesh, the brook of Egypt, Tahpanhes, Rameses, and all the land of Goshen, ¹⁰ beyond Tanis and Memphis, and all those living in Egypt as far away as the borders of Ethiopia. ¹¹ But all those living in that entire area ignored the call of Nebuchadnezzar king of the Assyrians and would not join him in the campaign; for they did not fear him but regarded him as an ordinary man. Therefore, they sent his envoys away, empty-handed and mortified.

¹² Nebuchadnezzar was so incensed at this entire region that he swore by his throne and kingdom that he would get revenge on all the territories of Cilicia, Damascene, and Syria, and would put to the

sword all those living in the land of Moab, the Ammonites, all Judea, and all those living in Egypt as far as the shores of the two seas.

¹³ In the seventeenth year he marshaled his forces against King Arphaxad; and in this battle he defeated him, routing Arphaxad's entire army and all his cavalry and chariots. ¹⁴ He occupied his towns and then turned to Ecbatana, subduing its towers and looting its bazaars, thereby reducing its magnificence to a mockery. ¹⁵ He caught Arphaxad in the mountains of Rages and riddled him with his javelins, thus making an end of him, once and for all. ¹⁶ Then he returned with his spoils to Nineveh, he and his entire motley army, an enormous horde of soldiers. There he and his army recuperated and feasted for four whole months.

II. Nebuchadnezzar Plots His Revenge
Against the West
(2:1–13 [Vg 2:1–6])

2 ¹ Then, in the eighteenth year on the twenty-second day of the first month, the decision was made in the palace of Nebuchadnezzar king of the Assyrians to take revenge on the whole region, just as he had promised. ² Summoning all his ministers and nobles, he presented them with his secret strategy; and with his own lips he reviewed for them the full insult of that entire region, ³ so that they resolved to destroy everyone who had not answered his appeal.

⁴ After he had perfected his plan, Nebuchadnezzar king of the Assyrians summoned Holofernes, the general in command of his armies and second in command to himself, and said to him, ⁵ "Thus says the Great King, lord of the whole world: Leave our presence and take with you experienced soldiers, as many as one hundred and twenty thousand infantry and twelve thousand cavalry, ⁶ and march out against all the region to the west, for they ignored my call. ⁷ Tell them to prepare for me earth and water, because in my rage I am about to come upon them, and I will cover every square inch of land with the feet of my army, and I will let them be looted by my troops. ⁸ Their wounded will fill their ravines and gullies! Every river will be filled to overflowing with their corpses! ⁹ I will send them away as captives to the ends of the whole world. ¹⁰ As for you, go and occupy all their

territory for me in advance. If they surrender to you, hold them for me until the time comes for me to punish them. [11] But on the rebellious show no mercy. Let them be slaughtered and looted throughout your territory. [12] For as surely as I and my powerful kingdom live, I have spoken! I will accomplish these things by my own hand. [13] As for you, don't neglect a single one of your lord's commands but execute them fully, just as instructed. And don't delay in doing it!"

III. General Holofernes Undertakes His Campaign Against the West
(2:14–3:10 [Vg 2:7–3:15])

2 [14] After withdrawing from his lord's presence, Holofernes summoned all the marshals, generals, and officers of the Assyrian army [15] and mustered picked men by divisions as his lord had instructed him, one hundred and twenty thousand infantry and twelve thousand mounted bowmen. [16] He organized them as a great army is marshaled. [17] He also took an enormous number of camels, asses, and mules for carrying their baggage and innumerable sheep, oxen, and goats for their food [18] as well as ample rations for every man and a generous amount of gold and silver from the royal palace.

[19] He then set out on his campaign, he and his entire army, to go ahead of King Nebuchadnezzar and to smother the whole western region with their chariots, cavalry, and picked infantry. [20] Along with them there went out a motley crowd like locusts, like the dust of the earth, countless because of their numbers.

[21] They set out from Nineveh on a three-day march to the plain of Bectileth, and they encamped opposite Bectileth near the mountain north of Upper Cilicia. [22] From there, Holofernes advanced into the highlands with his whole army: infantry, cavalry, and chariots. [23] He cut his way through Put and Lud and plundered all the Rassisites and Ishmaelites living on the edge of the desert south of Cheleon. [24] Then, crossing the Euphrates and proceeding through Mesopotamia, he razed all the walled towns along Wadi Abron as far as the sea. [25] He occupied the territory of Cilicia and slaughtered all who resisted him. Then he came to the southern borders of Japheth, facing Arabia. [26] Surrounding all the Midianites, he set their tents on fire and plun-

dered their sheepfolds. ²⁷ Descending upon the plain of Damascus during the wheat harvest, he set fire to all their fields, destroyed their
flocks and herds, sacked their towns, stripped their plains, and put all
their young men to the sword.

²⁸ So fear and dread of him possessed those living along the seacoast:
those in Sidon and Tyre, those living in Sur and Okina, and all those
living in Jamnia. Those living in Azotus and Ascalon were also terrified of him.

3 ¹ Therefore, they sent him envoys to sue for peace and say, ² "We,
the servants of the great king Nebuchadnezzar, lie prostrate before
you. Treat us as you please. ³ Our buildings, all our land, every wheat
field, the flocks and herds, all the sheepfolds of our encampments—
they are yours! Treat them as seems best to you. ⁴ Our towns and their
inhabitants are your slaves. Come and treat them as you see fit."

⁵ After the envoys had come and reported to Holofernes this mes-
sage, ⁶ he went down with his army to the coast, stationed garrisons in
the walled towns, and took choice men from them as auxiliaries.
⁷ These people and all those in the surrounding countryside welcomed
him with garlands and dancing and tambourines. ⁸ Yet he demolished
all their sanctuaries and cut down all their sacred poles. It was granted
to him to destroy all the gods of the area so that all the nations should
worship Nebuchadnezzar alone—that every dialect and tribe should
call upon him as god!

⁹ Then he advanced toward Esdraelon, near Dothan, which is oppo-
site the great ridge of Judea. ¹⁰ He encamped between Geba and
Scythopolis and stayed there a full month so as to collect all the supplies for his army.

IV. Israel's Reaction to Holofernes' Threatened
Invasion of Judea
(4:1–15 [Vg 4:1–16])

4 ¹ When the Israelites living in Judea heard of how Holofernes, the
ranking commander of Nebuchadnezzar king of the Assyrians, had
treated the nations, sacking and destroying their sanctuaries, ² they

were terrified at his approach and alarmed for Jerusalem and the Temple of the Lord their God. [3] (For they had returned from exile only a short time before; and all the people of Judea had been reunited, and the sacred utensils, the altar, and the Temple had just recently been rededicated after they had been defiled.) [4] So they alerted all the territory of Samaria, Kona, Beth-horon, Belmain, Jericho, Choba, Aesora, and the valley of Salem. [5] They went ahead and secured all the summits of the high hills, fortified the villages on them, and stored up their food in preparation for war (for their fields had just been harvested).

[6] Joakim the high priest, who was in Jerusalem at that time, wrote to those living in Bethulia and Bethomesthaim, which is opposite Esdraelon facing the plain near Dothan, [7] telling them to occupy the passes up into the hill country because access into Judea was through them; and it would be easy to prevent an army from entering (for the approach was only wide enough for two men at a time to pass).

[8] The Israelites did as they had been ordered by the high priest Joakim and the Council of all the people of Israel in session at Jerusalem. [9] Most fervently they cried out to God, every man of Israel, and they humbled themselves with much fasting. [10] They put on sackcloth, they and their wives and children, their cattle, every resident alien, and every hired or purchased servant. [11] All the Israelite men, women, and children living in Jerusalem prostrated themselves before the Temple and put ashes on their head and spread out their sackcloth before the Lord. [12] They even draped the altar with sackcloth; and with one voice they cried out to the God of Israel, fervently begging that he not allow their children to be carried off or their women raped or the towns of their heritage destroyed or the Temple profaned and reviled to the malicious delight of the heathen. [13] So the Lord heard their prayers and looked kindly on their distress.

For many days the people throughout Judea and in Jerusalem kept on fasting before the sanctuary of the Omnipotent Lord. [14] Wearing sackcloth around their loins, Joakim the high priest and all the priests who officiated before the Lord and those who ministered to the Lord offered the regular burnt offering, the votive, and the voluntary offerings of the people. [15] With ashes on their turbans, they cried to the Lord with all their might to look favorably on the whole House of Israel.

V. Achior, the Ammonite, Reviews for Holofernes the Religious History of the Jews (5:1–21 [Vg 5:1–25])

5 ¹ When it was reported to Holofernes, the ranking commander of the Assyrian forces, that the Israelites had prepared for war and that they had closed the mountain passes, garrisoned all the high hilltops, and laid traps in the plains, ² he was furious. Summoning all the rulers of Moab and the generals of Ammon and all the governors of the coastal region, ³ he said to them, "Now tell me, you Canaanites, who is this people that lives in the hill country? What towns do they inhabit? How big is their army? In what does their strength or power consist? Who is their king? Who commands their army? ⁴ And why have they, of all the people living in the West, refused to come and meet me?"

⁵ Then Achior, the leader of the Ammonites, said to him, "May my lord please listen to the advice of your servant. I will tell you the truth about this people living in the hill country near here. Nothing false shall come from your servant's mouth.

⁶ "These people are descended from the Chaldeans. ⁷ At one time they settled in Mesopotamia because they did not want to worship the gods of their ancestors who were in Chaldea. ⁸ (They had abandoned the ways of their ancestors and worshiped the God of Heaven, the god they had come to know. When the Chaldeans drove them out from the presence of their gods, they fled to Mesopotamia and settled there for a long while.) ⁹ Later, their god told them to leave the place where they were staying and go on to the land of Canaan. So they settled there and accumulated much wealth in gold, silver, and livestock.

¹⁰ "When a famine spread over the land of Canaan, they went down to Egypt and settled there as long as there was food. There they became so numerous that it was impossible to count them. ¹¹ So the king of Egypt turned against them and exploited them by forcing them to make bricks. He degraded them by making them slaves. ¹² But they cried out to their god, and he afflicted all the land of Egypt with incurable plagues. So the Egyptians expelled them.

¹³ "Then God dried up the Red Sea for them ¹⁴ and led them by the way of Sinai and Kadesh-Barnea. They drove out all the inhabitants of

the desert [15] and lived in the land of the Amorites. So strong were they that they destroyed all the Heshbonites; and crossing the Jordan, they took possession of all the hill country, [16] driving out before them the Canaanites, the Perizzites, the Jebusites, the Shechemites, and all the Girgashites. There they settled for a long while. [17] And as long as they did not sin against their god, they prospered; for theirs is a god who hates wrongdoing. [18] But when they abandoned the path he had laid down for them, they were devastated in many battles and were carried off as captives to a foreign land. The temple of their god was leveled to the ground, and their towns were occupied by their enemies. [19] But now that they have returned to their god, they have come back from the places where they had been scattered. They have regained Jerusalem, where their sanctuary is, and have reoccupied the hill country because it was uninhabited.

[20] "So now, my master and lord, if there is any oversight in this people, if they are sinning against their god and we can detect this offense among them, then we may go up and force them to fight. [21] But if this nation is not guilty, then let my lord please bypass them. For their lord and god will defend them, and we shall become the laughingstock of the whole world."

VI. Holofernes Rewards Achior for His Sound Advice
(5:22–6:21 [Vg 5:26–6:21])

5   [22] When Achior had finished saying all these things, all the people standing around the tent began muttering; and Holofernes' officers as well as those inhabiting the coastal region and Moab suggested thrashing him, [23] saying, "We're not afraid of the Israelites! They're a weak people, unable to wage war. [24] So let's go ahead, Lord Holofernes. Your army will eat them up!"

6   [1] After the hubbub of the men outside the council had died down, Holofernes, the ranking commander of the Assyrian army, said to Achior in front of all the assembled foreigners, [2] "So who are you, Achior and you Ephraimite mercenaries, that you play the prophet among us as you have done today, advising us not to make war against the people of Israel because their god will protect them? Who is god

except Nebuchadnezzar? He will send his forces and wipe them off the face of the earth! Their god won't save them. ³ On the contrary, we, Nebuchadnezzar's servants, will strike them down as if they were one man. They cannot withstand the strength of our cavalry. ⁴ With it we will destroy them. Their hills will be drunk with their blood, and their plains filled with their corpses. Not even their footsteps will survive! They will be completely wiped out! So says King Nebuchadnezzar, lord of the whole world. For he has spoken, and his commands will not be in vain.

⁵ "As for you, Achior, you Ammonite mercenary who has said these things in your day of insults, you shall not again see my face from this day until I take my revenge on this nation which came out of Egypt. ⁶ When I return, then the sword of my army and the spear of my servants will run you through, and you shall fall among their wounded. ⁷ My servants will now 'deliver' you to the hill country and leave you at one of the towns in the passes. ⁸ You will not die—until you are destroyed with them! ⁹ And if in your heart you believe that they won't be taken, then don't look so depressed. I have spoken, and not one of my words will fail to come true." ¹⁰ Then Holofernes ordered those servants who waited on him in his tent to seize Achior and take him away to Bethulia and hand him over to the Israelites.

¹¹ So his servants seized him and took him out of the camp into the plain; and from the plain they went up into the hill country and came to the springs below Bethulia. ¹² As soon as the men of the town saw them, they grabbed their weapons and went out of the town to the top of the hill; and all the slingers were pelting them with stones to prevent them from coming up. ¹³ But ducking under the hill, Holofernes' men tied Achior up, left him at the foot of the hill, and returned to their lord.

¹⁴ When the Israelites came down from their town and found him, they untied him and took him back to Bethulia and brought him before the magistrates of their town, ¹⁵ who at the time were Uzziah son of Micah from the tribe of Simeon, Chabris son of Gothoniel, and Charmis son of Melchiel. ¹⁶ These called together all the elders of the town, and all their young men and their women came hurrying to the assembly. They stood Achior in the center of all the people, and Uzziah questioned him about what had happened. ¹⁷ He answered by relating to them the decisions of Holofernes' war council, what he himself had said in the presence of the Assyrian leaders, and how

Holofernes had boasted of what he would do to the House of Israel. [18] Then the people prostrated themselves in worship of God and cried out, [19] "Lord God of Heaven, consider their arrogance and pity the sorry plight of our nation. Look kindly this day on those consecrated to you." [20] They then reassured Achior and commended him highly. [21] Uzziah took him from the assembly to his own home and gave a banquet for the elders, and throughout that night they called upon the God of Israel for help.

VII. Holofernes Begins an Effective Siege Against Bethulia (7:1–32 [Vg 7:1–25])

7 [1] The next day Holofernes ordered his entire army and all the people who had joined him as allies to break camp and move on Bethulia and to seize the passes up into the hill country and so make war against the Israelites. [2] So every able-bodied man of them marched off that day, and the strength of their fighting force was a hundred and seventy thousand infantrymen and twelve thousand cavalry, not counting the baggage train and the men who managed it, an enormous number. [3] They encamped in the valley near Bethulia, beside the spring; and they deployed on a wide front from Dothan to Belbaim, and in depth from Bethulia to Cyamon, which faces Esdraelon. [4] When the Israelites saw this horde, they were quite alarmed and said to one another, "They will now strip clean the entire land. Neither high mountains nor valleys nor hills will bear their weight!" [5] After getting their weapons and lighting beacons on their towers, they stood on guard all that night.

[6] On the second day Holofernes deployed his entire cavalry in full view of the Israelites who were in Bethulia. [7] He reconnoitered the approaches to their town; he found the water sources, seized them, and after posting detachments of soldiers over them, he returned to his main army.

[8] All the rulers of the children of Esau, the leaders of the people of Moab, and the generals of the coastal region then came to him and said, [9] "If our master will listen to our advice, then his army will suffer no losses. [10] For this people, the Israelites, do not rely on their spears

but on the height of the mountains where they live, since it is no easy task to get to the top of their mountains. [11] So now, master, don't fight them in a pitched battle, and not a single man of your army will fall. [12] Remain in camp and keep all your men with you while your servants take possession of the spring which flows from the foot of the mountain [13] because it is from there all the people of Bethulia get their water. So thirst will destroy them, and they will surrender their town. Meanwhile, we and our people will go up onto the surrounding hilltops and camp there so as to prevent any man from leaving the town. [14] They and their women and children will starve, and before the sword touches them they will be lying in the streets outside their homes. [15] So you will make them pay dearly for rebelling against you and for not being conciliatory."

[16] Because this advice was agreeable to Holofernes and his entire staff, he ordered it to be done just as they had recommended. [17] So a contingent of Ammonites, along with five thousand Assyrians, moved forward; they encamped in the valley and secured the Israelites' water sources and springs. [18] Meanwhile the children of Esau and the Ammonites went up and encamped in the hill country opposite Dothan, and they sent some of their number to the southeast toward Egrebel, which is near Chous on the Wadi Mochmur. The rest of the Assyrian army encamped in the plain and covered every square inch of it; their tents and supplies formed an immense encampment, since they constituted such a very great number.

[19] The Israelites then cried out to the Lord their God, for their courage had failed them because all their enemies had surrounded them, and there was no escape from them. [20] The entire Assyrian army (the infantry, chariots, and cavalry) had blockaded them for thirty-four days, and all the water reserves were depleted for all the inhabitants of Bethulia. [21] The cisterns were going dry, and no one could quench his thirst for even a day because the water had to be rationed. [22] Their children were listless, and the women and young men fainted from thirst and were collapsing in the town's streets and gateways, for they no longer had any strength.

[23] So all the people, including the young men, women, and children, gathered around Uzziah and the other town leaders and shouted in protest. And in the presence of all the elders they said, [24] "May God judge between you and us! For you did us a great injustice by not making peace with the Assyrians. [25] We have no one to help us now.

Rather, God has sold us into their hands, to sprawl before them in thirst and utter helplessness. ²⁶ Contact them at once and hand over the whole town to be sacked by Holofernes' people and all his army, ²⁷ for it is better for us to be sacked by them. For although we shall become slaves, our lives will be spared; and we shall not witness with our own eyes the death of our little ones or our wives and children breathing their last. ²⁸ We call to witness against you heaven and earth and our God, the Lord of our ancestors, who punishes us for our sins and for the sins of our fathers, that you do what we have said, today."

²⁹ Then there arose a bitter and general lamentation throughout the assembly, and they cried loudly to the Lord God. ³⁰ Uzziah then said to them, "Courage, my brothers! Let us hold out for five more days. By then the Lord our God will have pity on us, for he will not abandon us altogether. ³¹ But if these days go by and no help comes to us, then I will do as you say." ³² He then dismissed the men to their various stations (they went on the walls and towers of their town) and sent the women and children to their homes. But throughout the town they were very dejected.

VIII. Judith, a Pious Widow of Bethulia, Gets Permission to Carry Out Her Secret Plan (8:1–36 [Vg 8:1–34])

8 ¹ News of what had just happened reached Judith daughter of Merari son of Ox, son of Joseph, son of Oziel, son of Elkiah, son of Ananias, son of Gideon, son of Raphain, son of Ahitub, son of Elijah, son of Hilkiah, son of Eliab, son of Nathanael, son of Shelumiel, son of Zurishaddai, son of Israel. ² Her husband Manasseh, who belonged to the same tribe and family, had died during the barley harvest. ³ (He was supervising those binding the sheaves in the field when he suffered sunstroke. He took to his bed and died in his hometown of Bethulia, and was buried with his ancestors in the field between Dothan and Balamon.) ⁴ Now Judith had been a widow in her home for three years and four months. ⁵ She had made a shelter for herself on the roof of her home and wore sackcloth around her waist and dressed in widow's clothing. ⁶ She fasted every day of her widowhood, except for sabbath eve, the sabbath itself, the eve of the new moon, the new moon itself, and the joyous feasts of the House of Israel. ⁷ She was also shapely and beautiful. Moreover, her husband Manasseh had left her gold and silver, male and female servants, livestock, and fields; and she had remained on her estate. ⁸ Yet there was no one who spoke ill of her, so devoutly did she fear God.

⁹ In any event, she heard about the people's bitter attack against the magistrate because they had been demoralized by the lack of water. Judith had also heard about the response which Uzziah had made to them, how he had promised them to surrender the town to the Assyrians after five days. ¹⁰ She sent the maid in charge of all her property to summon Uzziah, Chabris, and Charmis, the elders of her town.

¹¹ After they had arrived, she said to them, "Please hear me out, magistrates of the citizens of Bethulia. For the advice you offered the people today is not sound. And you confirmed this oath you made between God and yourselves, promising to surrender the town to our enemies unless the Lord comes to your aid within that time. ¹² But now who are you to test God this day and to set yourselves above God among mortals? ¹³ You are putting the Omnipotent Lord to the test, but you will never learn anything! ¹⁴ If you cannot plumb the depths of a person's heart or understand the thoughts of his mind, then how can you fathom God, who made all these things, or read his mind or understand his reasoning? No, my brothers, do not provoke the anger of the Lord our God. ¹⁵ For if he does not choose to help us within those five days, he still has the power to protect us as long as he wants or even to destroy us in the presence of our enemies. ¹⁶ But as for you, do not impose conditions on the Lord our God; for God is not to be threatened as a man is or to be cajoled as a mere mortal. ¹⁷ Rather, as we wait for his deliverance, let us call upon him to help us. He will listen to our voice, if he is so disposed.

¹⁸ "For there has not been in our generation, nor is there among us today a tribe or family, a rural area or town that worships man-made gods, as was the case in former times. ¹⁹ That is why our ancestors were handed over to be slaughtered and sacked and so fell in a great catastrophe before our enemies. ²⁰ But as for us, we recognize no other God than him; therefore we may hope that he will not spurn us or any of our nation. ²¹ For if we are captured, then all Judea will be exposed, and our sanctuary will be looted; and we will answer with our blood for their desecration. ²² The slaughter of our brothers, the captivity of the land, the desolation of our heritage—all this he will bring upon our

heads among the nations wherever we serve as slaves; we shall be an offense and a disgrace in the sight of our masters! [23] For our servitude will not develop into favor; rather, the Lord our God will turn it into disgrace.

[24] "So then, my brothers, let us set an example for our countrymen. For their lives depend upon us; and the sanctuary, both the building and its altar, rests upon us. [25] All this being so, let us give thanks to the Lord our God, who is putting us to the test, just as he did to our ancestors. [26] Remember how he treated Abraham; how he tested Isaac; and what happened to Jacob in Syrian Mesopotamia while he was working as a shepherd for Laban, his mother's brother? [27] For he has not tested us, as he did them, to search their hearts; nor is he taking vengeance on us. Rather, the Lord scourges those who come near him so as to admonish them."

[28] Then Uzziah said to her, "All that you have said you have spoken with good intentions, and there is no one who can take issue with you. [29] For today is not the first time that your wisdom has been evident; for from your earliest days all the people have recognized your good sense and sound judgment. [30] But the people were terribly thirsty and so forced us to say what we told them and made us take an oath we cannot violate. [31] So now you pray for us, for you are a devout woman! Then God will send a downpour to fill our cisterns, and we will no longer be fainting from thirst."

[32] "Listen to me," said Judith to them, "I am going to do something which will go down among the children of our people for endless generations. [33] As for you, stand at the gate tonight, and I will leave with my maid. But within the period after which you promised to surrender the town to our enemies, the Lord will deliver Israel by my hand. [34] But you must not inquire into the affair; for I will not tell you what I am going to do until it is accomplished."

[35] "Go to it!" said Uzziah and the magistrates to her, "May the Lord God go before you to take revenge on our enemies!" [36] So they left her rooftop shelter and went to their posts.

IX. Judith Prays God to Help Her
(9:1–14 [Vg 9:1–19])

9 ¹ Then Judith prostrated herself, put ashes on her head, and uncovered the sackcloth she had been wearing. And just as the evening's incense offering was being offered in the Temple at Jerusalem, Judith cried aloud to the Lord and said, ² "Lord, the God of my ancestor Simeon, into whose hand you put a sword to take revenge on the foreigners who had violated the virgin's womb, uncovering her thighs to her shame and polluting her womb to her dishonor. For you said, 'This shall not be done!' Yet they did it. ³ So you handed over their leaders to slaughter and their bed, blushing for her deceived, to bloodshed. You struck down the slaves with the princes and the princes upon their thrones. ⁴ You handed over their wives for rape and their daughters for slavery and all their spoils for distribution among your beloved children, who had been so zealous for you and had been appalled at the pollution of their blood and had called upon you for help. God, my God, hear me also—a widow!

⁵ "For you are responsible for all these things and for what preceded and what followed them. You designed the present and the future; and what you had in mind has happened. ⁶ The things you have planned present themselves and say, 'Here we are!' For all your ways are prepared beforehand, and you judge with foreknowledge.

⁷ "Here are the greatly reinforced Assyrians, boasting of their horses and riders, priding themselves in the strength of their infantry, trusting in shields and javelins, in bows and slings! They do not know that you are 'the Lord who crushes wars; ⁸ the Lord is your name.' Dash their might by your powers; in your anger bring down their strength! For they plan to desecrate your sanctuary, to defile the tabernacle, the resting place of your glorious name, to knock off the horns of your altar with the sword! ⁹ Observe their arrogance and bring your fury on their heads: put into my hand—a widow's—the strength I need. ¹⁰ By the guile of my lips strike down the slave with the ruler and the ruler with his servant. Break their pride by the hand of a female! ¹¹ For your strength does not depend upon numbers nor your might upon powerful men. Rather, you are the God of the humble; you are the ally of the

insignificant, the champion of the weak, the protector of the despairing, the savior of those without hope.

12 "Please, please, God of my father and God of Israel's heritage, ruler of heaven and earth, creator of the waters, king of all your creation, hear my prayer: 13 Grant me a beguiling tongue for wounding and bruising those who have terrible designs against your covenant and your sacred house, even against Mount Zion and the house your children possess. 14 Demonstrate to every nation and every tribe that you are God, the God of all power and might, and there is no one who protects the people of Israel but you."

X. After Prettying Herself Up, Judith Goes to the Camp of the Enemy (10:1–17 [Vg 10:1–16])

10 1 When Judith had stopped calling on the God of Israel and had finished saying all these things, 2 she arose from her prostrate position, summoned her maid, and went down into the house where she spent her sabbaths and feasts. 3 She removed the sackcloth she had been wearing and took off her widow's dress. Then she bathed all over with water, anointed herself with rich perfume, fixed her hair, put a tiara on it, and dressed herself in the clothes she used to wear on the joyous occasions when her husband Manasseh was alive. 4 Then she slipped sandals on her feet and put on her anklets and bracelets, her rings and earrings, and all her jewelry. (She had made herself very fetching so as to catch the attention of the men who would see her.) 5 She then handed her maid a skin of wine and a jug of oil, filled a bag with roasted grain, dried fig cakes, and pure bread; then she packed all her dishes and had her maid carry them.

6 They then went toward the town gate of Bethulia and found Uzziah standing there with the other town elders, Chabris and Charmis. 7 And when they saw her (for her face was so transformed and her clothes so different), they were much struck by her beauty. They said to her, 8 "May the God of our ancestors grant you favor and fulfill your plans so that the Israelites may glory and Jerusalem exult!" She bowed to them and 9 said to them, "Order the town gate to be opened for me, and I will go out and accomplish the things you have just

mentioned to me." So they ordered the young men to open up for her, just as she had asked, [10] and they did so. When Judith went out, accompanied by her maid, the men of the town kept staring after her until she had gone down the hill and crossed the valley, where they lost sight of her.

[11] As the women were going straight on through the valley, an Assyrian patrol came upon her, [12] took her into custody, and demanded, "What is your nationality? Where are you coming from? And where are you going?" "I am a daughter of the Hebrews," she replied, "and I am running away from them because you are about to eat them up! [13] So I am on my way to Holofernes himself, the general in command of your army, with reliable information, and only in his presence will I indicate a way by which he can go and conquer all the hill country without risking life or limb of his men."

[14] As the men listened to her explanation and studied her face, they were much struck by her beauty, so they said to her, [15] "By hurrying down to our lord's presence you have saved your life. So now proceed to his headquarters, and some of us will escort you and deliver you into his hands. [16] And when you are standing before him, don't be afraid. Tell him what you have just told us, and he will treat you well." [17] They then detailed from their number a hundred men to conduct her and her attendant, and these led them to Holofernes' quarters.

XI. Judith Goes to Holofernes Himself and Presents "Inside" Information (10:18–11:23 [Vg 10:17–11:21])

10   [18] There was a general stir throughout the camp as word of her arrival spread from tent to tent. And they came and crowded around her as she stood outside Holofernes' tent until they told him about her. [19] They were struck by her beauty; and judging by her, they speculated on the Israelites, saying to one another, "Who can despise these people when they have such women among them? It is not wise to let a single male of theirs survive; for if they are let go, they will be able to beguile the whole world!"

[20] Then Holofernes' bodyguard and all his personal servants came out and led her into the tent. [21] Holofernes was resting on his bed

under a canopy, which was woven of purple, gold, emeralds, and other precious stones. [22] When they had announced her, he came out into the front part of the tent, preceded by silver lamps. [23] When Judith came before him and his attendants, all were struck by her beautiful face.

When she had prostrated herself and done obeisance to him, his servants helped her to her feet. **11** [1] Then Holofernes said to her, "Courage, woman! Don't be afraid. For I have never hurt anyone who chose to serve Nebuchadnezzar, king of the whole world. [2] But as for your people who occupy the hill country, if they had not insulted me, I would not have raised my spear against them. They brought this upon themselves! [3] In any event, tell me, why did you run away from them and come to us? You are safe now. Don't worry; you will live through this night and for a long while to come, [4] for no one is going to hurt you. Rather, you will be well treated, just like all the servants of my lord, King Nebuchadnezzar."

[5] "Accept the words of your servant," said Judith to him; "permit your maidservant to speak to you, and I will say nothing false to my lord this night. [6] And if you follow the advice of your maidservant, God will accomplish something through you, and my lord will not fail to achieve his ends. [7] For I swear by Nebuchadnezzar, king of all the earth, and by the might of him who has sent you to correct every person, that because of you not only do human beings serve him, but also the beasts of the field, the cattle, and the birds of the heavens. Thanks to you, Nebuchadnezzar and all his house shall prosper. [8] For we have heard of your wisdom and your adroitness. The whole world knows that you, above all others in the kingdom, are brave, experienced, and dazzling in the arts of war.

[9] "We have also heard Achior's account of the advice he offered in your war council; for the men of Bethulia rescued him, and he told them everything he had said to you. [10] Don't ignore his advice, my lord and master, but take it to heart. For it is true: our nation cannot be punished nor can the sword subdue them, unless they sin against their God. [11] But as it is, my lord need not be exposed or unsuccessful, and death will fall upon them. Sin has them in its power; and they are about to enrage their God when they commit a sacrilege. [12] Because their food supply is exhausted and their water almost gone, they have resolved to kill their cattle. Moreover, they have decided to consume all that God in his laws has forbidden them to eat. [13] They have de-

cided to eat the firstfruits of the grain and the tithes of wine and oil which they had consecrated and reserved for the priests who officiate in the presence of our God at Jerusalem, even though it is not lawful for any of the laity so much as to touch these things with their hands. [14] They have sent men to Jerusalem to get permission from the Council, because even there the people have been doing the same things. [15] The result will be that when they get permission and they act upon it, on that day they will be given to you to be destroyed.

[16] "Knowing all this, I, your servant, made my escape from their presence. God has sent me to accomplish with you things which will astonish the whole world whenever people hear about them. [17] For your servant is devout and serves the God of Heaven night and day. So I will remain with you now, my lord; and every night your servant will go out into the valley and pray to God, and he will tell me when they have perpetrated their offenses. [18] I will then come and report it to you; and you shall march out with your whole army, and there won't be a single one of them to resist you. [19] I will guide you through the heart of Judea until you reach Jerusalem; and I will set your throne right in the middle of her. You will lead them like sheep that have no shepherd! Nor will a dog so much as growl at you! I have been given foreknowledge of this; it was announced to me, and I was sent to tell you."

[20] Her words delighted Holofernes and all his attendants. They were struck by her wisdom and exclaimed, [21] "In terms of beauty and brains, there is not another woman like this from one end of the earth to the other!" [22] Then Holofernes said to her, "God did well to send you before the people to give strength to our hands and destruction to those who insulted my lord. [23] You are both beautiful and eloquent. If you do as you have promised, your god shall be my god; and you shall live in King Nebuchadnezzar's palace and be famous throughout the world."

XII. Judith as a Guest of Holofernes
(12:1–9 [Vg 12:1–9])

12 [1] He then ordered them to bring her into where his silver dinnerware was set out and to serve her from his own delicacies and wine.

[2] But Judith said, "I will eat none of that lest it be an offense to God. Besides, I have enough with what I brought with me." [3] But Holofernes said to her, "But if you run out of what you have, how can we get you more of the same? For there is no one of your nationality here among us." [4] Judith replied, "As sure as you live, my lord, your servant will not exhaust her supplies before the Lord God accomplishes by my hand what he had planned."

[5] Holofernes' attendants then brought her into the tent, where she slept until midnight. Toward the morning watch she got up [6] and sent word to Holofernes, saying, "Let my lord please give orders for your servant to be allowed to go out and pray." [7] Holofernes then ordered his guards to let her pass. So she stayed in the camp three days, and each night she would go out into the valley of Bethulia and at the spring would bathe herself from the uncleanness. [8] When she had finished bathing, she would pray to the Lord, the God of Israel, to guide her in her plan to deliver the children of her people. [9] Having made herself ritually pure, she would go back and stay in the tent until her meal was brought to her in the evening.

XIII. Filled with Lust and Wine, Holofernes Loses His Head to Judith (12:10–13:10 [Vg 12:10–13:12])

12   [10] On the fourth day Holofernes gave a party for his retinue only and invited none of his commanders. [11] He said to Bagoas, the eunuch in charge of his personal affairs, "Go 'persuade' the Hebrew woman who is in your care to join us, and to eat and drink with us. [12] For we will be disgraced if we let such a woman go without having her, because if we do not make her, she will laugh at us."

[13] Bagoas then withdrew from Holofernes' presence and went to Judith and said, "May this lovely maid not hesitate to come before my lord to be honored in his presence and to enjoy drinking wine with us and act today like one of the Assyrian women who serve in Nebuchadnezzar's palace."

[14] "Who am I," responded Judith, "that I should refuse my lord? I will do whatever he desires right away, and it will be something to boast of until my dying day."

[15] So she proceeded to put on her dress and all her accessories. Her servant preceded her and spread on the ground opposite Holofernes the lambskins which Bagoas had provided for her daily use to recline on while eating.

[16] When Judith entered and lay down, Holofernes was beside himself with desire, and his brain was reeling; and he was very eager to have relations with her. (From the day he had first seen her he had been watching for an opportunity to seduce her.) [17] So Holofernes said to her, "Do have a drink. Enjoy yourself with us!"

[18] "I will indeed drink, my lord," said Judith, "for today is the greatest day of my whole life."

[19] Then she took what her servant had prepared, and ate and drank in his presence. [20] Holofernes was so delighted with her that he drank a great deal of wine, much more than he had ever drunk on a single day since he was born. **13** [1] It grew late, and his retinue hurried away. Then Bagoas closed the tent from outside and dismissed those attending his lord, and they went to bed; for they were all very tired, since the party had lasted so long.

[2] So Judith was left alone in the tent with Holofernes sprawled on his bed, dead drunk. [3] (Now Judith had instructed her servant to stand outside her bedroom and wait for her to come out as usual; for she had said she would be going out for her prayers. She had also said the same thing to Bagoas.) [4] So all had left them, and no one, either important or insignificant, was left in the bedroom.

Then Judith, standing beside his bed, prayed silently, "Lord, God of all power, look in this hour upon the work of my hands for the greater glory of Jerusalem, [5] for now is the opportunity to come to the aid of your inheritance, and to carry out my plan for the destruction of the enemies who have risen up against us." [6] She went up to the bedpost by Holofernes' head, and took down from it his sword; [7] and approaching the bed, she grabbed the hair of his head and said, "Lord God of Israel, give me the strength, now!" [8] Then she struck at his neck twice with all her might, and chopped off his head. [9] Next, she rolled his body off the bed and yanked the canopy from the poles. A moment later she went out and gave Holofernes' head to her servant, [10] who put it in her food sack.

The two of them then went out, as they always did, "to pray." They passed through the camp, bypassed that valley, and climbed up the slope to Bethulia and approached its gates.

XIV. After Recounting Her Night's Work, Judith Reveals Her Plans for the Next Day's Battle (13:11–14:10 [Vg 13:13–14:6])

13 11 While still some distance away, Judith called out to the sentries at the gates, "Open! Open the gate! God our God is with us, still displaying his strength in Israel and his might against our enemies, as he has today!" 12 When her townsmen heard her voice, they hurried down to the city gate, and called the elders of the town. 13 So everyone, regardless of status, came running (for they were surprised she had returned); they opened the gate and welcomed them; they lit a fire to give some light and crowded around them.

14 Then she raised her voice and said, "Praise God! Praise him! Praise God, who has not withdrawn his mercy from the House of Israel, but has shattered our enemies by my hand this very night!" 15 She then produced the head from the sack. And holding it up, she said to them, "Here's the head of Holofernes, the general in command of the Assyrian army. And here's the canopy under which he lay in his drunken stupor! The Lord has struck him down by the hand of a female! 16 Yet I swear by the Lord, who protected me in the course I took so that my face tricked him and brought his downfall, Holofernes committed no sin with me to defile me or to disgrace me." 17 The people were all quite amazed. And bowing down and worshiping God, they said, "Blessed are you, our God, who this day has mortified the enemies of your people!"

18 Uzziah then said to her, "My daughter, more blessed are you by God Most High than all other women on earth! Blessed also is the Lord God, who created the heavens and the earth, who guided you in crushing the head of the leader of our enemies! 19 People will never forget to praise you when they remember the power of God. 20 May God make your deed redound to your everlasting honor, and grant you every blessing! For you risked your own life when our nation was brought to its knees. You went out boldly to meet the disaster that threatened us, walking a straight line before our God." Then all the people said, "Amen! Amen!"

14 ¹ Then Judith said to them, "Please hear me out, my brothers. Take this head and hang it from the battlements of our wall. ² And as soon as day breaks and the sun comes out over the land, each of you take up your weapons, and let every able-bodied man leave the town. Appoint a commander for them as if you were about to descend upon the plain against the Assyrian outpost. Only you must not descend! ³ Then the Assyrian outpost will grab their weapons and make for camp. They will rouse the officers of the Assyrian army and then rush into Holofernes' tent, and not find him! Then they will panic and retreat at your advance; ⁴ and you and all who live within Israel's borders will pursue them and cut them down in their tracks. ⁵ But before doing all this, bring Achior the Ammonite to me so that he may see and recognize the one who despised the House of Israel and sent him to us as if to his death."

⁶ So they summoned Achior from Uzziah's house. But when he arrived and saw Holofernes' head held by one of the men in the assembly of the people, he collapsed; and his breathing was faint. ⁷ But when they picked him up, he threw himself at Judith's feet and did obeisance to her, saying, "Blessed are you in every tent of Judah! In every nation those who hear your name will be in dread. ⁸ Now tell me all that you have done these past few days."

So Judith related to him in the people's presence everything she had done from the day she left up to the moment she was speaking to them. ⁹ When she had finished speaking, the people shouted at the top of their lungs and made the town ring with their cheers. ¹⁰ When Achior saw all that the God of Israel had done, he believed in God completely. So he was circumcised and was admitted to the community of Israel, as are his descendants to the present day.

XV. On Learning of Holofernes' Death,
the Assyrians Panic and Are Decisively Defeated
(14:11–15:7 [Vg 14:7–15:8])

14 ¹¹ When dawn came, they hung Holofernes' head from the wall. Then every man of Israel picked up his weapons, and they went out by groups to the mountain's passes. [12] When the Assyrians saw them, they sent word to their superiors, who reported to their generals, their commanders of thousands, and all their other officers. [13] They arrived at Holofernes' tent and said to the one in charge of all his affairs, "Please rouse our lord, for these slaves have dared to come down and fight against us so that they may be wiped out to a man!"

[14] So Bagoas went in and shook the curtain partitioning the tent (for he had supposed that he was sleeping with Judith). [15] When no one answered, he drew aside the curtain and went into the bedroom and found him on top of the bedstool—a discarded corpse, with his head missing! [16] He let out a yell; and with wailing, groaning, and shouting ripped his clothes. [17] He then went into the tent which Judith had occupied; and when he did not find her, he rushed out to the people, shouting, [18] "The slaves have duped us! A single, Hebrew woman has brought shame on the House of King Nebuchadnezzar. Look! Holofernes is lying on the ground! And his head is missing!"

[19] When the officers of the Assyrian army heard this, they tore their clothes in consternation; and their cries and shouting were very loud throughout the camp. 15 [1] And when those who were in their tents heard, they were appalled at what had happened. [2] Then, quivering with fear, no man stood firm with his comrade, but with common impulse they tried to escape along every path in the plain and the hill country. [3] Those who were encamped in the hills around Bethulia were fleeing, too. Then the Israelites, every fighting man among them, sallied out after them. [4] Uzziah dispatched men to Bethomasthaim, Chobai, Chola, and all the territory of Israel to tell them what had been accomplished and to urge them all to rush upon the enemy and annihilate them. [5] As soon as the Israelites heard the news, then as one man they fell upon them and cut them to pieces as far as Choba. Those in Jerusalem and all the hill country also rallied, for they had been told what had happened in the enemy camp. The men in Gilead and those in Galilee outflanked them, causing heavy losses until they were past Damascus and its borders. [6] Meanwhile, the rest, who had stayed in Bethulia, fell upon the Assyrian camp and looted it, making themselves very rich. [7] When the Israelites returned from the slaughter, they seized what was left. Even the villages and hamlets in the hill country and the plain got a lot of booty, for there was a tremendous amount of it.

XVI. The Israelites Celebrate Their Victory, and Judith Offers Her Hymn of Praise (15:8–16:20 [Vg 15:9–16:24])

15   8 Joakim the high priest and the Israelite Council who lived in Jerusalem came to see for themselves the wonderful things the Lord had done for Israel, and to see Judith and to wish her well. 9 When they came to her, they blessed her with one voice and said, "You are the glory of Jerusalem! You are the great pride of Israel! You are the great boast of our nation! 10 For by your own hand you have accomplished all this. You have done well by Israel; God is well pleased with it. May the Omnipotent Lord bless you in all the days to come." And all the people said, "Amen!"

11 It took the people a month to loot the camp. They gave to Judith Holofernes' tent, with all his silver dinnerware, beds, bowls, and gear. She took them and loaded her mule; then she hitched up her carts and piled the things on them. 12 All the women of Israel flocked to see her and sang her praises; some of them performed a dance in her honor. She took branches in her hands and distributed them to the women who accompanied her. 13 She and those who accompanied her crowned themselves with olive leaves. Then, at the head of all the people, she led all the women in their dancing while all the men of Israel, armed and garlanded, followed, with songs of praise on their lips. 14 In the presence of all Israel Judith began this thanksgiving, and all the people lustily sang this hymn of praise. 16   1 And Judith sang,

> Begin a song to my God with tambourines.
> Praise the Lord with cymbals.
> Raise to him a psalm of praise.
> Extol him and invoke his name.

> 2 For the Lord is a God who crushes wars;
> Bringing me into his camp among his people,
> He delivered me from the power of my pursuers.
> 3 Assyria came from out of the mountains of the north;
> He came with myriads of his warriors.
> Their numbers blocked up the wadis;

And their cavalry covered the hills.

4 He boasted that he would set fire to my territory,
Kill my young men with the sword,
Dash my infants to the ground,
Seize my children as spoil,
And would carry off my maidens.

5 The Omnipotent Lord has foiled them
By the hand of a female.

6 For their champion did not fall at the hands of young men;
Nor did the sons of Titans strike him down,
Nor did towering giants set upon him;
But Judith daughter of Merari
Undid him by the beauty of her face.

7 For she took off her widow's dress
To rally the distressed in Israel.
She anointed her face with perfume

8 And fixed her hair with a tiara
And put on a linen gown to beguile him.

9 Her sandal ravished his eyes;
Her beauty captivated his mind.
And the sword slashed through his neck!

10 The Persians shuddered at her audacity,
And the Medes were daunted by her daring.

11 When my oppressed ones raised their war cry
And my weak ones shouted,
The enemy cowered in fear,
Screamed and ran.

12 Mere boys ran them through
And wounded them like deserters' children.
They were destroyed by the army of my Lord!

13 I will sing to my God a new song:
Lord, you are great and glorious,
Marvelous in strength, invincible.

14 Let all your creation serve you!
For you spoke, and they were created;
You sent forth your spirit, and it formed them.
And there is none who can resist your voice.

15 For the mountains will be moved from their foundations like
water;

The rocks will melt before you like wax.
Yet to those who fear you
You will show mercy.
16 For any sacrifice for its pleasant smell is a little thing,
And any fat for a whole burnt offering is to you insignificant;
But he who fears the Lord is always great.
17 Woe to the nations which rise against my people!
The Omnipotent Lord will take vengeance on them on the day of
   judgment;
He will consign their flesh to fire and worms,
And they will wait with pain forever.

18 When they arrived at Jerusalem, they worshiped God. As soon as the people were purified, they offered their burnt offerings and their votive offerings and their gifts. 19 Judith dedicated all the possessions of Holofernes, which the people had presented her. The canopy which she had taken for herself from his bedroom she also gave to God as a votive offering. 20 For three months the people continued their celebrations in Jerusalem in front of the sanctuary; and Judith stayed with them.

XVII. Epilogue
(16:21–25 [Vg 16:25–31])

16   21 After that everyone went back home. So Judith returned to Bethulia and lived on her own estate. In her time she was famous throughout the whole country. 22 Many men wanted her, but for the rest of her life (from the day Manasseh her husband died and was gathered to his people) no man had relations with her. 23 Her fame continued to increase, and she lived in her husband's house until she was a hundred and five years old. She emancipated her trusted servant. And when she died in Bethulia, she was buried in the same cave as her husband Manasseh; 24 and the House of Israel mourned her for seven days. (Before she died she had distributed her property among those most closely related to her husband Manasseh and to her own nearest relatives.) 25 Not again did anyone threaten the Israelites during Judith's lifetime, or for a long time after her death.

INTRODUCTION

INTRODUCTION

Both Jews and Christians are accustomed to hearing about saints who died for their people, men like Jeremiah or Stephen. Judith is the story of the saint who murdered for her people—or at least, so the book bearing her name would have its readers understand. Even more ironic, although almost every chapter of the book breathes a spirit of intense Jewish nationalism and Pharisaic piety, Judith was accepted as canonical by Christians, only to be rejected as such by the Jews themselves. Such an outcome, however, was not an inappropriate result for a book which is itself essentially ironic: having conquered many great peoples and cities, the mighty Assyrian army under General Holofernes was decisively defeated by Bethulia, a small Israelite town. Moreover, wanting only to seduce the "helpless" widow Judith, Holofernes ended up losing his head to her; for she decapitated him!

RÉSUMÉ OF JUDITH

The following synopsis, which is somewhat more detailed than might ordinarily be expected, is designed to do two things: (1) to refresh the reader's memory of the Judith-story, and (2) to provide him with some specific clues as to what scholars have generally regarded as the book's relative strengths and weaknesses.

When King Nebuchadnezzar of Assyria left his capital city of Nineveh in the twelfth year of his reign to wage war against the great Median king Arphaxad, various peoples of the East marched along with him, including those from the highlands and those living along the Tigris, Euphrates, and Hydaspes rivers, as well as the king of the Elymaens. The various countries in the West—the peoples from Cilicia and Damascus down through Palestine to the southernmost borders of Ethiopia—were also invited to join him. However, they not only refused to do so, but they even abused his envoys, with the result that Nebuchadnezzar swore that someday he would avenge himself on them. Five years later Nebuchadnezzar finally defeated Arphaxad and destroyed the "invulnerable" city of Ecbatana (chap. 1).

The following year, Nebuchadnezzar commissioned Holofernes, his highest-ranking general, to initiate his revenge against the West. With an army of one hundred twenty thousand infantry and twelve thousand cavalry, Holofernes was to quell the rebellious spirit and to receive from the offending nations the customary tokens of submission, namely, offerings of earth and water.

Commanded to show no mercy on those who continued to rebel, Holofernes was told by the king, "If they surrender to you, hold them for me until the time comes for me to punish them."

When Holofernes left Nineveh with his enormous army, its ranks now swollen by porters, baggage, and various kinds of animals for working and eating, his army was as countless as the locusts in the sky. After a three-day march of about three hundred miles to Bectileth in northern Cilicia, where he cut through the lands of Put and Lud to plunder the Rassisites and Ishmaelites, Holofernes crossed the Euphrates and proceeded through Mesopotamia to Cilicia and Damascus. By late spring, he was wreaking total havoc against the Midianites and those in the Damascus Plain.

The peoples along the Mediterranean coast, in cities like Sidon, Tyre, Jamnia, Azotus, and Ascalon, were now so terrified of Holofernes (chap. 2) that they promptly sued for peace and put themselves completely at his mercy. Holofernes not only occupied their lands and drafted their best men into his growing army, but he also demolished their sanctuaries and cut down their sacred poles, insisting that everyone worship Nebuchadnezzar—and Nebuchadnezzar only—as god.

As Holofernes advanced toward the plain of Esdraelon, he encamped between Geba and Scythopolis for a month while he consolidated his forces (chap. 3). Having heard what Holofernes had done to other peoples and their gods, the Israelites in Judea, who themselves had just returned from exile, were very concerned about the safety of their temple in Jerusalem. On the orders of the high priest, Joakim, all the Israelites prepared for war. Towns such as Bethulia and Bethomesthaim were urged to make special efforts to secure their mountain passes, for through them the Assyrians had access to Judea and Jerusalem. Meanwhile the priests in Jerusalem continued to offer the prescribed sacrifices while all the Israelites clothed everyone in sackcloth and ashes and begged their God with prayer and fasting to spare them and their temple (chap. 4).

On learning that the Israelites had decided to resist, Holofernes asked his staff about them. Achior, commander of the Ammonites, then gave an extended report. He said that the Israelites were descendants of the Chaldeans and that, for religious reasons, they had immigrated to Canaan, where they had thrived. Later, during a terrible famine, they had resettled in Egypt, where they subsequently became slaves. Thanks to miraculous acts of their god, they were expelled from there. Their god even dried up the Red Sea for them so that they could escape the Egyptians. After wandering in the Sinai for a short time, they invaded and settled again in Canaan. There, they had their ups and downs; but as long as they remained faithful to their god—and to him only—they prospered. But because of their increasing wickedness, their god had allowed them to be conquered, their temple to be destroyed, and the people to go into exile. Just recently they had returned to the hill country and rebuilt their temple in Jerusalem. Achior concluded his account by advising Holofernes to bypass the Israelites; for unless they were sinning against their god (which Achior thought unlikely), their god would not allow anyone to defeat them.

After Holofernes' staff had listened to all this, they were incensed and begged him to wage war against the Israelites (chap. 5). Holofernes, too, was offended and went on to insist that the Israelites' god could not save them because Nebuchadnezzar alone was god. The Israelites, he assured Achior, would be totally destroyed. Moreover, since Achior had shown such confidence in the Israelites and their god, his fate would be tied to theirs, that is, Achior would be "delivered" into the hands of the Israelites and so would ultimately share their lot.

Later, the scouts of Bethulia, a small Israelite city south of Esdraelon and near Dothan, found Achior, all tied up, at the bottom of their hill and brought him to town. There Uzziah, the town's chief magistrate, interrogated him in the people's presence. After Achior had repeated everything that had been said and done at Holofernes' staff meeting, everyone commended him highly; and Uzziah took him home as his guest (chap. 6).

Two days later, on the advice of the commanders of the Edomites and the Moabites, Holofernes, whose huge army was now deployed in the valley near Bethulia, seized the town's water supply outside its walls. Meanwhile, Edomites and Ammonites occupied the hill country opposite Dothan and to the southeast as far as Egrebel, near Chous.

After thirty-four days of this siege, both the water and the courage of the Bethulians were just about gone. Dying of thirst, the people reprimanded Uzziah and his two colleagues for not making peace with the Assyrians on their first appearance before Bethulia, and they demanded that the town be surrendered immediately; for they felt it was better to be living slaves than dead Bethulians. However, Uzziah succeeded in making a compromise with them, to the effect that if God did not somehow come to the town's rescue within the next five days, then the magistrates would surrender it. Satisfied with that promise, the people returned to their assigned tasks. But their morale was very low (chap. 7).

Unfortunately, one of Bethulia's wisest and most prominent citizens had not been present at the meeting, namely, Judith, the daughter of Merari and widow of Manasseh. Wealthy and quite beautiful, she was also very religious, constantly fasting and always wearing sackcloth, except on special occasions. Everyone, without exception, had always spoken well of her.

When this Judith learned of the compromise, she was appalled. She immediately sent for the magistrates and chided them, insisting that they had erred in trying to force God's hand. God, she argued, could do whatever he wanted with his people; but, unlike mortals, he could not be threatened or cajoled. True, she conceded, the entire Israelite nation had, in the past, experienced many terrible things. But it was always their own fault, that is, they had not been faithful to their God. But ever since their return from exile the people had remained faithful. Therefore, the Bethulians should now stand firm, setting an example of righteousness and of confidence in their God. Besides, the security of the Temple rested directly on Bethulia, which now blocked Holofernes' route to Jerusalem. Their present predicament should not be viewed as punishment, Judith maintained, but as a test and an admonishment by their God.

Although not disagreeing with Judith's logic, Uzziah still insisted that he had had no other choice in the matter. "So now you pray for us," said Uzziah to Judith, "for you are a devout woman!" Ignoring that slight gibe, Judith revealed that she had a secret plan involving herself and her trusted servant. The two women would have to be absent from the town for the next five days. "But you must not inquire into the affair," she said, ". . . until it is accomplished." Desperate and willing to try anything, the magistrates quickly gave her their permission (chap. 8).

At the precise moment when the evening's incense was being offered in the Temple at Jerusalem, Judith was praying to God. In her prayer, Judith found comfort in the fact that her ancestor Simeon, through God's help, had avenged himself on the Shechemites for Hamor's raping of his sister Dinah. Judith asked that God would grant her, a female *and* a widow, the courage and guile to carry out her plan against the cruel Assyrians. That way, Jerusalem would be spared, and all the world would know that the Lord God, alone, protects Israel (chap. 9).

Her prayers finished, Judith removed her widow weeds, bathed and perfumed herself, and then put on her sabbath best, that is, the expensive clothes and jewelry she had worn in the days when her husband Manasseh was still alive. Now, dressed to kill, she gave the trusted maid who was to accompany her their very simple provisions: a skin of wine, a jug of oil, some roasted grain, dried fig cakes, and some kosher bread. As the two women departed through the town gates that night, the elders, as well as the young men standing guard, were struck by Judith's beauty.

The two women had not gone too far through the valley when they were discovered by an Assyrian patrol. Judith explained to them that she was running from the Bethulians, and that she had a message only for their general's ears. So struck were these soldiers by her beauty, they not only detailed a hundred men to accompany her but even instructed her on how best to conduct herself before Holofernes. Her arrival in the main camp caused quite a stir; and everyone, including Holofernes, who left the comforts of his luxurious canopy to see her, was struck by Judith's great beauty (chap. 10).

Assuming that such a woman would be frightened of him, Holofernes tried to reassure Judith, promising that nothing evil would happen to her. Judith proceeded to assure Holofernes that if he would follow her advice to the letter, then "God will accomplish something through you, and my lord will not fail to achieve his ends." Then, after flattering Holofernes shamelessly, Judith underscored the fact that Achior was absolutely correct: no evil could befall the Israelites as long as they did not sin against their God. Unfortunately, however, in order to assuage their hunger and thirst, the Bethulians were about to commit a sacrilege by drinking the blood of slain cattle and eating certain foods prohibited by God. Because she placed loyalty to God above loyalty to her people, she had deserted them and fled to the Assyrians. Moreover, when God would reveal to her within the next few days that the sacrilege had indeed occurred, she would inform Holofernes; and then the Assyrians could, without any difficulty, bring God's punishment upon the Israelites. In fact, she herself would be willing to lead Holofernes into Jerusalem! Needless to say, the delighted Holofernes commended Judith on her beauty and good sense, and promised her that she would soon be rewarded appropriately (chap. 11). Offered some of his food served on his best dinnerware, Judith declined, insisting that she must use only that which she herself had brought. Moreover, she assured him, "Your servant will not exhaust her supplies before the Lord God accomplishes by my hand what he had planned."

For the next three days, with Holofernes' permission, Judith followed this routine. While it was still dark, Judith and her servant would go out into the valley of Bethulia, where she would bathe, pray, and await God's guidance. Purified, she would then return to her tent and stay there until she ate in the evening.

Four days later, Holofernes, determined to seduce Judith that night, had Bagoas, his majordomo, invite her to a very small party in his tent. "Who am I that I should refuse my lord?" purred Judith. "I will do whatever he desires right away, and it will be something to boast of until my dying day."

As she lay there on her fleece at Holofernes' feet, Judith so bewitched him that Holofernes drank more wine than he had on any other occasion in his entire life (chap. 12). By the time everyone had withdrawn and left the two of them by themselves for the night, Holofernes was sprawled on his couch, dead drunk! Taking Holofernes' own sword and praying for strength, Judith grabbed Holofernes by the hair of his head; and with two swipes she cut off his head. Rolling his body off the couch, Judith grabbed his splendid canopy, summoned her maid, who was standing just outside with a sack, and plopped Holofernes' head in it. Then, as on the three preceding nights, the two women passed by the sentries, unchallenged, as they went out "for prayer."

Only this time, they took a different route, finally ending up before the gates of Bethulia. When her townspeople heard Judith's victorious shouts, they opened the gates and quickly surrounded her. "Here's the head of Holofernes. . . . And here's the canopy under which he lay in his drunken stupor!" exclaimed Judith. "The Lord has struck him down by the hand of a female!" Moreover, she assured them, she had done it without losing her honor!

The people were amazed, and they praised God, who had done all this. Uzziah offered the highest accolades, claiming that Judith was the most honored woman in the world and that she would always be remembered whenever Israelites thought about the power of God, to all of which the people shouted, "Amen! Amen!" (chap. 13).

Judith then outlined a ruse for the next day. At sunrise, Holofernes' head was to be hung on the town walls, and every able-bodied Bethulian was to act as if he and his comrades were going to go down and fight against the Assyrians. When the Assyrians would see them and go to awaken Holofernes, they would find him (and themselves) headless and so would panic. *Then,* the Bethulians would attack!

Judith suddenly remembered about Achior and asked that he be brought from Uzziah's home. On seeing Holofernes' head, Achior almost passed out with shock, thereby confirming that the head was indeed that of Holofernes. Achior then insisted on hearing her whole story from beginning to end, much to the people's delight. Achior was so impressed with what God had done for Israel that he converted to Judaism and was circumcised (his descendants were still Israelites at the time of the writing of Judith).

The next day the Bethulians did exactly as Judith had said they would. And so did the Assyrians! For when Bagoas went to rouse Holofernes and tell him about the impending Israelite attack, he found Holofernes alone in his bedroom, a discarded corpse without a head (chap. 14). At first immobilized by fear, the Assyrians soon panicked and ran. As word of the rout quickly spread throughout the land, Israelites from every town and city rallied and joined in the pursuit. The men from Galilee and Gilead, for instance, outflanked the retreating Assyrians and continued to inflict heavy losses on them until the enemy had retreated beyond Damascus. Meanwhile, those Bethulians who, by virtue of age or sex, had not participated in the battle itself went down and looted the enemy camp. The returning victorious Israelites also shared in the looting, for the Assyrians had left behind a tremendous amount of booty.

Joakim the high priest and the Council also came down from Jerusalem to share in the victory and to congratulate Judith. Joakim said to her, "You are the great boast of our nation! For by your own hand you have accomplished all this. You have done well by Israel; God is well pleased with it." And all the people answered, "Amen!"

The looting of the enemy camp went on for about a month. Out of gratitude for Judith's efforts, the people presented her with all of Holofernes' personal possessions. As they all made their way toward Jerusalem, Israelite women sang and danced in Judith's honor while she herself took branches from the trees and distributed them among the women. The women also crowned themselves with olive leaves. As for the men, armed and garlanded, they sang as they brought up the rest of the triumphant procession (chap. 15).

In special honor of their great victory, Judith sang a new hymn of thanksgiving. Her song told how the Assyrians had made terrible boasts about what they would do to Israel and how God had foiled them by the hand of a female. Holofernes had not fallen victim to warriors or towering giants but to the beauty of Judith. "Her sandal," they sang, "ravished his eyes; her beauty captivated his mind. And the sword slashed through his neck!" According to the song, the Persians and Medes shuddered at her daring, but the weak and oppressed Israelites were inspired by it. Thus the enemy was routed and destroyed by the army of the Lord. Judith's song also spoke of God's invincible strength and the glory of his creative acts. She concluded it by insisting that God values reverence for him much more than sacrifices or burnt offerings, and that God will take revenge on the wicked nations on the day of judgment, consigning their flesh to fire and worms forever!

After arriving in Jerusalem, the people were purified from their defilement by the dead bodies and all the other defiled things they had touched. Then they offered up countless sacrifices and gifts. Judith dedicated to God all the gifts the people had given her as well as the canopy she herself had taken from Holofernes. After three months of celebration in the holy city, everyone went back home.

Although Judith's fame continued to grow, she spent the rest of her long life—she lived to be a hundred and five years old!—on the estate of her deceased husband. (Many men wanted Judith, but from the day Manasseh died, no man possessed her.) Before she herself died, she emancipated her most faithful servant and distributed all her property to her closest relatives on both sides of the family. She was buried in the same cave as her husband, and Israel mourned her for seven days. As the result of Judith's heroic actions against the Assyrians, no one threatened Israel for the rest of her life or for a long time thereafter (chap. 16).

A PRELIMINARY ASSESSMENT

In assessing the value of the book of Judith, scholars have often observed, on the credit side, that it is a well-told story, especially chaps. 10–13, which are a masterpiece of irony and fast action. Then too, the character and personality of both the heroine and the villain are drawn effectively. Finally, the story, with its skillful use of prayers, speeches, and plot, is an effective means of expressing the author's own theological concerns and religious ideas (a point conceded even by those readers who do not particularly agree with the book's religious views).

On the debit side, the book has a number of glaring historical and geographical errors of "fact,"[1] inconsistencies, and improbabilities, all of which scholars have accounted for in a variety of ways. Then too, the story seems, at least to most Western readers, unbalanced, that is, the author takes far too much time getting to "the heart" of the story (Judith herself is not even mentioned until 8:1). Finally, and this is obviously a very subjective area of scholarship, many students of Judith have been quite critical of the book's theological views, as well as its moral and ethical stance. Inevitably, scholarly comments in this area sometimes tell us as much (or more!) about a particular author and his times as they do about the book itself. In any event, all the above strengths and weaknesses must now be investigated in the INTRODUCTION, although not always in the same sequence as noted above.

THE HISTORICITY OF JUDITH

Evidence for

The book purports to be a historical account. Moreover, it has all the outward trappings of one, including various kinds of dates, numerous names of well-known persons and places, and, most important of all, a *quite* believable plot. Each of these features must now be examined in detail.

Typical of genuine historical accounts, Judith includes a number of quite specific dates (for details on any of the matters below, see the relevant NOTE):

the twelfth year of . . . Nebuchadnezzar (1:1)
In [Nebuchadnezzar's] seventeenth year (1:13)
in the eighteenth year on the twenty-second day of the first month (2:1)

and exact periods of time:

feasted for four whole months (1:16)
stayed there a full month (3:10)
blockaded them for thirty-four days (7:20)
hold out for five more days (7:30)
a widow . . . for three years and four months (8:4)
It took the people a month to loot the camp (15:11)
For three months the people continued their celebrations in Jerusalem (16:20)

as well as some vague and imprecise expressions of time:

---

[1] I.e., data known only from the Bible. The word "fact" is in quotation marks because some of the facts that the book of Judith contradicts are *biblical* facts, which may or may not be historically true, there being no extrabiblical evidence to establish them as such. To give a clear, if irrelevant, example: it is a *biblical* fact that Methuselah died at the age of 969 years (Gen 5:27). Whether that person actually existed and whether the number given is accurate are matters on which people, including scholars, disagree.

during the wheat harvest (2:27)

they had returned from exile only a short time before . . . Temple had
just recently been rededicated (4:3)

For many days the people . . . kept on fasting (4:13)

At one time they settled (5:7)

and settled there for a long while (5:8)

settled there as long as there was food (5:10)

There they settled for a long while (5:16)[2]

died during the barley harvest (8:2)

For there has not been in our generation (8:18)

today is the greatest day of my whole life (12:18)

more than he had ever drunk on a single day since he was born (12:20)

Then too, like many genuine historical accounts, Judith features a number
of individuals whose names were those of well-known Gentiles (e.g., Nebuchadnezzar [1:1], Holofernes [2:4], and Bagoas [12:11]) and Israelites (e.g.,
Joakim [4:6] and Uzziah [6:15]), not to mention the names of some otherwise
unknown Gentiles (namely, Arphaxad [1:1] and Achior [5:5]) and Israelites
(e.g., Chabris and Charmis [6:15]).[3] As for Judith's own historical roots, she
claims for herself the longest genealogy of any woman in the Bible, sixteen
known ancestors (see 8:1 and COMMENT II, pp. 187–88).

Because there is a plethora of geographical names in Judith, only a representative sampling will be cited. Suffice it to say, some place names are quite
well known:

Nineveh and Ecbatana (1:1)	Damascus (1:7)
Rages (1:5)	Esdraelon (1:8)
Samaria and Tahpanhes (1:9)	Sidon, Tyre, and Azotus (2:28)
Memphis (1:10)	Dothan (3:9)
Cilicia (1:12)	Scythopolis (3:10)
Euphrates (2:24)	Jerusalem (4:2)

while other sites are uncertain:

the river Hydaspes (1:6)	Bectileth (2:21)
the brook of Egypt (1:9)	Put and Lud (2:23)
the two seas (1:12)	Beth-horon and Jericho (4:4)

while many others are totally unknown:

---

[2] The last four examples, which are from Achior's account of Israel's history, are appropriately imprecise; for even an informed Gentile could not be expected to be well versed on specific
dates of Israel's past.

[3] Although each of the preceding persons is mentioned more than once in Judith, the particular citation refers to that place in the NOTES where that name is discussed in some detail.

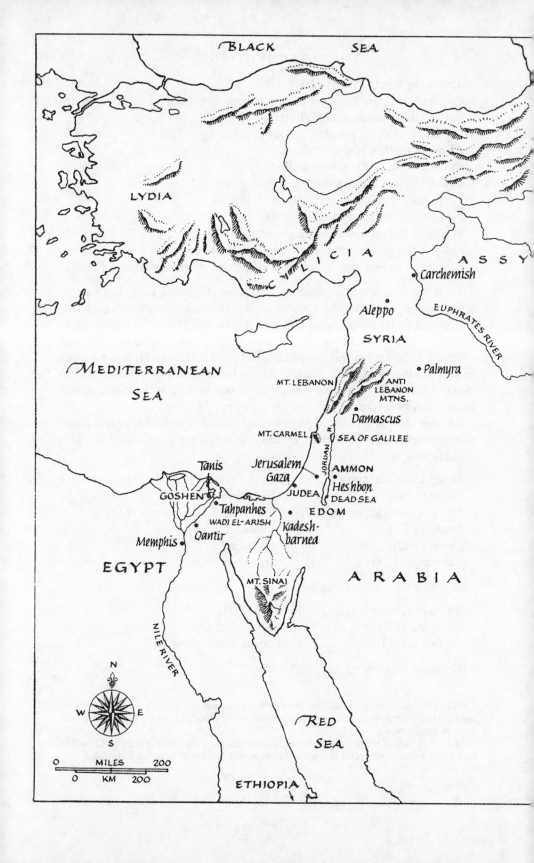

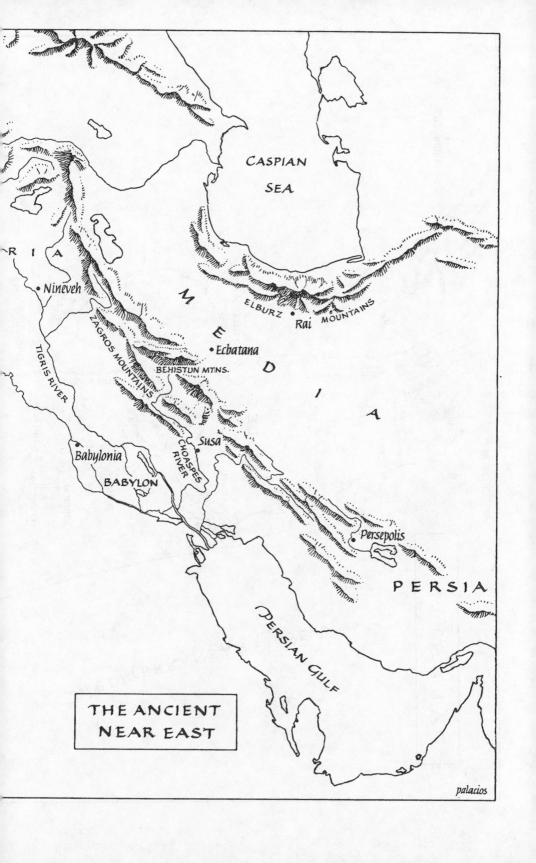

CASPIAN
SEA

R I A

• Nineveh

TIGRIS RIVER

ZAGROS MOUNTAINS

M
E
D
I
A

ELBURZ • Rai MOUNTAINS

• Ecbatana

BEHISTUN MTNS.

Susa

CHOASPES RIVER

Babylonia

BABYLON

Persepolis

P E R S I A

PERSIAN GULF

THE ANCIENT
NEAR EAST

palacios

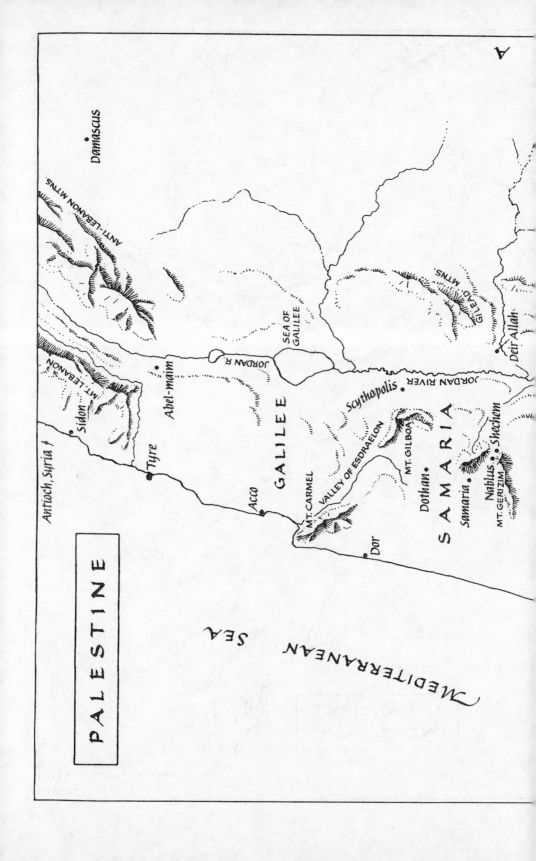

PALESTINE

Antioch, Syria ↑

Sidon •
Tyre •
Acco •
Dor •

MEDITERRANEAN SEA

Damascus •

ANTI-LEBANON MTS.
MT. LEBANON

Abel-maim •

SEA OF GALILEE

JORDAN R.

GALILEE

MT. CARMEL
VALLEY OF ESDRAELON
Scythopolis •
MT. GILBOA
Dothan •

SAMARIA

Samaria •
Nablus •
MT. GERIZIM
Shechem •

GILEAD MTNS.

JORDAN RIVER

Deir 'Allah •

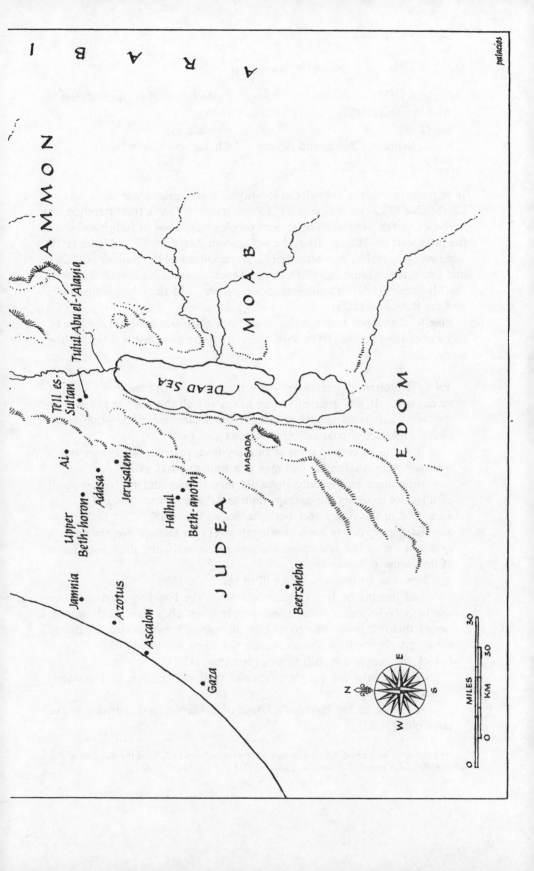

ARABI

AMMON

Tulul Abu el-'Alayiq

Tell es-Sultan

Ai.

Upper
Beth-horon

Adasa

Jerusalem

Beth-anoth

Halhul

MASADA

DEAD SEA

MOAB

EDOM

JUDEA

Jamnia

Azotus

Ascalon

Beersheba

Gaza

MILES

KM

N
W — E
S

0   30

0   KM   30

palacios

Cheleon (2:23)   Bethulia(!) and Bethomesthaim
Wadi Abron (2:24)   (4:6)
Sur (2:28)   Cyamon (7:3)
Kona, Belmain, Choba, and Aesora   Chobai and Chola (15:4)
(4:4)

In some instances, the difficulty in identifying a particular place name may be attributable to its corruption in its Hebrew stage, its Greek transliteration, or both (see NOTES *passim*).[4] The ancient peoples mentioned in Judith also span the full spectrum, ranging from the well-known Assyrians (1:1), Medes (1:1), Persians (1:7; 16:10), Moabites (1:12), Ammonites (1:12), Midianites (2:26), and Edomites or Idumeans (7:8); through such questionable identifications as the Elymaeans (1:6); to totally unknown peoples, like the Cheleoudites (1:6) and the Rassisites (2:23).

Finally, the plot of Judith is simple and straightforward enough for it to be fact rather than fiction. To be sure, there are some improbable details in the story:

Yet he [Holofernes] demolished all their sanctuaries and cut down all their sacred poles. It was granted to him to destroy all the gods of the area so that all the nations should worship Nebuchadnezzar alone—that every dialect and tribe should call upon him as god! (3:8)

. . . it would be easy to prevent an army from entering (for the approach was only wide enough for two men at a time to pass). (4:7)

. . . a hundred and seventy thousand infantrymen and twelve thousand cavalry, not counting the baggage train and the men who managed it. . . . encamped in the valley near Bethulia, beside the spring. . . . (7:2–3)

She fasted every day of her widowhood, except for sabbath eve, the sabbath itself, the eve of the new moon, the new moon itself, and the joyous feasts of the House of Israel. (8:6)

Yet there was no one who spoke ill of her. . . . (8:8)

. . . and judging by her, they speculated on the Israelites, saying to one another, "Who can despise these people when they have such women among them? It is not wise to let a single male of theirs survive; for if they are let go, they will be able to beguile the whole world!" (10:19)

It took the people a month to loot the camp. (15:11)

For three months the people continued their celebrations in Jerusalem. . . . (16:20)

. . . she lived in her husband's house until she was a hundred and five years old. (16:23)

---

[4] For example, Belmain of 4:4 may or may not be the Belbaim of 7:3 and the Balamon of 8:3; and Choba of 4:4 *may* be the same as Choba of 15:5 and Chobai of 15:4.

What is so striking about the above list is that *this* is all there is. There are no other "details of fact" to strain a modern reader's credulity. Moreover, with the exception of the statements in 3:8 and 4:7 (see NOTES), the rest of this material remains well within the bounds of realism and could be essentially true, i.e., just slightly exaggerated. As G. T. Montague has so rightly observed:

> The absence here of the supernaturally miraculous is remarkable. Quite unlike the book of Tobit and other works of the period, the book of Judith knows of no angelic intervention, no frightening display of supernatural power. The very panic of the Assyrian army is quite plausibly explained as due to the death of its leader. The real powers locked in combat in this book are, on the one hand, ambition, power, sensuality and passion, and, on the other, faith, courage and daring. Providence acts through natural courage here, and this is all the more surprising, since the author alludes to ancient narratives in which the miraculous element played an important role. *(Books of Esther and Judith,* p. 11)

The destruction of Holofernes and his army was accomplished through human efforts rather than by divine or miraculous intervention. To be sure, both Judith and her people called upon God in prayer and fasting (4:11–13; 9:1); nonetheless, it was mortal courage and guile that brought about the victory. While all Israel, including Judith, gave the primary credit to God, they all simultaneously recognized Judith as the means:

> "The Lord has struck him down by the hand of a female!" [cried Judith] (13:15)
> "Blessed also is the Lord God . . . who guided you in crushing the head of the leader of our enemies!" [exclaimed Uzziah] (13:18) Then all the people said, "Amen! Amen!" (13:20)
> "The Omnipotent Lord has foiled them/By the hand of a female." [sang Judith and the people] (16:5)

Perhaps this absence of the miraculous and the supernatural in the book can better be appreciated by comparing it with the LXX's Esther, where we read that as Esther appeared before the king, unannounced, "God changed the king's spirit to gentleness" (Add Esth D 8).[5] Also, there is an implied intervention by an angel in Judas Maccabeus's defeat of Nicanor, a narrative with strong affinities to the Judith-story: "And he [Judas] called upon [God] in these words: 'O Lord, you did send your angel in the time of Hezekiah king of Judea, and he killed a hundred and eighty-five thousand in the camp of

---

[5] Evidently the Aramaic text used by Jerome did make mention of an angel's protecting Judith (see NOTE on "the Lord, who protected me" in 13:16). The Vg, and probably Jerome's Aramaic source, also had Judith's physical beauty miraculously enhanced by God once she undertook her dangerous mission (see NOTE in 10:4 on "to catch the attention of the men").

Sennacherib. So now, O Sovereign of the heavens, send a good angel to carry terror and trembling before us.' " (2 Macc 15:22–23; see also 1 Macc 7:41)

Not surprisingly then, there are present-day scholars who regard Judith as having "a certain historicity"; for instance Montague has written:

> The author, writing resistance literature under the rule of a foreign power, has used the Assyrians as types of the Greeks and used Nebuchadnezzar as a coded symbol for Antiochus the Illustrious, the Greek Seleucid king who persecuted the Jews. . . . *the author reworked for this purpose a story whose historical nucleus went back two centuries, to the Persian period.* . . . Thus, we can conclude that the book of Judith is historical in two senses: one, there is a historical nucleus which gave rise to the Judith tradition, *though this nucleus is now difficult to recover;* the other, the story witnesses to the way believing Jews of the post-exilic period understood the challenge of their existence when pressured by tyrants to abandon their sacred traditions. [italics added] *(Books of Esther and Judith,* p. 8)

Evidence Against

However, since Martin Luther, who viewed Judith as a poem and an allegorical passion play, scholars have noted the book's shocking carelessness with well-established historical and geographical facts. As early as 1689, Capellus delivered a scathing evaluation of Judith: "a most silly fable invented by a most inept, injudicious, impudent and clownish Hellenist" *(Commentarii et notae criticae in Vet. Test.* [Amsterdam], p. 575). Oddly enough, although as early as the fifth century A.D. a few writers had reservations about the authenticity of Judith's Nebuchadnezzar (Sulpicius Severus, for instance, thought that he should be identified with Artaxerxes III), the Church Fathers did not question the book's essentially historical character (see Biolek, *Weidenauer Studien* 4 [1911]: 335–68).

The very first verse of chap. 1 contains two of the most egregious "blunders" of the entire book: "It was the twelfth year of the reign of Nebuchadnezzar, who ruled over *the Assyrians* from his capital, *Nineveh,* that Arphaxad was ruling over the Medes from Ecbatana" (italics added). But as any student of the Bible knows, Nebuchadnezzar was king of the Babylonians, not the Assyrians. And most students of OT history know that Nineveh was destroyed in 612 B.C.—seven or eight years prior to Nebuchadnezzar's becoming king. Moreover, according to Jer 32:1 the twelfth year of Nebuchadnezzar would have been the fourth year of the reign of Zedekiah, Judah's last king in the *pre*exilic period; however, elsewhere in Judith the setting for the events of the story is placed in the *post*exilic period (see, for example, NOTES on 4:3, 6; 5:18–19). Finally, neither secular nor biblical history knows of any Median king named Arphaxad. To be sure, Ecbatana was a great city, just as the book affirms (1:1–4); but the city was actually "conquered" in 554 B.C.[6] by Cyrus the Great, not Nebuchadnezzar (see NOTE on "its magnificence to a mockery" in 1:14). Such an opening verse should raise in any reader's mind some reservations about the book's historical accuracy, not to mention its author's intent.

Chaps. 2 and 3 of Judith continue to offer serious errors in fact but of a different kind, namely, geographical. Holofernes' entire army marched from Nineveh to northern Cilicia, a distance of about three hundred miles, in just *three days* (2:21), after which they cut their way through Put and Lud (usually identified by scholars with Libya in Africa, and Lydia in Asia Minor, respectively; see NOTE on 2:23), only to find themselves crossing the Euphrates River and proceeding west *through Mesopotamia* (2:24) before arriving at Cilicia and Japheth, facing Arabia (2:25)! Either something is now missing from that itinerary, or the author knew nothing about Mesopotamian geography (see NOTES *passim*).

Once Holofernes reached the eastern coastline of the Mediterranean, his itinerary becomes more believable even though a number of the cities and peoples mentioned are unknown, e.g., Sur and Okina (2:28) and Geba (3:10). Just exactly what route Holofernes' army took to get from the coastal cities of Azotus and Ascalon (2:28) to the place where they could encamp and besiege Bethulia is unknown. The LXX seems to suggest that Holofernes' attack on Bethulia came from the north (cf. 4:6; 8:21; 11:14, 19), while the Vg's account, which was based on an Aramaic version of Judith (see INTRODUCTION, pp. 95–100), has Holofernes' attack coming from the south (see NOTE on 3:1). The presence of Edomite, Moabite, and Ammonite soldiers in Holofernes' army (7:17–18) gives credence to the southern-route theory.

Starting with chap. 4, the problem shifts from the author's errors and confusion over geographical names and locations to the reader's ignorance and confusion as to the geographical locations of sites near Bethulia. For instance, of the eight Israelite places named in 4:4, five are totally unknown, namely, Kona, Belmain, Choba, Aesora, and the valley of Salem (see NOTES). However, it is two verses later that the full extent of our ignorance is revealed; for in spite of all the geographical and topographical clues given elsewhere (see NOTE on 4:6), the location of Bethulia—*the* local setting for the story of Judith and mentioned nineteen times in the text—is unknown! Nor is the town mentioned anywhere else in the Bible.

By chap. 5, the interests of the author have shifted from so-called secular to sacred history. By using only a few place names and no personal names, he was able to have Achior present a brief survey of Israel's long history, largely

---

[6] Justification of this date for the assumption of Cyrus as king of Ecbatana may be found in Drews, *Historia* 18 (1969): 1–11. In the clause "the city was actually 'conquered,'" the word "conquered" was put in quotes because the fall of Astyages had all the ingredients of an internal dynastic change or palace revolt; moreover, apart from the king, the Median kingdom continued without virtually any change (see Graf, *Medism*, especially Chapter One).

from a Deuteronomistic point of view.[7] Achior told of how the ancestors of
the Israelites had left Chaldea and settled in northern Mesopotamia so that
they might freely worship the God of Heaven, and how they later settled in
Canaan and prospered until a great famine drove them down into Egypt (vv
6–10). Although the Israelites eventually became slaves there, their God finally heard their prayers. Achior spoke of their miraculous escape from
Egypt, their crossing of the Red Sea, their wanderings in the Sinai, and their
invasion and settlement in Canaan (vv 11–17), where they prospered as long
as they did not sin against their god. But finally, so great was Israel's sin that
God allowed their state and temple to be destroyed and the people carried off
into exile. Just recently the people had returned, reoccupied the land, and
rebuilt Jerusalem and its temple (vv 18–19).

As a brief survey of Israelite history, Achior's account raises no historical
problems, that is, it does not disagree with the most general outline of Jewish
history as presented in the OT. The two possible exceptions to the preceding
generalization (i.e., "the Chaldeans drove [the Hebrews] out" [v 8], and [the
Hebrews] "accumulated [in Canaan] much wealth in gold, silver, and livestock" [v 9]) are not really exceptions (see relevant NOTES).

What *is* exceptional about Achior's account is that he had recited Jewish
history down into the *post*exilic period. In other words, without mentioning
Nebuchadnezzar by name, Achior had been describing Nebuchadnezzar's
total destruction of the Temple in 586 B.C. and its recent rebuilding seventy-
some years later to Holofernes, whose king—the same Nebuchadnezzar—*had
not yet* destroyed the Temple at Jerusalem! One can scarcely imagine a more
glaring anachronism than that! In fact, it is so blatantly obvious that it is
difficult to imagine how an author who had Achior do such an acceptable job
of telling an internally consistent historical account of the Jews (i.e., vv 6–19)
could have made such a blunder unknowingly. As will be shown later, the
storyteller quite deliberately constructed this and other anachronisms, such
as those already noted in 1:1 (see INTRODUCTION, pp. 78–79).

As for the rest of Judith, apart from the location of a few places which,
while unidentified, may very well be actual sites,[8] there are no other serious
geographical or historical blunders or improbabilities that would raise anew
the question of the historicity of the Judith-story (not even the allusion to
Persians and Medes in 16:10 [see NOTE]). The reason for this is that from
chap. 8 on, Judith herself has center stage; and her activities, which are of a

---

[7] I.e., "And as long as they did not sin against their god, they prospered. . . . But when they
abandoned the path he had laid down for them, they were devastated in many battles and were
carried off as captives to a foreign land." (5:17–18a) See also 5:20–21. Judith will use a slightly
modified version of this argument with the magistrates of Bethulia (8:18–20) and then, later, with
Holofernes (11:10).

[8] See NOTES on Belbaim and Cyamon (7:3); Egrebel, Chous, and Wadi Mochmur (7:18);
Balamon (8:3); Chobai and Chola (15:4).

rather restricted scope, get the author's spotlight. Nonetheless, the damage to the book's claims to historicity has already been done by the historical and geographical difficulties in the first third of the book.

To the question "Is the Judith-story historical?" D. N. Freedman has, perhaps, given the best answer:

> Perhaps in the end we will come out approximately where Shakespeare did: Hamlet and Lear were real people, but the plays have little to do with factual history, and the story and characters in the plays have a life of their own which bears little resemblance to the original historical figures, or the various characterizations in the sources which Shakespeare used. (private correspondence with this writer)

One need not look to distant times, however, for examples of how real people are fictionalized into legends almost overnight. Many Americans still thrill to John Greenleaf Whittier's account of how Barbara Frietchie defied Stonewall Jackson's soldiers as the Confederates tried to prevent her from displaying the American flag as they marched through Frederick, Maryland:

> She leaned far out on the window-sill,
> And shook it forth with a royal will.
> "Shoot, if you must, this old gray head,
> But spare your country's flag," she said.
> A shade of sadness, a blush of shame,
> Over the face of the leader came;
> The nobler nature within him stirred
> To life at that woman's deed and word;
> "Who touches a hair of yon gray head
> Dies like a dog! March on!" he said.

The account is true, to the extent that there actually was a Barbara Frietchie living in Frederick when Lee's troops marched through that town. Whittier's account is untrue, in that it was not Frietchie who waved the flag in defiance, and the gallant Jackson was not even in town at the time. (For an amusing yet instructive discussion of the historical facts behind the Frietchie legend, see Tristram Potter Coffin, *Female Hero*, pp. 5–12).

THE TIME OF THE NARRATIVE

Not surprisingly, however, some scholars have tried to solve this problem of historicity by dividing the book into at least two parts, making the first portion, which concerns a foreigner's invasion of the West, dependent upon one historical source[9] and the story of Judith herself dependent upon another.

[9] For a discussion of the particular invasions suggested, see INTRODUCTION, pp. 54–55.

Aside from the mention of "Nebuchadnezzar king of the Assyrians" and "Nineveh" (1:1 *et passim),* all the data in Judith presuppose, at the very least, a postexilic setting for the story. Certain of the features immediately suggest a Persian setting. For instance, both major and minor characters have names common in the Persian period:[10] Judith, Holofernes, Bagoas, and Joakim (see NOTES on 8:1; 2:4; 12:11; and 4:6, respectively). There are also allusions to certain Persian practices and terms (e.g., "to prepare . . . earth and water" [2:7]; *kidaris,* "turban" [4:15]; *satrapes,* "governor" [5:2]; and *akinakēs,* "sword" [13:6]), not to mention allusions to the Medes (1:1; 16:10) and Persians themselves (1:7; 16:10). Then too, the appellation "God of Heaven" (see 5:8) was an expression common in the Persian period. Finally, the information in 4:3, while vague and imprecise (i.e., "they had returned from exile only a short time before; . . . and the Temple had just recently been rededicated") strongly suggests a Persian setting.

On the other hand, the book of Judith unquestionably contains some Hellenistic elements, notably, such practices as wearing garlands and olive wreaths (see NOTES on 3:7 and 15:13, respectively), worshiping a king as a god (3:8), and reclining while eating (12:15). Certain institutional arrangements seem to have developed after 165 B.C., with the rise of the Maccabees: the sweeping military and political powers of the high priest (4:6) and the supremacy of the Jerusalem Council over other Jewish councils (4:6, 8; 11:14). Some scholars would regard it as no coincidence that Judith's life span of a hundred and five years (16:23) was exactly the same length of time as the Maccabean period (i.e., 168–163 B.C.; see NOTE on 16:23). More specifically, a number of items in the Judith-story are strikingly reminiscent of the story of Judas Maccabeus (167–161 B.C.) as recorded in 1 and 2 Maccabees,[11] especially with reference to Judas's defeat of Nicanor:

> So the armies met in battle on the thirteenth day of the month of Adar. The army of *Nicanor* was crushed, and he *himself was the first to fall in the battle. When his army saw that Nicanor had fallen, they threw down their arms and fled.* The Jews pursued them a day's journey, from Adasa as far as Gazara, and as they followed kept sounding the battle call on the trumpets. *And men came out of all the villages of Judea round about, and they outflanked the enemy* and drove them back to their pursuers, so that they all fell by the sword; not even one of them was left. *Then the Jews seized the spoils and the plunder, and they cut off Nicanor's head* and the right hand which he had so arrogantly stretched out, *and brought* them and *displayed* them just outside *Jerusalem. The people rejoiced greatly and celebrated* that day as a day of great gladness. And they decreed that this day should be celebrated each year

---

[10] Apart from "Scythopolis" and "Azotus" (see NOTES on 3:10 and 2:28), none of the personal names or place names are incontestably Greek.

[11] For brief but perceptive observations on the difference in perspective between the books of 1 and 2 Maccabees in general, see Momigliano, *Alien Wisdom,* pp. 103–6.

on the thirteenth of Adar. *So the land of Judah had rest for a few days.* [italics added] (1 Macc 7:43–50)

Those items in italics are especially reminiscent of the Judith-story. In addition, a number of the Judean towns mentioned in Judith are mentioned also in the Judas-story. For example, Judas put Jamnia to the torch and devastated Azotus in 164 B.C. (see NOTES on 2:28); and at Beth-horon he won a couple of battles against the Seleucids (see Jdt 4:4) and later defeated the Idumeans and forced them to convert to Judaism (see NOTE on 7:8). Last but not least, there are certain motifs in the book of Daniel (a work composed in the days of Judas), which are also present in Judith, for example, Nebuchadnezzar as a symbol for Antiochus IV, Epiphanes (see Daniel 3 and, especially, the NOTE on "call upon him as god" in Jdt 3:8), Nebuchadnezzar as one consciously served by all the animals (so Jdt 11:7; cf. Dan 2:37–38), and a strong emphasis on Jews refraining from eating forbidden foods (Jdt 10:5; 11:13; 12:2, 19; cf. Dan 1:8). In short, the book of Judith has a number of affinities with the general "plot," spirit, terminology, and traditions of the days of Judas Maccabeus. It is not surprising, then, that Martin Hengel describes Judith as a "narrative romance . . . where material from the Babylonian Diaspora is used . . . with strong nationalistic colouring inspired by the Maccabean war of liberation" *(Judaism and Hellenism,* I, 140).

There is, however, some other evidence which suggests a historical setting for Judith (or at least for the date of the book's final form) somewhat later than the early Maccabean period (168–135 B.C.). For instance, certain Palestinian cities mentioned in Judith were independent of Israel until they fell victim to the expansionary activities of the first Hasmonean king, John Hyrcanus I (135–104 B.C.), who, among other things, devastated Azotus (2:28), conquered Scythopolis (3:10), annexed all the territory of Samaria (4:4), and by 107 B.C. had destroyed Shechem and, earlier, its Samaritan temple at Mount Gerizim (so Josephus, *Ant.* 13.9.1; and *Jewish Wars* 1.2.6; for further details on Gerizim, see R. J. Bull, "Tell er-Ras," EAEHL, IV, 1015–22). The open and friendly attitude of Jerusalem toward Samaria and its territories (cf. 4:4 and 6) strongly suggests that the Judith-story received its final form sometime after Samaria had been conquered and integrated, so to speak, into the Judean state. Significantly, apart from an allusion to Shechem as a Canaanite city in the period of the Judges (see NOTE on 5:16), the city itself is not mentioned by name in Judith (for a brief discussion of C. C. Torrey's idea that Bethulia is actually Shechem, see NOTE on "Bethulia" in 4:6; for details on Shechem itself, see G. E. Wright, "Shechem," EAEHL, IV, 1083–94).

The best hypothesis to explain the pronounced Persian elements in Judith as well as the undeniable presence of Greek and even Hasmonean elements is that the book's setting is the Persian period and the date of the book's composition, or final form, is in the Hasmonean period (for more on the date of composition, see INTRODUCTION, pp. 67–70). Failure to distinguish carefully between the period of the book's setting and the date of Judith's composition has occasioned considerable confusion over the years.

THEORIES TO ACCOUNT FOR HISTORICAL CONTRADICTIONS

Over the past century, scholarly efforts to preserve some semblance of historicity for Judith have taken several tacks. The evolving-text theory explains the conflicting historical data within Judith as being the result of various "details of fact" being added, over the centuries, to what was originally a brief but consistent tale. Although it was Hugo Winckler[12] who in 1901 first suggested for Judith an evolutionary development extending over a long period of time,[13] Franz Steinmetzer is the principal name associated with the evolving-text theory *(Neue Untersuchung)*. According to Steinmetzer, the original story concerned events in the time of the Assyrian king Ashurbanipal (668–627 B.C.); the second edition of the story was set in the days of Cyrus the Great of Persia (550–530 B.C.), thereby accounting for such troublesome data as the Temple's destruction and the exile, as well as the relatively recent return and establishment of the Jews in the early postexilic period (cf. Jdt 5:18–19); the third stage in the text's evolution added certain features from the reign of Artaxerxes I, Longimanus (465–424 B.C.), while the final edition was adapted to the atmosphere and events in the time of Antiochus IV, Epiphanes (175–163 B.C.).[14] Thus, the story, starting from a brief and simple tale with very few personal or place names, gradually picked up at various points additional names, details, and local coloring, to which were added finally extended passages, including prayers, hymns, and conversations.

While the gradual evolution of a story is, in principle, easy enough to believe in, and with some biblical stories even documentable, Steinmetzer's theory as applied to Judith has not been well received, although it was better received by Catholic than Protestant scholars, many of the latter evidently regarding it as a type of literary "gerrymandering" in the interest of preserving the story's initial historicity. Steinmetzer's theory would probably have been accepted by more scholars had there not been other more viable and less complicated explanations for the same phenomena (see below).

In the late nineteenth century especially, a number of scholars subscribed to what might be called the pseudonym theory, which maintains that, for one reason or another, all the characters in Judith are deliberately disguised his-

---

[12] *Altorientalische Forschungen* 2 (1901): 267, 272–75.

[13] Winckler had taken his clue from Gaster, who in 1894 had suggested for Judith an evolution of short duration; see INTRODUCTION, pp. 103–5.

[14] For exactly what could have been added from each of these four reigns, see INTRODUCTION, pp. 54–55.

torical personages. The best-known elaborations of this kind of hypothesis are those of Gustav Volkmar *(Handbuch der Einleitung)*, Moses Gaster,[15] and Charles J. Ball.

	Volkmar	Gaster	Ball
The Cast			
NEBUCHAD-NEZZAR	Emperor Trajan	Pompey	Antiochus IV, Epiphanes
ASSYRIANS	Syrians		Syrians
NINEVEH	Rome or Antioch[16]	Rome	Antioch
ARPHAXAD	Arsaces, a Parthian king	Mithridates	Arsaces
MEDES	Parthians		Parthians
ECBATANA	Nisibis		
HOLOFERNES	Lusius Quietus	Scaurus, a Roman general	Nicanor, a general under Antiochus IV and Demetrius I
JUDITH	the Judeans		Judas Maccabeus
JOAKIM		Onias, a Pharisee	Alcimus, a Hellenist
The Time	A.D. 117[17]	A.D. 63	The Hasmonean period

The pseudonym theory could be correct, especially in light of the well-known practices in the book of Daniel and the Dead Sea Community at Qumran, where historical personages and peoples were given disguised names and titles. However, there are some difficulties with the particular systems noted above. In each of the "Cast of Characters" and especially in Gaster's, a complete correspondence could not be established, i.e., a full and exact parallel is lacking. Then too, even within a particular cast of characters, such as in Ball's, there are certain anomalies, if not contradictions: for instance, we know that Alcimus was the sworn enemy of Judas Maccabeus (cf. 1 Macc 7:5–7, 12–16; see also J. C. Swaim, "Alcimus," IDB, I, 76); yet Ball would have these two people represent Joakim and Judith (respectively), who were on excellent terms with one another (or at least so we may infer from 15:8 and 16:19).[18] Finally, Volkmar's theory has an insurmountable difficulty: his historical situation postdates by more than a quarter of a century the first

[15] *Encyclopaedia Biblica,* III, cols. 2642–46.
[16] I.e., the capital of the Seleucids.
[17] According to Volkmar, the references in Jdt 5:18–19 to the destruction of the Jewish Temple and the recent return of the exiles really applied to Titus's destruction of the Second Temple in A.D. 70, and "the return" of the Jews in the days of either Trajan or Hadrian.
[18] Steinmann, who also subscribed to this particular identification, was correct when he observed that "this would not be the first time that inspired writers presented contradictory aspects of the same event or of the same personality" (p. 32).

Christian allusion to Judith, namely, that of Clement I of Rome (30?–?99).[19] Not surprisingly, then, while each of the above theories has had its supporters, especially about three quarters of a century ago, present-day scholars have not found the pseudonym theory particularly persuasive.

Perhaps the most popular hypothesis among scholars has been what might be called the two-accounts theory, that is, the book of Judith consists of two parts of unequal length: (1) a "historical" account of a pagan king's war in the East and/or his subsequent invasion of the West (chaps. 1–3); and (2) the story of Judith's deliverance of her people (chaps. 4–16). While these two sections of the Judith-story are sometimes thought to reflect the same historical period, more often scholars have thought otherwise, especially those scholars who view the story of Judith itself as being essentially fictitious. Although a large number of Assyrian, Babylonian, Persian, and Syrian kings have been suggested by scholars as the particular pagan king in question,[20] several rulers have had a goodly number of scholars supporting their identification with Judith's "Nebuchadnezzar," notably, Ashurbanipal of Assyria; Artaxerxes III, Ochus, of Persia; Antiochus IV, Epiphanes, of Syria; and Demetrius I, Soter, also of Syria. Ironically, the two Babylonian kings with the actual name "Nebuchadnezzar" (i.e., Nebuchadnezzar II and "Nebuchadnezzar IV") have won virtually no supporters.[21]

Not only Winckler and Steinmetzer (see above) but also a number of other scholars[22] have thought that chaps. 1–3 of Judith contain historical elements from various campaigns of Ashurbanipal of Assyria, who, among his many accomplishments in his invasion of the West, actually succeeded in sacking Egypt's Thebes in 663 B.C. According to this hypothesis, Judith's Arphaxad would have represented either the Median king Phraortes II (see NOTES on 1:15) (or his father Deioces)[23] or Ashurbanipal's brother Shamashshumukin, the deputy king of Babylon who led an empire-wide revolt against Ashurbanipal in 662 B.C. In either case, the profanation of the Temple and the return from exile alluded to by Achior in Jdt 5:18–19 (= Vg 5:22–23) would have referred to events in the days of King Manasseh of Judah (687–642 B.C.).[24] It is precisely here that the principal weakness of the theory lies, i.e., in Manas-

[19] Volkmar got his original inspiration from Ferdinand Hitzig *(Über Johannes Markus,* p. 165), who dated the story of Judith to an even later event, namely, Bar-Kochba's revolt (132–35 A.D.) against the Roman emperor Hadrian.
[20] See Pfeiffer, pp. 295ff., and Soubigiou, p. 490 for lists of ancient candidates and the scholars up to their own day who had nominated them for that honor. Scholarly support for many of the candidates has been almost limited for the most part to the scholar who first made the proposal.
[21] Movers *(AfAuk Theo* 13 [1835]) was alone in his support for Nebuchadnezzar II; as for "Nebuchadnezzar IV," see NOTE on "Nebuchadnezzar . . . ruled over the Assyrians from . . . Nineveh" in 1:1.
[22] For a fairly long list of them, most of whom are Roman Catholic, see Soubigiou, p. 490.
[23] See NOTE in 1:2 on "Arphaxad."
[24] For brief but helpful background information on Ashurbanipal as well as Manasseh, see Bright, *History of Israel,* pp. 310–16.

seh's reign the Temple was *profaned,* not destroyed; and it was Manasseh himself, not his people, who went into exile and returned a few years later (cf. 2 Chr 33:1–20). Besides, there seems to be a stronger candidate than Ashurbanipal.

Many scholars, past and present, have argued that chaps. 1–3 of Judith have drawn upon the campaigns and accomplishments of the energetic but ruthless Artaxerxes III, Ochus (358–338 B.C.), who, early in his career, had to establish himself in the East.[25] This Achaemenian ruler did, in fact, invade the West, wreaking terrible destruction on such Phoenician cities as Sidon (see NOTE on 2:28); and by 343 B.C. he had reconquered Egypt. Artaxerxes III actually had a general by the name of Holofernes (see NOTE on 2:4) and an advisor named Bagoas (see NOTE on 12:11). Thus, the postexilic setting of Judith; the presence of Persian practices, terms, and names (see INTRODUCTION, pp. 49f.); plus the absence of Greek personal and place names—all these considerations make it quite likely, in the judgment of the present writer, that the author utilized information, possibly oral in character, from the time of Artaxerxes III. But if so, then—as many supporters of this identification quickly concede—the year of Judith's composition does not date to this period.

That both "sections" of the Judith-story have Maccabean elements cannot be denied. There is in Judith, for instance, the religious crisis, i.e., the potential destruction of the Temple and the compulsory worshiping of "Nebuchadnezzar" as god.[26] However, it is the second part of Judith (chaps. 4–16) that is more clearly Maccabean in its spirit, in its religious practices and political institutions.[27] Not surprisingly then, some scholars would equate Judith's "Nebuchadnezzar" with one of the Syrian kings during the lifetime of Judas Maccabeus,[28] namely, Antiochus IV, Epiphanes (175–163 B.C.) or Demetrius I (162–150 B.C.). "Parallels" between the activities of Antiochus IV and "Nebuchadnezzar" would be that both had a Western campaign against Egypt and Judea (Jdt 1:9–12 and 1 Macc 1:16) and an Eastern one (against Media and Ecbatana in Jdt 1:14; against Persia and Persepolis in 1 Macc 3:31 and 2 Macc 9:2–3). And, just as "Nebuchadnezzar" had Holofernes cross the Euphrates and destroy great cities and temples (Jdt 2:24 and 3:8), so Antiochus (see Plate 2) and General Nicanor tried to do the same (1 Macc 3:37; 6:1–2; 7:33–35). Generally speaking, however, scholars who believe that one of the Syrian kings was the model for "Nebuchadnezzar" are not particularly interested in establishing the historicity of the events attributed to him or his

[25] To Soubigiou's list of scholars supporting this identification with Judith's "Nebuchadnezzar" (p. 492) should be added such names as Cowley, Delcor, Eissfeldt, Grintz, and Keil.

[26] See NOTES on 3:8; also on "Who is god except Nebuchadnezzar?" in 6:2.

[27] See, for example, the NOTE on 12:2, the first two NOTES on 4:6; and the NOTE on 4:8.

[28] But Miller *(Buch Judith)* would date Judith to the time of either Antiochus III, the Great (223–187 B.C.), or his successor, Seleucus IV, Philopater (187–175 B.C. [so also Steinmann]).

wicked general. Rather, these scholars tend to see the book as being more of one piece. In this respect, they are certainly correct.

THE SO-CALLED IMBALANCE OF THE NARRATIVE

In the eyes of many, Judith consists of two very unequal parts (chaps. 1–7 and 8–16), "unequal" not so much with respect to their length[29] as to their respective importance, interest, and literary quality. Perhaps the "kindest" cut by a critic was that of Paul Winter: "The narrative is slightly dispropor- tionate in its parts" (IDB, II, 1024). Regarding the first seven chapters as providing introduction and background for Judith's activities, Alonso- Schökel (p. 3) concluded that the great length of the first part was not justi- fied by the narrative function it fulfilled. Dancy was even more critical and specific with regard to the first seven chapters: ". . . duller in thought and flatter in style [than chaps. 8–16]. . . . The historical setting has few merits. Dramatically it is spoiled by tedious descriptions (especially 1:2–4, 4:9–15) and confusions (e.g., 2:21–27), stylistically by exaggerations (e.g., 1:16) and empty rhetoric (e.g., 2:5–13)."[30] (p. 68) W. O. E. Oesterley in effect deni- grated the first part of Judith when he wrote: ". . . from chapter viii on- wards one is carried along in almost breathless excitement; it is a masterpiece of narration" (Books of the Apocrypha, p. 374). Perhaps it is worth noting that the thirteen midrashim on the Judith-story, as recorded in André Dubarle's work, suppress the first part (although there may be other than mere literary considerations for this "suppression"; see INTRODUCTION, pp. 103–8).

However, recently (and rightly) there has been a gradual shift toward a greater appreciation of chaps. 1–7, especially as scholars view Judith more as a literary tale rather than as a historical novel. Montague, for instance, writes: "This section [chaps. 1–7] sets the stage for Judith's intervention by describ- ing in heightening strokes the desperate situation of the Jews. . . . [Nebuchadnezzar's] swallowing up of Arphaxad (otherwise historically un- known) dramatizes the practically cosmic threat which he presents to the western world, of which Israel is part." (Books of Esther and Judith, p. 15) It is unfortunate, perhaps, that the book is always called "Judith," for that simple fact naturally puts the spotlight on the adventures of the heroine. If the book had another name, such as Beast and the Beauty or, in the more contemporary idiom, "Two Interrelated Case Studies: A Servant of Man Vis- à-vis a Servant of God," then we would undoubtedly have an entirely differ-

---

[29] In the LXX edition of Brooke, McLean, and Thackeray (Esther, Judith, Tobit), chaps. 1–7 consist of 291 lines of actual Greek; chaps. 8–16, of 413 lines, thereby making the second section longer by 42 percent.

[30] For a radically different assessment of 2:5–13, see COMMENT on SECTION II, p. 134.

ent perception of the book; for a title often tells the audience what they are expected to see or hear.

Regardless of whether the book is actually misnamed, recent scholarship indicates a new appreciation for chaps. 1–7. These seven chapters fulfill a structural function, namely, in a number of ways and levels they serve as a foil to chaps. 8–16. More specifically, in the first part of Judith, Nebuchadnezzar and Holofernes won all the battles; in the second part, Judith and the Israelites (so Wayne Peters in Alonso-Schökel, p. 34). Then too, raw masculine power prevailed in the first part; "soft" feminine beauty and wiles in the second. All the Israelite males—the magistrates and the men of Bethulia, as well as the men in all the other Israelite towns and cities, not to mention the high priest and the entire religious and political hierarchy in Jerusalem (chaps. 4–6)—hid behind the safety of their town walls, but Judith and her slave left the security of their city to go out and meet the enemy. In chap. 5, Achior was honest, straightforward, and totally unsuccessful in convincing Holofernes of the truth, while Judith in her dealings with Holofernes was deceitful, dishonest—and totally successful. By chap. 5, the Gentile Achior knew Israel's God better than did the Israelite magistrates of Bethulia (see NOTES *passim* in chap. 8). Holofernes, the undisputed master of men and nations (chaps. 2–7), was mastered by a female! The preceding contrasts and ironies are, by no means, the only ones within the two parts (see INTRODUCTION, pp. 78–85).

Thanks to the excellent rhetorical criticism done on Judith by Toni Craven (she herself prefers the term "compositional analysis"),[31] it becomes increasingly clear that the book of Judith is made of a whole cloth and was intended as a balanced and proportional narrative. Craven's study shows that the book has in each of its parts a threefold chiastic structure and a distinctive thematic repetition. More specifically, each part has as its major chiastic feature its own repeating theme: in chaps. 1–7, the theme is *fear* or its denial (cf. 1:11; 2:28 [twice]; 4:2; 5:23; 7:4), and men play all the leading roles; in chaps. 8–16 it is *beauty,* mentioned or implied, and a woman has center stage.[32] Thus, just as *fear of the Assyrians* had a "domino effect," knocking down successive nations and peoples in chaps. 1–7, so *Judith's beauty* bowled over one male after another (see NOTE on 10:7). Craven has schematized the two parts as follows:

[31] Craven first presented her views in a brief article, "Artistry and Faith in the Book of Judith," *Semeia* 8 (1977): 75–101. A detailed treatment of her views may be found in her Ph.D. dissertation published by Scholars Press as part of the SBL dissertation series, which, unfortunately, has the same title as her article and in this commentary is designated AFBJ.

[32] Cf. Jdt 8:7; 10:4, 7, 10, 14, 19, 23; 11:21; 12:12, 16, 20; 16:6, 9.

Chapters 1–7
1. Introduction to Nebuchadnezzar and his campaigns against Arphaxad (1:1–16)
2. Nebuchadnezzar commissions Holofernes to take vengeance on the disobedient nations (2:1–13)[33]
3. Development
   A. The campaign against the disobedient nations; the people surrender (2:14–3:10)
   B. Israel hears and is "greatly terrified"; Joakim orders war preparations (4:1–15)
   C. Holofernes talks with Achior. Achior is expelled from the Assyrian camp (5:1–6:11)
   C′ Achior is received into Bethulia; he talks with the people of Israel (6:12–21)
   B′ Holofernes orders war preparations; Israel sees and is "greatly terrified" (7:1–5)
   A′ The campaign against Bethulia; the people want to surrender (7:6–32)

. . . Each unit in this chiastic pattern is defined by a major geographic shift of scene and an alternation between the nations of Assyria and Israel. Each of the sections is introduced by a temporal clause indicated either by a pleonistic *kai* in simple juxtaposition with a second verb in the pattern of the Hebrew *waw-conversive* or by the particle *de* followed by a temporal phrase. *(Semeia* 8 [1977]: 81f.)[34]

Chapters 8–16
   A. Introduction to Judith (8:1–8)
   B. Judith plans to save Israel (8:9–10:8)
   C. Judith and her maid leave Bethulia (10:9–10)
   D. Judith overcomes Holofernes (10:11–13:10a)
   C′ Judith and her maid return to Bethulia (13:10b–11)
   B′ Judith plans the destruction of Israel's enemy (13:12–16:20)
   A′ Conclusion about Judith (16:21–25)

[33] Craven offers the following explanation for the historical and geographical difficulties in the opening chapters of Judith: "The Book of Judith simply does not yield literal or even allegorical data. Instead, its opening details seem to be a playful manipulation of both histori- and geographical facts and inventions. The author's proclivity to imaginative fabrications continues throughout the entire story, even to the making up of the town so important in the story, Bethulia. The historical and geographical absurdities point not to ineptitude on the part of the author, but rather to skillfulness in focusing attention on something other than a historical recitation." (SBLDS 70, pp. 73–74)

[34] At first glance, Craven's singling out of these distinctive syntactical features at the beginning of each "scene change" in this chiasm and the next might seem impressive and even persuasive. Unfortunately, the same characterizations concerning syntax could be made about many verses throughout Judith. In other words, the syntactical features Craven notes here are in no way distinctive or conclusive for her general position.

. . . The heart of this chiastic structure (D) is the heart of the story, and both form and content signal the climactic significance of Judith's triumph over Holofernes. *(Semeia* 8 [1977]: 88)

Because Craven, in contrast to most commentators, was perceptive enough to notice that nowhere does Judith's Nebuchadnezzar actually instruct Holofernes to have people worship him as a god (see COMMENT on SECTION II, p. 134), Craven has noted another "thematic relationship" which also ties the two parts together, namely:

Each [i.e., Holofernes and Judith] acts out a "commission" not explicitly ordered from on high. No word of Yahweh confers authority for Judith to deliver Israel; no word of Nebuchadnezzar grants Holofernes the right to acclaim him God. Nebuchadnezzar is not party to the religious struggle of the story. . . . Holofernes himself demands the worship of Nebuchadnezzar, for it is he—not Nebuchadnezzar—who is punished. . . . The beheading of Holofernes provides both literary and theological resolution; Holofernes is overcome; Yahweh triumphs at the hand of the woman Judith. *(Semeia* 8 [1977]: 93)

Craven might also have observed that Achior is a crucial character for uniting both sections of the book. For Achior has one foot solidly planted in the first part (chaps. 5–6) and his second foot resting in the other (11:9–19; 14:6–10). Achior is a splendid study in contrasts and an effective foil for several of the book's characters. For example, in comparison to the wicked Holofernes, Achior is "the Righteous Gentile" who was saved by the Jews (see NOTE on his name in 5:5). When compared with Judith, Achior is the honest but ineffective advisor. An experienced soldier, Achior fainted when he saw the head that Judith had cut off with her own two hands. Yet Achior had more faith in the character and ways of Israel's God than did the magistrates of Bethulia. If his name really was Achior and if it is really Hebrew, then Achior was well named (i.e., "Light is my [divine] brother"; see NOTE on 5:5); for his survey of Jewish history in chap. 5 was a means whereby the author could express his own theology. Moreover, that same survey also provided the orientation necessary for Holofernes to "understand" and believe Judith when she explained to him why she was betraying her people (see 11:9–19, especially the second NOTE on 11:13). Finally, after confirming for the Bethulians that the severed head was indeed Holofernes', Achior then converted to Judaism, thereby making himself—an accursed Ammonite (see first NOTE on 14:10)—one with God and his people.

RELIGIOUS VIEWS AND VALUES IN THE BOOK

The theological views and values of the author are skillfully conveyed by him in two ways: (1) explicitly by statements in the speeches, prayers, and conversations of the characters; and (2) implicitly in the actions of the characters, especially Judith. God has a variety of names and titles in Judith, including such frequently used ones as "the Lord" (4:11; 8:11; 9:1), "God" (8:11; 11:6), "the God of Israel" (6:21; 9:12; 10:1; 12:8; 14:10), and "the Lord [their/our] God" (4:2; 7:19; 8:14; 13:18),[35] as well as those used but once or twice: "the God of Heaven" (5:8), "Lord God of Heaven" (6:19), "the Lord [God] who crushes wars" (9:7; 16:2), "the Lord of our ancestors" (7:28), "the God of my ancestor Simeon" (9:2), "the God of the humble" (9:11), "God of my father" (9:12), "ruler of heaven and earth" (9:12), "creator of the waters" (9:12), "King of all your creation" (9:12), and "God Most High" (13:18).

As for God's attributes, he is the one, true (8:20), omnipotent Lord (4:13; 8:13; 15:10; 16:5, 17), invincible (16:13b), unfathomable and inscrutable (8:14), as well as vengeful and wrathful (9:2; 9:8; 16:17), yet also merciful to those who fear him (16:15), and the God of the underdog (9:11). The Creator of the universe *and* the Lord of history (9:12; 13:18), Yahweh has guided Israel from its patriarchal period (5:6–9; 8:26; 9:2–4), through its stay in and escape from Egypt (5:10–13) and its wandering in the wilderness and its conquest of Canaan (5:14–16), into its preexilic, exilic, and postexilic periods (5:17–19; 8:18–20). The God of Israel is also the one who is in control of world history (9:5), including its end (16:17).

Although the word "covenant" occurs only once in Judith (9:13), the concept itself is quite basic, and is interpreted largely in Deuteronomistic terms (see Jdt 5:17–18, 20–21; 8:20; 11:10). Consistent with such a theological perspective is the book's strong emphasis on the importance of Jerusalem (4:2; 10:8; 11:19; 15:9; 16:18, 20) and its Temple (4:2–3, 12; 8:21, 24; 9:8, 13; 16:20).[36] The cultus in Jerusalem is depicted as being in full operation, complete with the temple complex (16:20), altar and sacred utensils (4:3), high priest (4:6), priests and Levites (4:14–15), various kinds of sacrifices and offerings, including the evening incense offering (4:14; 9:1; 16:18), and the firstfruits of grain and the tithes of wine and oil for the priests (11:13). In Jerusalem the priests and laity (and the Israelites elsewhere) prayed, fasted, and wore sackcloth (4:11–15). In short, except for almsgiving and the baptism of Gentile converts to Judaism (see NOTE on "he was circumcised and was admitted" in 14:10), virtually all the traditional Jewish practices of both

---

[35] The citations for each of the preceding titles are not exhaustive.

[36] It is curious that in the Song of Judith (16:1–17) neither Jerusalem nor the Temple is mentioned. (Nor is Holofernes mentioned by name.)

the cultus and individuals are mentioned. In fact, nothing noted thus far about God's titles or attributes in the book of Judith or about the cultus or the religious practices of individuals is at all unusual or noteworthy. More specifically, all of it is essentially typical of Maccabean Judaism. (Were it not for the sweeping political and military authority of the high priest, Joakim, and the very strenuous fasting practices of Judith in 8:6, a much earlier date could be assigned [see NOTES in 4:6 on "Joakim" and "who was in Jerusalem at that time"].)

In Judith, it is not what the Israelites believed about God or how they practiced their religion that is in any way unusual. Rather, it is who the heroine was, and what she did. By the standards of her day, Judith lived a saintly life ("there was no one who spoke ill of her, so devoutly did she fear God" [8:8]). Once her husband had died, Judith devoted herself to constant prayer and fasting (8:4–6). Beautiful and wealthy, she lived simply (12:4) and as a celibate to her dying day (16:22). Judith emancipated her trusted servant (16:23), and before she died she distributed her wealth in the approved fashion (16:24). With the passing of time her fame increased rather than diminished (16:23). Judith was a saint.

She was also—for the sake of her God and her people—a shameless flatterer (11:7–8), a bold-faced liar (11:12–14, 18–19), and a ruthless assassin (13:7–8), with no respect for the dead (13:9–10, 15). While such aphorisms as "All's fair in love and war" and "The end justifies the means" have frequently been voiced by men and women down through the ages, they have rarely been subscribed to by "the saints." But Judith is an exception: she was the saint who murdered for her people! (see 13:20) While such a characterization may strike the reader as oxymoronic, one should remember that what one person regards as an oxymoron, someone else may call a "paradox."

Unquestionably, the application of the term "saint" to Judith will also be objectionable to some readers. Certainly, every religious community has its particular definition of the word, but the concept usually includes one who is eminent for piety or virtue as defined by the particular group in question. In Judith's case, her total and lifelong devotion to her God and her people is indisputable; and her people's acceptance of her as deeply religious is equally clear (see 8:8, 28–31; 13:18–20; 16:23). Interestingly enough, in discussing the question of why the book of Judith was denied admission to the Jewish canon, neither ancient nor modern scholars suggest that her deceitful and murderous conduct toward Holofernes was what made the book unacceptable for inclusion in the canon.[37] In other words, while some scholars have questioned the morality of Judith's conduct, they have not questioned her devo-

---

[37] It is true, however, that Jerome was at pains to explain that Judith was praised not because of her successful lying but because of her devotion to her people (*Adversus Rufinum* 1).

tion to God or her people. Like it or not, then, for the ancient author, Judith was a saint.

Perhaps the word "murdered" (i.e., "the saint who murdered for her people") will strike some readers as too strong a term. After all, a variety of English words are used for the act of depriving a person of his or her life. For instance, "to execute" often has the connotation of carrying out a legal sentence without any personal malice, while "to assassinate" suggests a sudden and treacherous attack for personal or political reasons.[38] "To kill" is a relatively neutral term for depriving someone of life, while "to murder" means to kill unlawfully and, often, with premeditated malice. Inasmuch as Judith was already in the hands of the enemy (and, if things did not go right, in the arms of Holofernes), the term "murder" seems more accurate than "assassinate." In short, Judith was the saint who murdered for her people.

Judith, like many heroes past and present, had a goodly share of desirable qualities: a very attractive physical appearance, intelligence, resourcefulness, and great personal courage, to name only a few. Like many natural-born leaders, Judith had great confidence in herself. What makes her unique among biblical heroines is her piety and the particular outward forms that piety took, i.e., strenuous fasting, constant prayer, celibacy, and great concern for observing the laws of kašrût.[39] In this respect, none of the other biblical heroines are like her, not Miriam, Deborah, Jael, or Esther.[40] Evidently, the author intended Judith's piety as well as her confidence in God to be an inspirational example to his readers. That is, in the face of any present or future threat to the Jewish religion or state, Jews should follow Judith's example of courage, Pharisaic piety, ardent nationalism, and confidence in God. Judith, as her name suggests (i.e., "Jewess"; but see first NOTE on 8:1), was the personification of the Jewish people, loyal to their God and to one another.

But if Judith is the heroine of the tale, God is the hero. (Neither the magistrates of Bethulia nor Joakim the high priest qualifies for that title.) Ultimately, it was not Judith who saved her people. Rather, it was God, using

---

[38] A good example of a female assassin is Charlotte Corday, who in 1793 stabbed to death in his bathtub Jean-Paul Marat, one of the most bloodthirsty leaders of the French Revolution. Corday had met Marat for the first time only minutes before.

[39] I.e., laws concerning ceremonial, ritual, or dietary "cleanness" (cf. Jdt 10:5; 11:13; 12:2, 7, 19). In the OT, foods were either clean or unclean. For example, among the meats, ruminants with cloven hooves, and fish with fins and scales were clean (see Lev 11:2–12), while other meats were unclean, including pork, certain birds and insects, all reptiles (see Lev 11:13–44). For a brief discussion of dietary laws in the OT and more technical aspects of kašrût, see L. E. Toombs, "Clean and unclean," IDB, I, 641–48.

[40] Queen Esther apparently ate the delicacies from the king's cuisine (see Esth 2:9). However, in Add C 28 of the LXX Esther, she tries to avoid eating the king's food, some of which was certainly not kosher. But even here, Esther's abstinence is not as total as Daniel's (cf. Dan 1:8, 13, 15) or Judith's.

her as his means.[41] The author is very emphatic on this point, having Judith herself affirm it on three separate occasions: when speaking to Uzziah ("Rather, as we wait for [God's] deliverance, let us call upon him to help us. He will listen to our voice, if he is so disposed" [8:17]), when praying to God ("bring your fury on their heads: put into my hand—a widow's—the strength I need. By the guile of my lips strike down the slave with the ruler and the ruler with his servant. Break their pride by the hand of a female!" [9:9–10]), and when addressing the Bethulians on her safe return ("God our God is with us, still displaying his strength in Israel and his might against our enemies, as he has today" [13:11]; "Praise God, who has not withdrawn his mercy from the House of Israel, but has shattered our enemies by my hand this very night" [13:14]; "Here's the head of Holofernes . . . and here's the canopy. . . . The Lord has struck him down by the hand of a female" [13:15]). Uzziah makes the same point in 13:18b: "Blessed also is the Lord God, who created the heavens and the earth, who guided you in crushing the head of the leader of our enemies!" Finally, the point is emphatically made in the Song of Judith:

> For the Lord is a God who crushes wars;
> Bringing me into his camp among his people,
> He delivered me from the power of my pursuers. (16:2)

> The Omnipotent Lord has foiled them
> By the hand of a female. (16:5)

Another theological emphasis in the book, while not peculiar to Judith in the OT, is very well expressed, namely, sometimes human suffering is a means of divine *testing* rather than punishment (see NOTES on 7:28 ["who punishes us for our sins"] and 8:18–27 and COMMENT I on SECTION VIII). In A. Kolenkow's apt description of this aspect: "Achior is putting forth a typical Deuteronomic notion of what the natives understand about Israel: 'either win or sin.' The Israelites say, 'Oh, yes!' because Deuteronomy is part of their heritage. Judith then has to enlarge their understanding because there is a third category, 'being sinless and yet things go badly.' . . . The mere retribution idea of punishment is the idea Judith is speaking against. Judith tells the people, 'You are the righteous' (almost too strongly)." (Alonso-Schökel, p. 66)

---

[41] This is true even though, as Alonso-Schökel points out: "Only once is God the subject of a sentence uttered by the narrator (4:13); but he is ever present in the prayers and blessings and the thanksgivings of the Jews. . . . God is present in the faith, and he acts through the confidence of man. He is not the God of the priestly tradition (especially typified by Chronicles)." (p. 17)

THE HEROINE'S CHARACTER

In commenting on Judith's character and conduct, scholars have often said, in effect, as much about themselves and their times as about Judith. For example, at a time when Christians found themselves mortally threatened by pagan persecutions, scholars like Clement of Rome (30?–?99) saw Judith as a brave and godly woman:

> Many women have received power through the grace of God and have performed many deeds of manly valor. The blessed Judith, when her city was besieged, asked the elders to allow her to go out into the camp of the strangers. So she gave herself up to danger, and went forth from love of her country and her people in the siege, and the Lord delivered over Holofernes by the hand of a woman. (1 *Clem.* 55:45)

Later, in the days when religious persecutions were not so much a threat to the Church Fathers as sexual temptations to a celibate priesthood, such theologians as Tertullian (160?–?230), Methodius of Tyre (third cent.), and Ambrose of Milan (339–97)[42] praised Judith highly, not so much for her courageous assassination of Holofernes as for her self-imposed celibacy.[43] A good example of their attitude toward Judith's celibacy is expressed in the admonishment of St. Fulgentius of Ruspe to the widow Galla:

> Chastity went forth to do battle against lust, and holy humility forward to the destruction of pride. [Holofernes] fought with weapons, [Judith] with fasts; he in drunkenness, she in prayer. Accordingly, a holy widow accomplished by virtue of chastity what the whole people of the Israelites were powerless to do. One woman cut down the leader of such a great army, and restored unhoped-for freedom to the people of God. (Epistle 2.29)

Clearly, Judith was their type of woman.

The values and priorities of a Victorian England, with its patronizing and protective attitude toward "the fairer sex," are well exemplified in the observations of Edwin Cone Bissell, writing in 1886:

> The character [of Judith], moreover, is not simply objectionable from a literary point of view, but even more from a moral stand-point. . . . Her way is strewn with deception from first to last, and yet she is represented as taking God into her counsels and as having his special blessing in her enterprise. . . . she assents to his [i.e., Holofernes'] request to take part in a carousal at his tent and to spend a night in his embrace. . . . In fact, it would seem to have been a mere matter of chance

---

[42] Tertullian, *De monogamia* 17; Migne, *Patrologia Latina,* II, 952; Methodius, *Convivium decem virgin, Oratio* 11.2; Migne, *Patrologia Graeca,* XVIII, 212; Ambrose, *De virginibus* 1.2.4; Migne, *Patrologia Latina,* XVI, 213.

[43] The early Church Fathers were by no means the only Christians who praised Judith primarily in terms of her chastity. For example, the Anglo-Saxon Aelfric (ca. 1000 A.D.) so viewed her in the famous Old English poem "Judith" (for details, see Pringle, *Traditio* 31 [1975]: 83–97).

that Judith escaped an impure connection with Holofernes, and something which she could by no means have counted on as certain—not to say probable—when she went to his tent. Indeed, her entire proceeding makes upon us the impression that she would have been willing even to have yielded her body to this lascivious Assyrian for the sake of accomplishing her purpose. That God by his providence interposed to prevent such a crime, cannot relieve her of the odium attaching to her conduct. . . . And she exposes herself in this manner to sin, simply for the present purpose of gaining the confidence of a weak slave of his passions that she may put him to death. . . . there are elements of moral turpitude in the character of Judith. (p. 163)

Clearly, Judith was not Bissell's kind of lady.

Although the women's movement is recent, it has already provided some new insights and radically different perspectives on Judith. According to Patricia Montley,[44] Judith is the archetypal androgyne. She is more than the Warrior Woman and the *femme fatale,* a combination of the soldier and the seductress. As Montley has rightly noted:

The androgyne possesses the characteristics usually attributed to males and the characteristics usually attributed to females. Androgynous gods are not uncommon in Eastern or Western cultures. . . . In the ancient Greek pantheon, Hermes, Hermaphrodite, and Eros were male-female. . . . The Babylonian moon god Sinn *[sic]* was addressed by worshippers as "Mother Womb, begetter of all things, O Merciful Father who hath taken into his care the whole world." (p. 39)

What makes Judith's androgyny so unusual and fascinating, argues Montley, is that her "masculinity" and her "feminity" are sequential rather than simultaneous. That is, as a widow she is asexual; in Bethulia with the elders, Judith "plays the man"; in the Assyrian camp, she acts the woman until she resumes her manly role by cutting off Holofernes' head; then back in Bethulia she continues to act the man until the defeat of the Assyrian army, after which she reverts permanently to the asexuality of her widowhood. "In her marvelous androgyny, Judith embodies yet somehow transcends the male/female dichotomy. To this extent, she is a heroine who rises above the sexism of her author's culture." (p. 40) Clearly, Judith is the feminist's kind of person!

Just as the brilliance of a cut diamond is the result of many different facets, so the striking appeal of the book of Judith results from its many facets. The various interests and parochial assessments noted above are not necessarily untrue or mutually exclusive. After all, by the standards of her day and her people, Judith *was* deeply religious; and by the standards of any time or place, she was courageous and clever. And by the standards of most people, except perhaps those whose lives depended upon her saving act, Judith was brutal. Last but not least, she does not fit nicely into our conventional molds of

[44] *Anima* 4 (1978): 37–42. The article contains a very useful bibliography on Judith in the fine arts.

masculinity or femininity; but, as Montley rightly notes, Judith combines and
transcends them. Of such diversity are literary gems made.

THE ORIGINAL LANGUAGE OF THE BOOK

Regardless of the original language of the Judith-story,[45] the LXX version
of Judith gives every indication of being a translation of a Hebrew text.
Unfortunately, no such text has survived (see INTRODUCTION, pp. 101–2).
However, the LXX offers considerable internal evidence for a Hebrew
Vorlage. There are variant readings in the LXX which reflect different underlying Hebrew terms. These, in turn, are often similar in sound and spelling,
and probably arose through some common scribal error from a common
original; see, for example, NOTES on "will suffer no losses" (7:9); "will be
exposed" (8:21); "fixed her hair" (10:3); "have relations with her" (12:16);
"to praise you" (13:19); "cowered in fear" (16:11); and "like water" (16:15).
See also the NOTE in 15:12 on "performed a dance," where the Syr reading
presupposes a Hebrew reading similar in appearance to the Hebrew phrase
posited for the *Vorlage* of the LXX. Then too, in the LXX there are several
awkward words and phrases which are best explained by positing the translator's misreading of a Hebrew word which resembled in appearance (but not
meaning) the one presupposed by the extant Greek rendering (see NOTES on
"among the peoples of" [1:8]; "he reviewed for them the full insult" [2:2];
and "from the uncleanness" [12:7]). Whether we should also include in this
category such readings as "Dothan, which is opposite the great ridge" in 3:9
and "Ephraimite mercenaries" in 6:2, both of which are usually regarded by
scholars as being examples of the same phenomenon, is debatable (see
NOTES). Perhaps it should be noted in passing that most of the readings cited
above come from the second part of the Judith-story, not from the section
featuring Nebuchadnezzar's war against Arphaxad and Holofernes' general
campaign against the West (i.e., chaps. 1–3).

Further evidence of a Hebrew *Vorlage* is to be found in the LXX's quite
literal rendering of Hebrew idioms, such as "all flesh" (2:3); the many idioms
involving the word "face" (2:7, 19, 25; 3:2, 9; 10:23 [three times!]; 11:5;
16:15);[46] the various expressions involving the "eye" (2:11; 3:4; 12:14; 13:20);
"as *someone/something* lives" for oaths (2:12; 11:7; 12:4; 13:16); "it was with-

[45] Scholars have been unpersuaded (and rightly so) of Scholz's view of over a century ago that
the book of Judith was originally composed in Greek *(Commentar über das Buch "Judith").*
Edgar J. Bruns (CBQ 16 [1954]: 12–14) believed that the story was originally in Elephantine
Aramaic; but he offered no philogical or linguistic evidence for this view. Even though the
assertion runs contrary to her general thesis, T. Craven is "no longer convinced that we should
assume a Hebrew original. . . . the Greek text could have been written from the outset in
elegant hebraicised Greek." (SBLDS 70, p. 5).

[46] According to Enslin's count (p. 131), there are sixty-eight occurrences of the Gk *prosōpon* in
Judith.

out number" (2:17); "on the left" for "north" (2:21); "put to the mouth of the sword" (2:27); "a month of days" (3:10); "image of the heart" (8:29); "generation to generation" (8:32); "from small to great" (13:4, 13); "Amen" (13:20; 15:10); "to speak peace" (15:8); and "many days" (16:25).

The reader of the Greek Judith is constantly reminded of its Hebrew *Vorlage*, primarily because of the book's literalistic rendering of Hebrew syntax. For instance, there is the ubiquitous paratactic construction, with almost every other sentence beginning with a *kai*, "and," followed immediately by the verb (i.e., the so-called *waw* consecutive of Hebrew). Equally obvious Hebraisms are *kai egeneto*, which renders Heb *wayĕhî* (2:4; 5:22; 10:1, 18; 12:10; 13:12; 16:21); the reinforcing repetitious infinitive, or infinitive absolute construction (2:13; 6:4; 7:15; 9:4); the *ou . . . ekei* rendering (= the *'šr . . . šm* construction; see 5:19; 7:10); and resumptive pronouns (10:2; 16:3, 5), not to mention a superabundance of *spodra* (= Heb *m'd*, "very") and various forms of *pas* (= Heb *kl*, "all," "every"). Also quite frequent are the appearances of *kai nun* (= Heb *w'th*, in 5:19, 20; 7:11, 25, 26; 8:12, 13, 24, 31; 10:15; 11:2, 3, 9, 11, 17, 23; 14:8) and of *idou* (= Heb *hnh*, in 2:5; 3:2, 3, 4; 9:6, 7; 12:12; 13:15). Less obvious are the instances of hendiadys (2:12; 7:18; 8:5; 9:8, 13, 14; 10:3, 13; 14:10; 16:1, 16), and the variety of ways in which *en* (= Heb *b*, "in," "at," "among," "with," "by," "according to," etc.) is used (see NOTES *passim*).

DATE OF THE BOOK

Judith was probably composed in the Hasmonean period, most likely either toward the end of the reign of John Hyrcanus I (135–104 B.C.) or at the beginning of the reign of Alexander Janneus (103–78 B.C.). Converging lines of evidence, both historical and theological in character, support such a date. But before considering them, one should be mindful of certain distinctive features and accomplishments in the reigns of these two kings.

John Hyrcanus I, who on the death of his father Simon (143–135 B.C.) assumed the offices of high priest and ethnarch of the Jews, may have been the first of the Hasmoneans to regard himself as king.[47] In any event, Hyrcanus certainly played that role quite successfully: he minted coins, concluded a treaty with Rome and Sparta, enriched his kingdom, and extended its borders. Not only did he devastate such cities as Azotus and conquer Scythopolis, both of which were mentioned in Judith (2:28 and 3:10, respectively), but he also defeated the Idumeans and compelled them to convert to Judaism. But even more important for our purposes here, by 107 B.C. Hyr-

---

[47] There is no question that his son and successor, Judas Aristobulus I (103 B.C.), referred to himself as "King of the Jews."

canus had annexed all the territory of Samaria, having destroyed earlier the Samaritan temple on Mount Gerizim,[48] as well as Samaria and Shechem.

However, the religious zeal that had characterized the early Maccabeans had now grown weaker. Or perhaps "become divided" is a better expression; for in the subsequent period three distinct sects seem to have emerged: the Pharisees, who were the spiritual and cultural descendants of the Hasidim ("the pious") of Judas Maccabeus's days; the Sadducees, who were landed gentry and/or Hellenists; and the Essenes, whose famous Dead Sea Scrolls were found at Qumran. As Hyrcanus's reign progressed, he found himself increasingly siding with the Sadducees against the Pharisees.

Nevertheless, John Hyrcanus did not spill any Pharisee blood. The same cannot be said of his successor, Alexander Janneus.[49] Janneus (Gk *Jannai* = "Jonathan") was a Hellenist in sympathies; or at least he was strongly pro-Sadducee. Unlike John Hyrcanus, Janneus is remembered more for the grief he caused his own countrymen than for the difficulties he created for his Gentile neighbors. When on one terrible occasion the Pharisees pelted him with rotten fruits for his drunken and outrageous behavior as he conducted a high-priestly ritual,[50] his troops fell upon the rioting people and killed six thousand of them. Not surprisingly, a few years later a civil war broke out between the Pharisees and the Sadducean supporters of Janneus. Some six years later (ca. 88 B.C.), Janneus, along with Demetrius III (a Seleucid ally and descendant of Antiochus IV, Epiphanes!), was defeated at Shechem. Nonetheless, several years after that, Janneus had again gained the upper hand; and if Josephus may be believed, on one occasion Janneus crucified eight hundred rebellious Pharisees, allowing his soldiers to rape and kill the wives and children of the condemned men as they hung helpless on their crosses![51] In short, sectarian differences and violent hostility of one Jewish group for another were exceedingly prevalent during Janneus's reign.

Janneus had greater success against his Gentile neighbors, for under his rule Israel enjoyed greater territorial holdings in all directions than it had under any other Maccabean/Hasmonean ruler. According to Josephus *(Ant.* 13.15.4), Janneus ruled over Azotus, a city which according to Jdt 2:28 was not in Israelite hands at the time, a fact of some relevance for dating Judith. A fighting man to the end, Janneus died while fighting in Transjordan in 78 B.C.

A word should be said here about Janneus's queen and successor, Salome

---

[48] So Josephus, *Ant.* 13.9.1; and *Jewish Wars* 1.2.6.

[49] Actually, Judas Aristobulus I was the immediate successor to Hyrcanus, but he reigned for only one year.

[50] According to the Talmud Tractate *Sukka,* Janneus, during a ritual designed to insure that rain would fill the cisterns of Jerusalem, deliberately poured the libation waters on his own feet instead of on the altar.

[51] Small wonder that Janneus has been identified by some scholars with two of the worst villains of the Dead Sea Scrolls, namely, "the Wicked Priest" and/or "the Lion of Wrath."

Alexandra. Fortunately for the Pharisees, she was very sympathetic to their cause; and during her reign (76–67 B.C.) the Pharisees had nine years in which to recover from the ravages of Janneus. Her brother and advisor was Simeon ben Shetah (so *Ber.* 48a), a layman and fanatical leader of the Pharisees. A man of very strong religious convictions and actions, Simeon more than once counseled and carried out harsh acts against those with whom he disagreed. Everything that is known about Simeon suggests that he was the kind of person who would have approved of the murderous conduct and punctilious observance of the Jewish law as practiced by a Judith. Moreover, Simeon seems to have championed certain rights for women, notably in the area of divorce, where they were especially vulnerable (see Y. D. Jilat, "Simeon ben Shetah," EncJud, XIV, 1563–65).

The preceding remarks on the reigns of Hyrcanus and Janneus may be of some value in helping the reader to determine to what extent the political and religious milieu of each is compatible with various elements in the book of Judith.

If Judith's appraisal of the religious situation of her day is accurate, then her people were not guilty of idolatry (see 8:18–20), nor had they committed any sacrilege (11:11–19 notwithstanding). In other words, the author of Judith thought that the crisis that confronted Judea *and Samaria* was more political than religious. Apostasy was not a problem. It was the political independence of their country and the physical well-being of the Temple that were being threatened, not their faith in God. All this suggests that the story took its final form sometime after the days of Judas Maccabeus.

Just as the NT had its "Good Samaritan" (see Luke 10:29–37) so did the OT. And Judith was her name. Ironically, she was also a good Jew. In fact, in the book of Judith *all* the inhabitants of the territory of Samaria were good *Jews,* ready to block Holofernes' path to Jerusalem (4:4–8) and prompt to join in the rout of the Assyrian army (15:3–5). Like the man who missed seeing the forest while looking for a particular tree, many scholars, in their understandable concern to establish the exact location of Bethulia, have overlooked the most significant fact, namely, Bethulia was in *Samaritan* territory! The author has a quite open and friendly attitude toward the Samaritans (cf. 4:4, 6). Such an attitude makes far more sense after 107 B.C. rather than before, that is, some time after John Hyrcanus had annexed and integrated, so to speak, the territory.

With some justice, however, D. N. Freedman has argued that a Judean conquest of Samaritans

> would hardly improve feelings between the two parties unless they were different from the rest of mankind. The NT reflects the bitter and deep-hostility between Samaritans and Judeans. The more or less friendly atmosphere must be fictitious, or deliberately reflective of a time when such relations were thought to be friendly.

There would have been periods before the Exile, and also in the Persian Period when high priests of Jerusalem were on good terms with the Sanballats of Samaria. (private correspondence with this writer)

Nonetheless, it is not an uncommon attitude of conquerors to overestimate the "goodwill" of the vanquished or to underestimate their hostility. It seems likely that this is what happened to the author of Judith sometime after Judea's annexation of Samaria.

Just as significant for dating Judith is the fact that the religious views of the book, while essentially those of early Pharisaism (see INTRODUCTION, p. 60), are not belligerently sectarian in character, that is, they are Pharisee in spirit rather than anti-Sadducee or anti-Essene in emphasis. The author, with his irenic attitude toward all Jews, seeing them as being essentially one people and one religion, reflects more the religious situation in the days of John Hyrcanus than of Alexander Janneus, when sectarianism was so rampant and vicious. Given the divisiveness and meanspiritedness of sects in Janneus's day, we find it improbable that an author as conciliatory in spirit toward Ammonites and residents of Samaria as Judith's would have written then. Certainly the later Pharisees, the group ultimately responsible for fixing the Jewish canon, were not pleased with the book's conciliatory spirit.

AUTHOR AND PLACE OF COMPOSITION

Various lines of evidence suggest that the author of Judith was a Palestinian Jew, probably an early Pharisee.[52] First, the central events of the story (i.e., chaps. 4–16) take place in Palestine itself, where the author evidences a more accurate and precise knowledge of geography than he does of his geography outside of Palestine (see INTRODUCTION, p. 47).[53] Second, the *Vorlage* of the Greek Judith was unquestionably Hebrew (see INTRODUCTION, pp. 66–67), and this writer knows of no linguistic evidence that indicates that the story originally was in either Aramaic (see fn. 45) or Greek. (The view of Hans J. Priebatsch ZDPV 90 [1974]: 50–60), who maintains that Judith's identification of Nebuchadnezzar as the "king of the Assyrians" whose residence was at "Nineveh" and who crossed the "Hydaspes" [rather than the Choaspes] is proof that the author of Judith used Eupolemos [a Jewish-Hellenistic scholar of the Hasmonean period], does not constitute a contradiction to the preceding statement.) Finally, the book's religious ideas are Palestinian and Phari-

[52] The author is anonymous, although Wolff *(Buch Judith* pp. 188–96) maintained that the book was written by Achior himself.

[53] Zeitlin (in Enslin, pp. 31–32) opted for the place of writing as Syrian Antioch, maintaining that because the Palestinian Jews are regularly called "Israelites" throughout Judith rather than by the more accurate term "Judeans," the author must have been living in the Diaspora, in a city where Hebrew and Aramaic were spoken with sufficient frequency to justify writing the story. It is more likely, however, that the term "Israelites" is merely an archaism in Judith.

saic in character (see INTRODUCTION, p. 61), with no traces of Alexandrian or Sadducean influence.

To the objection that the author said little, if anything, about a belief in resurrection (see first NOTE on 16:17) or the importance of almsgiving (two major tenets of Pharisaism), it should be observed that almsgiving nowhere naturally fits into the story, and neither does belief in the resurrection of the body. Sadducean authorship of Judith has been argued recently by Hugo Mantel,[54] who regards Judith's repeated emphasis on activities centering around Jerusalem and its Temple (i.e., tithing, sacrifices, ablutions, ritual foods, Levites, high priest, etc.), with no mention of either synagogues or the importance of the study of Torah, as indicative of that particular sectarian group. But there is as little justification for concluding that the author of Judith was a Sadducee as for thinking that he might have been an Essene (after all, Judith did live a disciplined and celibate life) or a Zealot.

That the author had a very positive attitude toward Jews in the Samaritan territory is certainly true, but whether he was himself a native of that particular area, as Torrey long ago suggested, is impossible to say.[55]

THE BOOK'S GENRE

Once scholars stopped regarding Judith as a purely historical account, they started looking for a more accurate characterization of its literary genre. Starting with Martin Luther, who characterized Judith as a poem, "a kind of allegorical . . . passion play,"[56] scholars have had continued difficulty in establishing the precise genre of the story. To say that the book is a fictional account where historical and geographical details serve a literary purpose, while somewhat helpful, is not precise enough. In other words, exactly what kind of fiction is it?

In the last century or so, three general types of answers have been advanced, each having a number of variations and even permutations. Understandably, many scholars have characterized the book as being some form of a *novel*. However, those who subscribe to the word "novel" have not been in agreement as to the proper adjective to modify it. For example, to W. von

[54] *Studies in Judaism* (1976): 60–80. The twelve arguments used by Mantel in his Hebrew article are conveniently summarized by Craven in SBLDS 70, pp. 118–20.

[55] Early in his career, Torrey raised the possibility that our author was actually a Samaritan, possibly from Shechem (JAOS 20 [1899]: 171); later, *Apocryphal Literature*, Torrey proposed that Dothan might be the author's home. Both suggestions are just speculations.

[56] "Judith," wrote Luther in his Preface to Judith, "is the Jewish people . . . Holofernes is the heathen, the godless, and unchristian Lord of all ages." Actually, the allegorical approach to Judith had been advanced as early as Jerome, who compared Judith's actions to the Church's "decapitation" of the Devil; but the allegorical approach, at least as applied to Judith, was not in vogue throughout the Middle Ages, Church Fathers preferring to regard the book as a historical account.

Wilamowitz's argument that Judith is "a typical hellenistic novel," Altheim and Stiehl agreed, but quickly added that the book was, even more so, a *Jewish* novel (pp. 200–1). What Andrews simply called "a religious novel" (p. 35) Dancy describes as "a short historical novel which carries a strong religious message" (p. 67). Dancy went on to say that Judith is "most closely related to popular drama" (p. 127) and "common to all popular literature . . . the basic ingredients of the plot are (i) love and (ii) *either* a journey (quest) or a conflict (military or political); the sequence of events contains (iii) at least one reversal of fortune, and it leads to (iv) a 'happy' ending" (p. 127). Craven *(Semeia* 8 [1977]: 75–101) has gone even further, maintaining that the book *is* "fictional drama, in which history, geography, and characterizations serve a narrative purpose" (p. 95). Finally, Metzger has characterized the book as "a quasi-historical novel" (p. 51).

Folktale is another literary genre suggested for the story. But "folktale" is a rather broad characterization, covering, for example, the book of Jonah which shares certain similarities with Judith and yet is quite different from it (see COMMENT II, p. 130). Exactly what type of tale Judith might be is much debated. Mary P. Coote (in Alonso-Schökel, pp. 21–26) described the book in rather grandiose terms, categorizing it as essentially "an epic rescue story" which combines features of the Faithful Wife[57] and the Female Warrior,[58] both popular folk motifs. By contrast, Alan Dundes (in Alonso-Schökel, pp. 28–29) viewed Judith in more down-to-earth terms. For him, Judith is a tale exemplifying "the perennial battle of the sexes" where, ordinarily, a virgin (rather than a widow) has to sleep with the intoxicated general.[59] In keeping with his identification of Judith's genre, Dundes made certain comparisons which will strike many readers, including the present writer, as quite strained; for example:

> Holofernes wishes to penetrate the city, but Judith prevents him from doing so. . . . Judith penetrates Holofernes' camp rather than Holofernes penetrates her city. . . . The reference to the inability of the land to bear the weight of the invaders [7:4] would appear to be a thinly veiled sexual metaphor. . . . Not only did he not penetrate the narrow passage of the city, but he lost his head over a pretty woman, with the loss of his sword and head constituting symbolic castration. . . . The invaded becomes the invader. . . . The functional equivalent of a "virgin" does not lose her maidenhead but rather she wins the head of the male oppressor. (in Alonso-Schökel, pp. 28–29)

[57] That is, the enslaved husband is rescued by his chaste wife who, in her disguise, wins the favor of her husband's captors and secures his release (Grimm, #218).

[58] The ideal of femininity and beauty, the Female Warrior derives her power from assuming a male role; independent of male authority, she remains chaste, and her name has special significance.

[59] See K. 872, in Thompson, *Motif-Index of Folk-Literature.*

While the present writer has, in principle, no objections to the idea that conscious as well as unconscious libidinous energy may affect a storyteller's narrative, he finds the particular examples cited by Dundes as strained and unpersuasive.

Moreover, sometimes a Freudian analysis of a literary work may say more about the analyst than the thing analyzed, Erich Fromm's interpretation of a well-known version of "Little Red Riding Hood" being a case in point. In his *The Forgotten Language* Fromm argued that

> Most of the symbolism in this fairy tale can be understood without difficulty. The "little cap of red velvet" is a symbol of menstruation. The little girl of whose adventures we hear has become a mature woman and is now confronted with the problem of sex.
>
> The warning "not to run off the path" so as not "to fall and break the bottle" is clearly a warning against the danger of sex and of losing her virginity.
>
> The wolf's sexual appetite is aroused by the sight of the girl and he tries to seduce her by suggesting that she "look around and hear how sweetly the birds are singing." . . . The wolf, masquerading as the grandmother, swallows innocent Little Red-Cap. When he has appeased his appetite, he falls asleep. . . .
>
> How, then, is the wolf made ridiculous? By showing that he attempted to play the role of a pregnant woman, having living beings in his belly. Little Red-Cap [having been cut out of the wolf by the woodsman] puts stones, a symbol of sterility, into his belly, and the wolf collapses and dies. . . . This fairy tale, in which the main figures are three generations of women . . . speaks of the male-female conflict; it is a story of triumph by man-hating women, ending with their victory. (pp. 240–41)

For an amusing but biting criticism of Fromm's analysis of this much-loved fairy tale, see Coffin, *Female Hero,* pp. 152–57.

With respect to Judith, Coote has rightly observed, "the man-woman issue . . . is part of the meaning but only a part. . . . it's a rescue story, basically. The male versus female dichotomy is the issue which defines the conflict in a certain way and lends the central character special power" (in Alonso-Schökel, p. 54). Finally, Ernst Haag,[60] while categorizing the story as "an example narrative," went on to say that Judith has "suprahistorical" (lit. *übergeschichtliches)* or metahistorical dimensions. Using a phenomenological analysis, Haag regards the book of Judith as a free, parabolic historical representation, where Nebuchadnezzar is "a type of Anti-Yahweh," a representative of God's Enemy in the Final Times, although Judith's Nebuchadnezzar does not represent *the* final battle. In some ways, Haag's characterization of the book approaches the third genre.

The third basic type of genre, and by its very nature the most difficult to describe with precision, is *apocalypse.* In the late nineteenth century, Anton

---

[60] Haag's views are clearly expressed in a brief article *(Bibel und Kirche* 19 [1964]: 38–42), and worked out in greater detail in his *Studien zum Buche Judith.*

Scholz *(Buch Judith)*, while still viewing Judith as an allegory, even more emphasized the eschatological aspects of the story. According to Scholz, Holofernes' attacks are those of the Anti-Christ against the Kingdom of God, with Bethulia and Judith representing Israel and the Church, respectively.[61] Other Roman Catholic scholars have also subscribed to an apocalyptic interpretation. A. Lefèvre viewed Judith as "an apocalyptic parable . . . without even an ounce of the miraculous" *(Supplément au Dictionnaire de la Bible,* IV, col. 1319), and Barucq, readily conceding that the book has none of the conventional characteristics or marks of an apocalypse (i.e., no esoteric or baffling imagery, no symbolic numbers, etc.), insisted that "the fundamental idea of the book is plainly *[franchement]* apocalyptic" (p. 11).

Although eschewing such terms as "apocalyptic" and "eschatological" and preferring instead to view Judith primarily as an expression of *Heilsgeschichte,* Joseph Dreissen *(Ruth, Esther, Judith)* nonetheless regards Judith as portraying a battle essentially between Yahweh and the Anti-Yahweh. While there is in Judith "a double dialectic between King Nebuchadnezzar and King Yahweh on the one side, and between Holofernes and Judith on the other," ultimately, there "is only one dialectic: Nebuchadnezzar—Yahweh, or 'gods'—God" (p. 81). Dreissen may be correct in his conclusion; but if so, he has arrived at it while misapplying some of the evidence. To be sure, in Jdt 2:5 Nebuchadnezzar spoke of himself in rather grandiose terms ("Thus says the Great King, lord of the whole world"), and his certainty of success in 2:12b is also quite presumptuous ("I have spoken! I will accomplish these things by my own hand"); but nowhere in chap. 2 does Nebuchadnezzar *himself* lay any claims to divinity. Nor, contrary to Dreissen, do the two passages elsewhere in Judith which claim divinity for Nebuchadnezzar attribute the claim to Nebuchadnezzar himself. Those two passages are:

3:8 Yet he [Holofernes] demolished all their sanctuaries and cut down all their sacred poles. It was granted to him to destroy all the gods of the area so that all the nations should worship Nebuchadnezzar alone—that every dialect and tribe should call upon him as god!

6:2 "Who is god [said Holofernes to Achior] except Nebuchadnezzar? He will send his forces and wipe them off the face of the earth! Their god won't save them."

In 3:8 it is *the narrator* who makes the assertion. It is, at best, an inference he has drawn, for the fact is that Nebuchadnezzar made no such claim in chap. 2

---

[61] While frankly conceding that the typological interpretation of the OT "has fallen into disuse today," McNeil nonetheless insists that "in the case of a book like Judith, . . . it is only the *sensus plenior* [i.e., the fulfillment in Christ and his Church] that justifies our giving it serious theological consideration. . . . Unless Judith is to be seen as a type of Christ, and her killing of Holofernes as a type of cross, why read the book in Church as canonical scripture? . . . The idea of Judith as a type of Christ may be slightly startling to those who would more naturally take her as a type of his Mother. This was the interpretation of the Roman liturgy, which applied to our Lady the praises addressed to Judith." *(The Downside Review* 96 [1978]: 203)

of Judith. (To be sure, in the book of Daniel, Nebuchadnezzar himself claims to be divine.) As for the claim in 6:2, it is Holofernes, not Nebuchadnezzar, who ascribes divinity to the king; and, appropriately, it is Holofernes, not Nebuchadnezzar, who dies in the book of Judith.

Finally, Jean Steinmann *(Lecture de Judith)*, followed by Mathias Delcor,[62] viewed Judith as a brand new genre, "a synthesis of two genres [i.e., the Haggada and the apocalyptic vision] . . . without any appeal to marvelous or miraculous visions" (p. 129). For Steinmann, Judith's "Nebuchadnezzar"

> is a synthetic figure, an example, symbolic and apocalyptic. He is the adversary of God. . . . He is contemporaneous with the author of Judith. He is not of any time. He is not a man; he is a force, an idea incarnate, such as Napoleon. . . . He is Pride, and he is Satan. (p. 24)

In the opinion of the present writer, some of the confusion and disagreement among previous interpreters of the book of Judith, especially those who subscribe to the apocalyptic theory, is rooted in two things: (1) the disproportionate weight some of those scholars have given to a few phrases in two verses of Judith's Song (16:15a, 17); and (2) the excessive importance some scholars have attached to certain similarities between Judith and the book of Daniel, the latter unquestionably an apocalypse. To be sure, there are a couple of verses in the Song of Judith which *may* be of an apocalyptic or eschatological character, namely:

> For the mountains will be moved from their foundations like water;
> The rocks will melt before you like wax. (16:15a)
> Woe to the nations which rise against my people!
> The Omnipotent Lord will take vengeance on them on the day of
>   judgment;
> He will consign their flesh to fire and worms,
> And they will wail with pain forever. (16:17)

But even if these verses should be interpreted in an apocalyptic or eschatological sense, an interpretation which is surely open to question (see NOTES *passim* on 16:15–17), they still stand in sharp contrast to the entire thrust of the book and its central message that mere mortals can, and should, defeat evil through their own efforts rather than just passively wait for God himself to act. In the eyes of this writer, the so-called apocalyptic/eschatological materials in the Song are roughly analogous to the Epilogue of Ecclesiastes, where the "author's" summary of the book is almost the exact antithesis of the entire book, namely:

[62] According to Delcor (Klio 49 [1967]: 151–79), at times Judith is apocalyptic; at times, midrashic. It has certain similarities to the book of Daniel; but, unlike that apocalypse, Judith contains no revelations or visions.

The end of the matter; all has been heard. Fear God, and keep his command-
ments; for this is the whole duty of man. For God will bring every deed into
judgment, with every secret thing, whether good or evil. (Eccl 12:13–14)

Then too, the apocalyptic/eschatological elements in Jdt 16:15a and 17 (if
indeed they really are that) occur in a section which may not have been
composed by the author of Judith, that is, vv 13–17 of the Song may have had
a separate existence prior to the writing of Judith or they may have been
added later (see COMMENT II, pp. 252–57). In any event, to call the book a
kind of apocalypse because of 16:15 and 17 is a classic example of the tail
wagging the dog.

As for Judith's recognized similarities to the apocalyptic book of Daniel, in
both books "Nebuchadnezzar" obviously represents a person or force other
than the historical Nebuchadnezzar of the Neo-Babylonian Empire; and Jdt
11:7[63] seems to be influenced by Dan 2:37–38.[64] But such similarities between
Judith and the book of Daniel do not, at least in this writer's judgment,
transform a folktale into an apocalyptic parable or *quasi*-apocalypse, especially when it is Holofernes, not Nebuchadnezzar, who is *the* villain in Judith.
Recently, Craven has also argued that the apocalyptic interpretation of Steinmann and others "on internal grounds . . . is insupportable" (SBLDS 70, p.
110, n. 81).

THE BOOK'S PURPOSE

While most scholars of the last one hundred years have agreed that the
author of Judith was concerned more with theology than with history and
that he did not intend that his account be taken as describing actual events,
their agreement ends right there. Some indication of the wide range of opinion on this matter may be gained from the following quotations, arranged in
chronological order:

[The author made] an attempt to recommend Pharisaic principles by a sort of
historical novel. (Ball, p. 246 [1888])

The chief concern of the writer is with the telling of the story rather than with the
painting of a moral, in which the wish to interest takes precedence even of the desire
to instruct. . . . The book is well calculated to inspire patriotism and piety. . . .

[63] "For I [said Judith to Holofernes] do swear by Nebuchadnezzar, king of all the earth . . .
that because of you not only do human beings serve [Nebuchadnezzar], but so also the beasts of
the field, the cattle, and the birds of the heavens."
[64] Daniel said to King Nebuchadnezzar, "You, O king, the king of kings, to whom the God of
heaven has given the kingdom, the power, and the might, and the glory, and into whose hand he
has given . . . the beasts of the field, and the birds of the air, making you rule over them all.
. . ."

Views and doctrines which have nothing to do with the progress of the story are not introduced. (Torrey, *Jewish Encylopedia,* VII, 388–89 [1904])

The author is concerned with theology rather than with history. . . . It is, however, possible that the author adopted an existing story or popular tradition, purposely confusing his historical allusions in order to disguise it. (Cowley, p. 243 [1913])

The main purpose of the book is, therefore, clearly to inculcate and to forward Pharisaic Judaism. (Oesterley, *Books of the Apocrypha,* p. 38 [1914])

The apocryphal Book of Judith was written to prove that insistent prayer and unswerving fidelity to the Law can enable even a woman to overcome the most powerful of armies. (Johnson, *Prayer in the Apocrypha,* p. 7 [1948])

Indeed, the author's purpose is not to tell a story but to preach; he exalts national and religious patriotism, armed resistance against the enemies of the country and the religion of the fathers. (Lods, *Histoire de la littérature hébraïque et juive,* p. 789 [1950])

Purpose: 1) God does not abandon his people as long as they are faithful to him . . . ; 2) The Jews ought to struggle energetically against those who want to restrain those observances, strange customs, and to profane their sanctuary; 3) The author intends to present us in Judith the example of a heroic woman who loves God and places her confidence in him. (Soubigou, pp. 495–96 [1952])

Representatives of God and of Satan, Judith and Holofernes are made to illustrate the profound character of these two antagonistic forces. (Steinmann, p. 131 [1953])

The intention of the writer was to celebrate recent victories, to entertain as well as to inspire resistance. (Winter, IDB, II 1025, [1962])

But the object of the book was to carry the same message as the rest of the Old Testament—that "we are his people, and he is our God." (Dancy, p. 69 [1972])

Judith serves as a model, plus affirmation of success, of mortal action in time of difficulty, if man will but grasp the opportunity God has prepared. . . . The hero-story serves as a promise of what can be done if one rejects fear or does not rely on heavenly action in the present. (A. Kolenkov, in Alonso-Schökel, pp. 41–42 [1973])

[Judith is] the homiletic model of a man who preaches or advocates active resistance and not passive surrender. (Alonso-Schökel, p. 66 [1973])

Judith is a fictional drama in which history, geography, and characterizations serve a narrative purpose. By design, the story teaches readiness for the unexpected. (Craven, *Semeia* 8 [1977]: 95)

Scholarly differences concerning the exact date of Judith's composition help to account for the broad range of views regarding the author's intent. In other words, the date one assigns does much to determine one's understanding of the book's purpose, although, in all fairness, it should be granted that the reverse would also be true. In any event, the author's intent as defined, for example, by Lods and Steinmann is more compatible with a date of Judith's composition during or shortly after the days of Judas Maccabeus, while the definitions by Ball, Oesterley, and Craven would seem more appropriate for a somewhat later period, such as during the reign of John Hyrcanus I or the early days of Alexander Janneus. In point of fact, the five aforementioned scholars do subscribe to a date which is compatible with their date for Judith's composition.

All things considered, Judith appears to be a folktale in which its author, a Pharisee and an ironist *extraordinaire* (see INTRODUCTION, pp. 78–84), offered an example story featuring the least likely of models, a pious widow, who by courageously taking matters into her own hands, defeated the enemy and won lasting fame for herself. Such a message is always in vogue, in a period of peace as well as in time of war. The author was intent on telling an interesting and well-crafted story, and every detail of his narrative was designed to serve a literary or theological purpose. By skillfully combining the seemingly incompatible motifs of the Faithful Wife/Widow and the Female Warrior (see fns. 57 and 58, respectively), the author fashioned a heroine who looms larger than life.[65]

IRONY: THE KEY TO THE BOOK

A number of biblical books, including Esther (see AB 7B, p. lvi), make effective use of irony. But few, if any, are as quintessentially ironic as Judith. Failure to recognize this fact has been a primary reason for so many misinterpretations of the book, for whatever else the author of Judith may have been, he was an ironist. Because an ironist often *means* the exact opposite of what he *says,* he runs the risk of being misunderstood, especially if his readers are of too literal a cast of mind or if, as is so often the case with biblical passages and even whole books, the reader is unfamiliar with the *Sitz im Leben,* i.e., the full context or total situation in which the ironic statement is made.[66] The

---

[65] Even if there really was, as some scholars think, a kernel of historicity to the story (i.e., a Jewish woman somewhere, somehow rescued her people by assassinating an enemy leader), the question of Judith's historicity seems irrelevant. D. N. Freedman has taken issue with this view: "Perhaps you are right about the historicity being irrelevant, but that is only because we do not know enough about the background and origin of the story. . . . It may be pure fiction, but even that would be of interest if we knew where the author came from and where he got his background materials. My personal guess is that there was such a woman somewhere, and that while the story has been inflated to international proportions, some of the features are realistic enough to be true. Perhaps in the future more information will be available, perhaps in the form of earlier versions of Judith, or a Hebrew fragment, or something of earlier sources to give us a clue as to the origin of the story and its original setting." (private correspondence with this writer)

[66] Where the total context for an ironic statement is clear, there is little chance of the words being taken literally. When, for example, a young boy sees his father entering the house with his

earliest audience of the Judith-story, which may very well have heard the story rather than read it, would have known its *Sitz im Leben,* while later readers have had to infer it, often taking quite literally as "clues" for understanding the book the very information which originally was understood as ironic. A prime example of this phenomenon is the very first verse of Judith:

> It was the twelfth year of the reign of *Nebuchadnezzar, who ruled over the Assyrians from his capital, Nineveh,* that Arphaxad was ruling over the Medes from Ecbatana. [italics added; for details, see NOTES on 1:1]

The mention of Nebuchadnezzar here as "king of the Assyrians" is no slip of the pen; for he was so identified at least five more times in Judith (cf. 1:7, 11; 2:1, 4; 4:1). Moreover, that any biblical author would not have known that Nebuchadnezzar was king of the Babylonians rather than the Assyrians is improbable; and it is impossible for the author of Judith not to have known of the historical Nebuchadnezzar. After all, the storyteller was an author who knew his people's history well enough to have written a quite creditable survey of it (see Achior's account of Jewish history in Jdt 5) and to have provided Judith with an accurate awareness of certain periods of Israel's past, as evidenced in her confrontation with the magistrates of Bethulia (see NOTES on 8:25–27) and her prayer (especially 9:2–4). If modern readers of Judith could have been present when the story was first told, it is not unlikely that as the author began his account of "Nebuchadnezzar, king of the Assyrians," he would have given his listeners a slight smile or a sly wink. Torrey maintains, with considerable justification, that the effect of 1:1 on Judith's ancient readers (who knew its *Sitz im Leben)* would have been the same as that on modern readers from a story which began: "It happened at the time when Napoleon Bonaparte was king of England, and Otto von Bismarck was on the throne in Mexico" (p. 89). Torrey also suggests that the storyteller might have given his audience "a solemn wink" as he spoke the words. This is not to say that everyone in that audience understood the rest of the story as fiction. In other words, in spite of the caveat in 1:1, many hearers and readers probably took the story essentially at face value.

Definitions of irony are numerous and varied, for "irony, like love, is more readily recognized than defined" (Thompson, *Irony: An Historical Introduc-*

---

clothes soaking, dripping wet, with the lightning flashing outside and the thunder crashing overhead, and hears his father exclaim, "Beautiful day for a walk," there is little likelihood of the boy's taking those words literally. The details of the total situation—that is, the obvious signs of inclement weather, the father's wet clothes, his facial expression and body posture, his tone of voice, the particular emphasis the father gives the various words—all enable the boy to understand that his father does not really mean what he literally says, but the exact opposite. If, however, we ourselves had not witnessed the actual scene and had only read about it, then the fewer details we knew, the greater the likelihood of our taking the father's observation as literally true, especially if we read only: "The boy went to the door, and his father exclaimed, 'Beautiful day for a walk!' "

tion, p. 13). Useful for our purposes here are the definitions of "irony" in Webster's Third New International Dictionary:

1 a: feigned ignorance designed to confound or provoke an antagonist. . . .
   b: DRAMATIC IRONY [irony produced by incongruity between a situation developed in a drama and accompanying or preceding words or actions whose inappropriateness it reveals]
2 a: humor, ridicule, or light sarcasm that adopts a mode of speech the intended implication of which is the opposite of the literal sense of the words. . . .
   b: this mode of expression as a literary style or form. . . .
   c: an ironic utterance or expression
3 : a state of affairs or events that is the reverse of what was or was to be expected: a result opposite to and as if in mockery of the appropriate result. . . .

Given the above definitions of "irony," one can see that the book of Judith is ironic in nature, from the beginning to the end. Literally "to the end." For although Judith was a beautiful and desirable woman, she lived the life of a celibate from the time of her husband's death until her own much later (16:22–23).

Judith's entire life was ironic. A childless widow, she gave spiritual and political life to her people. A wealthy woman after her husband's death, she lived very simply, sometimes almost to the point of starving herself. In a sexist society where the roles of men and women were sharply delineated and kept quite separate, Judith played both roles with eminent success. Unwilling to eat food which was not kosher, she did not hesitate to tell bold-faced lies (see COMMENT I on SECTION XI, p. 212). A "soft" and feminine woman, she murdered Holofernes herself, praying to God to give her the strength to do so. In short, Judith was the saint who murdered for her people.

Holofernes is an ironic figure, too. Able to conquer the entire West,[67] he was unable to defeat the small town of Bethulia. Intending to master a defenseless widow, he was mastered by her. Wanting to use and, if necessary, abuse Judith, Holofernes' body was used and abused by her. His personal sword, which had taken the lives of so many of his enemies, also claimed his.

The minor characters in the story also have something ironic about them. Even before his conversion to Judaism, Achior, a pagan, had more faith in Yahweh's protecting the Israelites as long as they were guiltless than did Uzziah, the chief magistrate of Bethulia, a man who knew firsthand that his people had not yet been guilty of any sacrilege. Although an Ammonite and therefore prohibited by Deut 23:3 from joining the Jewish faith, Achior converted to Judaism. A battle-seasoned warrior, he nonetheless collapsed when Judith unexpectedly showed him Holofernes' head, which she had cut off with her own hands.

---

[67] As Nebuchadnezzar's first in command (2:4), Holofernes would have contributed to the defeat of the Medes and the destruction of their great city of Ecbatana.

It is ironic that Uzziah, whose name means "God is my defense," trusted God in a weak and "womanly" way, sitting behind the safety of the town walls and passively putting everything into God's hands, while Judith, a woman and a widow, acted in "manly" fashion, taking matters into her own hands by leaving the city to go out and face the enemy.

King Nebuchadnezzar claimed that he himself was the "lord of the whole world" (2:5); but the events at Bethulia proved that the God of Israel was actually *the* Lord. And when the Assyrian outpost discovered and arrested Judith, they were soon won over to her side, with the result that they instructed her on how to conduct herself, to best effect, before Holofernes (10:15–16)—a perfect example of the captive capturing her captors! Finally, while all the males of Bethulia hid behind the protection of its walls, it was a *nameless maid* who, because she went out with her mistress to the enemy camp and came back carrying the head of Holofernes in a sack (13:9–10, 15), will be remembered forever.

Writing on the subject of irony in the OT, Edwin M. Good *(Irony in the Old Testament)* maintained that there were several forms of irony in biblical narrative:

> *punctual* irony, the use of words and expressions of ironic intention at particular, more or less isolated, "points." . . . *episodic* irony, the perception of an entire episode with an ironic aim or intent, . . . *thematic* irony, the conjunction of a number of episodes all of which point to an ironic theme or motif. These three types of narrative irony may be interrelated. (pp. 81–82)

Good went on to observe that the techniques of ironic expression in the OT include the juxtaposition of the same word in irony, two forms of the same verb with different meanings, double entendres, the use of words to mean their opposite, the play on sounds (especially alliteration), understatement, and exaggeration (pp. 121–30). Virtually all of these techniques appear in Judith (see NOTES *passim*).

Each of the ironic statements below will be discussed in some detail at its appropriate place in the NOTES, but their ironic character should be reasonably clear even now, although in some instances scholars might debate as to exactly which particular type of irony the saying represents. (The ironic elements have been italicized by the present writer.)

> Holofernes to Achior: "So who are you, Achior and you Ephraimite mercenaries, that *you play the prophet* among us as you have done today, advising us not to make war against the people of Israel because their god will protect them? *Who is god except Nebuchadnezzar? He will send his forces and wipe them off the face of the earth! Their god won't save them."* (6:2) But Achior was not playing the prophet: he was speaking the truth, whereas all that Holofernes said here turned out the exact opposite.

"As for you, Achior, . . . *you shall not again see my face from this day until I take my revenge* on this nation out of Egypt." (6:5) Achior never again saw that face alive, but he did see the severed head.

"My servants will now 'deliver' you to the hill country and leave you at one of the towns in the passes. *You will not die—until you are destroyed with them!"* (6:7–8) Holofernes thought he was sentencing Achior to certain death; but he gave Achior —in the finest sense of the expression—"a life sentence!"

These views, which Good would characterize as "punctual irony," help to create a splendid example of what he calls "episodic irony." The same phenomenon is to be seen in Judith's first personal encounter with Holofernes:

Said Holofernes to Judith: "Courage, woman! Don't be afraid. . . . *You are safe now.* Don't worry; *you will live through this night and for a long while to come,* for no one is going to hurt you." (11:1, 3b–4a) Holofernes was correct: she was safe. *He* was the one whose life was in danger!

"God did well to send you before the people to give strength to our hands and destruction to those who insulted my lord. . . . If you do as you have promised, your god shall be my god; and you shall live in King Nebuchadnezzar's palace and *be famous throughout the world."* (11:22–23) God did do well by sending Judith, and she did become famous; but not for the reasons that Holofernes would have thought.

But if Holofernes spoke the truth (but not in the sense that he had intended it), Judith shows herself to be the master of irony in this episode, as the passages below so brilliantly illustrate:

"permit your maidservant to speak to you, and *I will say nothing false to my lord* this night." (11:5) Because God was *her* lord, Judith's statement was literally true— but totally misleading to Holofernes.

"And if you follow the advice of your maidservant, *God will accomplish something through you,* and *my lord will not fail to achieve his ends."* (11:6) Because Holofernes *did* follow Judith's advice, her lord achieved the destruction of Holofernes and his army.

"For I swear by Nebuchadnezzar . . . that because of you not only do human beings serve him, but also the beasts of the field, the cattle, and the birds of the heavens. Thanks to you, Nebuchadnezzar and all his house shall prosper." (11:7) To swear by Nebuchadnezzar's name meant everything to Holofernes—and nothing to Judith!

"Knowing all this, I, your servant, made my escape from their presence. God has sent me *to accomplish with you the things which will astonish the whole world* whenever people hear about them." (11:16) Holofernes understood Judith to be referring to what she would be doing *for him* when, in actual fact, she was talking about what she would do *to him.* And when asked by Holofernes what she would do when her scant provisions had run out, Judith replied, "As sure as you live, my lord, your servant will not exhaust her supplies *before the Lord God accomplishes by my hand what he had planned.*" (12:4) Holofernes understood Judith to be referring to his victory over Israel; Judith meant her victory over him.

The entire scene is a masterpiece of episodic irony. When Holofernes praised Judith for her beauty and brains ("You are both beautiful and eloquent" [11:23]), he was correct as far as he went. Only Holofernes did not go far enough: he failed to see that Judith was also clever, ruthless, and ironic.

To characterize these statements of Judith as "ironic" is in no way to deny that they were also lies, clever words designed to deceive. But just as shrewdness rather than dishonesty is the most striking feature of the "hero" in Jesus' Parable of the Dishonest Steward (Luke 16:1–9), so Judith's cleverness, albeit wrapped in deceit, is being celebrated here.

While the two scenes described above are *the* masterful episodes in the Judith-story, they are not the only places where irony occurs. Consider the following brief statements:

Judith cautions Uzziah before she leaves Bethulia: "But you must not inquire into *the affair;* for I will not tell you what I am going to do until it is accomplished." (8:34)

On being "invited" by Holofernes to attend his small party, Judith said to the eunuch, "Who am I . . . *that I should refuse my lord? I will do whatever he desires right away,* and *it will be something to boast of until my dying day.*" (12:14) Just as Judith said, her entire life was dedicated to doing *her* lord's will.

"I will indeed drink, my lord," said Judith, "for *today is the greatest day of my whole life.*" (12:18) Not because of what Holofernes was going to do to her, but because of what *she* was going to do to him!

"and approaching the bed, she grabbed the hair of his head and said, *'Lord God of Israel, give me the strength, now!'* Then she struck at his neck twice with all her might, and chopped off his head." (13:7–8) Praying for help to pull off a successful murder is not exactly a routine petition to the God of Israel.

In the Song of Judith, the people sang:
Her sandal *ravished* his eyes;
Her beauty *captivated* his mind.
And the sword slashed through his neck! (16:9)

How ironical! The would-be ravisher is ravished and killed! Sometimes the ironic effect results from a comparison of two separate episodes. For instance, in chap. 5 Achior tells Holofernes the truth and is disbelieved (so 6:2–4), while Judith dissimulates, equivocates, and lies (see NOTES *passim* on 11:5– 12:4, 14, 18)—and is believed. Finally, the theme for the entire book is well stated in 16:5: "The Omnipotent Lord has foiled them by the hand of a female." What could be more ironic than that!

The total effect of all the preceding passages, plus a number of others (see

NOTES *passim)*, is to create a work which contains Good's three categories: punctual, episodic, and thematic irony. Thus, the book of Judith is a perfect example of what Northrop Frye *(Anatomy of Criticism,* p. 162) has characterized as the last of the four categories of narrative literature, namely, the tragic, the comic, the romantic, and the ironic.

It should be noted that, despite the fact that Holofernes is a larger-than-life antagonist who was murdered and in spite of the fact that thousands of Assyrians also died,[68] Judith is comic irony. "Comic" is used here simply as the antonym of "tragic."[69] Humor is a notoriously difficult quality to define. For a word or scene which one person might regard as offensive or slightly embarrassing might make someone else smile or chuckle, while another person might roar with laughter. Scholarly reactions to such scenes as Judith's two encounters with Holofernes run almost the full gamut of emotional reactions. Oesterley, for example, felt that there were "some distinctively revolting passages" in Judith (p. 176); and Pfeiffer found the book to be "unrelieved by a sense of humor" (p. 299); while Louis André saw in it a "bellicose humor" *(Apocryphes,* p. 155); and Dancy thought the humor was "bitter," with "no forgiveness" (p. 130); yet Solomon Zeitlin characterized Judith as "a charming story" (in Enslin, p. 1).

But varied though emotional reactions to the book have been, rare is the scholar who has expressed any sympathy for Holofernes. D. N. Freedman, however, is such an exception; for he has written:

> An appropriate comparison of the principal characters in Judith would be the characters in the Song of Deborah: Sisera and Jael. The circumstances are not exactly the same, but the theme is similar. In some ways, Jael is worse because she invites the man to enter her home, which signifies both hospitality and protection, and then cold-bloodedly kills him when he is helpless. In Judith, the hospitality is extended by Holofernes, but Judith certainly violates the law of guests in a stranger's home. Certainly there is no sympathy for Sisera in the poem or the prose account, but he is an oddly appealing figure: a beaten warrior, but a warrior nevertheless, and one whose mother is concerned about him.
>
> Holofernes has some admirable characteristics in terms of his generalship and his devotion to his master, as well as less ingratiating traits. That he succumbed to the temptations of Judith is hardly surprising; how many others would have resisted (like Joseph who certainly is unusual in the Bible)? One can chiefly criticize his gullibility and stupidity in failing to take ordinary precautions with a foreigner. But that is the basic paradox. Everyone, even Holofernes, knows Judith's reputation for piety and devotion to the God of Israel. As a woman of honor, her word should be

[68] However, the author does not really delight in fighting *per se* (see COMMENT on SECTION I, p. 129f.; and COMMENT on SECTION XV, p. 241).

[69] "Comic" can be used in a wide variety of senses (see Corrigan, *Comedy).* That Pauline passages of great seriousness such as 1 Cor 1:18–2:5 and Rom 9:30–10:21 can be called "comic" is some indication of just how far the term can be from the sense of being funny or laughable (see Via, *Kerygma and Comedy in the New Testament,* especially pp. 40–69).

true, so Holofernes should believe her. At the same time, her devotion to the Law of Moses would rule out the possibility of any kind of contact with a foreigner like Holofernes, so the question of deception has to be raised from the beginning. Her showing up in the Assyrian camp violates so many rules that Holofernes should have been on guard. But then his head was turned by her beauty.

I think that one could muster some sympathy for Holofernes, in spite of the author's obvious and blatant prejudice, namely that Holofernes got exactly what he deserved. I think it is quite possible to have mixed feelings about the leading figures in this story, which perhaps the author did not intend to create, but then his characters are not paper figures but have turned into three-dimensional people with lives and wills of their own. (private correspondence with this writer)

In spite of this eloquent defense by Freedman, many scholars, including this writer, will conclude that Holofernes simply got what he deserved. He is just not perceived as a tragic figure. Nor is a reader of Judith "purged of emotions" as were the ancient Greeks after seeing a tragedy by Aeschylus or Sophocles. Rather, the author expected his readers to be amused as well as inspired by the words and deeds of the heroine.

Judith's advice to the magistrates in 8:14 ("you cannot plumb the depths of a person's heart or understand the thoughts of his mind") is certainly also relevant for the biblical scholar who would presume to explain to his readers the author's intent or the workings of his mind. Nonetheless, the fact remains that, among the people each of us comes in contact with, some have "mathematical" minds or special verbal ability;[70] some folks are "artistic" or "mechanically inclined"; some minds are "prosaic" while others are "imaginative"; some individuals are "rational" while others are analytical, "synthetical," or dialectical in nature. The position of the present writer is that the storyteller had a mind and a perspective which are best described as essentially and profoundly ironic in character. That simple "fact" shaped the whole as well as the major and minor parts of Judith.

To recognize the sweeping applicability of the "ironic theory" does not mean the immediate resolution of all the perplexing problems in Judith. The theory is no procrustean bed; for while it may help to resolve such historical problems as the presence of mutually exclusive preexilic and postexilic data in Judith, the theory does not resolve all the difficulties in the text, the notorious geographical problems being a case in point (see NOTES *passim*). Nonetheless, it does help the reader better to understand and to enjoy Judith when he or she realizes that its original author was an ironist who knew, as did many in his ancient audience, that he was writing fiction rather than fact.

---

[70] To what extent these various attributes, intellectual and psychological, are due to nature, nurture, or both, is beside the point, that is, whatever the reason/s may be, individuals do seem to "have" this or that ability or perspective.

STYLE AND SYNTAX

Very little need be said here about these matters in reference to the original book of Judith (i.e., the Hebrew *Vorlage* of the Greek version [see INTRODUCTION, pp. 66–67]), primarily because a number of significant comments relevant to Judith's syntax and style have already been made in this commentary, albeit in a variety of other contexts. Thus it might be helpful to recapitulate briefly.

As a folktale of the example type, Judith contains the usual elements appropriate for that genre and its subtype;[71] moreover, historical and geographical "details of fact" serve essentially literary and/or theological purposes.[72] From a literary (if not a psychological) point of view, both "sections" of Judith (i.e., chaps. 1–7 and 8–16) represent a balanced and proportional narrative (see INTRODUCTION, pp. 56–59). Irony, of various shapes and shades, is *the* pervasive literary technique in Judith, which is a fact too frequently overlooked.

THE CANONICITY OF JUDITH

Among Jews

The book of Esther had a long and difficult time attaining Jewish canonicity, but it finally did so.[73] Yet the book of Judith, which in its Semitic form had all the essentials of Palestinian Judaism (i.e., God, prayer, dietary scrupulousness, sacrifice, Temple, Jerusalem—*none* of which are even so much as mentioned in the MT of Esther[74]), was never admitted to the Palestinian canon, nor is the book known to have been present at Qumran.[75] Judith may have been excluded from the Hebrew canon because the Rabbis, who were responsible for fixing the canon in the last stages of the canonizing process, disapproved of the book's universalism, i.e., its accepting attitude toward the towns of Samaria and its approval of an Ammonite's admittance into the Jewish faith (so Steinmann, pp. 61–62).

[71] See INTRODUCTION, pp. 72–73; and NOTES *passim.*

[72] Again, the INTRODUCTION is useful (pp. 77–78), but even more so are the NOTES *passim.*

[73] For details, see Moore, *Studies in the Book of Esther,* pp. xxiv–xxvii.

[74] For a brief but accurate comparison of the religious "deficiencies" of the book of Esther *vis-à-vis* Judith, see Gordis, JBL 100 (1981): 359–88, especially p. 360.

[75] According to Delcor (Klio 49 [1967]: 170), the Essenes rejected Judith because of its Pharisaic elements. Nor was the book mentioned by either Philo or Josephus. Given all the heroes and books of the OT not mentioned by Philo, we should not be surprised by his silence concerning Judith (as a matter of fact, he does not mention any books of the Apocrypha). On the other hand, Josephus not only tells the story of Esther, but he even includes several of the Additions to Esther (see AB 44, p. 154). Thus his silence about Judith *may* be an argument against the book's antiquity.

There is genuine merit to Craven's view that Judith was simply too radical a woman for the rabbis who fixed the Jewish canon to memorialize:

> To accept the Book of Judith as a canonical book would be to judge the story holy and authoritative. And to judge the story of the woman Judith holy and authoritative could indeed have been deemed a dangerous precedent by the ancient sages. . . . she is faithful to the letter of the law but not restricted to traditional modes of behavior. . . . she fears no one or thing other than Yahweh. Imagine what life would be like if women were free to chastise the leading men of their communities, if they dared to act independently in the face of traumas, if they refused to marry, and if they had money and servants of their own. Indeed if they, like Judith, hired women to manage their households what would become of all the Eliezers of the world? I suspect that the sages would judge that their communities simply could not bear too many women like Judith. The special genius of this story is that it survived and grew in popularity despite its treatment at the hands of the establishment. (SBLDS 70, pp. 117–18)

However, the most likely reason for Judith's omission from the Hebrew canon is, as H. M. Orlinsky *(Essays in Biblical,* pp. 279–81) has noted, that the Rabbis could not accept it because the book ran counter to their *halakah*[76] that a Gentile convert to Judaism had to be circumcised *and baptized* in order to become a Jew.[77] In other words, not only did Judith have Achior, an Ammonite, accepted into Judaism, which in itself ran counter to Deut 23:3 (but see NOTE on 14:10), but he was not baptized.

> To canonize a book—that is, to make it officially a source of doctrine—when the doctrine did not conform to that of the canonizers, was too much to ask. The Book of Esther, with all its "faults," offered nothing specific that violated Pharisee *halakah.* (p. 218)

Then too, as the festival of Hanukkah fell into disfavor after the Hasmonean dynasty had ended, so the book of Judith, which was associated with the festival (see INTRODUCTION, pp. 105–6) also diminished in importance. Ball (p. 243) went so far as to suggest that the Pharisees may have deliberately suppressed the original Hebrew account, so great was their hatred of the Hasmonean family. Certainly, Judith's setting in Samaritan territory would not have made her story more popular among the Pharisees who fixed the canon (so Winter, IDB, II, 1026).

While scholars naturally look for *the* reason why Judith was not included in the Jewish canon while Esther was, the simple fact may be that just as in secular elections the individual voters cast their ballots for or against a particular candidate for one or more reasons, so the "voting" of the sages for or

---

[76] *Halakah* is that body of Jewish Law in the Talmud which interprets and supplements the laws of the OT.

[77] The latter requirement was made mandatory sometime after A.D. 65 (see Zeitlin, "Proselytes and Proselytism").

ILLUSTRATION OF THE
CANONICAL STATUS
OF JUDITH IN THE
EARLY CHRISTIAN CHURCH

✝ Canonical   ▪ Noncanonical

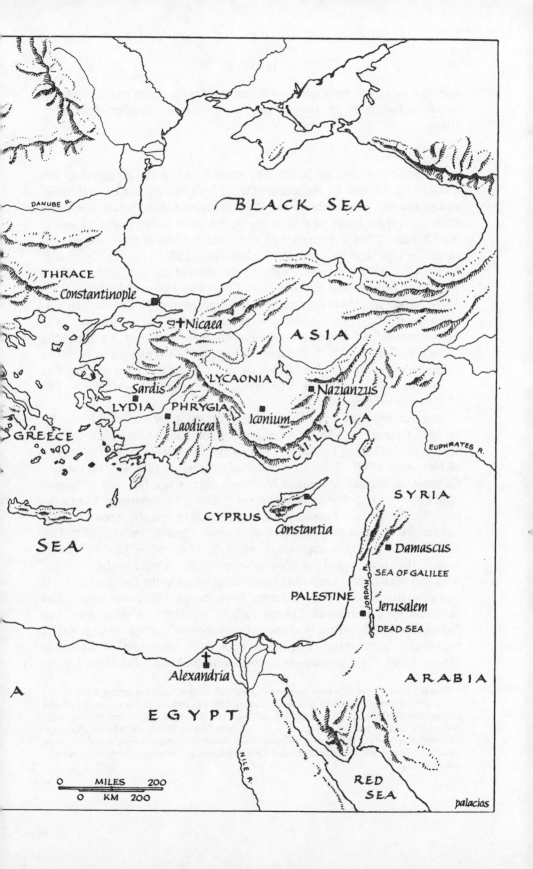

BLACK SEA

THRACE
Constantinople
Nicaea
ASIA
DANUBE R.

LYCAONIA
Sardis
Nazianzus
LYDIA PHRYGIA
Laodicea Iconium
GREECE
CILICIA
EUPHRATES R.

SYRIA
CYPRUS
Constantia
SEA
Damascus
SEA OF GALILEE
PALESTINE
Jerusalem
DEAD SEA

Alexandria
ARABIA

A
EGYPT

NILE R.

JORDAN R.

RED
SEA

0   MILES   200
0   KM   200

palacios

against a particular book's inclusion into the Jewish canon (see Freedman's caveat on Jamnia on pp. 140–41) may have involved a number of considerations.

Among Christians

The Semitic version of Judith, like other books of the Apocrypha, was translated into Greek for the benefit of those Jews who did not know Hebrew, and so became part of the so-called Alexandrian Canon.[78] And again like other apocryphal books of that canon, Judith got a mixed reception among the Christian Church Fathers.[79] In the Eastern Church, the book was regarded as canonical by Clement of Alexandria (150?–?215); the Council of Nicaea (A.D. 325); Anonymi, *Dialectica Timothei et Aquilae;* Junilius (fl. ca. 542); and Ebedjesu; and in the Western Church by Hilary of Poitiers (315?–?367); Augustine (354–430); Innocent I (reigned 401–417); Pseudo-Gelasius; Cassiodorus (485?–?585); Isidorus of Miletus (560–636); the lists in *Codex Claromontanus* and *Liber sacramentorum* (sixth–seventh cent. A.D.); and the Council of Carthage (397). Clement of Rome (30?–?99) alluded to Judith as an example of a brave and godly woman in 1 *Clem.* 55:4–5; but whether this necessarily implies canonicity is uncertain. (Jude's use of Enoch 1:9 in vv 14–15 is certainly comparable.)

However, the book was not regarded as canonical by Melito of Sardis (fl. ca. 167); Origen (185?–?254); Athanasius of Alexandria (293?–373); Cyril of Jerusalem (315?–386); Epiphanius, bishop of Constantia (315?–403); Gregory of Nazianzus (330?–?389); Amphilochius of Iconium (339?–?394); Pseudo-Chrysostom; Pseudo-Athanasius (fl. fourth cent. A.D.); Leontius of Byzantium (485?–?543); John of Damascus (645?–?749); Nicephorus of Constantinople (758?–829); the Laodicean Canons (343–381); and the Apostolic Canons (ca. 380)—all of these being of the Eastern Church. Jerome (340?–420) seemed to be speaking approvingly when he observed in his "Preface to Judith" that Jews regard the book as uncanonical. In sum, in the West, the book was nearly always regarded as canonical, while in the Eastern Church it was generally denied canonical status. Even though Judith was regarded as canonical by a number of Church Fathers, especially by those who, like Judith (see 16:22), willingly chose celibacy (see INTRODUCTION, p. 64), a book-length commentary was not written on it until that of Rhabanus Maurus (780?–856), *Expositio in librum Judith* (in Migne, *Patrologia Latina,*

---

[78] Judith does not seem to have been used by any NT writer (but see NOTE on 8:14).

[79] Complete lists of the canonical books of Church Fathers, councils, and synods may be found conveniently in IOTG, pp. 200–14; and in Sundberg, HTS, XX (1958), 58–59. For brief introductions to the Church Fathers named below, the interested reader should see Altaner, *Patrology.* The original texts of the Fathers may be found in J. P. Migne, *Patrologiae cursus completus,* series *Graeca* and *Latina.* For the dates of relevant Church Fathers, and of classical writers, see APPENDIX II, p. 263f.

CIX, 539–92). In keeping with the spirit of his age, Maurus's approach was allegorical.

Perhaps a word should be said here about the relationship of the books of Judith and Esther with respect to canonicity in the Christian Church. Given the similarity of the two books, especially in Esther's LXX form with its six Additions (see n. 131, p. 214), we should not be surprised to find that among the Church Fathers Judith and Esther were frequently listed side by side, regardless of whether the particular Father regarded them as canonical.[80] Nor should it be surprising to the reader that the three earliest allusions to the book of Judith among the Fathers are intimately tied up with the story of Esther, namely, in 1 *Clem.* 55, dating from the first century A.D.; *Stromata* 4.19 of Clement of Alexandria; and the *Constitutions of the Holy Apostles* 5.3.20 (ca. 380). In all three of these works allusions to the bravery of Judith and Esther are mentioned in the same breath. Then too, the fact that ancient Christian congregations often kept their biblical scrolls in boxes *(cistae* or *kitōbos)* to protect and preserve them also served to help organize them into sets of a chronological or topical character, e.g., legal, historical, prophetic, didactic collections. Thus, the fact that the books of Judith and Esther featured a woman as hero and had other similarities as well would have prompted some "scroll-keepers" to have kept the two scrolls in the same box, all of which would have predisposed some Church Fathers to associate the two books (so IOTG, pp. 225, 229, n. 1). If one book did have a strong influence on determining the canonical status of the other, it is probable that Judith, which could lay no claim to having been accepted as canonical by the Jews,[81] did more to detract from Esther's canonical claims than did Esther's claims to canonicity contribute to strengthening the canonical status of Judith's.

THE SEPTUAGINT TRANSLATION OF JUDITH

Text and Recensions

The original Greek text of Judith is best represented by three uncials: codices Vaticanus (LXX[B]), Alexandrinus (LXX[A]), and Basiliano-Vaticanus (LXX[N]).[82] More so than the other three uncials, Codex Sinaiticus (LXX[S]) has been contaminated by later recensional activity, in part because, originally, it

---

[80] So Athanasius of Alexandria, Augustine, Innocent I, Pseudo-Gelasius, Cassiodorus, Anonymi, *Dialectica Timothei et Aquilae,* Junilius, Isidorus, *Liber sacramentorum,* Nicephorus, and Ebedjesu; so also the Council of Carthage and LXX[B] (LXX[SA] have Tobit separating the two).

[81] So Origen in *Ad Africanum* 13, and Jerome in his "Preface to Judith."

[82] For the dates of these and other Greek manuscripts, see pp. xx–xxi.

carelessly omitted a number of words, phrases, and even clauses (see textual fns. *passim*).[83]

Robert Hanhart, working with twice the number of Greek minuscules as the Cambridge editors (thirty-four versus eighteen),[84] has detected in these cursives four recensions of the LXX: (1) the Origenic or Hexaplaric (e.g., LXX^k), on which type of text both the OL and Syr versions were based (see Hanhart, *Text und Textgeschichte*, pp. 14–45); (2) the Lucianic (e.g., LXX^b);[85] (3) Recension A (e.g., LXX^{gp}), which shares a number of readings with LXX^N, especially;[86] and (4) Recension B (e.g., LXX^{cejw}), which not infrequently agrees with LXX^A (see Hanhart, *Text und Textgeschichte*, pp. 57–60).

Character

Stating clearly his position but offering no documentation to support it, Montague, a Roman Catholic scholar, has written:

> Judith . . . needs no apology for its presentation in Greek. It is not a translation but a free reworking of the earlier Hebrew stratum. This fact argues strongly for the superiority of the Greek text in determining the Word of God to the Church. *(Books of Esther and Judith, p. 13)*

There is a certain risk involved in characterizing a translation whose *Vorlage* is not extant, for it is like trying to judge the fidelity of an apprentice's copy of his master's painting when we have never seen the original. In such a situation, we are denied complete certainty in assessing the copy's fidelity to the original; but we are not left in total ignorance, either. For sometimes clues to the original's composition, balance, color, and detail may be reasonably inferred from a copy.

In the case of Judith, at least, proof of the LXX's faithful rendering of the Hebrew syntax and idiom is unmistakable (see INTRODUCTION, pp. 66–67). Moreover, the Greek is so literalistic a translation of the Hebrew that many of the niceties of "good" (i.e., classical) Greek are either lacking or underrepresented. For instance, there are only a couple of genitive absolutes (e.g., *stenēs tēs prosbaseōs ousēs* in 4:7) and relatively few subordinate clauses and participial phrases. In comparison with the rest of the LXX, Judith is especially lacking in Greek particles. More specifically, there are only fourteen instances of *dē* (so Enslin, p. 86) and forty occurrences of *de* (so Soubigou, p. 487), relatively small numbers for 704 lines of Greek. The particle *an* occurs either four (11:2, 15; 12:4; 14:2) or seven times, depending upon which

---

[83] For detailed discussion and numerous examples of recensional contamination of the uncials, see Hanhart, *Text und Textgeschichte*, pp. 60–74.

[84] See INTRODUCTION, pp. xx–xxi.

[85] Hanhart, *Text und Textgeschichte*, pp. 46–52. For further background information on the Lucianic Recension in general, see OTTV, pp. 141–43.

[86] Hanhart, *Text und Textgeschichte*, pp. 52–57.

uncial is used for the counting. The particle *men* appears but once (5:20), while *ara, oun,* and *te* do not occur at all. The conjunctions *alla,* "however," and *gar,* "for," are used only twenty-one and thirty times, respectively (so Soubigou, p. 487).

And yet, in this area, as in so many others in Judith, contradictory truths must be affirmed. In spite of the translator's very literal rendering of Hebrew idioms and syntax, he displays a rather rich and flexible vocabulary. Enslin, who has taken the trouble of actually counting many of the various words in the text, reports that our Greek translator used 1,250 different words. Enslin (p. 41) helps to put that particular statistic into clearer perspective by noting that of the 183 words beginning with the letter *alpha (a),* 102 are used in the book but once. Also, as any reader familiar with the LXX quickly recognizes, the LXX of Judith has its fair share of *hapax legomena* (see NOTES *passim).* The translator's vocabulary was rich in those areas which were of special interest to him, notably military terms (see NOTES *passim)* and words for "sin" (see NOTE on "is not guilty" in 5:21), the people of Israel (see NOTE on "the House of Israel" in 6:17), and the Temple at Jerusalem (see NOTE on "sanctuaries" in 4:1).

The translator liked to use a wide variety of verbs, also. Instead of employing the same one again and again, he preferred to use a related verb, one which was made by adding to or changing a prefix to the verbal root (see, for example, 5:6–9, where he used *oikō, katoikō,* and *paroikō;* or 14:6, 8, and 14, where he used *ēlthen, exēlthen,* and *eisēlthen,* respectively; see also NOTE on "rush upon" in 15:4). Predictably, the translator relied on the already established LXX translation for OT passages rather than translating anew (see NOTES on "to be cajoled" in 8:16; and on "the Lord who crushes wars" in 9:7 and 16:2).

Date

The *terminus a quo* for the Greek translation must be at some point after the Hebrew text was written (see INTRODUCTION, pp. 67–70), i.e., ca. the early first century B.C.). As for the *terminus ad quem,* the LXX version was in existence by at least the first century of the Christian Era; for Clement of Rome refers to the Judith-story as if it were quite well known to his readers (see INTRODUCTION, p. 64).

The oldest extant text of Judith is probably an ostracon (a potsherd on which there is writing) dating to the second half of the third century A.D., on which 15:1–7 are preserved, unfortunately in a fragmentary condition (Schwartz, RB 53 [1946]: 534–37). Even more unfortunate, the only "interesting" reading derived from it is that the town's name was *Batuloua,* a reading shared by LXXᵏ in 4:6.

OTHER ANCIENT VERSIONS OF JUDITH

Biblical scholars are always interested in the ancient versions of whatever books of the Bible they are studying at the time. Today, if a particular scholar is working on a book of the OT, then he or she can use the MT of the Hebrew Bible as printed in *BH³*, which has at the bottom of each page an *apparatus criticus* containing variant readings from the ancient versions. That same scholar would also use (and if working on a book of the OT Apocrypha would have to use) the Larger Cambridge and/or Göttingen Septuagint (see BIBLIOGRAPHY), which also have their *apparatus criticus* at the bottom of each page. Because the *apparatus* in the LXX editions are so much more extensive and detailed than in *BH³*, one might conclude that much help can be gained from them for explicating and emending the Greek text. Unfortunately, however, that is not always the case, primarily because the ancient versions represented in the *apparatus criticus* of many biblical books are either so fragmentary,[87] late,[88] mixed, or unscientific.[89] With these caveats made, certain generalizations concerning the ancient versions of Judith are in order.

The Vetus Latina, *or Old Latin*

As is the case with the OL of other books of the Bible (see OTTV, pp. 237–46), the OL of Judith is a translation of the LXX rather than of a Semitic text. The evidence for such a conclusion takes two forms. First, the OL closely adheres to the content and sequence of the LXX, especially to LXX^k. Second, throughout Judith the OL has readings which are clearly a transliteration of a Greek rather than a Semitic text, for example:

In 3:9 (and 4:6 of some minuscules), the OL has the proper name "Prionem" for the LXX's *prinos*, "ridge."

In 4:15 the OL's *cidares/cidarim* is a transliteration of Gk *kidareis*, "turban," a Persian loanword.

In 8:10 and 10:2, the OL uses the otherwise unknown Latin word *abra*, which is obviously a transliteration of Gk *abra*, "maid."

E. E. Voigt, who has done the most detailed analysis of the Latin versions (i.e., the OL and the Vg) of Judith in this century *(Latin Versions of Judith)*, has shown that the OL of Judith is best called the OL version*s*. There are, he

---

[87] For instance, while the Larger Cambridge Septuagint of Judith uses five OL "manuscripts" and Hanhart's Göttingen Septuagint uses thirteen, the manuscripts are often incomplete, fragmentary, or only extended quotations from the Church Fathers.

[88] The manuscripts for the Eth version of Judith, for instance, date from no earlier than the seventeenth century.

[89] With the exception of the LXX and the Vg, none of the ancient versions of the Bible is represented by what might be properly called a critical, scientific edition.

maintained, three largely independent recensions of the OL, with some contamination between the first and second recensions (both of which are dependent, but in different ways, upon a Greek text of the same family as LXX^k), and the third recension (OL^c) entirely independent of the first two recensions but contaminated considerably by the *later* Vg version of Jerome.[90] Because the OL is based on the LXX, only those variants in the OL that are helpful or of special interest will be noted in the present work.

The Latin Vulgate

The nature of the text used by Jerome for his Latin translation and its relationship to the LXX are among the most debated and perplexing problems in Judithian studies. The statistical approach is one way to illustrate the first problem; for as Voigt has rightly reported:

> Of the 340 verses in the Greek text the Vulgate omits 42 entirely and large parts of 45 more. In the remaining verses the Vulgate agrees with the Greek more or less closely only about one half of the time, and literally reproduces the material in the Greek in relatively few instances. As for the rest of the book, about one-third in amount, the same trend of narrative can be recognized, sometimes abbreviated (as in 7:23; 8:9f; 9:14; 11:13, etc.), and sometimes expanded (as in 6:21; 6:3; 8:34, etc.), but on the whole the method of expression and the order of the words is so completely changed in the Vulgate that it is hard to believe that it came from the Greek. . . . Furthermore, the Vulgate adds 32 verses (e.g., 4:12–14; 5:15–19; 6:16–18; 7:1–22; 8:24f; 9:7–9; 14:9f; etc.), which are unattested by Greek or [Old] Latin. This material as a matter of fact adds nothing new in sense, but merely enlarges on the topic under discussion. (pp. 46–47, 48)

The reason for this great disparity between the Vg and the LXX is well known, for Jerome wrote in his "Preface to Judith":

> By the Hebrews the Book of Judith is placed with the Apocrypha. . . . Written in the Chaldean language, it is placed with the histories. But because the Council of Nicea is said to have counted this book in the numbers of Sacred Writings, I have succumbed to your request, nay rather your demands; and after my occupations with which I am so much hindered were laid aside, I gave one short night's work to it, rendering the sense of it rather than a literal translation. I have cut out the most faulty variant readings of the many manuscripts. I have expressed in Latin only those readings which I could find in Chaldean without doing violence to the sense.[91]

---

[90] See Voigt, *Latin Versions of Judith*, pp. 13–45, especially, pp. 44–45.

[91] So my colleague, Professor Ruth Pavlantos, has translated the Latin: *Liber Judith inter Apocrypha legitur. . . . Chaldaeo sermone conscriptus inter historias computatur. Sed quia hunc librum Synodus Nicaena in numero Sanctarum Scripturarum legitur computasse, acquievi postulatione vestrae, imo exactioni, et sepositis occupationibus quibus vehementur arcetabar, huic unam lucubratiunculum dedi, magis sensum e sensu quam ex verbo verbum transferens. Multorum codicum varietatem vitiosissimam amputavi; sola ea, quae intelligentia integra in verbis Chaldaeis invenire potui, Latinis expressi.*

On the basis of internal evidence, there is every reason to accept Jerome's claim that he used an Aramaic text for his translation. For example, the Latin word *ut* occurs seventy times in the Vg's Judith and only fifteen times in the corresponding passages of the OL; and "In every case where the Vg makes use of this particle, it stands where one would find the Aramaic *dî*" (Voigt, p. 52). *Dî*, of course, is a very common particle in Aramaic for introducing a subordinate clause.[92] Further evidence of a Semitic *Vorlage* is indicated by the presence of Semitic idioms in the Vg's "additions," i.e., those phrases, clauses, or passages which do not occur in either the LXX or the OL (e.g., "mouth of the sword" in Vg 2:16 and 15:6; and *tradens tradet* in 5:20 [24]). More will be said about these "additions" on p. 99.

Certain aspects of Jerome's translating procedures for Judith are well known, thanks to his "Preface to Tobit." (Like Judith, Tobit was available to Jerome in Aramaic but not Hebrew or Greek.) Both apocryphal books were translated by him in Bethlehem (A.D. 398). Far less at home with Aramaic than Hebrew, Jerome utilized what is called today "simultaneous translation." As the Aramaic text was being translated aloud into Hebrew by a Jewish scholar, Jerome was dictating to his secretary a Latin translation of it. Jerome reports that by using this process the book of Tobit took him "a day's labor"; and Judith, "one short night's work" *(unam lucubratiunculum)*. For Jerome to have translated the two books in such a short period of time (even if it was only a first draft) means that his translations of Tobit and Judith were more likely to have errors and imprecisions than if he had spent more time on them. Evidently Jerome felt he had given them all the time they deserved, neither book being part of the Jewish canon.

Jerome's translating procedures as outlined in his "Preface to Tobit" and his comments in his "Preface to Judith" suggest that his translation of Judith was more of a paraphrase, aiming at the general sense, than a literal, word-for-word rendering of the Aramaic. That fact alone might make one more cautious about using the Vg for emending the LXX. However, the problem is further complicated by our uncertainty as to exactly how Jerome utilized in his translation the OL, which, being based upon the Greek (see above), may very well have been different from his Aramaic text at a number of points. Ball (p. 243), for instance, thinks Jerome was more concerned with bringing the OL into greater conformity with the Aramaic than he was interested in translating the Aramaic *per se*, all of which would explain, maintained Ball, why the Vg "not seldom coincides with the Old Latin," that is, Jerome did not change that which the OL already in essence had. On the other hand, because the extant manuscripts of the OL are relatively late for most books of

---

[92] E.g., *melius est enim ut viventes serviamus* (3:2); *quod gens Israel defendatur a Deo suo, ut ostendam tibi* (6:2); *ut autem noveris quia* (6:6); *quod est hoc verbum . . . ut tradat* (8:10); *mox autem ut ortus est dies* (14:7); *et mox ut purificati sunt* (16:22). The word *quod* in 6:2 and 8:10 is also a rendering of the Aram *dî.*

1. Present-day Tel Dothan, a site mentioned in 3:9 and elsewhere in Judith.

2. A silver tetradrachm coin, with the head of Antiochus IV, Epiphanes (175–163 B.C.). Minted at Antioch.

3. Silver coin, ca. 158 B.C., with the inscription "Orophernes King Victorious." From Pirene.

4. Bronze statue by Donatello (1386–1466). Judith about to cut off Holofernes' head. *Piazza della Signoria, Florence*.

5. *Judith* by Cristofano Allori (1577–1621). A serene Judith holding the severed head while her admiring maid looks on.

6. *The Story of Judith and Holofernes* by Michelangelo (1475–1564). Judith and her maid carrying off Holofernes' head. *Sistine Chapel, Vatican.*

7. *Below:* Bronze Hanukkah lamp. Judith holding the severed head of Holofernes, sixteenth century.

8. *Judith and Holofernes* by Andrea Mantegna (1431–1506). A watchful Judith dropping Holofernes' head into a bag held by her rather homely servant.

9. *Judith and Holofernes* by Botticelli (1444–1510). The servants of Holofernes discovering their decapitated lord.

the Bible, contamination of the OL by the Vg is not an uncommon phenomenon, either; and as Voigt (pp. 42–44) has argued, that is exactly what happened with Judith, namely, OL^c was contaminated very much by the Vg.

The problem of the nature of the relationship of the Vg to the OL is well illustrated below, where the two versions of chap. 1 are printed one after the other for purposes of comparison. Even if the reader does not know Latin, he or she can easily see that the Vg has omissions and transpositions, as well as differences in words and phrases even in parallel passages. It should be underscored here that the nature and extent of the variations between the versions are typical of the rest of Judith, with one exception, namely, the Vg in chap. 1 has no "additions" to the LXX or the OL, a not surprising fact, since it is four verses shorter than the LXX. (Because the OL follows the LXX so closely, an English translation of it is not provided here.)

OLD LATIN

¹ *Anno duodecimo regni Nabuchodonosor qui regnavit Assyriis in Ninive civitate magna, in diebus Arfaxath regis, qui regnavit in Medis in Ecbathana civitate, et aedificavit turrem in Ecbathana.*

² *Et in circuitu muros ejus, ex lapidibus excisis, latitudine cubitorum trium, et longitudine cubitorum sex: et fecit altitudinem muri cubitorum sexaginta, et turres constituit supra portas ejus cubitorum centum:*

³ *Altitudinem et latitudinem earum fundavit in cubitis sexaginta: et fecit portas ejus exsurgentes in altum cubitis sexaginta, et latitudinem earum cubitis quadraginta,*

⁴ *Ad exitum quadrigarum suarum.*

⁵ *Et fecit bellum in diebus illis rex Nabuchodonosor adversus regem Arfaxath.*

⁶ *In campo magno, hic est campus Ragau. Et convenerunt in pugnam omnes habitantes in montanis, et Euphrate, et Tigri, et Ydaspi, in campis Arioth regis Elimeorum: et collegerunt se gentes multae ad bellum filorum Chelleuth.*

⁷ *Et misit Nabuchodonosor rex Assyriorum ad omnes inhabitantes Jamnae, Persidis, et Ciliciam, et Damascum, Libanum et Antelibanum, et contra faciem maris,*

⁸ *Et qui sunt in nationibus Carmeli et Galaad, et superiori Galileae in campo magno Esdrelon.*

⁹⁻¹⁰ *Et ad omnes qui erant in Samaria, et in civitatibus ejus, et trans Jordanem usque Hierusalem, et Bathana, et Chelus, et Cades, et flumina Aegypti, et Tafnas, et Ramesses, et omnem terram Gessen, donec veniatur supra Thaneos et Memphis, et omnes qui inhabitant Galilaea maritima in Jordanen, in totam terram Aegypti, donec veniatur ad fines Aethiopiae.*

¹¹ *Et contempserunt omnes inhabitantes terram illam, verbum Nabuchodonosor regis Assyriorum, neque convenerunt cum illo in praelium, quia non timerunt eum: sed erat adversus eos quasi vir unus. Et remiserunt legatos ejus vacuos, sine honore facies eorum.*

[12] *Et iratus est rex Nabuchodonosor ad omnem terram illam vehementer, et juravit per sedem regni sui, animadversurum se in omnes fines Ciliciae et Damasci et Scythiae, et interfecturum gladio suo inhabitantes Moab et filios Ammon et omnem Judaeam et omnes qui in Aegypto sunt, usque dum veniatur montanam, et ad finitima duorum aequorum.*

Et praeparavit se in virtute sua adversus regem Arfaxath in anno septimo decimo: et invaluit in pugna sea, et redegit in potestate sua omnem virtutem regis Arfaxath, et omnen equitatum ejus, et omnes currus ipsius, et dominatus est civitatum ejus.

Et abiit usque Ecbatham, et obtinuit turres ejus, et praedatus est plateas ejus, et ornamenta ejus, et posuit ea in opprobrio; et cepit regem Arfaxath in montibus Ragau, et percussit illum in lanceis suis, et disperdidit eum usque in hodiernum diem.

Et reversus est Nabuchodonosor rex in Niniven, ipse et exercitus, multitudo virorum bellatorum copiosa nimis; et erat illic securus habitans; et epulatus est ipse et virtus ejus per dies centum viginti.

THE VULGATE

[1] *Arphaxad itaque, rex Medorum, subjugaverat multas gentes imperio suo, et ipse aedificavit civitatem potentissimam quam appellavit Ecbatanis,*

[2] *Ex lapidibus quadratis et sectis; fecit muros ejus in latitudinem cubitorum septuaginta, et in altitudinem cubitorum triginta, turres vero ejus posuit in altitudinem cubitorum centum.*

[3] *Per quadrum vero earum, latus utrumque vicenorum pedum spatio tendebatur, posuitque portas ejus in altitudinem turrum;*

[4] *Et gloriabatur quasi potens in potentia exercitus sui, et in gloria quadrigarum suarum.*

[5] *Anno igitur duodecimo regni sui Nabuchodonosor rex Assyriorum qui regnabat in Ninive civitate magna, pugnavit contra Arphaxad et obtinuit eum,*

[6] *In campo magno qui appellatur Ragan circa Euphraten et Tigrim et Jadason in campo Erioch regis Elicorum.*

[7] *Tunc exaltatum est regnum Nabuchodonosor, et cor ejus elevatum est; et misit ad omnes qui habitabant in Cilicia et Damasco et Libano,*

[8] *Et ad gentes quae sunt in Carmelo et Cedar et inhabitantes Galilaeam in campo magno Esdrelon,*

[9] *Et ad omnes qui erant in Samaria, et transflumen Jordanem usque ad Jerusalem, et omnem terram Jesse quousque perveniatur ad terminos Aethiopiae.*

[10] *Ad hos omnes misit nuntios Nabuchodonosor rex Assyriorum;*

[11] *Qui omnes uno animo contra dixerunt, et remiserunt eos vacuos, et sine honore abjecerunt.*

[12] *Tunc indignatus Nabuchodonosor rex adversus omnem terram illiam juravit per thronum et regnum suum quod defenderet se de omnibus regionibus his.*

VULGATE TRANSLATION (Douay Version)

[1] Now Arphaxad king of the Medes had brought many nations under his dominions, and he built a very strong city, which he called Ecbatana,

[2] of stones squared and hewed: he made the walls thereof seventy cubits broad, and thirty cubits high; and the towers thereof he made a hundred cubits high. But on the square of them, each side was extended the space of twenty feet.

[3] And he made the gates thereof according to the height of the towers.

[4] And he gloried as a mighty one in the force of his army and in the glory of his chariots.

[5] Now in the twelfth year of his reign, Nabuchodonosor king of the Assyrians, who reigned in Ninive the great city, fought against Arphaxad and overcame him

[6] in the great plain which is called Ragua, about the Euphrates, and the Tigris, and the Jadason, in the plain of Erioch the king of the Elicians.

[7] Then was the kingdom of Nabuchodonosor exalted, and his heart was elevated. And he sent to all that dwelt in Cilicia and Damascus, and Libanus,

[8] and to the nations that are in Carmelus, and Cedar, and to the inhabitants of Galilee in the great plain of Esdrelon,

[9] and to all that were in Samaria, and beyond the river Jordan even to Jerusalem, and all the land of Jesse till you come to the borders of Ethiopia.

[10] To all these Nabuchodonosor king of the Assyrians sent messengers.

[11] But they all with one mind refused, and sent them back empty, and rejected them without honor.

[12] Then king Nabuchodonosor being angry against all that land, swore by his throne and kingdom that he would revenge himself of all those countries.

Regardless of whether the Vg is a faithful translation of the Aramaic or a paraphrase influenced by the OL, we must still account for the Vg's "additions," i.e., those passages which have no equivalent in either the Greek or the OL. Were all of them part of the Aramaic text, or did Jerome create some of them himself? In general, when translating other books of the Bible Jerome did just that, that is, he translated rather than edited. Thus, it is highly unlikely that in Judith many of the "additions" are expressions of Jerome's own flights of imagination. One can hardly imagine, for instance, Jerome's inventing such a detail as in 7:6 of the Vg: "Now Holofernes, in going around, found that the fountain which supplied them with water, *ran through an aqueduct outside the city on the south side; and he commanded their aqueduct to be cut off*" (italics added). Given the brief amount of time Jerome devoted to translating Judith (so his "Preface"), most scholars think it unlikely that he would have taken the time to create *de novo* some of the more extended homiletical additions (Jdt 4:12–14; 5:11–16; 7:7–10). Even 10:4 of the Vg, while certainly appealing to Jerome in principle, sounds very much midrashic in character: "And the Lord gave [Judith] more beauty; because all this dressing up did not proceed from sensuality, but from virtue; and therefore the Lord increased this her beauty, so that she appeared to all men's eyes incomparably lovely." This is not to say, however, that Jerome might not have "reshaped"[93] or toned down a passage here and there. Compare also the Vg's "And the heart of Holofernes was smitten, for he was burning with desire for her" (12:16) with the corresponding verse in the LXX: "When Judith entered and lay down, Holofernes was beside himself with desire, and his brain was reeling; and he was very eager to have relations with her. (From the day he had first seen her he had been watching for an opportunity to seduce her!)"

In sum, Jerome's translation gives every indication of being a paraphrase of an Aramaic text which, when compared to the LXX (and the OL), had a considerable number of additions and omissions,[94] as well as a number of other differences. All this being the case, the Vg will rarely be used in the present work for emending the LXX.

The Aramaic Vorlage *of the Vulgate*

To say that the Vg is of very limited use for emending the LXX of Judith does not automatically rule out its use for other purposes, especially if the Aramaic text behind it can illuminate the origins or evolution of the Judith-story. The crucial question here is simply this: Was Jerome's Aramaic text a translation of an older Hebrew account (so Ball and Dubarle) or was it a free translation of the Greek?[95]

This is obviously not the place for a detailed discussion of such a complex problem, let alone its "solution." But some indication of the difficulties involved in such a question can be seen by considering two verses in the Song of Judith (chap. 16), a psalm which may or may not have had an independent existence prior to the composition of Judith (see COMMENT on SECTION XVI, pp. 252–57). In 16:2a, where the author quotes Exod 15:2, Jerome unquestionably rendered the LXX version of that passage; for the LXX is radically different from the MT:

Exod 15:2

    MT   *yhwh 'yš mlḥmh yhwh šmw*
          "Yahweh is a man of war; Yahweh is his name."

    LXX *kurios suntribōn polemous, kurios onoma autō*
          "The Lord crushes wars; the Lord is his name."

---

[93] *"And chastity was joined to her virtue,* so that she knew no man all the days of her life, after the death of Manasses her husband" (italics added; 16:26 of Vg) sounds suspiciously Christian.

[94] This includes geographical details, e.g., the LXX material in Jdt 2:28; 3:9; 4:4, 6; 15:4.

[95] This appears to be the majority opinion and is subscribed to by, among others, Cowley, Enslin, Grintz, Pfeiffer, and Voigt.

Vg   *dominus quasi vir pugnator, omnipotens nomen eius*
     "The Lord is as a man of war, Almighty is his name."

Judith 16:2

LXX *oti theos suntribōn polemous kurios*
     "For the Lord is a God who crushes wars."

Vg   *dominus conterens bella; dominus nomen est illi*
     "The Lord puts an end to wars; the Lord is his name."

This verse, as much as any in the Vg of Judith, has persuaded many scholars that Jerome's Aramaic text was a free paraphrase of the LXX (but see first NOTE on 16:2).

On the other hand, in 16:13, where the LXX has *kurie, megas ei,* "Lord, you are great," the corresponding verse in the Vg (i.e., 16:16) has *Adonai, Domine, magnus est tu,* "O Adonay, Lord, great are you." The presence of the title "Adonay" is curious. It is the standard Jewish substitute word for the sacred name *Yhwh,* which in the LXX is routinely translated as *kurios,* "Lord." Thus, the presence of the title "Adonay" *may* indicate that behind Jerome's Aramaic text was a Hebrew *Vorlage;* otherwise, had Jerome been translating from an Aramaic translation of the Greek, the word "Adonay" would not have been present.

With some justice, F. C. Porter has argued that in Jerome's Aramaic *Vorlage* it was Jerusalem, not Bethulia, that was the site for our story.

> The Vulgate never gives a clear description of Bethulia (cf. LXX 4:6, 7; 6:7, 10, 11; 7:3; 8:3; 10:13; 11:2); it omits or changes all passages which clearly distinguish Bethulia and Jerusalem up to 15:9 (cf. LXX 4:6, 7; 11:19, 11:13; 15:5); and Vulgate omits LXX 8:21, 22, 24; 9:1b; 11:14, 15). Further, Vulgate contains some positive suggestions that Jerusalem is the besieged city (Vulg. 3:14 [cf. LXX 3:9, 10]; 7:3, 6, 7, 9; 15:4; and Ozias [Uzziah] is "prince of Judah" [Vulg. 8:34; 13:23]). Only in 15:9 and perhaps 16:22–25 does Vulgate *require* the distinctions. This suggests that the identification is not due to Jerome but to his source. (HDB, II, 822)

Here, as in a number of other places in Judith (see NOTES *passim),* Jerome's Aramaic *Vorlage* (as inferred from his Latin paraphrase of it) seems similar to the "ancient" Hebrew version/s and midrashim on Judith.

The "Ancient" Hebrew

There are at least five important Hebrew texts of Judith. Their agreement with the Vg is so pronounced that most scholars, including Carl Meyer and Jehoshua Grintz,[96] simply regard them as very free Hebrew translations of the Latin. Dubarle, who has studied the matter as much as any twentieth-century scholar, is quite accurate in saying of the five texts that "they often follow [the Vg] verse for verse; more rarely, but not exceptionally, they follow it word for word" (VT 8 [1958]: 351).

[96] Meyer, *Biblica* 3 (1922): 193–203; Grintz.

As for the *Vorlage* of these texts, Dubarle, more so than anyone else, has taken the minority view, maintaining that these Hebrew texts, along with the Aramaic material preserved in the Vg, are a separate and independent witness to another and possibly older tradition of the Judith-story. When Dubarle first advanced his theory (VT 8 [1958]: 344–73), he designated the five Hebrew texts as A, B, C, D, and E. In a subsequent article (VT 11 [1961]: 62–87), he felt compelled to report that Text A had turned out to be a "modern" Hebrew translation of Luther's German translation of Judith, the Hebrew translation having been done by L. J. Zeeb in 1799.[97] Later, in Dubarle's two-volume study of Judith *(Judith)*, three of the Hebrew texts (B, C, and E) and the Latin text of the Vg were printed side by side (II, 8–97), so that the similarities and differences among the Hebrew texts are quite evident, as is their striking agreement with the Vg *vis-à-vis* the LXX.

Whether these Hebrew texts are ultimately free translation/s of the Vg or, as Dubarle has argued, an independent witness to another and older tradition of the Judith-story is a subject too complex and removed from the central problems of the LXX of Judith to be treated in any detail here. However, the present writer does not think that Dubarle has made his case; for Grintz has offered some of the most convincing evidence for the Hebrew texts being based upon the Vg:

> In 7:3 of Text B, the Heb "place name" *'d 'pyṣm*, "to Aphitsim," actually represents a misinterpretation of the Vg's *ad apicem*, "to the top."
>
> In Text C, *'brh*, which is taken in the Hebrew text as a personal name and is always followed by *špḥth*, "her servant," represents a misreading of the Latin word *abra*, which is merely a transliteration of Gr *abra*, "maid."
>
> In 6:21 and 7:18, where the Vg translates the LXX's *ekklēsia*, "the assembly," i.e., a group of people, as *ecclesia*, the Text C has *hykl*, "temple," i.e., a building, a theoretically possible but here an obviously erroneous translation of the Latin.[98]

Meyer *(Biblica* 3 [1922]: 199) saw proof of the reliance of Text C on the Vg in the fact that only they mention "an aqueduct" instead of "the water sources" (7:6); both say "twenty days," not "thirty-four" (7:11); both have the word "cheese" after the word "bread" (10:5); both specify "the drinking of their blood" (11:11); and both refer to the Israelites as "the mice" instead of "the slaves" (14:13; but see NOTE). Finally, it should be noted that the man named "Joakim" in 4:6, 8, and 14 of the LXX is called *Heliachim* in the Vg (4:5, 7, 11), and *'lyqym* in Texts B, C, and E.

In sum, because the ancient Hebrew version seems to be little more than a very free translation of the Vg's loose rendering of its Aramaic *Vorlage*, read-

---

[97] Actually, as Dubarle points out, Luther's collaborator, Philipp Melanchthon, translated Judith.

[98] For other examples from Grintz, as well as Dubarle's efforts to explain them away, see Dubarle, *Judith,* I, 62–67.

ings from the "ancient" Hebrew version will rarely appear in the present commentary.

The Midrashim

A midrash is "an ancient Jewish narrative that has the form characteristic of a midrash [a Hebrew word meaning "exposition"] and the purpose of setting forth or illustrating a religious teaching."[99] There are well over a dozen ancient midrashim of the Judith-story; and they, or at least their oldest extant copies, date to the Middle Ages. Thus, the question of how old and authentic their contents actually are can be a real problem. Published in widely scattered and often difficult to secure books and journals, the Hebrew text of thirteen of them has been conveniently printed (but hardly ever *in toto)* and analyzed in some detail in Dubarle's *Judith* (his discussion is in Vol. I; the texts themselves in Vol. II).[100] Although Dubarle found sixteen instances where one or more midrashim shared readings with the "ancient" Hebrew texts B and/or C, as well as (sometimes) with the Vg,[101] he concluded that the midrashim and the Hebrew Texts B and C "constitute two different branches in the evolution of a primitive story" (p. 104).

Even though the midrashim will not play any significant role in the present commentary, a few more words should be said here about them. For students of Judith have regularly expressed interest in them, especially since 1894, when Gaster (PSBA 16 [1893/94]: 156–63) published one, dating to the tenth or the beginning of the eleventh century, which he regarded as representing the earliest and most accurate version of the Judith-story. Gaster's translation is as follows:

A tale. Our teachers taught: on the eighteenth day of Adar *[i.e.,* one is not allowed to fast];[102] it is the day on which Seleukos[103] went up. As we are told, at the

[99] *Webster's Third New International Dictionary,* Unabridged (1971).
[100] The interested reader should consult the standard work in the field, Jellinek, *Bet ha-Midrasch;* also Grintz.
[101] Dubarle, *Judith,* pp. 102–4. Lest the reader be misled, it should be noted that most of these shared readings are quite brief (e.g., Text B, Vg 6:9, and Midrashim 3 and 4 have "They tied Achior to a tree by his hands and feet"; the Vg and Texts B and C have in 8:34 a reading which Midrash 9 also shares, namely, "Go in peace, and the Lord be with you"). None of the fourteen readings is even half again as long as either of the two preceding examples.
[102] The material inside the square brackets was supplied by Gaster, who had concluded that the midrash had originally been a part of *Megilat Taanit* (i.e., an ancient writing containing the calendar of the festivals of the Maccabean period) and that because Judith's victory occurred on the eighteenth of Adar (= March/April), the Jews could not fast on that day. However, Meyer *(Biblica* 3 [1922]: 200–1) was probably correct in arguing that since the liberation of Bethulia seems to have occurred in the late fall (see Jdt 4:5) rather than in the early spring (Adar), this midrash was not part of *Megilat Taanit.*
[103] I.e., King Seleucus IV, Philopator, unless the term simply means "a Seleucid king," which is most unlikely.

time when he besieged Jerusalem,[104] the Israelites were fasting and had put sacks on. There was a very beautiful woman Judith, daughter of Ahitob.[105] On every day she used to pray to God in ashes and sackcloth. God inspired her with the thought that a miracle would happen through her.[106] So she went to the porters of the gate and said to them: "Open the gates for me, may be that a miracle will happen through me." They said to her, "Have you, perhaps, turned to the other side?" She answered, "God forbid." So they opened the gates to her, and she went to the camp of Seleukos, she and her handmaid with her. She said to them (i.e., the soldiers of Seleukos), "I have a secret errand to the king." They went and told the king, and said to him, "A beautiful maiden[107] has come from Jerusalem, and she says that she has a secret errand to the king." He said, "Let her come in." She went before the king, and fell down upon her face before him. He said to her, "What is that you want?" She answered and said, "My lord king, I belong to a great family in Jerusalem, and my brothers and my father's house were kings and high priests.[108] I have now heard them speaking concerning you, that the time has arrived when this town is to fall in your hands, therefore I have come first to find favour in your eyes."[109]

When the king beheld her beautiful countenance and heard her words, she found favour in his eyes; and he rejoiced at the tidings she had told him. Then he commanded his servants to prepare a great feast. While they were preparing it, he ordered all the princes to leave, as he wished to have the company of the damsel. He asked her to sin. She answered and said, "My lord king, for this very thing I have come here with all my heart, but now it is impossible, as I am in my impurity;[110] tonight is the time of my purification; I therefore desire the king to herald throughout the camp, that no one should stay the woman and her handmaid, when she goes out in the night to the fountain of water. When I return I will give myself over to the king, that he do what is pleasing in his sight."[111]

The wicked man did accordingly. In the night he invited all the princes, his generals and his servants, and they ate and rejoiced at that great feast and got drunk. When they saw that the king was nodding his head, they said, "Let us depart, for he wishes to have the company of the Hebrew maiden." So all went forth and left the king alone with the maiden and with her handmaid. She then took the falchion and cut off his head. She took the head and went out. When they left the soldiers noticed them, and said to one another, "No one is to touch them, such is the command of the king." So they passed (the camp) and reached Jerusalem in the middle of the night. They called upon the porters and said, "Open the gates for us, for the miracle has already come to pass." The porters replied, "Is it not sufficient

[104] Throughout this midrash (and the others), it is Jerusalem, not Bethulia, that is being besieged.

[105] The name, but not this particular person, is mentioned in 1 Sam 22:9; 1 Chr 6:12; 9:11.

[106] Evidently Jerome's Aramaic text also spoke of an angel's help; see NOTE on "the Lord, who protected me" in 13:16.

[107] Here, as in some other midrashim, Judith is unmarried rather than widowed.

[108] In some other midrashim, the heroine is a daughter of one of the Hasmonean kings.

[109] Judith offers here the very plausible reason of wanting to save her own neck rather than, as in the LXX, of wanting to be an instrument for God's righteous punishing of his people.

[110] See Lev 15:13, 19–28.

[111] Neither shy nor coy, Judith freely admitted to being quite willing to have intercourse with the king, once she was purified.

for you to have defiled yourself, that thou wish to deliver the blood of Israel (to their enemies)?" So she did swear to them; but they would not believe her until she showed them the head of that wicked king; only then they believed her and opened the gates to her. That day they kept as a day of feasting; on the morrow the Israelites went forth against that army and slew them until they had destroyed them completely. The residue left their horses and their money and ran away. And the Israelites came and spoiled everything.[112]

This particular midrash is brief, clear, and to the point. It is also quite old; but no one, except Gaster and Scholz (see BIBLIOGRAPHY), has been persuaded it represents *the* earliest form of the Judith-story.

Because it is so difficult to appreciate fully a midrash in isolation, one more midrash can be included here *in toto,* this one a bit more like the LXX and with clear connections with Hanukkah, the Feast of Dedication established by Judas Maccabeus on the occasion of his liberation of Jerusalem and its Temple in 165 B.C. The translation, with some slight twentieth-century editing by this writer, is Ball's:

The Rabbis have handed down as follows. In the days of the kingdom of the wicked Javan [i.e., the Greeks; see H. F. Beck, "Javan," IDB, II, 805], they decreed against Israel that . . . whoever married a wife, she should be wedded to the governor first, and afterwards, go back to her husband. And they went on this way for three years and eight months, until the daughter of John the High Priest was wed.[113] When they led her to this governor, she uncovered her head, tore her clothes, and stood bare in the presence of the people. Immediately Judas and his brothers were filled with indignation against her, and said, "Bring her out and burn her; and do not let this matter be revealed to the government, on account of the danger to lives; for she has hardened her face to become naked in the presence of all this people." Then she said to him, "How shall I be exposed to scorn before my brothers and my friends, and not be exposed to scorn in the eyes of the uncircumcised and unclean person, since you are willing to betray me, and to bring him to lie with me?"

When Judas and his confederates heard that, they took counsel together to kill the governor. Immediately they dressed the maiden in royal attire, and made a bridal canopy of myrtle from the house of Hasmoneus to the house of the governor; and all the masters of harp and lyre came, as well as the masters of music; and they were playing and dancing until they came to the governor's house. When the king heard that, he said to his princes and servants, "Behold, they are of the great ones of Israel, of the seed of Aaron the priest; how glad are they to do my will! They are worthy of great glory." And he made his princes (captains) and his servants go outside, and Judas and his confederates went in with his sister to the governor. And they cut off his head, and looted all that he had, and killed his princes and his servants, and completely trampled the Javanim, except the root of the kingdom.

[112] Gaster, PSBA 16 (1893–94): 160–61; his Hebrew text is printed on pp. 162–63 of his article.
[113] According to *Megilat Taanit,* VI, she was the only daughter of Mattathias ben Johanan, the high priest.

And Israelites who were in the city were in terror and trembling on account of those young men of Israel. A voice from heaven came forth and said, "The young men, who went forth to make war with Antiochus, have gained the victory!" And those young men returned, and shut the gates, and showed repentance, and occupied themselves with the Law, and with works of mercy.

When the king of the Greeks heard that Israel had killed his governor, he gathered all his people, and besieged Jerusalem; and the Jews were quite terrified. And there was there a widow woman, Judith by name; and she took her maid and went to the gates of Jerusalem, and said, "Let me go forth, that Heaven may work a miracle by my hand."[114] And they opened up for her, and she went out, and went to the troops. And they said to her, "How beautiful you are!" She said to them, "My pleasure is to speak to the king."

And she went before the king. And he said to her, "What do you want?" And she said, "My lord, I am a daughter of the great ones of Israel, and my brothers are prophets. When they were prophesying, I heard that tomorrow Jerusalem will fall into your hand." When he heard it, he was exceedingly happy. And he had one of his wise men[115] who used to watch the signs of heaven, and he was accustomed to say, "I see that Israelites are returning (to God) in penitence, and that you will not prevail over them. Return to your place." And the king was filled with indignation against him; and the king ordered him to be seized and to bind his hands and feet and hang him on the tree beside Jerusalem.[116] And the king said, "Tomorrow, when Jerusalem falls into our hands, we will kill him."

And the king believed this Judith, and loved her, and said to her, "Is it your pleasure to be married?" And she said to him, "My lord, oh king, I am not worthy, except to be one of your servants. But truly, since you are so inclined, have a herald to pass through all the camp that everyone who sees two women going to the fountain not touch them because I must go there to wash myself and to bathe."[117] Immediately they had the herald to pass through (the camp), and she did so.

And the king made a great banquet, and they drank and got drunk; and afterwards all went, one by one, to their tents. And the king was lying on her bosom *[whmlk yšb bhyqh]*, and slept. And this Judith went and lifted his sword and cut off his head, and stripped off the linen garment upon him.[118]

And she went with the king's head to the gates of Jerusalem, and said, "Open the gates for me; for already the Holy One has performed a miracle by my hand." And they said to her, "Is it not enough for you that you have played the whore and acted corruptly, that you also come among us with guile?" Immediately she showed them the king's head. When they saw it, they opened the gates and came out and raised the cry, "Hear, O Israel, Yahweh our God, Yahweh is One!" When the Greeks heard that, they said, "Tomorrow they will come against us." And they went to the

[114] In the midrashim, as in the Vg, Judith's work is perceived, from beginning to end, as miraculous, a perspective totally lacking in the LXX.

[115] I.e., Achior, although not named as such.

[116] Achior was also tied to a tree in the Vg.

[117] Here, in contrast to the preceding midrash, Judith does not say yes to the king's proposal; nor, however, does she say no.

[118] Not his embroidered mosquito net of the LXX.

king, and brought him out headless; and there fell upon them terror and dread, and they all fled. And Israel pursued after them, and killed ever so many of them.

So may the Holy One (blessed be He!) quickly work vengeance on our enemies, and hasten for us salvation according to that which is written, "And there shall come to Zion a Redeemer. . . ." Said R. Simeon ben Yochai [who lived about A.D. 120]: "These are the Greeks who made war with the house of Hasmoneus and his sons. And in the hour that they entered into the temple, a Greek went and took the book of Law, and brought into Hannah the daughter of John the High Priest, whose beauty was peerless in the world; and she was wedded to Eleazar ben Hasmoneus. And this Greek intended to go in to her, in the presence of her husband and her father. Said John, "I am the High Priest, and my sons are three; and you are Hasmoneus, and your sons are seven; lo (we are) twelve, according to the Twelve Tribes. I trust the Holy One will work a miracle by our hands." Immediately Eleazar drew the sword and killed this Greek; and he said, "My help is from the Lord, who made heaven and earth."[119]

This midrash, entitled "Midrash for Hanukkah," shares several common features with other, much longer midrashim. First, little or no attention is given to the villain's activities prior to his siege of the city, that is, what would correspond to Jdt 1–7 is lacking. Second, the besieged city in question is always Jerusalem. Third, the heroine, regardless of whether she is described as a maiden, a princess, or a widow, is usually living in the Maccabean period rather than the Persian. Fourth, the names of minor characters mentioned in the LXX are often omitted (e.g., Achior, Joakim, Uzziah, etc.) or different.

The longer midrashim agree much more closely with the LXX and/or the Vg than do the two preceding midrashim, so much so that many scholars regard the longer midrashim as very free Hebrew versions of either the Greek or, more likely, the Vg. For example, the *M'sh Yhwdyt* begins:

It was in the days of Holofernes the king of Javan, a great and powerful king (he had subdued many provinces and strong kings, and razed their fortresses and burned down their palaces), in the twelfth year of his reign that he decided to go up and subdue the Holy City of Jerusalem.[120]

In typical midrash fashion, it goes on to include and expand upon, as well as to "omit," material found in the Greek and Latin versions. Interestingly enough, Judith is called "Judith daughter of Beeri," and Uzziah is described as a "prince of Israel," while Chabris and Charmis are called "priests." Achior plays his appropriate role, but is not mentioned by name. Joakim is not mentioned at all, Uzziah having taken over his function in the story.

[119] Ball, pp. 254–56; for portions of Hebrew text, see Dubarle, *Judith*, II, 110–13; for the full Hebrew text, see Jellinek, I, 132–36.
[120] For the entire Hebrew text, see Enslin, pp. 82–90.

The Others

The Syr versions of Judith,[121] the Copt (the Sahidic, or southern dialect, only), and the Eth are, like other books of the OT and the Apocrypha, literal translations of their Greek *Vorlagen.*[122] Readings from these versions will be cited in the textual footnotes and/or the NOTES only when they offer an especially interesting or important variant.

Fortunately for the interested student, Judith is one of the few books of the LXX which has had critical editions of it prepared by both the Cambridge[123] and the Göttingen Septuagint projects. In keeping with their standard procedures established earlier for other books of the LXX, the editors of the Cambridge Septuagint have printed one manuscript as its text (LXX[B]) and recorded the variants of the Greek and ancient versions in its *apparatus criticus,* while the Göttingen Septuagint, edited by Hanhart (see p. 92), has created an eclectic text, with its variants noted in the *apparatus.* The present commentary is based upon the Cambridge Septuagint of Judith; but the present writer, as well as many other students of Judith, has profited from Hanhart's excellent companion volume to his Göttingen Judith *(Text und Textgeschichte).*

---

[121] I.e., the Peshitta and the Syro-Hexaplar, the latter a very literal Syrian translation of Origen's text done by Paul of Tella in Alexandria in 116–117 (see OTTV, pp. 227–28).

[122] For background information on these versions in general, see OTTV, pp. 229–35; on Judith in particular, see Hanhart's *Iudith,* VIII 4, 16–19.

[123] I.e., The Old Testament in Greek (see BIBLIOGRAPHY, Brooke et al.), the so-called Larger Edition of the Cambridge Septuagint (in contrast to Henry Swete's "smaller" Cambridge Bible).

BIBLIOGRAPHY

Commentaries

Alonso-Schökel, Luis. *Ruth, Tobias, Judith, Ester.* Los Libros Sagrados, VIII, 99–163. Madrid: Ediciónes Cristiandad, 1973.

Ball, Charles James. *Judith.* Apocrypha of the Speaker's Commentary, ed. Henry Wace, I. London: John Murray, 1888. Cited as Ball.

Barucq, André. *Judith, Esther.* 2d ed. La Sainte Bible de Jérusalem, XIV. Paris: Cerf, 1959. Cited as Barucq.

Bissell, Edwin Cone. *The Book of Judith.* The Apocrypha of the Old Testament. New York: Charles Scribner's Sons, 1886. Cited as Bissell.

Bückers, Hermann. *Die Bücher Esdras, Nehemias, Tobias, Judith und Esther.* Herders Bibelkommentar, IV. Freiburg im Breisgau: Herder, 1954.

Cowley, Arthur E. *The Book of Judith.* In APOT, I, 242–67. Cited as Cowley.

Craghan, John. *Esther, Judith, Tobit, Jonah, Ruth.* Old Testament Message: A Biblical-Theological Commentary, ed. C. Sluhl-Mueller and M. McNamara, 16. Wilmington, Del.: Michael Glazier, 1982.

Dancy, J. C. *Judith.* The Shorter Books of the Apocrypha, The Cambridge Bible Commentary, ed. P. R. Ackroyd, A. R. C. Leaney, and J. W. Parker. Cambridge University Press, 1972. Cited as Dancy.

Dimmler, Emil. *Tobias, Judith, Esther, Makkabäer.* Munich: Gladback, 1922.

Dumm, D. R. *Jerome Biblical Commentary.* Englewood Cliffs, N.J.: Prentice-Hall, 1968.

Eichrodt, Walther. *Ezekiel: A Commentary.* Translated by Coslett Quinn. Philadelphia: Westminster Press, 1970.

Enslin, Mortin S. *The Book of Judith.* Jewish Apocryphal Literature, VIII. Leiden: E. J. Brill, 1972. Cited as Enslin.

Fritzsche, Otto F. *Die Bücher Tobias und Judith.* Kurzgefasstes exegetisches Handbuch zu den Apokryphen des Alten Testamentes, ed. O. Fritzsche and C. Grimm, II. Leipzig: Hirzel, 1853. Cited as Fritzsche.

Grintz, Jehoshua M. *The Book of Judith: A Reconstruction of the Original Hebrew Text with Introduction, Commentary, Appendices, and Indices* (in Hebrew with English summary). Jerusalem: The Bialik Institute, 1957. Cited as Grintz.

Grzybek, Stanislaw, and Sylvester Baksik. *Ksiega Tobiasza; Ksiega Judyty; Ksiega Estery.* Pismo Swiete Starego Testamentu, VI/1–3. Lublin, 1963.

Lamparter, Helmut. *Das Buch Judith.* Die Apokryphen II, in Die Botschaft des Alten Testaments, XXV/2, 135–82. Stuttgart: Calver, 1972. Cited as Lamparter.

Löhr, Max. *Das Buch Judith.* In APAT, I, 147–64.

Miller, Athanasius. *Das Buch Judith übersetzt und erklärt.* Die Heilige Schrift des

110 JUDITH

Alten Testaments, ed. F. Feldmann and H. Herkenne, IV/3. Bonn: Peter Hanstein, 1940.

Montague, George T. *The Books of Esther and Judith.* Pamphlet Bible Series, 21. New York: Paulist Press, 1973.

Priero, Giuseppe. *Giuditta.* La Sacra Bibbia: Volgate Latina e Traduzione Italiana dai Testi Originali. Torino: Marietti, 1959.

Scholz, Anton. *Commentar über das Buch "Judith" und über "Bel und Drache."* 2d ed. Leipzig: Leo Wörl, 1898.

Simon, Mose. *SPR YHWDYT.* HSPRYM HḤYṢWNYM. 2d ed. Abraham Kahana, ed. Tel Aviv: Masadah, 1956.

Soubigou, L. *Judith.* La Sainte Bible de Louis Pirot et Albert Clamer, IV, 481–575. Paris: Letourzey et Ané, 1952. Cited as Soubigou.

Stummer, Friedrich. *Tobias, Judith, Esther.* Die Heilige Schrift des A. T. in deutscher Übersetzung (Echter Bibel), II. Würzburg: Echter Verlag, 1956.

Zenger, Erich. "Das Buch Judith." In *Historische and legendische Erzahlungen.* Judische Schriften aus hellenistisch-römischer Zeit, ed. Werner Georg Kümmel et al., I, 6. Gütersloh: Mohn, 1981.

Zöckler, Otto. *Judith,* Die Apokryphen des Alten Testamentes. Kurzgefasstes Kommentar zu den Heiligen Schriften des Alten und Neuen Testamentes sowie zu den Apokryphen, ed. O. Zöckler and H. Strack, I, 185–213. Munich: Oskar Beck, 1891.

Other Books

Abel, Félix M. *Géographie de la Palestine.* 3d ed. Paris: J. Gabalda, 1938.

Aharoni, Yohanan, and Michael Avi-Yonah, eds. *The Macmillan Bible Atlas.* New York: The Macmillan Company, 1968.

Alonso-Schökel, Luis. "Narrative Structure in the Book of Judith." *Protocol Series of the Colloquies of the Center for Hermeneutical Studies in Hellenistic and Modern Culture* XII/17 (March 1974). Cited as Alonso-Schökel.

Altaner, Berthold. *Patrology.* Translated by H. C. Graef. Edinburgh and London: Nelson, 1960.

André, Louis E. T. *Les Apocryphes de l'Ancien Testament.* Florence: O. Paggai, 1903.

Andrews, Herbert T. *An Introduction to the Apocryphal Books of the Old and New Testaments.* 5th ed., rev. Edited by C. H. Pfeiffer. Grand Rapids: Baker Book House, 1954. Cited as Andrews.

Avi-Yonah, Michael. *Hellenism and the East: Contacts and Interrelations from Alexander to the Roman Conquest.* Ann Arbor, Mich.: University Microfilms, 1978.

Booth, Wayne C. *A Rhetoric of Irony.* Chicago: The University of Chicago Press, 1975.

Bright, John. *A History of Israel.* 3d ed. Philadelphia: The Westminster Press, 1981.

Brockington, Leonard H. *A Critical Introduction to the Apocrypha.* Studies in Theology. London: Duckworth Press, 1961.

Brunner, Gottfried. *Der Nabuchodonosor des Buches Judith.* Berlin: Rudolph Pfau, 1940, 1959 (2d ed.). Cited as Brunner.

Coffin, Tristram Potter, *The Female Hero in Folklore And Legend.* New York: The Seabury Press, 1975.

Corrigan, Robert W. *Comedy.* San Francisco: Chandler Publishing Co., 1965.

Dandamaev, M. A. *Persien unter den ersten Achämeniden.* Wiesbaden: Reichert, 1967.

Di Lella, A. A., and Louis F. Hartman. *Daniel,* AB, vol. 23. Garden City, N.Y.: Doubleday, 1978.

Dreissen, Joseph. *Ruth, Esther, Judith in Heilsgeschichte.* Paderborn: F. Schoningh, 1953.

Dubarle, André Marie. *Judith: Formes et sens des diverses traditions.* Analecta Biblica Investigationes Scientificae in Res Biblicas, XXIV. Rome: Institut Biblique Pontifical, 1966.

Eissfeldt, Otto. *The Old Testament: An Introduction, Including the Apocrypha and Pseudepigrapha, and Also the Works of Similar Type from Qumran.* Translated from the 3d German edition by Peter R. Ackroyd. New York: Harper & Row, 1965. Cited as Eissfeldt.

Fromm, Erich. *The Forgotten Language: An Introduction to the Understanding of Dreams, Fairy Tales and Myths.* New York: Grove Press, 1957.

Frye, Northrop. *Anatomy of Criticism.* Princeton, N.J.: Princeton University Press, 1957.

Ghirshman, Roman. *The Arts of Ancient Iran from Its Origins to the Time of Alexander the Great.* Translated by Stuart Gilbert and James Emmons. New York: Golden Press, 1964.

Goldstein, Jonathan A. *I Maccabees,* AB, vol. 41. Garden City, N.Y.: Doubleday, 1976.

Good, Edwin M. *Irony in the Old Testament.* Philadelphia: Westminster Press, 1965.

Goodspeed, Edgar J. *The Story of the Apocrypha.* Chicago: The University of Chicago Press, 1939. Cited as Goodspeed.

Gowan, Donald E. *Bridge Between the Testaments: A Reappraisal of Judaism from the Exile to the Birth of Christianity.* 2d ed., rev. Pittsburgh: Pickwick Press, 1980.

Graf, David F. "Medism: Greek Collaboration with Achaemenid Persia," a University of Michigan dissertation, 1979.

Groom, Nigel. *Frankincense and Myrrh: A Study of the Arabian Incense Trade.* London: Longman, 1981.

Haag, Ernst. *Studien zum Buche Judith: Seine theologische Bedeutung und literarisches Eigenart.* Trierer Theologische Studien, XVI. Trier: Paulinus Verlag, 1963. Cited as Haag.

Hanhart, Robert, ed. *Text und Textgeschichte des Buches Judith.* Mitteilungen des Septuaginta-Unternehmens, XIV. Göttingen: Vandenhoeck & Ruprecht, 1979.

Hengel, Martin. *Jews, Greeks and Barbarians: Aspects of the Hellenization of Judaism in the pre-Christian Period.* Philadelphia: Fortress Press, 1980.

———. *Judaism and Hellenism: Studies in the Encounter in Palestine During the Early Hellenistic Period.* 2 vols. London: SCM Press, 1974.

Hitzig, Ferdinand. *Über Johannes Markus und seine Schriften.* 1843.

Hoftijzer, Jacob, and G. van der Kooij. *Aramaic Texts from Deir 'Allā.* Documenta et Monumenta Orientis Antiqui, XIX. Leiden: Brill, 1976.

Jellinek, Adolph. *Bet ha-Midrasch, Sammlung kleiner Midraschim und vermischter Abhandlungen aus der ältern judischen Literatur.* 2d ed. 4 vols. Jerusalem, 1938.

Johnson, Norman B. *Prayer in the Apocrypha and Pseudepigrapha.* Journal of Biblical Literature Monograph Series, II. Philadelphia: Society of Biblical Literature, 1948.

Lange, Nicholas de. *Apocrypha: Jewish Literature of the Hellenistic Age.* New York: The Viking Press, 1978.

Lods, Adolphe. *Histoire de la littérature hébraïque et juive depuis les origines jusqu'à la ruine de l'état juif.* Paris: Payot, 1950.

Mendenhall, George E. *The Tenth Generation.* Baltimore: The Johns Hopkins University Press, 1973.

Metzger, Bruce. *An Introduction to the Apocrypha.* Oxford University Press, 1957. Cited as Metzger.

Migne, J. P. *Patrologia Graeca* (Collection of the Greek Fathers). 162 vols. Paris, 1857–66.

———. *Patrologia Latina* (Collection of the Latin Fathers). 217 vols. Paris, 1844–55.

Momigliano, Arnaldo. *Alien Wisdom: The Limits of Hellenization.* London: Cambridge University Press, 1975.

Moore, Carey A., ed. *Studies in the Book of Esther.* New York: KTAV, 1982.

Noth, M. *A History of Pentateuchal Traditions.* Englewood Cliffs, N.J.: Prentice-Hall, 1972.

Oesterley, W. O. E. *The Books of the Apocrypha.* New York: Ravel, 1914.

———. *An Introduction to the Books of the Apocrypha.* London: S. P. C. K., 1935. Cited as Oesterley.

Orlin, Louis L., ed. *Michigan Oriental Studies in Honor of George G. Cameron.* Ann Arbor, Mich.: University of Michigan Dept. of Near Eastern Studies, 1976.

Orlinsky, Harry M. *Essays in Biblical Culture and Bible Translation.* New York: KTAV, 1974.

Pfeiffer, Robert H. *History of the New Testament Times, with an Introduction to the Apocrypha.* New York: Harper, 1949. Cited as Pfeiffer.

Purdie, Edna. *The Story of Judith in German and English Literature.* Paris: Librairie Ancienne Honoré Champien, 1927.

Raboisson, Pierre A. *Judith: La véracité du livre de ce nom devant les documents cunéiformes et les histoires Hérodote.* Rome, 1898.

Reed, W. L. *Ashera in the Old Testament.* Fort Worth, Tex.: Christian University Press, 1949.

Rost, Leonhard. *Judaism Outside the Hebrew Canon: An Introduction to the Documents.* Translated by David E. Green. Nashville: Abingdon, 1971.

Ruskin, John. *Mornings in Florence: Being Simple Studies of Christian Art for English Travellers.* New York: John Wiley and Sons, 1877.

Russell, David. *Between the Testaments.* Philadelphia: Muhlenberg Press, 1960.

Scholz, Anton. *Das Buch Judith, eine Prophetie.* Würzburg: Leo Wörl, 1885.

Seux, Marie Joseph. *Epithètes royales akkadiennes et sumériennes.* Paris: Collège de France, 1967.

Speiser, A. E. *Genesis,* AB, vol. 1. Garden City, N.Y.: Doubleday, 1964.

Staerk, Willi. *Alte und neue armaïsche Papyri, Kleine Text* 94, 26. Altorientalische Texte zum Alte Testament, ed. Hugo Gressman. 2d ed. Berlin and Leipzig, 1926.

Steinmann, Jean. *Lecture de Judith.* Paris: J. Gabalda, 1953. Cited as Steinmann.

Steinmetzer, Franz. *Neue Untersuchung über Geschichtlichkeit der Judith-erzählung.* Leipzig: 1907.

Stummer, Friedrich. *Geographie des Buches Judith.* Bibelwissenschaftliche, III. Stuttgart: Katholisches Bibelwerk, 1947. Cited as Stummer.

Surburg, Raymond F. *Introduction to the Intertestamental Period.* St. Louis: Concordia Publishing House, 1975.

Tcherikov, Victor A. *Hellenistic Civilization and the Jews.* Philadelphia: Jewish Publication Society, 1959.

Thackeray, H. St. John. *Some Aspects of the Greek Old Testament.* London: Allen & Unwin, 1927.

Thompson, J. A. K. *Irony: An Historical Introduction.* Cambridge: Harvard University Press, 1927.

Thompson, Stith. *Motif-Index of Folk-Literature: A Classification of Narrative Elements in Folktales, Ballads, Myths, Fables, Mediaeval Romances, Exempla, Fabliaux, Jest-Books, and Local Legends.* Rev. and enl. ed. 6 vols. Bloomington: Indiana University Press, 1955–58.

Torrey, Charles C. *The Apocryphal Literature: A Brief Introduction.* New Haven: Yale University Press, 1945. Cited as Torrey.

Via, Dan O., Jr. *Kerygma and Comedy in the New Testament: A Structuralist Approach to Hermeneutic.* Philadelphia: Fortress Press, 1975.

Vivas, Eliseo. *Creation and Discovery: Essays in Criticism and Aesthetics.* New York: Noonday, 1955.

Voigt, Edwinn E. *The Latin Versions of Judith.* Leipzig: Drugulin, 1925. Cited as Voigt.

Volkmar, Gustav. *Handbuch der Einleitung in die Apokryphen,* I. Tübingen: Sumtibus Ludovici Friderici Tues, 1863.

Weissman, A. S. *Das Buch Judith, historisch-kritisch beleuchtet.* Vienna: 1890.

Will, Edouard. *Histoire du monde hellénistique.* Nancy: Faculté des lettres et des sciences humaines, 1966–67.

Wolff, O. *Das Buch Judith als geschichtliche Urkunde verteidigt und erklärt.* Leipzig: 1881.

Articles

Albright, W. F. "The Lachish Cosmetic Burner and Esther 2:2." In *A Light unto My Path,* ed. H. N. Bream, R. D. Heim, and C. A. Moore. Philadelphia: Temple University Press, 1974.

Alon, Gedalyahu. "The Levitical Uncleanness of Gentiles." In *Jews, Judaism, and the Classical World.* Jerusalem: Magnes Press, 1977.

Altheim, Franz and Ruth Stiehl. "Esther, Judith, und Daniel." In *Die aramäische Sprache unter den Achaemeniden* I, 195–213. Frankfurt am Main: V. Kostermann, 1963. Cited as Altheim and Stiehl.

Anderson, Bernhard W. "The New Frontier of Rhetorical Criticism: A Tribute to James Muilenburg: An Introduction." In *Rhetorical Criticism: Essays in Honor of*

James Muilenburg, ed. Jared J. Jackson and Martin Kessler, ix–xviii. Pittsburgh: Pickwick Press, 1974.

Avisar, S. "Sulla storicita di Giuditta." *Bibliotheca Orientalis* (1959): 22–25.

Barr, John. "Den teologiska varderingen av den efterbibliska judendormen." SEÅ 32 (1967): 69–78.

Bentzen, Aage. "Der Hedammu-Mythus, das Judithbuch und Ähnliches." *Archiv Orientâlní* 18 (1950): 1–2.

———. "*Epurōsen,* Judith 8:27." BiblOr 9 (1952): 174–75.

Biolek, Anton. "Die Ansicht des christlichen Altertums über dem literarischen Charakter des Buches Judith." *Weidenauer Studien* 4 (1911): 335–68.

Bruns, Edgar J. "The Genealogy of Judith." CBQ 18 (1956): 19–22.

———. "Judith or Jael?" CBQ 16 (1954): 12–14.

Cazelles, Henri A. "Le Personnage d'Achior dans le livre de Judith." RSR 39 (1951): 125–37, 324–27.

Colunga, Alb. L. "El género literario de Judit." *Ciencia Tomista* 74 (1948): 94–126.

Condamin, Albert. "Un Pseudonyme de Samarie dans le livre de Judith." RSR 14 (1910): 570f.

Craven, Toni. "Artistry and Faith in the Book of Judith." *Semeia* 8 (1977): 75–101.

Criado, R. "Judith, Libro de." *Encyclopedia Biblia* (1965), IV, 768–72.

Deprez, A. "Le Livre de Judith." *Évangile* 47 (1962): 5–69.

Delcor, Mathias. "Le livre de Judith et l'époque grecque." Klio 49 (1967): 151–79.

Drews, R. "The Fall of Astyages and Herodotus' Chronology of the Eastern Kingdom." *Historia* 18 (1969): 1–11.

Dubarle, André Marie. "L'Authenticité des textes hébreux de Judith." *Biblica* 50 (1969): 187–211.

———. "La Mention de Judith dans la littérature ancienne, juive et chrétienne." RB 66 (1959): 514–49.

———. "Rectification: Sur un text hébreu de Judith." VT 11 (1961): 86–87.

———. "Les Textes divers du livre de Judith. À propos d'un ouvrage récent." VT 8 (1958): 344–73.

———. "Les Textes hébreux de Judith: Un nouveau signe d'originalíte." *Biblica* 56 (1975): 503–11.

Duncan, James A. "A Hebrew Political Romance." *Biblical World,* n.s. 3 (1894): 429–34.

Dussaud, René. "Samarie au temps d'Achab." *Syria* 7 (1926): 9–29.

Edwards, Richard. "Concordance for the Book of Judith." Alphabetic listing prepared from *Thesaurus Linguae Graecae.* Irvine, Calif.: University of California Press, 1979. (Computer printout)

Free, Joseph P. "Dothan." RB 69 (1962): 266–70. Pl. XL.

———. "The First, Second, Third, Fourth, Fifth, Sixth, Seventh Season at Dothan." BASOR 131 (1953): 10–18; BASOR 156 (1959): 22–29; BASOR 160 (1960): 6–13.

Gaster, Moses. "An Unknown Hebrew Version of the History of Judith." PSBA 16 (1893/94): 156–63.

———. "Judith, The Book of." In *Encyclopaedia Biblica,* ed. Thomas K. Cheyne and J. S. Black, III, cols. 2642–46. New York: The Macmillan Company, 1901.

Gordis, Robert. "Religion, Wisdom and History in the Book of Esther—A New Solution to an Ancient Crux." JBL 100 (1981): 359–88.

Greenfield, Jonas C. "Nebuchadnezzar's Campaign in the Book of Judith" (in Hebrew). *Yediot* 28 (1964): 204–8.

Grintz, Jehoshua M. "Judith, Book of," EncJud, X, 451–59.

———. "On the Source of the Basic Motif in the Book of Judith" (in Hebrew). *Molad* 17 (1959): 564–66.

Gruber, Mayer I. "Was Cain Angry or Depressed? Background of a Biblical Murder." BAR 6 (1980): 35–36.

Haag, Ernst. "Die besondere literarische Art des Buches Judith und seine theologische Bedeutung." *Trierer Theologische Zeitschrift* 71 (1962): 288–301.

———. "Der Widersacher Gottes nach dem Buch Judith." *Bibel und Kirche* 19 (1964): 38–42.

Harris, Rendel. "A Quotation from Judith in the Pauline Epistles." ExpTim 27 (1915–16): 13–15.

Heltzer, M. "Eine neue Quelle zur Bestimmung der Abfassungszeit des Judithbuches." ZAW 92 (1980): 437.

Hicks, E. L. "Judith and Holofernes." *Journal of Hellenistic Studies* 6 (1885): 261–74.

Hinz, Walther. "Zur Behistun-Inschrift des Dareios." ZDMG 96 (1942): 326–49, esp. 326.

Hoftijzer, Jacob. "The Prophet Balaam in a 6th Century Aramaic Inscription." BA 39 (1976): 11–17.

Jansen, A. "Der verschollene Verfasser des Buches Judith." *Theologie und Glaube* (1912): 269–77.

Jansen, H. Ludin. "La Composition du chant de Judith." *Acta Orientalia* 15 (1936): 63–71.

Joüon, Paul. "Judith 16, 15 (Vg. 18)." *Biblica* 3 (1923): 112.

Kanael, Baruch. "Notes on Alexander Jannaeus' Campaigns in the Coastal Region" (Hebrew with English summary). *Tarbiz* 24 (1954/55): 9–15.

Klein, G. "Über das Buch Judith." *Notes du IIIe Congrès international des Orientalistes,* Sect. Sem. B, Leiden: 1891, p. 10.

Lefèvre, A. "Judith, Livre de." *Supplément au Dictionnaire de la Bible,* IV, cols. 1315–21. Paris: Letouzey et Ané, 1949.

Lewy, Julius. "Enthält Judith I–IV Trümmer einer Cronik zur Geschichte Nebukadnezars und seiner Feldzüge von 597 und 591?" ZDMG 81 (1927): lii–liv.

McCarter, P. Kyle, Jr. "The Balaam Texts from Deir 'Allā: The First Combination." BASOR 239 (1980): 49–60.

McNeil, Brian. "Reflections on the Book of Judith." *The Downside Review* 96 (1978): 199–207.

Mantel, Hugo. *"Hsydwt Qdwmh"* (Ancient Hasidim). *Studies in Judaism* (1976): 60–80.

Martin, R. A. "Syntax Criticism of the LXX Additions to the Book of Esther." JBL 94 (1975): 65–72.

Meyer, Carl. "Zur Enstehungsgeschichte des Buches Judith." *Biblica* 3 (1922): 193–203.

Milik, Jozef T. "Note additionnelle sur le contrat juif de l'an 134 après J.C." RB 62 (1955): 253–54.

Miller, Athanasius. "Der Nabuchodonosor des Buches Judith." *Biblica* 23 (1942): 95–100.

Momigliano, Arnaldo. "Biblical Studies and Classical Studies: Simple Reflections About Historical Method." BA 45 (1982): 224–28.

Montley, Patricia. "Judith in the Fine Arts: The Appeal of the Archetypal Androgyne." *Anima* 4 (1978): 37–42.

Moutsoulas, I. "Judith" (in Greek). *Thrēskeutikē kai Ethikē Enkuklopaideia* 6 (1965): 941–43.

Movers, C. F. "Über die Ursprache der deuterokanonischen Bücher des A.T." *AfAuk Theo* 13 (1835).

Neuman, Abraham A. "Josippon and the Apocrypha." JQR 43 (1952/53): 1–26.

Parker, S. Thomas. "The Decapolis Reviewed." JBL 94 (1975): 437–41.

Porter, Frank C. "Judith, Book of." HDB, II, 822–24.

Prat, F. "Livre de Judith." *Dictionnaire de la Bible,* III, (1903), 1824–33.

Priebatsch, Hans J. "Das Buch Judith und seine hellenistischen Quellen." ZDPV 90 (1974): 50–60.

Pringle, Ian. "Judith: The Homily and the Poem." *Traditio* 31 (1975): 83–97.

Schedl, Claus. "Nabuchodonosor, Arpakšad, und Darius." ZDMG 115 (1965): 242–54.

Schwartz, Julius. "Un Fragment grec du Livre de Judith (sur ostracon)." RB 53 (1946): 534–7. Pl. VII.

Sealey, R. "The Pit and the Well: The Persian Heralds of 491 B.C." CJ 72 (1976): 13–20.

Skehan, Patrick W. "The Hand of Judith." CBQ 25 (1963): 94–110.

———. "Why Leave Out Judith?" CBQ 24 (1962): 147–54.

Steuernagel, Carl. "Bethulia." ZDPV 66 (1943): 232–45.

Sundberg, Albert. "The Old Testament of the Early Church." HTS, XX (1958): 58–59.

Torrey, Charles C. "Judith, Book of." In *The Jewish Encyclopaedia,* ed. I. Singer, VII, 388–90. New York: Funk & Wagnalls, 1904.

———. "The Older Book of Esther." HTR 37 (1944): 8.

———. "The Site of Bethulia." JAOS 20 (1899): 160–72.

———. "The Surroundings of 'Bethulia.' " *Florilege Melchior de Vogüe.* Paris: 1909, pp. 599–605.

Tov, Emanuel. "The 'Lucianic' Text of the Canonical and the Apocryphal Sections of Esther: A Rewritten Biblical Book." *Textus* 10 (1982): 1–25.

Vaccari, Alberto. "Note critiche ed esegetiche, Judith xvi:11." *Biblica* 28 (1947): 401–04.

Volkmar, Gustav. "Die Composition des Buches Judith." TQ 16 (1857): 441–98.

Vuippens, J. de. "Darius I, le Nabuchodonosor du livre de Judith." *Estudis Franciscans* 31 (1927): 351–69.

Wilson, Robert R. "The Old Testament Genealogies in Recent Research." JBL 94 (1975): 169–89.

Winckler, Hugo. *Altorientalische Forschungen* 2 (1901): 267, 272–75.

Winter, Paul. "Judith, Book of." IDB, II, 1023–26.

Wright, G. E. "The Good Shepherd." BA 2 (1939): 44–48.

Zeitlin, Solomon, "The Book of Esther and Judith: A Parallel." In *The Book of Judith*, ed. Morton S. Enslin, Jewish Apocryphal Literature, VII. Leiden: Brill, 1972. Cited as Zeitlin.

————. "Jewish Apocryphal Literature." JQR 40 (1949–50): 223–50.

————. "The Names Hebrew, Jew and Israel: An Historical Study." JQR (1953): 365–79.

————. "Proselytes and Proselytism During the Second Commonwealth in the Early Tannaitic Period." In *Harry Austryn Wolfson Jubilee Volume*. 1965.

Zenger, E. "Der Juditroman als Traditionsmodell des Jahweglaubens." *Trierer Theologische Zeitschrift* (1974): 65–80.

Zimmermann, Frank. "Aids for the Recovery of the Hebrew Original of Judith." JBL 57 (1938): 67–74.

Zorell, F. "Canticum Judith, Vg 16, 1–2." *Verbum Domini* 5 (1925): 329–32.

Ancient Versions

Brooke, Alan E., Norman McLean, and H. St. John Thackeray, eds. *Esther, Judith, Tobit*. The Old Testament in Greek, III, Part 1. Cambridge University Press, 1940.

Hanhart, Robert, ed. *Iudith*. Septuaginta, Vetus Testamentum graecum, VIII 4. Göttingen: Vandenhoeck & Ruprecht, 1979.

Libri Ezrae, Tobiae, Iudith. Biblia Sacra iuxta Latinam Vulgatam versionem, ed. Ordinis Sancti Benedicti, VIII. Rome: Typsis Polyglottis Vaticanis, 1950.

Rahlfs, Alfred. *Ioudith*. Septuaginta, id est Vetus Testamentum graece iuxta LXX interpretes, 5th ed., Stuttgart: Württ. Bibelanstalt, 1952, 973–1002.

Swete, Henry Barclay, ed. *Ioudeith*. The Old Testament in Greek According to the Septuagint, II, 781–814. Cambridge: Cambridge University Press, 1907.

Thompson, H. F., ed. *A Coptic Palimpsest in British Museum Containing Joshua, Judges, Ruth, Judith, and Esther in the Sahidic Dialect*. London: Oxford University Press, 1911.

JUDITH

I. Nebuchadnezzar's War with King Arphaxad
(1:1–16 [Vg 1:1–12])

1 ¹ It was the twelfth year of the reign of Nebuchadnezzar, who ruled over the Assyrians from his capital, Nineveh, that Arphaxad was ruling over the Medes from Ecbatana. ² (Arphaxad[a] had surrounded Ecbatana with walls of hewn stones four and a half feet thick and nine feet long, and the walls he had made one hundred and five feet high and seventy-five feet wide. ³ At its gates he had placed towers one hundred and fifty feet high, with foundations ninety feet thick. ⁴ He had designed its gates, which were [b]one hundred and five[b] feet high and sixty feet wide, to allow his army of mighty men to parade forth, with his infantry in full formation.) ⁵ [c]In that year[c] King Nebuchadnezzar went to war against King Arphaxad in the Great Plain (this plain[d] is on the borders of Rages[e]). ⁶ [f]There rallied to him[f] all the inhabitants of the highlands, all those living along the Euphrates, the Tigris, and the Hydaspes[g], and in the plains, King Arioch of the Elymaeans. Thus, many nations [h]had mustered to join[h] the forces of the Cheleoudites[i].

⁷ Nebuchadnezzar king of the Assyrians also contacted all the inhabitants of Persia and all those living in the West: those living in Cilicia and Damascus, Lebanon and Anti-Lebanon, all those living along the coast, ⁸ those among the peoples of Carmel and Gilead and those in Upper Galilee and the great valley of Esdraelon[j], ⁹ all those in Samaria and its towns, and beyond the Jordan as far as Jerusalem, Betane[k], Chelus[l], Kadesh, the brook[m] of Egypt, Tahpanhes, Rameses,

---

[a] LXX and verss. "he."
[b-b] LXXˢ, OL, and Syr "90"; Vg "150."
[c-c] LXX "in those days"; see v 1.
[d] LXXᴬᴮ omit.
[e] Syr *Dura.*
[f-f] LXXˢ and OL "they met for war"; see NOTE.
[g] Gk *udaspēn;* Syr *ulai;* OL *hydnas/idas;* Vg *jadason.*
[h-h] LXX "they assembled"; Syr adds "to fight against."
[i] So LXXᴬᴺ and several mins.; LXXᴮ *cheleoul;* LXXˢ *cheslaiouda;* Syr "the Chaldeans"; Vg omits.
[j] So LXX and verss.; LXXᴮ *esrēm.*

and all the land of Goshen, ¹⁰ beyond Tanis and Memphis, and all those living in Egypt as far away as the borders of Ethiopia. ¹¹ But all those living in that entire area ignored the call of Nebuchadnezzar king of the Assyrians and would not join him in the campaign; for they did not fear him but regarded him "as an ordinary man". Therefore, they sent his envoys away, empty-handed and mortified.

¹² Nebuchadnezzar was so incensed at this entire region that he swore by his throne and kingdom that he would get revenge on all the territories of Cilicia, Damascene, and Syria, and would put to the sword all those living in the land of Moab, the Ammonites, all Judea°, and all those living in Egypt as far as the shores of the two seas.

¹³ In the seventeenth year he marshaled his forces against King Arphaxad; and in this battle he defeated him, routing Arphaxad's entire army and all his cavalry and chariots. ¹⁴ He occupied his towns and then turned to Ecbatana, subduing its towers and looting its bazaars, thereby reducing its magnificence to a mockery. ¹⁵ He caught Arphaxad in the mountains of Rages and riddled him with his javelins, thus making an end of him, once and for all. ¹⁶ Then he returned ᵖwith his spoilsᵖ ᑫto Ninevehᑫ, he and his entire motley army, ʳan enormous horde of soldiers. There he and his army recuperated and feastedʳ for four whole months.

ᵏ LXXᴮ *baitanē;* LXXᴬ *blitanē;* LXXˢ *batanē;* LXXᴺ *betanē.*
ˡ LXXᴬᴮᴺ *chelous;* LXXˢ *cheslous.*
ᵐ LXXˢ "torrents"; OL "rivers."
ⁿ⁻ⁿ So LXXᴮ; see NOTE.
° So LXX; LXXᴮ "Idumea."
ᵖᵖ Lit. "with them."
ᑫ⁻ᑫ LXXᴮᴺˢ and many mins. omit.
ʳ⁻ʳ LXXᴮ omits.

Notes

1:1. Like the opening sentence in Esther, the first sentence in Judith is actually several verses long, primarily because of the lengthy parenthetical description concerning the size of Ecbatana's walls (vv 2–4). Enslin somewhat overstates the case by writing: ". . . in the opening sentence, syntax vanishes in what seems a cluttered congeries of words" (p. 41), for the meaning of the opening verses is clear enough in the Greek. But when one tries translating them into another language, especially into a language like English, which is less highly inflected than Greek, then the translator must take certain liberties with the text, such as breaking it up into several sentences and supplying an additional word here and there (see textual notes ^e and [~]). To what extent the awkward flow of the Greek reflects accurately either the actual convolutions of a Semitic *Vorlage* or subsequent inner-Greek phenomena is impossible to say, there being no MT with which to compare the LXX.

While the extended parenthetical expression in vv 2–4 interferes with the smooth flow of events, especially with setting the date for those events, it does help to create in the reader anxious feelings about the implications of Nebuchadnezzar's irresistible power (i.e., if this seemingly invulnerable city of Ecbatana was destroyed with relative ease by him [v 14], how would the Israelites fare?). Jerome's Vg begins the story by saying: "Now Arphaxad king of the Medes had subjugated many nations in his empire, and he built a very strong city which he called Ecbatana . . ." (Vg 1:1), and puts what is v 1 of the Greek after v 4 of his Latin version. But, as Soubigou rightly noted, the Greek sequence preserves "the better order of grandeur" (p. 502).

the twelfth year. According to Jer 32:1, this would have been the fourth year of Zedekiah, the last king of Judah, who in that same year (593 B.C.) declined an invitation from his Palestinian neighbors to revolt against Nebuchadnezzar of Babylon (cf. Jer 27:3; 28:1). In other words, according to the dating here in v 1, the setting for the book of Judith is in the last years of the *pre*exilic period! Yet historical details elsewhere in Judith, especially from chap. 8 on, clearly presuppose a *post*exilic setting (see NOTES *passim*).

Nebuchadnezzar . . . ruled over the Assyrians from . . . Nineveh. Nebuchadnezzar II (605/4–562 B.C.), the most famous king of the Neo-Babylonian Empire, never ruled from Nineveh, that city having been utterly destroyed by his father Nabopolassar and Cyaxares of the Medes in 612 B.C., i.e., seven or eight years *before* Nebuchadnezzar ascended the throne.

According to the Behistun Inscription of Darius I, Hystaspes (522–486 B.C.), among the nineteen kings opposing Darius in the Magian Revolt of 522 B.C. was one Araka son of Haldita, an Aramaean who, after persuading the people of Babylon that he was actually a son of Nabonidus (556–539 B.C.), reigned as Nebuchadnezzar IV. This man, argued Gottfried Brunner, Walther Hinz (see BIBLIOGRAPHY), and Claus Schedl, is the Nebuchadnezzar mentioned in Judith. According to Schedl (ZDMG 115 [1965]: 242–54), who has worked most recently on the problem, "Arphaxad" in Jdt 1:1 is a Median title (probably "Lord of the Knights") rather than a personal name and, in all likelihood, refers to Frawartish (Bab Nidintu-bel), who also claimed to be Nabonidus's son and, as Nebuchadnezzar III, briefly reigned over Babylon until dethroned by Araka. As for the Aramaean Araka being described in Jdt 1:1 as ruling over "the Assyrians from his capital, Nineveh," Schedl argued that the word "Assyrians" was being used in the postexilic sense of "the Syrians," and that "Nineveh" actually represented *Ninos* (mod. Membidsch) between Aleppo and Carchemish, a city not so far from northern Cilicia that an army could not have gone from the one place to the other in a three-day march (see Jdt 2:21). Other arguments of Schedl are even more farfetched; for example, the troublesome references to the activities in "the seventeenth" and "eighteenth" years of Nebuchadnezzar's reign (see NOTES on 1:13 and 2:1, respectively) refer, argued Schedl (p. 246), to the seventeenth and eighteenth years *after the reign of Nabonidus(!),* the last legitimate king of Assyria. Not surprisingly, most scholars have rightly rejected any identification of Judith's Nebuchadnezzar with Araka, in part because of such questionable "explanations" as those offered above, but primarily because, according to the Behistun Inscription, Araka had reigned for less than a year when he was executed by Windaparna, Darius's general, in November of 521 B.C.

While the book of Judith abounds in historical and geographical errors and inconsistencies (see NOTES *passim*), these "slips" in v 1 can hardly be regarded as accidental, since in Judith Nebuchadnezzar is identified as being the king of the Assyrians at least six times. Moreover, inasmuch as today many laymen know that Nebuchadnezzar was king of the Babylonians rather than of the Assyrians, so the ancient author would have known also, as would many of his audience. That being the case, scholars have offered a variety of explanations for this deliberate anachronism. Possibly "Nineveh" really represents "the whole complex of towns in the angle formed by the Tigris and Zab" (Ball, p. 262), or "Assyrians" may represent a scribal failure to distinguish carefully between Assyria and Babylonia, as in 2 Chr 33:11 (so Goodspeed, p. 49). Or possibly, "Nebuchadnezzar" is a pseudonym for some king who, for reasons unknown to us, was not identified explicitly by the ancient author (for various candidates suggested, see INTRODUCTION, pp. 54–55). More likely, both "Nebuchadnezzar" and "Nineveh" are, at least from the point of view of the OT, symbols epitomizing the vilest arch-villain and the cruelest, mighty city, respectively (so Barucq). To accept this explanation is not to deny the correctness of Torrey's view that the information on the date in v 1 was an expression of the author's ironical humor: ". . . he gives his auditors a solemn wink. . . . [and] shows his humor, as well as his care for the right interpretation of his work." (p. 89) Given the great amount of irony throughout the book (see NOTES *passim*), Judith has no better place to express its pervasive irony than in its very first verse.

from his capital, Nineveh. Lit. "in Nineveh, the great city." The same Greek expression occurs in the LXX on Jonah 1:1 and 3:2, a book which has several connections with Judith (see COMMENT II, p. 130).

Arphaxad. Presumably, this is a totally fictitious character (see NOTE on v 2). Assuming that the name is not hopelessly corrupt, scholars know of no such Persian or Median king by this name, although Ball (p. 263) regarded it as a possible corruption of "Arbaces," the name of the first Median king, according to Ctesias. According to Herodotus *(Hist.* 1.96), it was Deioces who built Ecbatana. Some other scholars have thought it referred to Phraortes, founder of the Median Empire (so Barucq, p. 21). On the name in Gen 10:22, see A. E. Speiser, *Genesis,* p. 70.

Ecbatana. Cf. Ezra 6:2f.; 2 Macc 9:3; Tob 3:7. Approximately 300 miles northeast of Babylon and 325 miles southeast of Nineveh, Ecbatana (mod. Hamadān) was a capital city and favorite summer resort of the kings of the Achaemenian Empire and, later, of the Parthians. (For more details, see M. J. Dresden, "Ecbatana," IDB, II, 6f.)

2. *surrounded . . . with walls . . . seventy-five feet wide.* Although scholars have often compared the walls of Ecbatana with those of other great cities, such as Babylon (seventy-five feet wide [Herodotus *Hist.* 1.178]) or Nineveh (wide enough for three chariots to drive abreast on it [Diodorus Siculus, *Historical Library* 2.3]), to make such comparisons is really to miss the author's point: while Ecbatana's grandeur and massiveness attested to the almost superhuman power of Nebuchadnezzar, who was

able to conquer such a city, his army was still unable to take insignificant Bethulia, a town protected only by the God of Israel (so Steinmann, p. 48).

All the prodigious dimensions in vv 2–4 are totally fictitious, the invention of the author to evoke an atmosphere of grandeur. To date, no such protective walls have been found at Ecbatana, although, in all fairness, it must be noted that because the modern city of Hamadan now covers it, Ecbatana has not been scientifically excavated by arcıaeologists. On the other hand, other great Persian cities, such as Persepolis, have been excavated thoroughly; and no such protective walls have been found there, either. (For magnificent photographs of Achaemenian art and architecture in general, and of Persepolis in particular, see Roman Ghirshman, *Arts of Ancient Iran.*) Finally, according to Herodotus *(Hist.* 1.98), Ecbatana was fortified by Deioces (not Arphaxad) ca. 700 B.C., only to fall to Cyrus in 554 B.C.

four and a half feet. Lit. "three cubits." A unit of measurement, a cubit was the distance from the elbow to the fingertip, i.e., approximately eighteen inches. Then, as now, the standards of weights and measurements varied not only among the nations but also within the same nation, depending upon time, place, and circumstance. For further details, see O. R. Sellers, "Weights and Measures," IDB, IV, 828–39.

3. *towers one hundred and fifty feet high.* The number of these wall towers is not mentioned by the author; but according to Diodorus Siculus, a Greek historian of the first century B.C., Nineveh had fifteen hundred such towers, each of them two hundred feet high *(Historical Library,* 2.3).

5. *Great Plain.* Evidently Irak Ajemi in modern Iran, which starts about one hundred miles northeast of Ecbatana and extends to the mountain range of Elburz, south of the Caspian Sea.

Rages [ragau]. Cf. 1:15. The place where Arphaxad was killed (v 15) and where the Median Phraortes fled after being defeated by Darius I, Hystaspes, Rages was a well-known Median city. It is often identified with the modern town of Rai, which is about two hundred miles northeast of Ecbatana and six miles southeast of modern Teheran. If that identification is correct, its location is described most erroneously in the Vg: "near the Euphrates and the Tigris." The city is frequently mentioned in the book of Tobit (Tob 1:14; 4:1, *passim).* Instead of *ragau,* the Syriac has *dura,* which may represent, in part, the Syrian translator's misreading of a Heb *resh (r)* for a *daleth (d).*

6. In the Greek, the meaning of this verse is obscure, primarily because we are uncertain as to the proper interpretation of its two verbs and the true identity of at least three of its proper names.

There rallied to him. Sunēntēsan pros auton, lit. "they met him," can be taken in either a friendly sense (so many modern English translations) or in a hostile sense, especially in light of LXXˢ and the OL ("they met for war"), which the NEB, for instance, renders as "Nebuchadnezzar was opposed by . . ." The same ambiguity is found in the last verb of the verse (see textual note ᵇ⁻ᵇ).

high lands. Orinēn, lit. "hill country," refers to Iran's Zagros mountain range, the high plateau opposite the plains of Mesopotamia and Elam.

Hydaspes. Because the river of this name is actually located in far-distant India, i.e., the mod. Jhelam River (Sanskrit: *Vitasta),* and because the ancient versions offer quite varied readings (see textual note ᵉ), many scholars think that the river intended was actually the two-hundred-mile-long Choaspes (mod. Kerkheh), which flows west of

Susa into the Tigris-Euphrates (Herodotus, *Hist.* 1.188; 5.49) and is mentioned in Strabo, *Geog.* 15.3, in connection with the Eulaeus (a river near Susa) and the Tigris as being "far-distant rivers." The Syr's variant, *Ulai* (which is to be identified with the Eulaeus), is mentioned in Dan 8:2, 16.

Arioch . . . of Elymaeans. Cf. Gen 14:1, 9. Not only can this king(?) not be identified, but the phrase mentioning him is totally corrupt, a fact glossed over by most modern translations. According to Polybius (5.44.9), Elyma was a Persian district. On the name as it appears in Gen 14:1 and 9, see Speiser, *Genesis,* p. 107.

Cheleoudites. Since neither the LXX nor the ancient versions offer a name which is otherwise known (see textual note *'),* *uiōn cheleoud,* lit. "sons of Cheleoud," is either another name for the Assyrians or a corruption of "Chaldeans" (so Barucq and others), or, least likely, another group which joined the Assyrians (so NEB, Soubigou, and others). Dancy would resolve all the difficulties in this verse by observing: "The author's geography is no more accurate than his history" (p. 1).

7. *the inhabitants of Persia.* This is an anachronism, reflecting the fact that the author lived in the postexilic period. For in the preexilic period (i.e., in the days of Nebuchadnezzar) the area in question would have been designated as "Media." It was not until the middle of the fifth century B.C. that the Persian element took precedence over the Median; see also NOTE in 16:10 on "Persians . . . Medes."

8. *among the peoples of.* Correctly sensing a certain awkwardness in this phrase, a number of scholars, starting with Otto Fritzsche, have suggested that the Greek translator read Heb *b'my,* "among the peoples of," for either *b'ry,* "in the cities of," or *bhry,* "in the mountains of."

Gilead [galaad]. Presumably, the highland region in Transjordan through which the Jabbok River (mod. Nahr ez-Zerqa) flows.

Esdraelon. The Greek name for that western portion of the valley of Jezreel, including the valley of Megiddon, which separates Galilee from Samaria. For further details on this historic valley, see G. W. Van Beek, "Jezreel," IDB, II, 906–7.

9. *Betane.* Cf. Josh 15:58. Evidently a city south of Jerusalem, *baitanē* is better identified with Beth-anoth (mod. Beit-'Ainum), seven miles north of Hebron and one and a half miles southeast of Halhul, than with Bethany (so JB), which is one and a half miles east of Jerusalem.

Chelus [chelous]. Possibly to be identified with Halhul, four miles north of Hebron (cf. Josh 15:58), or with Chalutsa (mod. Khalasa), southeast of Beersheba (so Soubigou). See Stummer, pp. 12–13.

Kadesh. I.e., Kadesh-barnea, the oasis in the Wilderness of Zin, where the Israelites under Moses encamped for a while (Deut 32:51; Num 34:3–5; Josh 15:23). For further details on the site, see M. Dothan, "Kadesh-Barnea," EAEHL, III, 697–99.

the brook [lit. "the river"] *of Egypt.* The Greek probably refers not to the Nile itself but to "the brook [Heb *nḥl]* of Egypt" (mod. Wadi el-Arish), which geographically separates Palestine and Egypt (cf. 1 Kings 8:65; 2 Chr 7:8; Josh 15:4). In speaking about the brook of Egypt, the Assyrian kings Sargon I and Sennacherib expressly stated there was no water in it (cf. ANET², pp. 286, 290, 292).

Tahpanhes. This *taphnas* is almost certainly Tahpanhes (mod. Tell Defneh), an important frontier station near Lake Menzaleh in northern Egypt. Called "Daphnai" by Herodotus *(Hist.* 2.30), the site was quite important during the reign of Psammetichus (663–609 B.C.) and the period of the Persian occupation.

Rameses. Cf. Gen 46:28 of LXX; 47:11. The royal city of Rameses II (ca. 1290–1224 B.C.) and his successors for almost two hundred years, this city was the starting point of the Exodus (Exod 12:37; Num 33:3–6). However, because dozens of sites in the delta had the name "Rameses" as a component of their name, the exact location of this particular Rameses is uncertain, although both Tanis and Qantir are strong candidates (see J. A. Wilson, "Rameses, city of," IDB, IV, 9).

Goshen [gesem]. An area in the northeastern part of the Egyptian delta, Goshen was where the Hebrews lived from the time of Joseph until the Exodus (cf. Gen 47:4, 6).

10. *Tanis.* A historic city located in the eastern section of the delta, Tanis (mod. San el-Hajor) is the Greek name for the post-Ramesside city which in the OT is called "Zoan" (Isa 19:11, 13; 30:4; Ezek 30:14; Ps 78:12). According to the majority opinion of scholars, Tanis is to be identified with Per-Rameses of the Nineteenth Dynasty, and with Avaris of the Hyksos period.

Memphis. Located on the western side of the Nile about thirteen miles south of present-day Cairo, Memphis was the chief city of northern Egypt, especially from the Third through Fifth dynasties. It continued to be important, however, and Strabo *(Geog.* 17.1.32) states that in his own day (first century B.C.) Memphis's population was second only to that of Alexandria. Both Memphis and Tahpanhes (v 9) are mentioned in Jer 44:1.

The reasonably accurate sequence of place names in vv 7–10, i.e., Nebuchadnezzar's message proceeded first west and then south, is certainly no proof that the author of the story was using an oral or written source based upon an actual Assyrian or Persian campaign, as some scholars have contended (see INTRODUCTION, pp. 54–55); for anyone who knew his OT, especially Genesis, Exodus, Joshua, and Jeremiah (see NOTES *passim* above), could just as easily have constructed such a series of place names. Jerome's Vg greatly reduces the problem of identifying sites, primarily because so few are mentioned:

> He sent to all that dwell in Cilicia and Damascus, and Lebanon, and to the nations that are in Carmel and Cedar, and to the inhabitants of Galilee in the great plain of Esdraelon, and to all that were in Samaria, and beyond the river Jordan even to Jerusalem, and all the land of Jesse until as far as the borders of Ethiopia. (Vg 1:7b–9)

11. *that entire area.* Lit. "all the land." One of the rhetorical techniques used by the author to emphasize the awesome power and claims of Nebuchadnezzar is his use of this phrase eight times in the first two chapters (1:11, 12; 2:1, 2, 6, 7, 9, 11).

regarded him as an ordinary man. So also Grintz, who posits for the original Hebrew *k'ḥd h'dm* (p. 80). *Ēn enantiou autōn ōs anēr isos,* lit. "he was before them as an equal," i.e., they had thought of him as just one more in a long line of "great" kings and generals who, although no greater than themselves, always demanded more than they deserved, let alone could ever get. (In the case of the real Nebuchadnezzar, he was *extra*ordinary, a household word even today.) However, many scholars and versions, including the JB and NEB, read with most uncials and ancient vers. *ōs anēr eis,* "as one man," i.e., those who ignored Nebuchadnezzar had thought of him as being alone and unsupported. Far too paraphrastic is the GNB's "They thought he had no chance of winning the war so . . ."

12. *Damascene*. Although the Greek word here literally means "Damascus," probably the general region surrounding the city and not just the city itself was intended. The general area has a number of ancient tells.

Syria. This is the Greek word for Heb *'rm*, "Aram," a general term sometimes used for all the territory between Mesopotamia and the Mediterranean.

Moab, the Ammonites, all Judea. This singling out of Judea and her Transjordanian neighbors from all the many nations and peoples included in vv 7–10 is effective foreshadowing, suggesting to the reader that ultimately it will not be Nebuchadnezzar's war with Arphaxad that is central but his war with Judea, a war strongly influenced by Ammonites and Moabites (cf. 5:2; 7:8)!

the shores [ta oria] of the two seas. These bodies of water have been variously identified: The Red Sea and the Persian Gulf (Volkmar); the Red Sea and the Mediterranean (Cowley); or, most likely, the White and Blue Niles, i.e., the two branches of Egypt's great river (Bissell and others). The GNB's "from the Mediterranean Sea to the Persian Gulf" is simply an arbitrary interpretation, not a translation.

13. *seventeenth year*. To stress the fact that it took a full five years (cf. v 1) for Nebuchadnezzar, unaided by those mentioned in vv 7–10, to defeat Arphaxad (so Dancy, p. 76) is to miss the point; for unless one believes that an actual historical battle is being described here (Soubigou, for instance, argues that this is the year 341 B.C. [p. 511]; see INTRODUCTION, p. 55), then the year for ending Nebuchadnezzar's war with Arphaxad was probably determined by the biblical fact that Nebuchadnezzar was known to have besieged Jerusalem in his eighteenth year (cf. Jer 32:1).

14. *bazaars*. Lit. "broad streets."

its magnificence to a mockery [oneidos]. So JB; lit. "her beauty into her shame." The NEB's "to abject ruin" is too strong, at least as applied to the real city; for although Ecbatana was conquered by Cyrus the Great in 554 B.C.—and not by Nebuchadnezzar!—it was still a thriving city in the days of the Parthian Empire (so Strabo, *Geog.* 11.522; 16.743). Cowley (p. 248) posited for the phrase here a play on words in the Hebrew: *ypy bdpy.*

Shame (Gk *oneidos)* is an important theme in Judith, occurring also in 8:22; 9:2; and, in the form of *oneidismos,* in 4:12 and 5:21.

15. *in the mountains of Rages*. Evidently the mountain range of Elburz, six miles north of Rages. According to Craven:

> Activities on mountain tops are of undeniable importance in the Book of Judith. Nebuchadnezzar destroys his enemy Arphaxad in the mountains [1:15], Holofernes too moves against his enemies in the hills [2:22] and hilltop cities [3:6], continually narrowing the scene of combat . . . to a specific hill on which the town of Bethulia is built. . . . the interweaving of this imagery with the specific cultic notes about the destruction of places of worship (3:6–8) in spite of the prior surrender of these people (3:3) and the explicit fear of the people of Israel for their Temple in Jerusalem (4:2) transforms concern . . . to concern over religious survival. . . . This concatenation of the scenes of conflict gradually builds . . . to the climactic confrontation on the Israelite mountain top city of Bethulia. Holofernes' proud boast,

"Who is God except Nebuchadnezzar?" (6:2) voices the threat central to the story of the conflict told in the Book of Judith. (SBLDS 70, pp. 79–80)

In other words, *all* mountaintop activities in Judith are strictly symbolic, having no independent historicity. Just as it was appropriate that the representatives of Yahweh and Baal contend for Israel's loyalty on top of Mount Carmel (1 Kgs 18:17–46), so in Judith the question of "Who is Lord of all the earth?" *had to be* fought on high places. Craven may well be correct in this matter, and perhaps ancient as well as modern readers have on a subliminal level perceived this clever rhetorical device; but if so, Craven seems to be the first scholar to have isolated it so clearly.

riddled him with his javelins. In comparison with the rest of the account in chap. 1, the description seems needlessly detailed and bloodthirsty unless it reflects, as some scholars have argued, an actual, if unrelated, event: "It is improbable that the author of Judith is here giving the true details of the defeat and death of Phraortes, the second king of the Medes, when assailing the Assyrians of Nineveh (Hdt, I, 102). . . . Lipsius may be right in supposing a reminiscence of Darius' victory at Rhagae over Katrida, who pretended to desert from Cyaxares, the Arbaces of Ctesias." (Ball, p. 270)

making an end of him, once and for all. Lit. "he totally destroyed him, to this day."

16. *motley [summiktos] army.* Cf. the LXX of Exod 12:38; Jer 27:37; and 32:20. Herodotus uses the same term to characterize Xerxes's army *(Hist.* 7.55).

for four whole months. Lit. "one hundred and twenty days." Cf. Esth 1:4, where Xerxes celebrated at Susa for half a year.

Comment I

Starting with chap. 1, the ancient author was not "writing history" (an ominous-sounding activity to all but the learned) but telling an exciting story, a tale that in every time and place has fascinated both young and old, learned and illiterate. It is the failure to recognize this simple fact that has created for the informed person "the historical problems" of v 1, e.g., the historical Nebuchadnezzar was king of the Babylonians, not the Assyrians; he never ruled from Nineveh; Arphaxad is unknown outside the Bible (see NOTES). That the author was telling a good story rather than writing history is humorously underscored by his ironic words in v 1: "Nebuchadnezzar . . . ruled over the Assyrians from . . . Nineveh." Wayne Shumaker was, unfortunately, correct when he observed that "one of the values of being uninformed [about the details of ancient geography] may be in the ignorance which permits attention to be concentrated on the sweep of territory suggested ('from Egypt to Media,' we can all appreciate *that)* without being distracted by historical or geographical anomalies" (in Alonso-Schökel, p. 31).

Although chap. 1 ostensibly deals with Nebuchadnezzar's war with King

Arphaxad, the war itself was important only to the extent that it explains why later on Judea found Nebuchadnezzar's army camped at her gates. In fact, the war with Arphaxad is so peripheral to the author's interest that he devotes only six verses to it (vv 5–6 and 13–16).[124] Apart from providing in his opening chapter the "historical" setting for his story (v 1), the author was primarily interested in arousing in his readers two emotions: the Siamese twins of fear and fascination. More specifically, he wanted to awe his readers with Ecbatana's "invincibility" and her magnificence (vv 2–4), a grandeur which Nebuchadnezzar would destroy (vv 13–15); and he wanted to excite in his readers a fear concerning Nebuchadnezzar's subsequent frustration (vv 7–11) and desire for revenge against Judea (v 12). To these initial ingredients of humor, fear, and fascination the author will skillfully add later God, sex, and death. Small wonder so many people know the story of Judith!

Comment II

The first verse in Judith (see NOTE on "Nebuchadnezzar . . . ruled over the Assyrians from . . . Nineveh") as well as certain other features in the book (see NOTES *passim)* may remind some readers of the book of Jonah, which also contains a well-known folktale.[125] The detail in Judith most reminiscent of Jonah is in 4:10, where the Israelites expressed their repentance and mourning by putting sackcloth even on their cattle. However, whether the very puzzling length of time involved in Holofernes' march from Nineveh to northern Cilicia (i.e., three days [see the first NOTE on 2:21]) was actually affected by the length of Jonah's trek through Nineveh (also three days [Jonah 3:3]) is unknown. But, in all likelihood, this similarity is purely coincidental, the expression "three days" often being in the Bible a common expression for "several days."

Both books regard the Assyrians as the enemies of the Israelites (although in neither work does its author view the Assyrians in a totally unfavorable light), and both Jonah and Judith took their final form in the postexilic period. But if the author of Judith was influenced by the book of Jonah, that influence was largely indirect and unconscious, consisting primarily in the fact that Jonah was a romance written prior to the composition of Judith.

---

[124] The Vg is even more brief, there being but two verses devoted to Arphaxad's defeat (Vg 1:5–6). With regard to Holofernes' death, however, the Vg is more gruesome, in that it speaks of Holofernes "without his head wallowing in his blood" (Vg 14:4) and of his "lying upon the ground, without the head, weltering in his blood" (Vg 14:14).

[125] That the story of Jonah is a folktale is a characterization by no means subscribed to by all scholars. In fact, the book has been described as an allegory, a parable, and even as a historical account (for details, see W. Neil, "Jonah, Book of," IDB, II, 964–67).

II. Nebuchadnezzar Plots His Revenge
Against the West
(2:1–13 [Vg 2:1–6])

2 ¹ Then, in the *ᵃeighteenth year on the twenty-second*ᵃ day of the first month, the decision was made in the palace of Nebuchadnezzar king of the Assyrians, to take revenge on the whole region, just as he had promised. ² Summoning all his ministers and nobles, he presented them with his secret strategy; and with his own lips he reviewed for them the full insult of that entire region, ³ so that they resolved to destroy everyone who had not answered his appeal.

⁴ ᵇAfter he had perfected his plan, Nebuchadnezzar king of the Assyrians summoned Holofernes, the general in command of his armies and second in command to himself, and said to him, ⁵ "Thus says the Great King, lord of the whole world: Leave our presence and take with you experienced soldiers, as many as one hundred and twenty thousand infantry and twelve thousand cavalry, ⁶ and march out against all the region to the west, for they ignored my call. ⁷ ᶜTell them to prepare ᵈfor meᵈ earth and water, because in my rage I am about to come upon them, and I will cover every square inch of land with the feet of my army, and I will let them be looted by my troops. ⁸ Their wounded will fill their ravines and gullies! Everyᵉ river will be filled to overflowing with their corpses! ⁹ I will send them away as captives to the ends of the whole world. ¹⁰ As for you, go and occupy all their territory for me in advance. If they surrender to you, hold them for me until the time comes for me to punish them. ¹¹ But on the rebellious show no mercy. Let them be slaughtered and looted throughout yourᶠ territory. ¹² For as surely as I and my powerful kingdom live, I have spoken! I will accomplish these things by my own hand. ¹³ As for you,

---

ᵃ⁻ᵃ Syr "28th . . . 12th"; Vg "13th . . . 22nd."

ᵇ LXX *kai egeneto* (= Heb *wyhy).*

ᶜ Vg omits vv 7–9.

ᵈ⁻ᵈ So LXXˢ, many mins., Eth, OL, and Syr.

ᵉ Lacking in LXX.

ᶠ Most mins., OL, and Syr omit; see NOTE.

don't neglect a single one of your lord's commands but execute them fully, just as instructed. And don't delay in doing it!"

Notes

2:1. *eighteenth year.* This is the year after Arphaxad's defeat, during which period Nebuchadnezzar would have had time to nurse his desire for revenge. Because the Vg lacks 1:13–16, it dates this punitive campaign to Nebuchadnezzar's thirteenth year (cf. 1:5 of Vg). Those scholars who see this campaign of Nebuchadnezzar as being actually that of Ashurbanipal regard it as Ashurbanipal's reaction in 652 B.C., when, at the instigation of his brother Shamashshumukin, nations revolted against him throughout the empire, including Babylon, Elam, Syria, and Judah (cf. 2 Chr 33:11). That revolt was not quelled until after 640 B.C. (see Bright, *History of Israel,* pp. 310–14). On the other hand, Soubigou (p. 512) saw here one of the campaigns of Artaxerxes III, Ochus, possibly that of 345 B.C. More likely, however, the ancient author, with no intention of deceiving, simply preferred to invent for his account those trappings that usually accompany a "historical" tale.

As Craven quite correctly observes, the only true detail associated with Nebuchadnezzar's name in Jdt 1:1–2:13 is that he was involved in massive military aggression in his eighteenth year; but, as she also notes, that "military aggression" was actually the destruction of Jerusalem and the Israelite state (SBLDS 70, p. 71).

first month. I.e., Nisan (March/April). In the Near East, spring was the traditional time for military campaigns (cf. 2 Sam 11:1).

2. *he reviewed for them the full insult.* The translation is uncertain; but because the Gk *sunetelesen pasan tēn kakian,* "he completed all the wickedness," makes so little sense, the reading adopted here by most modern translators follows Fritzsche's suggestion that originally the Heb *wyglh,* "he revealed," was misread as *wyklh,* "he completed."

"And is it not high comedy to make Nebuchadnezzar an Assyrian and put him into an already destroyed capital city where he tells in detail his 'secret' plan and gives an order to his chief general which the latter soundly disregards?" (SBLDS 70, p. 115) Craven is certainly correct here, but her understanding of the definition of "comedy" is an academic and classical one, not that of the typical man on the street (see, for example, Wayne C. Booth, *Rhetoric of Irony*).

3. *everyone.* Lit. "all flesh," a common Hebraism, *kl bśr.*

4. *Holofernes [olophernēs].* The name's established anglicized form is based on the Vg, which aspirated the first syllable of this name even as it did others, such as Esther *(hester)* and Jerusalem *(hierusalem).* Possibly corrupted under the influence of the Greek compound *olo-,* "destroying," *orophernēs,* the correct Persian form, was used in both the Achaemenian and Seleucid periods for Persians, including one of the generals of Artaxerxes III who invaded Asia Minor and Egypt ca. 341 B.C. (Diodorus Siculus, *Hist.* 31.19.2–3). However, this Holofernes was said to have died in his own country, and several Cappadocian kings, one of whom supported Demetrius I, Soter, against Ariarathes V, ca. 158 B.C. (Polybius, *Hist.* 3.5.2). In the British Museum, the inscription "Orophernes King Victorious" appears on two silver coins from Pirene, ca. 158 B.C.; see Plate 3. (For an old, yet timely, discussion on the name as it appears in various ancient Greek writers, see G. A. Cooke, "Holofernes," HDB, II, 402.) While scholars dating the "events" of Judith to the time of Artaxerxes III's campaign in Asia Minor point out that a General Holofernes actually had an officer by the name of Bagoas (see NOTE on 12:11), scholars who date those same "events" to either the Maccabean or Hasmonean period point out that in the shortest recension of Judith, a King Seleucus appears in place of Holofernes (see p. 103).

5. *the Great King.* This Achaemenian title was borrowed from the Medes (see Dandamaev, *Persien,* p. 94), who, along with the Assyrians (see 2 Kgs 18:19; Isa 36:4), may have adopted it from the Hittites (see the entry on *šarru rabū* in Seux, *Epithètes royales,* pp. 298–300).

lord [kurios] of the whole world. "Lord," rather than "Master," as in some English translations, well expresses here the king's pretensions; for the audience of the ancient author knew that only God was "Lord of the whole world." "The cheap rhetoric with which Nebuchadnezzar instructs Holofernes (especially in vv 7–11) is part of the stock portrait of the heathen tyrant" (Dancy, p. 78).

experienced soldiers. Lit. "men confident in their (own) strength" rather than, by implication, trusting in God (cf. Pss 49:6; 52:7).

one hundred and twenty thousand infantry. This statistic is the same as that in 1 Macc 15:13, "a suggestive coincidence" (Ball, p. 272).

6. *region to the west.* I.e., Syria and Egypt, "the objects of the campaign of Artaxerxes Ochus" (Cowley, p. 249).

ignored my call. Lit. "disobeyed the command of my mouth"; cf. 1:11.

7. *prepare . . . earth and water.* A Persian, not an Assyrian or Babylonian, token of submission (cf. Herodotus, *Hist.* 6.48.2; 6.48.49), this detail is just one more of the Persian elements in the story. But according to Louis L. Orlin *(Michigan Oriental Studies),* the offering of earth and water "cannot simply be the equivalent of 'raising the white flag' or 'throwing down the sword' [but in Zoroastrian thought] . . . indicates the action of the one petitioning for the treaty or contract as properly humble, appropriate, and including the promise of inviolability" (pp. 265–66). For more on this Persian element in Greek tradition, see Sealey, CJ 72 (1976): 13–20.

I am about to come upon them. This is not so much a statement of fact as a most determined promise, like General MacArthur's famous vow at Bataan: "I shall return."

every square inch of land. Lit. "the whole face of the earth."

8. This verse, with its appropriate grandiloquence, may have been influenced by Ezek 35:8 and Isa 66:12. While the general sense of the verse is clear, a translator must, in the interest of eloquence, take certain liberties with its syntax. Since vv 7–9 are missing in the Vg, the reader misses there much of Nebuchadnezzar's bombast.

9. *send them away as captives.* Cf. Isa 20:4 of the LXX.

10. *occupy . . . in advance [prokatalēmpse].* Apart from Jdt 4:5; 7:1, 7, and 17, this verb does not occur in the LXX.

until the time comes for me to punish them. Lit. "till the day of their reproof *[elegmou]*."

11. *show no mercy.* Lit. "your eye shall not spare," as in the LXX of Deut 7:16 and Ezek 20:17. Vv 11–13 "underline well the cruel energy of the king" (Soubigou, p. 514).

your [sou] territory. I.e., the region entrusted to Holofernes. Because "your" is awkward here, some translators, following Fritzsche, posit here a misreading of Heb *'rṣh,* "wheresoever in the land" (i.e., with the old locative *h),* as *'rṣk,* "in your land."

12. *as I . . . live [zōn egō].* Here Nebuchadnezzar utters an oath which God himself has used (Deut 32:39–41 of the LXX). Believing the truth of God's claims in Deut 32:39–41, the ancient Jewish readers would have regarded all of Nebuchadnezzar's claims in vv 7–13 as pretentious, if not blasphemous.

my powerful kingdom. Hendiadys; lit. "the power of my kingdom."

by my own hand. Holofernes promises vengeance by his hand; Judith promises, with God's help, deliverance through hers (Jdt 8:33 and 12:4). Whether God's hand or Nebuchadnezzar's is mightier constitutes the central question posed by the book of Judith.

13. *execute them fully [epitelōn epiteleseis].* Lit. "completing, you will complete," this Hebraism represents the infinitive absolute construction in that language.

Comment

Nebuchadnezzar is not the villain in Judith. Holofernes is. Nonetheless, with just a few verses the author deftly sketched an unflattering, yet memorable, portrait of the one who had started it all. By Nebuchadnezzar's own words and actions he showed himself to be decisive (vv 1–2, 13) yet vengeful (vv 1, 6), proud and pretentious (vv 5, 12), unforgiving and cruel (vv 7–11). But although Nebuchadnezzar may have been grandiloquent (vv 7b–8) and pretentious, he was not quite the fool that Holofernes was; for in vv 1–13 (v 12 notwithstanding), Nebuchadnezzar made no claim to being divine. All of his orders to Holofernes in vv 5–13 were strictly of a political and military character, and in no instance did he require or even ask for divine honors. Yet Holofernes will try to enforce exactly that (3:8; 6:2). Thus, in the story at least, it will be Holofernes, the overzealous and blasphemous general, who is destroyed, not Nebuchadnezzar.

Be that as it may, the mighty Nebuchadnezzar has plotted a thoroughgoing revenge involving invasion and looting (v 7), killing and executions (v 8), and even deportation (v 9). And Judea (1:12) was expressly included!

III. General Holofernes Undertakes His Campaign Against the West (2:14–3:10 [Vg 2:7–3:15])

2 [14] After withdrawing from his lord's presence, Holofernes summoned all the marshals, generals, and officers[a] of the Assyrian army [15] and mustered picked men [b]by divisions[b] as his lord had instructed him, one hundred and twenty thousand infantry and twelve thousand mounted bowmen. [16] He organized them as a [c]great army[c] is marshaled. [17] He also took an enormous number of camels, asses, and mules for carrying their baggage and innumerable sheep, oxen, and goats for their food [18] as well as ample rations for every man and a generous amount of gold and silver from the royal palace.

[19] He then set out on his campaign, he and his entire army, to go ahead of King Nebuchadnezzar and to smother the whole western region with their chariots, cavalry, and picked infantry. [20] Along with them there went out a motley crowd like locusts, like the dust[d] of the earth, countless because of their numbers.

[21] They set out from Nineveh on a three-day march to the plain of Bectileth[e], and they encamped opposite Bectileth near the mountain north of Upper Cilicia. [22] From there, Holofernes[f] advanced into the highlands with his whole army: infantry, cavalry, and chariots. [23] He cut his way through Put and Lud and plundered all the Rassisites and Ishmaelites living on the edge of the desert south of Cheleon.[g] [24] Then, crossing the Euphrates and proceeding through Mesopotamia, he razed all the walled towns along Wadi Abron[h] as far as the sea. [25] He occupied the territory of Cilicia and slaughtered all who resisted him.

[a] LXX[s] "satraps."
[b-b] LXX "in battle array."
[c-c] LXX "a great number."
[d] LXX "sand."
[e] LXX[B] *baiteilaith;* LXX[A] *bekteleth;* LXX[NS] *bektileth.*
[f] LXX "he."
[g] LXX[AS] *cheleōn;* LXX[N] *chelleōn;* LXX[B] and Syr *chaldaiōn;* OL[S] *cheleonis terrae chaldaeorum;* Vg *cellon.*
[h] So LXX[BAN]: *abrōna;* LXX[S] *chebrōn;* L[cm] *mambrae;* Vg *mambre.*

Then he came to the southern borders of Japheth, facing Arabia.
26 Surrounding all the Midianites, he set their tents on fire and plundered their sheepfolds. 27 Descending upon the plain of Damascus during the wheat harvest, he set fire to all their fields, destroyed their
flocks and herds, sacked their towns, stripped their plains, and put all
their young men to the sword.

28 So fear and dread of him possessed those living along the seacoast:
those in Sidon and Tyre, those living in Sur^i and Okina, and all those
living in Jamnia. Those living in Azotus and Ascalon^j were also terrified of him.

3   1 Therefore, they sent him envoys to sue for peace and say, 2 ^{k}"We,
the servants of the great king Nebuchadnezzar, lie prostrate before
you. 'Treat us as you please.' 3 Our buildings, ^{m}all our land^m, every
wheat field, the flocks and herds, all the sheepfolds of our encampments—they are yours! Treat them as seems best to you. 4 Our towns
and their inhabitants are your slaves. Come and treat them as you see
fit."

5 After the envoys^n had come and reported to Holofernes this message, 6 he went down with his army to the coast, stationed garrisons in
the walled towns, and took choice men from them as auxiliaries.
7 These people and all those in the surrounding countryside welcomed
him with garlands and dancing and tambourines. 8 Yet he demolished
all their sanctuaries^o and cut down all their ^{p}sacred poles^p. It was
granted to him to destroy all the gods of the area so that all the nations
should worship Nebuchadnezzar alone—that every dialect and tribe
should call upon him as god!

9 Then he advanced toward Esdraelon, near Dothan, which is opposite the great ridge of Judea. 10 He encamped between Geba^q and
Scythopolis and stayed there a full month so as to collect all the supplies for his army.

^{i} So all mins. and uncials (Gk *sour*), except LXX^B *assour*; Eth *seir*.
^{j} LXX^S, OL, and Syr add "and Gaza."
^{k} Vv 2, 3, and 4 of LXX begin with *idou* (= Heb *hinnē*, "See!").
^{l} LXX^S omits.
$^{m-m}$ LXX^{BS} omit by haplography.
^{n} So OL and Syr; LXX "men."
^{o} So Syr; LXX "borders"; see NOTE.
$^{p-p}$ LXX "groves"; see NOTE.
^{q} LXX^B *gaibai*; LXX^N *gabai*; LXX^S *gaiban*; LXX^A, Eth *taiban*; OL^m *libda*.

Notes

2:14. *marshals [dunastēs].* Lit. "rulers"; cf. Wis 5:23; Sir 4:27; 2 Macc 9:25; 3 Macc 6:4.

Assyrian [assour]. In Judith, this form occurs thirteen times for the country itself while *uioi assour,* "sons of Asshur," and *assurioi,* "Assyrians," are "used with seeming indifference for the people" (Enslin, p. 69).

15. *one hundred and twenty.* According to Craven (SBLDS 70, pp. 75–76), the verbal repetition of that numeral found in 2:5 and 2:15 is a "serial concatenation" that the author used to unite the opening scenes in Judith. Repetition, according to Craven, is the major organizational feature of the book of Judith.

17. *innumerable.* Lit. "it was without number," a common Hebrew hyperbole (cf. Gen 41:49; Judg 6:5; 7:12).

19. *to smother.* Lit. "to cover." While "to blanket" has too many positive overtones, the JB's "to overwhelm" and the NEB's "to overrun" are too colorless, almost neutral: Holofernes' army was commissioned to do much violence.

20. *like locusts [akris].* Although the standard word in the LXX for "locusts," *akris,* is sometimes used there for other types of similar insects, including grasshoppers. Nonetheless, here locusts are a most appropriate image for Holofernes' army, symbolizing, as they do, destructiveness (cf. Deut 28:38; Joel 1:4) and countless numbers. For more on the subject, see Y. Palmoni, "Locust," IDB, III, 144–48.

like the dust ["sand"] *of the earth.* This is a mixed metaphor; for ordinarily the Bible speaks of "the sand of the sea" (Gen 32:12), "sand of the seashore" (Gen 22:17; Josh 11:4), or "the dust *['pr]* of the earth" (Gen 13:16; 28:14).

21. *a three-day march to . . . Bectileth.* An unidentified plain in or near northern Cilicia, Bectileth (see textual note *ʿ*) is sometimes identified with *bakatailloi,* south of Syrian Antioch (see Ptolemy, *Geography* 5.14), or with Beq'ah, a valley between Lebanon and Anti-Lebanon. The discussion of the problem long ago by Ball (p. 275) has not been superseded by more recent scholarship.

The recent suggestion of Craven to the effect that the three-day three-hundred-mile journey of the Assyrian army is but a humorous detail (SBLDS 70, pp. 115–16) strikes the present writer as unpersuasive. And while the observation of Montague is true enough, essentially he ignores the problem by saying: "The impossible zig-zagging of the campaign over the West simply sets the stage for the confrontation of a crushing world power with a people whose only faith is faith in their Lord?" *(Books of Esther and Judith,* pp. 15–16)

More likely, something is out of order here; for no ancient army could have traveled from Nineveh to northern Cilicia, a distance of approximately three hundred miles, in *just* three days. Either the order in vv 21–26 (i.e., Holofernes marches from Nineveh to northern Cilicia [v 21] through Mesopotamia [v 24] to Cilicia [v 25]) is no longer in its original sequence, or the ancient author was woefully lacking in his knowledge of non-Palestinian geography. The former explanation is more likely in this case.

north. Lit. "on the left," a Hebraism; see Gen 14:15.

23. *Put and Lud.* Traditionally, Put is thought by scholars to be located in Africa, probably to be identified with Libya (see Gen 10:6; 1 Chr 1:8; Jer 46:9), while Lud is usually identified with Lydia in Asia Minor (see Gen 10:22; Isa 66:19). Here in v 23, Put either refers to another Put (i.e., an unidentified one bordering Cilicia); or, what is more likely, the ancient author, ignorant of Put's actual location in Africa, mentioned it in relation to Lud because he knew from the Bible that Lud and Put were sometimes closely associated with one another (see Jer 46:9; Ezek 27:10;[126] 30:5). The close association of Put and Lud in the Bible may be due more to assonance than the geographical proximity of the two lands.

Rassisites. Lit. "the children of Rassis." Mentioned in the Bible only here, these people were evidently located near Cilicia. While some scholars regard the name as a corruption of "Tarsus" (OL, Vg *tharsis),* Stummer (pp. 24–25) identified it with Mount Rossos (mod. Arsus), where Alexander the Great and Darius III, Codomannus, fought the momentous Battle of Issus in 333 B.C.

Ishmaelites. Evidently a nomadic tribe in the Syrian desert. For further details, see G. M. Landes, "Ishmaelites," IDB, II, 748–49.

Cheleon. Some scholars identify this with ancient Cholle (mod. el-Khalle), between Palmyra and the Euphrates (see Stummer, pp. 24–25). In any event, the reading "Chaldeans" (see textual note *ᵍ)* cannot be right.

24. *crossing the Euphrates.* Something is seriously wrong here with the text; for as matters stand, we are asked to understand that Holofernes had been in northern Cilicia (v 21), then returned from there and recrossed the Euphrates—of which retracing of steps no mention is made in vv 22–23—and was now crossing the Euphrates a third time (v 24). Assuming that "the sea" mentioned at the end of the verse is the Mediterranean and not the Persian Gulf (so Soubigou, p. 516), we must either assume that v 24 is now out of order and originally preceded v 21, or we must conclude that the ancient writer was quite ignorant of non-Palestinian geography. In this case, the two explanations are not mutually exclusive.

The Vg reflects essentially the same impossible itinerary even though some of the place names are different:

> And when he had *passed through the borders of the Assyrians,* he came to the great mountains of Ange, which are *on the left of Cilicia.* . . . he took by assault the renowned city of Melothus, and pillaged all the children of Tharsis . . . and on the south of the land of Cellon. And *he passed over the Euphrates and came to Mesopotamia;* and he forced all the stately cities . . . till one comes to the sea; and he took the borders thereof, *from Cilicia* to the coasts of Japheth . . . south. [italics added] (Vg 2:12–15)

---

[126] According to Eichrodt *(Ezekiel,* p. 381, n. 9), the Lud in Ezek 27:10 is not to be identified with the Lydia of Gen 10:22 but is to be sought in Africa as in Ezek 30:5; Jer 46:9. But even if Eichrodt be correct in thinking that there were two countries named Lud, the one in Africa and the other in Asia Minor, the Put and Lud of Jdt 2:23 are still in close proximity to northern Cilicia (Jdt 2:21), in which case they are far removed from Africa and, thus, totally inappropriate for Holofernes' itinerary at this point.

Wadi Abron [cheimarrou abrōna]. In the Bible, Abron is mentioned only here. Attempts to identify it with the tiny stream Chaboras, which empties into the Euphrates some fifty miles above Dura, or to explain it as a misreading of Heb *'br hnhr,* "beyond the river" (so Movers, *AfAuk Theo* 13 [1835]), are unconvincing, especially since, according to vv 24–25, *abrōn* is in or near Cilicia. Certainly the ancient copyists could not agree on its name (see textual note *ʰ*).

25. *occupied . . . Cilicia.* This verse also seems out of place and better suited to following v 21, unless, as Ball suggested (p. 277), the author was simply recapitulating v 21.

Japheth, facing Arabia. Cf. Gen 9:27; 10:1–2. The identity of the first-named place is obscure. Judging from v 27, we may say that it was northeast of Damascus.

"Arabia" here designates not the large peninsula itself or even a part of it but the Syrian Desert or, as the geographer Ptolemy called it, *Arabia Deserta.* See 1 Macc 11:16, where Arabia, near Damascus, is part of the Nabataean territory; see also Gal 1:17.

26. *Midianites.* Although perhaps based in the northwestern portion of the Arabian Peninsula in the thirteenth century B.C. (see Exod 2:15), segments of these people wandered as far south as Mount Sinai (Num 10:29) and as far north as the Syrian-Arabian Desert (Judg 7:25); moreover, even in the eleventh century B.C. the Midianites were associated with "the people of the East" (Judg 6:3, 33; 7:12). For the argument that these people may have had their origins in Anatolia (mod. Turkey), see George E. Mendenhall, *Tenth Generation,* pp. 163–73.

27. *during the wheat harvest.* I.e., late spring or early summer. The wheat harvest occurs as early as April in the Jordan Valley and as late as August in the Upper Lebanons. Unless an entire year had passed since Holofernes had started out (and there is no indication that such is the case), then his broad swath of destruction had taken him only a few months, i.e., from March/April (2:1) to June.

put . . . to the sword. Lit. "strike with the mouth of the sword," a very common Hebraism (Gen 34:26; Josh 6:21; 1 Sam 15:8). While most scholars believe that the word "mouth" is used in this Hebrew idiom because the sword "devours" its victim, Theophile J. Meek (BASOR 122 [1951]: 31–33) suggested that the idiom means "up to the hilt," because Ancient Near Eastern "swords and battle-axes have been found in which the blade is represented as the tongue striking out of the open, ravenous mouth of a lion or dragon, which constitutes the base of the sword hilt" (p. 33).

28. The fact that exactly seven cities are mentioned in the verse is probably the author's way of underscoring the totality of the capitulation to Holofernes, the number seven being among the Hebrews a symbol of completeness. In other words, literary, not historical, considerations are at the base of the narrative.

Modern translators, perhaps in part as an expression of the Western emphasis on efficiency and the desire to get to the "important" parts quickly, sometimes erroneously abbreviate the original text in their translation. For example, while the JB's "The populations of Sidon and Tyre, of Sur, Ocina, Jamnia, Ozotus, Ascalon, were panic-stricken" may include all the vital information of v 28b, it misses the pregnant pauses created by the various syntactical structures of the Greek. Evidently the original author wanted his readers not just to "swallow" the facts but to savor them as well.

fear and dread [phobos kai tromos]. Compare 15:2, where the same two nouns (but in reverse order) are applied to the Assyrians.

Sidon and Tyre. The histories of these two great Canaanite cities have often been intertwined. Sidon, about twenty-five miles north of Tyre on the Mediterranean coast, was destroyed by the Assyrian king Esarhaddon (680–669 B.C.) in 677 B.C. It recovered and thrived, only to revolt against Artaxerxes III, Ochus, in 351 B.C. At that time over forty thousand of its citizens perished, so, not surprisingly, Sidon later surrendered to Alexander the Great in 333 B.C. without a struggle.

Tyre, originally a small rocky isle unconnected to the mainland, was also an old Canaanite city mentioned in the Amarna Letters of the fourteenth century B.C. Like Sidon, it too was a great maritime and commercial center. Unlike Sidon, Tyre avoided destruction by Esarhaddon in 677 B.C. by paying him tribute. Nebuchadnezzar, however, had to besiege Tyre for thirteen years before it "fell" to him in 572 B.C. (so Josephus; see however, Ezek 26:7–14, dating to ca. 587 B.C., and then to Ezek 29:17–20, dating to ca. 571 B.C. Judging from the latter passage and the silence of Babylonian sources, we might infer that Nebuchadnezzar's victory was less than total, possibly even a draw). However, unlike Sidon, Tyre chose to oppose Alexander the Great, with the result that Alexander built a mole from the mainland to the isle and conquered it after a seven-month siege, wreaking terrible revenge on the city. Both Tyre and Sidon were visited by Jesus (Matt 15:21; Mark 7:31) and Paul (Acts 21:3–4; 27:3).

Sur [sour] and Okina [okeina]. Unfortunately, both sites are unknown, probably because of corruption in the text (see textual note *ı*). *Sour* may be a corruption of *dōra* (Heb *d'r* or *dwr,* "Dor"), a seaport town about fifteen miles south of Mount Carmel (cf. Josh 12:23; 1 Kgs 4:11; 1 Macc 15:11–13, 25; see also G. Foerster, "Dor," EAEHL, I, 334–37); but, more likely, *sour* is a dittography, i.e., the Heb *ṣwr,* "Tyre," was read as *swr,* which was transliterated into Greek as *sour.* In any event, Vaticanus's "Assyria" cannot be correct.

As for *okeina,* the name occurs only here. It may be a corrupt form of Gk *akē,* "Acco" (= Heb *'kw;* mod. Acre), a very ancient harbor city north of Mount Carmel, which under the name "Ptolemais" was also important in the Hellenistic and Maccabean periods (cf. 1 Macc 5:15; 10:51–66). However, if Judith's "Sur" is actually Dor rather than a dittography for "Tyre," then what would otherwise have been a geographically accurate north-south progression (i.e., Tyre, Sidon, Acco, Jamnia, Ashdod, Ascalon) is ruined; for Acco is actually twenty-some miles north of Dor. Here such carelessness in the geographical sequence is somewhat surprising; for although the ancient author may not have had a strong command of non-Palestinian geography, scholars agree that he knew that of Israel (see NOTES *passim*).

Jamnia. Formerly called "Jabneel" (Josh 15:11) or "Jabneh" (2 Chr 26:6), Jamnia is nine miles north of Ashdod and about four miles inland from the Mediterranean. It served as a headquarters for several Seleucid generals: Georgias (1 Macc 4:15; 5:58), Appollonius (1 Macc 10:69), and Cendebeus (1 Macc 15:40). In 164 B.C., Judas Maccabeus put the torch to it.

It was at Jamnia, ca. 90–100 A.D., that the Jewish council fixed the authoritative text of the Hebrew Bible (i.e., the proto-MT) and excluded books from the Jewish canon (e.g., the Apocrypha). In this connection, the observations of D. N. Freedman about the matter are well worth repeating:

What do we really know about the Council of Jamnia? Everybody quotes everybody else about this famous or infamous Council, but what are the ancient sources, and what are reasonable inferences about its activity? Personally, I think it was a non-event, and not much happened, unlike the Council of Nicaea for example. . . . It would be refreshing if someone cited actually ancient sources for this Council and its work. (private correspondence with this writer)

Azotus. This city, which is about ten miles south of Jamnia and three miles inland from the Mediterranean Sea, was formerly called Ashdod, one of the five principal cities of the Philistines (Josh 13:3). Possibly the strongest of the pentapolitan cities in the Persian period (cf. Neh 4:7; 13:23–24), Azotus (as Ashdod was called in the Hellenistic period) was devastated in the Maccabean period by Judas (1 Macc 4:15; 5:68), Jonathan (1 Macc 10:77–85; 11:4), and John Hyrcanus (1 Macc 16:10); later, according to Josephus *(Ant.* 13.15.4), Alexander Janneus (104–78 B.C.) ruled over it. For further details on Ashdod/Azotus, see W. F. Stinespring, "Ashdod," IDB, I, 248–49; and M. Dothan, "Ashdod," EAEHL, I, 103–19.

Ascalon. Located on the Mediterranean Sea about ten miles south of Azotus and about twelve miles north of Gaza, Ascalon (formerly called Ashkelon) was also one of the cities of the Philistine Pentapolis (Josh 13:3); but it existed long before that time, having been mentioned in the Egyptian Execration Tablets, ca. 1850 B.C. In the Persian period, the city recognized the hegemony of Tyre (so Scylax, *Periplus* 104); and in the Maccabean period the city had reasonably peaceful relations with the Jews (cf. 1 Macc 10:86; 11:60; 12:33). For further details on this city, see articles by W. F. Stinespring, "Ashkelon," IDB, I, 252–54; and by M. Avi-Yonah and Israel Ephal, "Ashkelon," EAEHL, I, 121–30.

The absence of Gaza from Judith's list of conquered cities (but see textual note *j)* has prompted some scholars to infer that, because Gaza had been destroyed by Alexander Janneus in 96 B.C., the book of Judith must have been written after that event. Otherwise, the once great city, they argue, would surely have been mentioned in Judith. In any event, Gaza was restored by Pompey and rebuilt by Gabinus in 57 B.C. (see A. Ovadiah, "Gaza," EAEHL, II, 409), all of which suggests that Judith was composed sometime between 96 and 57 B.C. While such a date is acceptable to the present writer, it is only fair to point out that the entire argument is one based on silence, i.e., the omission of Gaza from the list of cities taken by Holofernes.

3:1. The list of Palestinian peoples given in the Vg, while analogous to the list in the LXX, is different (i.e., "Then the kings and the princes of all the cities and provinces, of Syria, Mesopotamia, and Syria Sobal, and Libya, and Cilicia sent their ambassadors, who coming to Holofernes, said" [Vg 3:1]). According to 3:14–15 of the Vg, Holofernes, after staying in Idumea for a month, launched from there his attack against Bethulia (cf. Jdt 3:10). In other words, his attack against Bethulia came *from the south;* yet in 3:3 of the Vg the attack against Bethulia came, as in the LXX, from the north. As Ball (p. 279) rightly noted, the presence of Idumeans (7:8), Moabites (5:2; 7:8), and Ammonites (5:2) in Holofernes' army presupposes their prior capitulation to him. Possibly, we should understand that in the earliest form of the invasion

account, Holofernes came down along the coast, turned east, and arrived at Scythopolis (3:10) by way of Idumea, Moab, and Ammon.

to sue for peace. Lit. "with peaceful words."

4. *as you see fit.* Lit. "as is good in your eyes." This expression and "Treat us as you
please" (v 2) as well as "Treat them as seems best to you" (v 3) are more than just
literary variations designed to avoid boredom in the reader. Actually, they represent
the envoys' skillful use of psychology, appealing as they do to Holofernes' conscious
and unconscious needs, namely, to his emotions (v 2), his prudence (v 3), and his sense
of justice (v 4). Although the overall effect of vv 2–4 is to create an image of terrified
grovelling, the envoys shrewdly present their case, appealing to various criteria by
which Holofernes might judge it.

5. *this message.* Lit. "according to these words." Asking no terms, the envoys
offered in vv 2–4 what amounted to complete and unconditional surrender.

6. *stationed garrisons [ephrourōse].* A rare word, occurring elsewhere in the LXX
only in 2 Esdr 4:56; Wis 17:15; and 1 Macc 11:3.

7. *garlands.* Lit. "crowns." Presumably of leaves and/or flowers (cf. Wis 2:8), such
wreaths belong to the Hellenistic period, not the Persian. Compare 16:30 of Jubilees, a
pseudepigraphical work of the Greek period, where crowns are mentioned in connection with the Jewish Festival of Booths.

8. *sanctuaries.* Although the LXX here has *oria*, "borders" (cf. Deut 19:14; Prov
22:28; Isa 10:13), most modern translations are probably correct in following the Syr's
"sanctuaries." Such an error in the LXX is best explained as an inner-Greek phenomenon, namely, an early Greek copyist misread *iera*, "temples," as *oria*. However, the
principal reason for preferring "sanctuaries" to "borders" is that "sanctuaries" is a
more appropriate word to parallel "sacred poles" (see below). See also NOTE on "sanctuaries" in 4:1.

sacred poles [alsē]. The translation is uncertain. Lit. "woods" or "groves," *alsē* is the
stock LXX translation for Heb *'šrh, 'šyrh, 'šyrm* (masc. pl.) and *'šrwt* (fem. pl.), which,
depending upon the context, refers to a Semitic goddess or to a cultic object which
represented her. Unfortunately, nowhere in the Bible is this cultic object described,
although that it was made all or partly of wood seems certain (for further discussion
on this complicated subject, see W. L. Reed, *Ashera in the Old Testament*). The
mention of the destruction of shrines/sanctuaries/high places together with Asherah/
Asherim/Asharoth is quite common in the OT (2 Kgs 18:4; 23:14–15; 2 Chr 14:3;
17:6; 31:1; 34:4). In the Hebrew Bible, for an Israelite king to tear down pagan shrines
and Asherah was quite commendable; but the author had no intention of saying
anything to Holofernes' credit. Rather, he had Holofernes do these things so that the
Israelites might know exactly what they could expect from Holofernes: his was not
just a political or military threat but a terrible religious menace, namely, the disrup-
tion of the worship and service of the one true God in favor of a human deity.

*It was granted [ēn dedomenon] . . . to destroy all the gods . . . so that all . . .
should worship Nebuchadnezzar alone.* Here in v 8 the people of the coast evidently
handed over to Holofernes their shrines and gods, even as they had handed over to
him themselves, all their possessions, their wives, and their children (vv 2–4). Both the
JB and NEB err here in saying that Holofernes was *commissioned* to do this (see

COMMENT, p. 134); rather, Holofernes, in his enthusiasm and his loyalty to his lord, went beyond the political and military mandate of Nebuchadnezzar.

should call upon him as god! In reality, neither Assyrian nor Babylonian nor Persian kings ever demanded that they be worshiped as gods; such demands for veneration were first made by the Hellenistic kings. To be sure, Nebuchadnezzar and Darius seem to demand such (so Dan 3 and 6, respectively), but it is generally understood by scholars that there these kings actually represented the Syrian king Antiochus IV, Epiphanes (but see A. A. Di Lella, *Daniel,* p. 13).

Contrary to popular understanding, however, the villainous Antiochus IV was not the first Hellenistic king to style himself a god. Not surprisingly, it was in Egypt, with its millennia-long tradition of Pharaoh as a god-king, that Ptolemies presented themselves to their subjects as gods, Ptolemy V (203–181 B.C.), even called himself *Theos Epiphanes,* "God Manifest." While content to refer to himself as "King Antiochus Epiphanes" outside the Seleucid kingdom, Antiochus IV presented himself to his subjects within his realm, both on coins and in a letter to the Samaritans (so Josephus, *Ant.* 12.5.258, 264), as "King Antiochus Theos Epiphanes," thereby making his claims to divinity quite explicit. For a detailed study of the epithet *epiphanes* as applied to Antiochus IV, see Mørkholm, Otto, *Studies in the Coinage of Antiochus IV of Syria,* Historisk-filosofiske Meddelelser udgivet af Det Kongelige Danske Videnskaberres Selskab, Bind 40, nr. 3, 1963; especially pp. 11–43, 47–56, and 68–74.

9. *Dothan [dōtaia], which is opposite the great ridge [prionos].* Cf. Gen 37:17; 2 Kgs 6:13. A classically shaped tell (see Plate 1) dating back to the Chalcolithic period, Dothan (mod. Dotha), is about eight miles south of Taanach and fifteen miles southeast of Scythopolis (see below). It is not, however, "opposite the great ridge of Judea" (v 9b). Thus Fritzsche, following Reland, suggested that the Gk *prionos,* "ridge," lit. "saw," represented a misreading of Heb *mîšôr* "plain," as *maśśôr,* "saw." The principal difficulty with this ingenious explanation is that in the Bible the area in question is always called "the valley *(['mq];* not "the plain") of Esdraelon." Equally unconvincing is Scholz's suggestion that "ridge" is correct because the valley "saws" the mountain range in two.

Perhaps of some relevance here is the Vg, which has:

> And when he had passed through all Syria Sobal, and all Apamea, and all Mesopotamia, he came to the Idumeans into the land of Gabaa, and he took possession of their cities, and stayed there for thirty days, in which days he commanded all the troops of his army to be united. (Vg 3:14–15)

On the basis of this passage one may legitimately wonder whether something is not missing in the LXX, possibly more information concerning some geographical points between those of v 6 and v 9. In any case, because Dothan is so frequently mentioned in Judith (4:6; 7:3, 18; 8:3), some scholars, such as Torrey, have thought that it might very well be the hometown of the ancient author. For further details on the city, see David Ussiskin, "Dothan," EAEHL, I, 337–39.

10. *Geba.* The site is uncertain, possibly because the name is corrupt (see textual note *ᵍ).* According to Yohanan Aharoni and Michael Avi-Yonah *(Macmillan Bible Atlas,* Index and Map 211), three towns in Israel were named Geba and the one near Mount Carmel (probably el-Harithiyeh) was most likely the Geba of Judith. Some

scholars have suggested that Judith's Geba is a corrupt form of "Mount Gilboa" (glbʿ), while others think that it was Jeba, a town about six miles south of Dothan, between Samaria and present-day Jenîn (see Torrey, JAOS 20 [1899]: 161).

Scythopolis. The only city in Judith mentioned by its Greek name, Scythopolis, lit. "City of the Scythians." According to Pliny (first century A.D.), Scythopolis got its name from the fact that that was "where a colony of Scythians are settled" (Pliny, *Natural History* 5.74; but see Tcherikov, *Hellenistic Civilization and the Jews,* pp. 102–3). Although Polybius (201?–?120 B.C.) referred to the city by its Greek name of Scythopolis (*Hist.,* 5.70.5), how much earlier than that the city was called by its Greek name is unknown. Its mention in Judith is, therefore, of little help in dating the book to any more precise period than "the Greek period." Known as Beth-shan (Tell el-Husn; mod. Beisan), it was the largest, most important, and most western of Rome's Decapolis (see D. C. Pellett, "Decapolis," IDB, I, 810–12; and S. Thomas Parker, JBL 94 [1975]: 437–41). Scythopolis occupied a most strategic position, guarding the eastern end of the valley of Jezreel and the northern end of the Jordan Valley as the Jordan River leaves the Sea of Galilee (Josh 17:16). Because of its strategic location, the city had been a very important one from before 3000 B.C. It was captured, but not destroyed, in 107 B.C. by John Hyrcanus I. For further details on the city, see M. Tyori, "Beth-Shean," EAEHL, I, 207–29.

a full month. Lit. "a month of days," a Hebraism (see Gen 29:14; Deut 21:13; 2 Kgs 15:13).

Comment

The preceding account should have one of two effects upon a reader, depending upon whether he or she is more interested in the fast-moving account of a military campaign or more distracted by the story's geographical errors and ambiguities. If the reader is primarily interested in the tale itself, then he or she will certainly be left with a clear impression of the awesome size, efficiency, and invincibility of Holofernes' army.

Reserving for his readers until later a more intimate description of Holofernes (see COMMENT on pp. 169 and 220), the ancient author skillfully provided his readers with some clues to Holofernes' character by painting a clear picture of Holofernes' army, which set out "to smother the whole western region with their chariots, cavalry, and picked infantry" (2:19); "cut . . . through Put and Lud and plundered" (v 23); "razed all the walled towns along Wadi Abron" (v 24); "occupied . . . Cilicia and slaughtered all who" (v 25); "set their tents on fire and plundered" (v 26); "set fire to all their fields, destroyed their flocks and herds, sacked their towns, stripped their plains, and put all their young men to the sword" (v 27); "demolished all their sanctuaries and cut down all their sacred poles. . . . so that all . . . should worship Nebuchadnezzar alone . . . and . . . should call upon him as god" (3:8). Clearly, Holofernes and his army were not making a perfunctory, show-of-strength march through the West: they were bringing death and destruction to all who resisted. And Judea was next in line!

However, for the ancient or modern reader who knows Near Eastern geography well, the errors in the "details of fact" may shout so loudly that they drown out what might otherwise be a fascinating account. More specifically, the account of Holofernes' progress from Nineveh to the Mediterranean Sea (2:21–25) is either incomplete and corrupt or composed in almost total ignorance of the geography of the area (see NOTES). Moreover, the exact itinerary (or even the general direction [!]) of Holofernes' army from the Mediterranean coast to his encampment between Geba and Scythopolis (3:5–10) is also confused, incomplete, or both (see NOTES). Thus, while one reader may be fascinated by the fast-moving events in 2:14–3:10, another reader, especially one knowledgeable in biblical geography, may be fascinated or exasperated by its flaws, all of which may help to explain, in part, the book's mixed reception among Christians as well as Jews (see INTRODUCTION, pp. 86–91).

IV. Israel's Reaction to Holofernes' Threatened Invasion of Judea (4:1–15 [Vg 4:1–16])

4 ¹ When the Israelites living in Judea heard of how Holofernes, the ranking commander of Nebuchadnezzar king of the Assyrians, had treated the nations, sacking and destroying their sanctuaries*, ² they were terrified at his approach and alarmed for Jerusalem and the Temple of the Lord their God. ³ ᵇ(For they had returned from exile only a short time before; and all the people of Judea had been reunited, and the sacred utensils, the altar, and the Temple had just recently been rededicated after they had been defiled.) ⁴ So they alerted all the territory of Samaria, Kona, Beth-horon, Belmainᶜ, Jericho, Choba, Aesora, and the valley of Salem. ⁵ They went ahead and secured all the summits of the high hills, fortified the villages on them, and stored up their food in preparation for war (for their fields had just been harvested).

⁶ Joakim the high priest, who was in Jerusalem at that time, wrote to those living in Bethuliaᵈ and Bethomesthaimᵉ, which is opposite Esdraelon facing the plain near Dothan, ⁷ telling them to occupy the passes up into the hill country because access into Judea was through them; and it would be easy to prevent ᶠan armyᶠ from entering (for the approach was only wide enough for two men at a time to pass).

⁸ The Israelites did as they had been ordered by the high priest Joakim and the Council of all the people of Israel in session at Jerusalem. ⁹ Most fervently they cried out to God, every man of Israel, and they humbled themselves ᵍwith much fastingᵍ. ¹⁰ They put on sackcloth, they and their wives and children, their cattle, every resident alien, and every hired or purchased servant. ¹¹ All the Israelite men,

---

ᵃ Gk *iera;* LXXᴬ, Eth "borders" *(oria).*
ᵇ Vg omits v.
ᶜ LXXᴮ *bailmain;* LXXᴬ *belmain;* LXXˢ *abelmain;* LXXᴺ *bemiaiōn;* Syr *abelmeholah.*
ᵈ LXXᴮ *baitouloua;* LXXˢ *baitoulia;* LXXᴬᴺ *betuloua;* OL, Vg *bethulia;* see NOTE.
ᵉ LXXᴮ *baitomaisthaim;* LXXᴬ *betomesthaim;* LXXᴺ *baitomesthai.*
ᶠᶠ LXX "them."
ᵍ⁻ᵍ So LXXˢᵇᶠᵏʳ, OLˢ, and Syr; LXXᴮᴬᴺ "most fervently," a dittography.

women, and children living in Jerusalem prostrated themselves before the Temple and put ashes on their head and spread out their sackcloth before the Lord. [12] They even draped the altar with sackcloth; and with one voice they cried out to the God of Israel, fervently begging that he not allow their children to be carried off or their women raped or the towns of their heritage destroyed or the Temple profaned and reviled to the malicious delight of the heathen. [13] So the Lord heard their prayers and looked kindly on their distress.

For many days the people throughout Judea and in Jerusalem kept on fasting before the sanctuary of the Omnipotent Lord. [14] Wearing sackcloth around their loins, Joakim the high priest and all the priests who officiated before the Lord and those who ministered to the Lord offered the regular burnt offering, the votive, and the voluntary offerings of the people. [15] With ashes on their turbans, they cried to the Lord with all their might to look favorably on the whole House of Israel.

Notes

4:1. *Israelites*. Lit. "the children of Israel." Had Judith been composed by a Palestinian Jew, argues Zeitlin (see in Enslin, pp. 31–32), then the Jews in the story would have been called by their proper name, Judeans, not "Israelites" or "Hebrews" (see also Zeitlin, JQR [1953]: 365–79). More likely, however, the term, in Judith at least, is merely an archaism; see also NOTE on "a daughter of the Hebrews" in 10:12.

nations. The *ethnē*, as here, represent the Gentiles (Heb *gwym)*, in contrast to "the people [Heb *'m* = Gk *laos]* of Israel."

sanctuaries. Occurring in Judith only here, *iera* can refer to shrines, temples, or holy things. In Judith, the Temple at Jerusalem is referred to as a *naos*, "temple" (v 2), *oikos*, "house" (v 3), *agiasma*, "sanctuary" (5:19), *agion*, "sanctuary" (4:12; 9:8), and *ta agia*, lit. "the holy things," i.e., the entire temple complex (4:12).

3. *returned from exile only a short time before; and . . . just recently.* For the ancient author to have established the general historical period for the events of his story by saying that it happened "a short time" after the Return (i.e., shortly after 538 B.C.) and "just recently" after the reconsecration of the Temple (i.e., sometime after 515 B.C.) is very curious, especially since elsewhere in his account the author offers an extended yet reasonably coherent history of his people (see Jdt 5:6–19; 8:26–27; 9:2–4). Thus, unless one regards these two phrases as a momentary lapse of the author's memory, a view which the present writer finds unpersuasive, then the easiest and most probable explanation is that the entire verse is an early gloss. Such a view is somewhat confirmed by the fact that the Vg omits this verse but not the verse preceding or

following it. Regardless of who was initially responsible for it, scholars generally agree that the passage was influenced by the account of Judas Maccabeus's cleansing of the Temple (see 1 Macc 4:36–61; 2 Macc 10:3–5). However, Enslin regards the mention of the Return and the reconsecration of the Temple as just "stage properties" for the author's story.

4. V 4 is a most troublesome verse, primarily because only three of the eight cities mentioned can be located with any certainty. This fact is especially unfortunate inasmuch as, depending upon their location, they might be crucial for establishing Judea's geographical boundaries at the time, a matter of central importance for determining the historical period in which Judith was written (see INTRODUCTION, pp. 67–70). In the corresponding verse of the Vg (i.e., Vg 3:3), only Samaria and Jericho are mentioned, thus making the geographical problems nonexistent for the Latin reader.

all the territory of Samaria. I.e., not just the city itself but also the adjacent cities and towns which, historically, were often regarded as being part of Samaria (for details, see G. W. Van Beek, "Samaria, Territory of," IDB, IV, 188–90). It was certainly appropriate in this verse for Samaria's name to head the list of cities to be contacted for Jerusalem's defense. Located about twenty-five miles east of the Mediterranean Sea and approximately forty-two miles north of Jerusalem, Samaria (mod. Sebastiyeh) dominated the north-south road which connected the plain of Esdraelon and the North, where Holofernes was, with Jerusalem in the South, where the Temple was located. Destroyed by Sargon II in 721 B.C., Samaria was soon repopulated and rebuilt, serving successively as a provincial administrative center for the Assyrian, Babylonian, and Persian empires. Throughout the Hellenistic period, the city had a most checkered history; but from 107 B.C. to 63 B.C., Samaria was in Jewish hands, it having been conquered by John Hyrcanus, who removed part of its walls (Josephus, *Ant.* 13.10.2–3). In the eyes of most scholars, the favorable attitude toward Samaria in Judith has great relevance for establishing the date of the book's composition (see INTRODUCTION, pp. 67–70). See NOTE on "Bethomesthaim" in v 6. For further details, see N. Avigad, "Samaria," EAEHL, IV, 1032–50.

Kona [konā]. Its location is unknown. Although several minuscules, Syr, and OL^s read "villages" (Gk *kōmas),* that reading probably represents an ancient correction rather than the survival of the original reading.

Beth-horon. Josh 21:22; 1 Chr 7:24; 2 Chr 8:5. Upper Beth-horon (Josh 16:5), which is 1,750 feet above sea level and about five miles northwest of Gibeon, is just two miles east of Lower Beth-horon (Josh 16:3), whose elevation is only about 1,000 feet above sea level (hence their respective names). Judas Maccabeus won two important battles there, one against Seron (1 Macc 3:16, 24) and the other against Nicanor (1 Macc 7:39). Beth-horon was later fortified by Bacchides (1 Macc 9:50; Josephus, *Ant.* 13.1.3).

Belmain. The site is unknown. The name may be corrupt (see textual note ^c). Whether this town is mentioned elsewhere in Judith is also uncertain (see 7:3; 8:3; 15:4). Avi-Yonah and Aharoni *(Macmillan Bible Atlas,* Map 211) would call it "Belaen" and identify it with Abel-maim, about thirteen miles south of Scythopolis.

Jericho. Actually, there were *two* Jerichos: OT Jericho (mod. Tell es-Sultan), located at the southern end of the Jordan Valley, and NT Jericho (mod. Tulul Abu el-'Alayiq), one mile to the south of OT Jericho, on the western edge of the Jordan Plain and about sixteen miles northeast of Jerusalem. Although the remains of a Hellenistic fortress have been found at NT Jericho (cf. 1 Macc 9:50; 1 Macc 16:14-16), the site did not come into its own until the days of Herod the Great. For more details on OT Jericho, see K. M. Kenyon, "Jericho," EAEHL, II, 550-64; for NT Jericho, ibid., 565-73.

Choba. Cf. 15:4, 5. The site is unknown. Some identify it with el-Mekhubbi, which is between Tubass and Besan. F. M. Abel *(Géographie,* p. 299) identified it with Hobah, north of Damascus (cf. Gen 14:15), which may be mod. Tell el-Salihiye. Avi-Yonah and Aharoni *(Macmillan Bible Atlas,* Map 211) identify it with el-Marmaleh, which is approximately thirty miles south of Scythopolis and about three miles west of the Jordan River.

Aesora. Site is also unknown. Of the five cities in the OT with the name "Hazor," this one may be Tell el-Qedah, about nine miles north of the Sea of Galilee (cf. Josh 11:1, 10; Judg 4:2, 17), or possibly the Hazor in Benjamin (Neh 11:33), i.e., Khirbet Hazzūr. Avi-Yonah and Aharoni would identify it with Jazer in Gilead (cf. Num 21:32; 32:35), at Khirbet es-Sar, about seven miles southwest of Philadelphia in Transjordan. (See S. Cohen, "Jazer," IDB, II, 805-6.)

valley of Salem. Cf. Gen 14:18. Again, the site is unknown. Avi-Yonah and Aharoni *(Macmillan Bible Atlas,* Map 211) identify this Salem with Salim (mod. Umm el-'Amdan[?]), a town near Aenon (cf. John 3:23). If this is the correct location for Salim and if Salim is the Salem of Judith, then the town would be about twelve miles south of Scythopolis.

Regardless of the actual location of the various places mentioned above, the favorable attitude toward Samaritans evidenced here and elsewhere in Judith (15:3-5) deserves comment. Since the collapse of the Northern Kingdom in 721 B.C., the relations between Judeans and those living in the territory of Samaria had been less than cordial. Possibly Samaritans were too hostile toward Jews for the people of Jerusalem to have warned them of an approaching pagan army, let alone to have counted on them to defend Jerusalem and its Temple. However, relations may have changed somewhat for the better after John Hyrcanus I had annexed all the territory of Samaria, having taken Shechem and having destroyed the Samaritan temple on Mount Gerizim by 107 B.C. (Dancy [pp. 82-83], however, thinks that "Samaria" may have been added by a later copyist so as to give the reader the impression that the area was under Jewish domination.) Worth quoting here is Enslin, who says of v 4:

> It is profitless to attempt to guess what places were in the author's mind or his reason for selecting them. The impression given that all of these districts were definitely Jewish and ready to resist one sent to destroy them is in sharp contrast to the attitude of their heathen neighbors (2:28) who had unhesitatingly surrendered and abjectly begged for mercy. This aroused district was to the north of Jerusalem in the path of the would-be conqueror who in good tradition was descending from the north. The reading in Vg: *Et miserunt in omnen Samariam per circuitum usque Jericho,* whether a faithful rendering of the Aramaic text which Jerome claims to have found or his own paraphrase avoiding unknown places, would seem a correct gloss on our text. (p. 79)

6. *Joakim.* Cf. Jdt 4:8, 14; 15:8. This name is another indication of the postexilic setting of the story, for there was indeed in the early days of the postexilic community

a high priest named Joiakim son of Jeshua (so Neh 12:26, but see 1 Esdr 5:5, and Josephus, *Ant.* 20.10.2.234). However, no high priest of that period exercised the sweeping military authority of Judith's Joakim. In fact, not until Maccabean times do we have religious and military responsibilities held by the same person, namely, Jonathan (cf. 1 Macc 10:18–21). But according to Montague: "The author contemporizes historical memories and stresses the totally religious nature of the threat to Israel. Again, Joakim (Judith 4, 6.8) was high-priest in Jerusalem under the Persian governor and is no doubt here recalled simply as a representative figure of the priesthood in general." *(Books of Esther and Judith,* p. 16)

Although in the Latin and the Syriac the high priest is called Eliachim, the meaning of that name is the same as that of Joakim, the theomorphic prefix *Jeho-,* "Yahu," being replaced by *Eli,* "God." Scholars who identify Judith's Nebuchadnezzar with Ashurbanipal explain the absence of any mention of an Israelite king here by saying that the story occurred during Manasseh's captivity (see INTRODUCTION, p. 54). It is more likely, however, that the story's setting was in the Persian period, and its composition in the Hellenistic.

who was in Jerusalem at that time. To say this about a high priest seems gratuitous, unless the ancient author was actually writing at a time when such was not always the case, namely, in the late Hasmonean period, when, because of their military role, high priests were not bound to the Holy City.

Bethulia [baitoula]. Cf. Jdt 7:3; 8:3. How ironic that the name and location of the most important site in Judith is unknown! Not surprisingly, we are not even sure of how it was spelled in Greek (see textual note *d*); more specifically, of the twenty-one uncials and minuscules collated in the Larger Cambridge Septuagint of Judith, there are nine Greek variants for the town's name.

Is the site's Hebrew name symbolic (= *byt 'l/wh,* "House of God"); or is it a pseudonym to disguise the site's true identity (= *byt 'lyh,* "House of Ascent," i.e., Shechem [so Torrey, JAOS 20 (1899): 164; so also T. Craven, for purely literary reasons, i.e., it emphasizes the concept of high places, an important theme in Judith (SBLDS 70, p. 73, n. 25)]); or is the Greek/Hebrew form simply corrupt? On the basis of the LXX translation of Ezra 2:28 (= 1 Esdr 5:21), where the Jewish towns of Bethel and Ai are transliterated as one word, *baitoliō,* Priebatsch (ZDPV 90 [1974]: 50–60) has suggested that Bethulia is really a doublet for "Bethel," the name of the famous shrine of Jacob.

Certain geographical and topographical clues within Judith should, at first glance at least, help to establish the site's location (i.e., Bethulia appears to be a walled town in the Samaritan hill country [6:11], overlooking a valley [10:10], south of the plain of Esdraelon [3:10; 4:6] and surrounded by mountains [10:10–11] with a spring nearby [7:12–13]; it is directly between Holofernes' army and Jerusalem [11:19], near Bethomesthaim and Dothan [4:6]). Scholars have identified it with Sânûr, which is almost five miles south of Dothan; or with Meseliah, also midway between Geba and Jenîn; or with *Kubâtje* (so Dussaud, *Syria* 7 [1926]: 9–29, especially 21–22; Steuernagel, ZDPV [1943]: 242); or with other sites in the area. "Apparently it is not the real name of any place with which we are familiar," wrote D. N. Freedman. "It may be modelled on some of the ideal names in Deutero Isaiah: e.g., Beul-land [Isa 62:4] or Hephzi-bah [Isa 62:4], but just what the root forms are is difficult to say." (private correspondence with this writer) Possibly because many twentieth-century scholars share the view of Fritzsche that Bethulia's existence is "a mere fiction," the list of possible candidates for the site has not increased since the days of Ball, who offered a detailed survey of the suggestions up to his day (Ball, pp. 284–85). Moreover, many would agree with A. Deprez: "But the topographical details are of little importance. That which counts for our author are the religious lessons which he wishes to give." (Évangile 47 [1962]: 20) While in essential agreement with Deprez and Freedman in this matter, the present writer believes that the author had some particular site in his mind's eye and that Shechem probably served as his general model.

With respect to Bethulia's location, Craven has concluded: "Torrey's argument that Bethulia is a pseudonym for Shechem is scarcely definitive. . . . It seems best to leave the details of the Book of Judith alone as the products of a fertile, creative imagination." (SBLDS 70, pp. 72–73, n. 24) Here, Craven is quite correct; but to practice what she counsels is a very difficult task, as witnessed by the fact that Craven herself (and doubtless also the present writer in this commentary) falls into the trap of historicizing various activities of the heroine: "[Judith's] faith is like that of Job after his experience of God in the whirlwind (cf. 42:1–6), yet in the story she has no special theophanic experience. *We can only imagine what happened on her housetop where she was habitually a woman of regular prayer* [italics added]." (SBLDS 70, pp. 88–89, n. 45) Craven's speculation here on the nature of Judith's rooftop experiences is not so much a reflection on Craven's methodology or approach as it is a tribute to the skills of the narrator, that is, his story is so well told that the characters come alive and take on a life of their own. In fact, if this kind of thing did not happen with readers of the book of Judith, then the book would not be the classic that it is.

Bethomesthaim. Compare Bethomasthaim in 15:4. Mentioned only in Judith, the site is unknown. Near Bethulia and Dothan, Bethomesthaim has long been thought to be an opprobrious pseudonym for "Samaria," namely, *byt mśṭmh,* "House of Shame" (so Condamin, RSR 14 [1910]: 570f.), or *byt mśṭm,* "House of the Devil" (so Torrey, p. 92). If one or the other of these explanations is correct, then either the name here or the mention of Samaria in 4:4 is a gloss. The latter is more likely, inasmuch as John Hyrcanus I destroyed Samaria ca. 107 B.C. (Josephus, *Ant.* 13.10.3).

7. *only wide enough for two men at a time.* The reason no one has been able to locate this Palestinian Thermopylae (see COMMENT II) is obvious: it never existed; it is simply a dramatic hyperbole. Ultimately, such military strategy would have been ineffective, serving only to delay Holofernes' destructive march. It will be Judith's piety and hand that will save the day, not narrow passes and brave fighting men.

8. *the Council [gerousia] . . . in session at Jerusalem.* Lit. "the senate . . . who sat in Jerusalem." Cf. Jdt 11:14 and 15:8. Regardless of whether the original Hebrew word for this council was *snhdryn,* "Sanhedrin," or, more likely, *hzqnym,* "Elders," (cf. Exod 3:16; Josh 23:2 of the LXX), the Gerousia as the supreme Jewish council is not mentioned until almost the Maccabean period, when Antiochus III, the Great (223–187 B.C.), speaks of it in a letter to Ptolemy (Josephus, *Ant.* 12.3.3). See also 2 Macc 11:27. According to Delcor (Klio 49 [1967]: 161) because *gerousia* was not replaced by *sunedria* as the term for the Jerusalem Senate until the time of John Hyrcanus II (67 B.C.), the use of *gerousia* here and in 11:14 and 15:8 indicates that

Judith was composed prior to John's day. For further details, see T. A. Burkill, "Sanhedrin," IDB, IV, 214–18.

9. *with much fasting.* Cf. v 13. Although required public fasting is not necessarily a rite in the Pentateuch (but see Lev 16:29, 31; 23:27; Num 29:7), Jews in the OT often resorted to fasting in periods of distress (Judg 20:26; 1 Kgs 21:9; Jer 36:9; Jonah 3:5; 2 Chr 20:3); so also the Diaspora Community at Elephantine (Staerk, *Alte und neue armäische Papyri,* 451). In the postexilic period, however, both public and private fasting became much more important (cf. 1 Macc 3:44–48; Esth 4:1–3, 15), especially among the Pharisees (for details, see H. H. Guthrie, "Fast, Fasting," IDB, II, 241–44).

10. *sackcloth . . . [on] their cattle.* Since such an all-encompassing act of penitence and supplication had worked for the citizens of wicked Nineveh (so Jonah 3:8, 10), surely the author was justified in having the Israelites do the same here. However, both Deprez *(Évangile* 47 [1962]: 22) and Craven (SBLDS 70, p. 115) view this allusion to the cattle not as something to be taken literally but as an expression of the author's sense of humor! (Sackcloth, however, is hardly a laughing matter, especially in light of v 12 [see NOTE]).

11. *Spread out their sackcloth before the Lord.* Compare 2 Sam 21:10, where Rizpah spreads out her sackcloth not only to lie upon but even more as an attention-getting device. The Vg has/adds: "And the priests put on sackcloth and they caused the little children to lie prostrate before the temple of the Lord, and the altar of the Lord they covered with sackcloth."

12. *draped the altar with sackcloth.* Like the sackcloth on the cattle in v 10, this is another extreme expression of the gravity of the situation. Such a gesture is nowhere else attested to in the Bible.

or their women raped [eis pronomēn, lit. "for booty"]. Whether the Israelite women were "just" raped or, worse, were carried off as wives for the Assyrians, either prospect was a terrible one for the men of Israel; cf. first NOTE on 9:4.

towns of their heritage [kleronomias]. The NEB's "their ancestral cities" fails to convey what is an important theological idea in Judith (cf. 8:22; 9:12; 13:5; 16:21), namely, the land of Canaan was ultimately inherited from God rather than acquired by men through force of arms or merit. See also Sir 46:8 and 1 Macc 15:33, 34.

Temple [agia]. In Judith, this plural adjective is used only for the Temple, or sanctuary, in Jerusalem (4:13; 8:21, 24; 9:8; 16:20).

13. Omitting this verse, the Vg has a reading whose idioms suggest a Semitic *Vorlage,* even as Jerome claimed:

> Then Eliachim the high priest of the Lord went about all Israel and spoke to them, saying, "Know ye that the Lord will hear your prayers, if you continue with perseverance in fastings and prayers in the sight of the Lord. Remember Moses, the servant of the Lord, who overcame Amalak, who trusted in his own strength, and in his power, and in his army, and in his shields, and in his chariots and in his horsemen; not by fighting with the sword but by praying with holy prayers. So shall all the enemies of Israel be, if you persevere in this work that you have begun."

Omnipotent Lord. Occurring in Judith here and in 8:13; 15:10; and 16:5, 17, *kuriou pantokratoros* is used in the LXX to translate both *YHWH ṣb 'wt,* "Lord Sabaoth," i.e., "Lord of hosts," and *šdy,* "Shadday." For a brief discussion on the troublesome epithet, see B. W. Anderson, "Hosts, Hosts of Heaven," IDB, II, 654–56.

14. *the regular burnt offering.* I.e., the *tāmîd.* This twice-daily sacrificing of a lamb was the most important of all Jewish sacrifices and offerings (cf. Exod 29:38–42; Num 28:6).

15. *turbans. Kidaris,* the Greek word used here for the headdress of the priests, is Persian in origin and denotes a "linen cap" (cf. Ezek 44:18).

Comment I

Upon hearing what Holofernes had done to peoples nearby, the Israelites, understandably, showed a natural fear for their own lives and property (so vv 1–2, 12). But according to the story, the Israelites were even more concerned about the religious threat that Holofernes posed (cf. vv 1b, 2, 12). Thus, although the Israelites made some military preparations against Holofernes (vv 4–5, 7), their primary response was a religious one, involving not only constant prayer (vv 9, 12) and sacrifice (v 14) but also the most severe forms of fasting (vv 9, 13) and the use of sackcloth (vv 10, 12, 14) and ashes (vv 11, 15). That it was the high priest rather than some purely secular figure who galvanized the Judeans into military action may be further proof of the essentially religious character of the threat as well as an indication of Judith's composition in the Hasmonean period.

But if the religious threads of this episode in the story are quite strong and distinct, the episode's total design is weakened and blurred (at least for many informed readers) by its anachronisms (see NOTES on vv 3, 6, 8) and geographical imprecisions (see NOTES on vv 4, 6). However, just as all but the most informed and persnickety modern person can read a historical novel about the American Civil War or some other fascinating and complex period without having the novel's anachronisms and imprecisions detract appreciably from his or her enjoyment of it, so presumably the ancient readers were not too distracted by "the difficulties" we have just pointed out. Or, to put it another way, if biblical books did not lay claim to being historical as well as religious in character, then most modern readers would probably give scant attention to the question of the historicity or accuracy of the events and persons described in the stories themselves.

Comment II

While this writer characterized the narrow pass at Bethulia [4:7] as "this Palestinian Thermopylae," using the expression in a figurative sense, Arnaldo Momigliano argues that Sparta's exploits at Thermopylae may very well have been in the mind of the author of Judith. His argument is sufficiently brief and thought-provoking to be quoted in full:

> In the last half of Herodotus' Book VII, the military scene is dominated by the defence of the pass of Thermopylae. The ideological scene is dominated by the conversation between Xerxes and the Spartan Demaratus, who explains to Xerxes why the Greeks, and especially the Spartans, will not yield to the Persians: they do not obey individual men, but the Law. In the book of Judith, before Judith herself appears on the scene, our interest is concentrated, on the military side, on the Jewish Thermopylae, the mysterious place Bethulia. The ideological background is filled by the conversation between Holophernes and Achior—the latter who is not a Jew, but unpredictably (because he is an Ammonite) will become one. Achior explains to Holophernes that the Jews will not yield so long as they obey their Law.
>
> When Judith appears, she presents herself to the Assyrians as the person who can reveal the secret path through the mountains, exactly as the traitor Epialtes does in Herodotus.
>
> The structure of the second part of Herodotus VII and of the first section of the book of Judith is articulated on the same sequence of an ideological dialogue and of a peculiar military situation. We must ask ourselves whether the author of the original Hebrew Judith knew Herodotus directly or indirectly. Here, as I have said, I am less sure about my answer, but my inclination to give again a positive answer is reinforced by another, better-known coincidence between the book of Judith and a Greek historical text. It has long been recognized that the five days the thirsty Jews who were besieged in Bethulia give to themselves before surrendering have their exact counterpart in the five days that the thirsty Greeks who were besieged by the Persians in Lindos give to themselves before surrendering. The Greek story is contained in the Chronicle of Lindos, a compilation from previous sources written in 99 B.C.
>
> Whatever his date, the author of the original Hebrew text of Judith seems to have been acquainted with stories reported by Greek historians about the wars of the Greeks against Persia. If there was anything which conceivably could interest the Jews, it was what the Greek historians thought about oriental empires and especially about Persia. Daniel and Judith may perhaps be defined as texts which in Hellenistic time and under Greek influence tried to present an image of the Jews as subjects of the previous universal empires: this image was of course very relevant to what the Jews could do or could hope under the Greco-Macedonian universal empire. (BA 45 [1982]: 227–28)

Certainly there is no compelling reason why Momigliano could not be correct in his thesis, especially since he declares that Greek writers may have influenced the author of Judith "directly or indirectly." While he does not define those two terms, they could, in their broadest sense, mean "consciously or unconsciously," as well as "read or heard about." Given how much ground the expression "directly or indirectly" covers, one is hard-pressed to imagine how his argument can be refuted, especially since a similar claim can be made for other biblical books, including Esther (see AB 7B, pp. xxxv–xliv and lii). However, Momigliano's claims do little to increase the probability of a kernel of historicity for the Judith-story.

V. Achior, the Ammonite, Reviews for Holofernes the Religious History of the Jews (5:1–21 [Vg 5:1–25])

5 ¹ When it was reported to Holofernes, the ranking commander of the Assyrian forces, that the Israelites had prepared for war and that they had closed the mountain passes, garrisoned all the high hilltops, and laid traps in the plains, ² he was furious. Summoning all the rulers of Moab and the generals of Ammon *and all the governors of the coastal region*, ³ he said to them, "Now tell me, you Canaanites, who is this people that lives in the hill country? What towns do they inhabit? How big is their army? In what does their strength or power consist? Who is their king? *Who commands their army*? ⁴ And why have they, of all the people living in the West, refused to come and meet me?"

⁵ Then Achior*, the leader of the Ammonites, said to him, "May my lord please listen to the advice of your servant. I will tell you the truth about this people living in the hill country near here. Nothing false shall come from your servant's mouth.

⁶ "These people are descended from the Chaldeans. ⁷ At one time they settled in Mesopotamia because they did not want to worship the gods of their ancestors who were* in Chaldea. ⁸ (They had abandoned the ways of their ancestors and worshiped the God of Heaven, the god they had come to know. When the Chaldeans* drove them out from the presence of their gods, they fled to Mesopotamia and settled there for a long while.) ⁹ Later, their god told them to leave the place where they were staying and go on to the land of Canaan. So they settled there and accumulated much wealth in gold, silver, and livestock.

¹⁰ "When a famine spread over the land of Canaan, they went down to Egypt and settled there as long as there was food. There they be-

---

⁻ LXXˢ and OLᵐ omit by haplography.
⁻ LXXˢ and Syr omit.
ᶜ Syr "Achiod"; see NOTE.
ᵈ Syr and Vg "were worshiped."
ᵉ LXX "they."

came so numerous that it was impossible to count them. [11] So the king of Egypt turned against them and exploited them by forcing them to make bricks. He[f] degraded them by making them slaves. [12] But they cried out to their god, and he afflicted all the land of Egypt with incurable plagues. So the Egyptians expelled them.

[13] "Then God dried up the Red Sea for them [14] and led them [g]by the way of[g] Sinai and Kadesh-Barnea. They drove out all the inhabitants of the desert [15] and lived in the land of the Amorites. So strong were they that they destroyed all the Heshbonites; and crossing the Jordan, they took possession of all the hill country, [16] driving out before them the Canaanites, the Perizzites, the Jebusites, the Shechemites, and all the Girgashites. There they settled for a long while. [17] And as long as they did not sin against their god, they prospered; for theirs is a god who hates wrongdoing. [18] But when they abandoned the path he had laid down for them, they were devastated in many battles and were carried off as captives to a foreign land. The temple of their god was leveled to the ground, and their towns were occupied by their enemies. [19] But now that they have returned to their god, they have come back from the places where they had been scattered. They have regained Jerusalem, where their sanctuary is, and have reoccupied the hill country because it was uninhabited.

[20] "So now, my master and lord, if there is any oversight in this people, if they are sinning against their god and we can detect this offense among them, then we may go up and force them to fight. [21] But if this nation is not guilty, then let my lord please bypass them. For their lord and god will defend them, and we shall become the laughingstock of the whole world."

---

[f] LXX "they."
[g-g] LXX *eis odon;* LXX[cejklvw], OL, and Syr read "to Mount" (Gk *eis oros*).

Notes

5:1. *laid traps.* In the LXX, Gk *skandala* is variously used to refer to baited traps (Josh 23:13), pitfalls (Wis 14:11), or barricades in general.

2. *rulers of Moab and the generals of Ammon . . . governors.* Although the historical Nebuchadnezzar did have the services of Moab and Ammon to use against Israel (cf. 2 Kgs 24:2), in Judith there has been no prior mention of these two nations

yielding to Nebuchadnezzar, a fact which *may* be another indication of corruption in the text (see NOTE on 3:9).

Rather than being precise designations of office or rank, the various Greek terms for leaders here, one of which is Persian *(satrapas,* "governors"), were evidently chosen for the sake of variety. However, Delcor (Klio 49 [1967]: 163–64) argues that because the officials of the coastal religion are called *satrapes,* "governors," in 5:2 and *stratēgoi,* "generals," in 7:8, the storyteller wrote during or after the days of Demetrius I, Soter (162–150 B.C.), that being the time when the older Persian term and its later Greek equivalent still existed side by side. One could be more persuaded by Delcor's argument if the Hebrew text of Judith were present, so that one could check on the Hebrew words behind the two Greek terms.

3. While scholars have disagreed as to whether or not the questions posed here were sincere or sarcastic, Deprez is certainly correct in observing that these questions "appear at the heart" of the story, the answers to them clearly explaining the nature and strength of the Jewish people. In answering these questions, Achior does not say who is king over Israel. For the author of the story and his readers the answer was self-evident: Yahweh is king.

you Canaanites. Lit. "sons of Canaan," the term here, while admittedly designating an ethnic or geographical group, is artificial and archaic, the term properly being confined to the early history of Israel (but see Neh 9:24).

5. *Achior.* The original form of this name is much debated. Many scholars interpret it as a rendering of Heb *'ḥy'wr,* "Light is my (divine) brother," an appropriate name inasmuch as Achior did indeed shed a bright, true light on the Israelites' history for Holofernes, and he did finally become a Jewish "brother," i.e., a Jewish convert (14:10). According to D. N. Freedman, "Achior" can even be interpreted to mean "the Sun (god) is my (divine) brother," which would be appropriate for a Yahwist ("since Yahweh is identified as the Sun-god in Ps 19") or for a Moabite such as Achior. Others, like Cowley and Steinmann, taking their cue from the Syr (see textual note *ͨ),* regarded "Achior" as a corruption of "Ahihud," "Brother of Judah" (as in the LXX of Num 34:27, where the MT's *Aḥyhwd* is rendered as *Achiōr,* the Heb *daleth* evidently being misread as the Heb *resh).* Henri Cazelles (RSR 39 [1951]: 125–37, 324–27) would see the name as a corruption of "Ahikar," the name of the famous pagan sage (see COMMENT II, pp. 162–63). Whether Cazelles is correct or not, the Achior in Judith is one of a well-known type, the *gôy ṣaddîq,* "righteous Gentile": Balaam (Num 22–24), Rahab (Josh 2–6), Naaman (2 Kgs 5), the Ethiopian eunuch (Acts 8:26–40), and others.

Achior is used most skillfully by the author of the story. He is the means whereby Holofernes learns enough about Israelites and their theological understanding of their history (5:5–21) so as to accept quite gullibly Judith's reasons for "betraying" her people (chap. 11). Also, in Achior's speech (chap. 5) the author of the story could express his own understanding of the sacred history of the Jewish people. Finally, having known Holofernes personally, Achior could confirm for the citizens of Bethulia the identity of the decapitated head brought by Judith (14:6–8).

the leader [o ēgoumenos] of the Ammonites. Because Achior's "title" is the same as that of Timothy, who fought against Judas Maccabeus (1 Macc 5:6), Delcor (Klio 49

[1967]: 156) maintained that Achior's title is another indication of the book's date of composition sometime after Judas Maccabeus.

please [dē]. Rather deficient in many stylistic features of good Greek (see INTRO-DUCTION, pp. 91–93), the Greek text of Judith does nonetheless contain fourteen instances of the use of *dē* (so Enslin).

7. *settled in Mesopotamia.* I.e., in Haran of northern Mesopotamia (see Gen 11:31 and Neh 9:7).

gods of their ancestors who were in Chaldea. The "who" evidently refers to "ancestors"; but the Syr and the Vg add "were worshiped," thereby making the pronoun refer to "gods."

8. *ways [odou].* Lit. "way," referring to cultic practices, as in 2 Kgs 16:3.

God of Heaven. Cf. Jdt 6:19; 11:17. This expression was common in Persian times, being found in 2 Chr 36:23; Ezra 1:2; 5:11, 12; Dan 2:37; and Tob 10:11, 12, as well as in the Elephantine Papyri.

the Chaldeans drove them out. According to Gen 11:31–12:5 (so also Neh 9:7–8 and Acts 7:2–4), Abraham left the land of the Chaldeans voluntarily, i.e., he was not driven out. The tradition of his forcible expulsion from Chaldea was a later midrashic development (cf. Josephus, *Ant.* 1.6.5). In any event, v 8 is best understood as a parenthetical expression, if not an actual gloss.

9. *accumulated . . . gold, silver, and livestock.* Compare Gen 13:2, where this is said of Abraham only *after* he had returned to Canaan from Egypt. Nonetheless, v 9 is not a contradiction of the Genesis account but the briefest statement of the "facts"; for not only was Abraham's visit to Egypt omitted by Achior (i.e., Gen 12:10–13:1) but so also was the entire Isaac-Jacob-Joseph story of Gen 13:3–46:4.

10. *as long as there was food. Dietraphēsan,* whose meaning here is obscure (lit. "while they were supported"), is possibly corrupt.

11. *by forcing them to make bricks.* Lit. "with hard work and brick," this phrase represents the author's "shorthand," which conveys well-known information through the use of a few key words.

12–14. Here the Vg offers an expanded version which may very well be based on the Chaldean manuscript used by Jerome (see INTRODUCTION, pp. 101–3):

> The God of Heaven opened the sea to them in their flight, so that the waters were made to stand firm as a wall on either side, and they walked through the bottom of the sea and passed it dry foot. And when an innumerable army of the Egyptians pursued after them in that place, they were so overwhelmed with the waters, that there was not one left, to tell what had happened to posterity. And after they came out of the Red Sea, they abode in the deserts of Mount Sinai, in which never man could dwell, or son of man rested. There bitter fountains were made sweet for them to drink, and for forty years they received food from heaven. (Vg 5:12–15)

15. *lived [ōkēsan] in the land of the Amorites.* Inasmuch as *ōkēsan* is used here (and in v 5) instead of either *katōkēsan* (v 9) or *parōkēsan* (v 10), the latter two words both meaning "settled," in a nonpermanent sense, "Amorites" here probably designates not just the land of the Heshbonites, as modern translators usually interpret it, but also part of the hill country as in Deut 1:19ff., 27, 44; Josh 10:5f. Compare Gen 15:16,

where "Amorite" refers to the pre-Israelite population of Canaan. For more on the meaning of this important but vague term, see A. Haldar, "Amorites," IDB, I, 115f.

So strong were they that. Lit. "in their might."

the Heshbonites. According to Num 21:25–26 and 34, the citizens of Heshbon inhabited an Amorite capital. Located in Transjordan south of Wadi Hesban in the northern part of Moab and about fifty miles due east of Jerusalem, Heshbon (mod. Hesban), after having been taken by the Israelites (Num 21:21–31), was occupied first by the tribe of Reuben (Josh 13:15–17) and then by the Gadites (Josh 21:39), only to be taken by King Eglon of Moab and then won back by Israel under Ehud (Judg 3:12–30), who retained it until the days of Mesha of Moab (mid-ninth century B.C.). Part of the Nabatean Kingdom in the Hellenistic period, Heshbon was conquered by Alexander Janneus (104–78 B.C.), who granted it full autonomy (Josephus, *Ant.* 13.15.4). For further details, see S. H. Horn, "Heshbon," EAEHL, II, 510–14.

16. *Canaanites, the Perizzites, the Jebusites, the Shechemites . . . Girgashites.* With one exception, this list is either identical or similar in content, if not in order, to other biblical lists of the dispossessed peoples (cf. Gen 15:20; Exod 3:8, 17; Deut 7:1; Josh 9:1; 11:3; Ezra 9:1; Neh 9:8). That one exception is "Shechemites," who are nowhere mentioned in the lists above. Their inclusion here may represent the author's hostility to the Samaritans and especially to Shechem, which John Hyrcanus I had taken (so Ball and others); or, more likely, it is a foreshadowing of Judith's denunciation in 9:2 of the rape of Dinah by Hamor the Shechemite (so Steinmann).

17. *they prospered.* The ancient author subscribed to the Deuteronomistic Creed of "Do good and prosper; do evil and be punished" (cf. Deut 28–30; Judg 2:11–15). For the author of Judith, "doing good" had almost as large a ritualistic component as a moral one (see INTRODUCTION, p. 62; but see also NOTE on 16:16). In this connection, D. N. Freedman offers an important caveat:

> Regarding the Deuteronomistic Code, ritual observance was also an integral part of obedience to the Covenant. The distinction between moral and ethical on one side and ritual and liturgical on the other is more a matter of modern analysis than ancient separation. (private correspondence with this writer)

18. *temple . . . was leveled to the ground.* An egregious anachronism! Here the well-known destruction of the Temple by Nebuchadnezzar in 586 B.C., a preexilic event of at least seventy-some years earlier (see 4:3), was now being described in postexilic times to a general of the very king who would be responsible for that act. This "detail of fact" is not in the Vg's Judith, possibly because Jerome, recognizing the contradictions involved, omitted it.

The best explanation for this anachronism is that the original setting of the Judith-story was in the early Persian period, but the final editor of Judith failed to straighten out or remove some of the inevitable contradictions growing out of having Nebuchadnezzar and the Assyrians as villains in the tale.

19. *where they had been scattered.* Lit. "where [ou] they were scattered there [ekei]," an obvious Hebraism (Heb '*šr* . . . *šm*).

20. *master [despota].* In Judith, this very deferential term is applied five times to Holofernes (5:20, 24; 7:9, 11; 11:10) and, ironically, only once to God (9:12). Possibly the word should be seen in its larger content (i.e., "my master and lord"), in which

case we might have hendiadys and translate the phrase as "my imperious lord."
Aware of the possible effect of the advice, he, Achior, was about to give Holofernes,
the Ammonite leader might well have used as deferential and flattering expression of
address as he could think of.

oversight [agnoēma] . . . *are sinning [amartanousin].* The Greek translator made
Achior very theologically sophisticated by having him distinguish between a sin of
omission ("oversight," as in Gen 43:13 of the LXX) and one of commission. See Tob
3:3, where the two words appear side by side but evidently not as synonyms.

21. *But.* According to Soubigou, the conjunctive particle *de* occurs forty times in
Judith.

is not guilty. Lit. "there is no lawlessness." The ancient Greek translator's extensive
vocabulary is well illustrated by the variety of terms he used for any offense by Israel:
adikia (v 17); *apestēsan apo tēs odou* (v 18); *agnoēma, amartanousin, skandalon* (v 20);
and *anomia* (v 21); see also *amartia* (7:28); and *amartēma* (11:11). His rich vocabulary
is in sharp contrast to the more limited one of the author of the Hebrew book of
Esther (see AB 7B, pp. livf.).

my lord. . . . *their lord.* With this antithesis the ancient author had Achior set up
here a nice theological question. Only time will tell which is the greater lord: the one
who will attack Israel or the one who will defend her.

Comment I

Achior's speech appears to have served two purposes. It informed Holofernes
of the nature and history of the Israelites, thereby making it easier for him
later on to believe Judith when she explains why she has deserted her people
and come over to his side (11:9–19). The speech also reminds the reader of
the sacred history of the Jewish people as interpreted from a Deuteronomistic
view: faithfulness to God is rewarded; infidelity *always* punished.

While Achior's survey of the sacred history of the Jews is general and
imprecise, perhaps because it is so brief, his historical account is not in error;
or at least it agrees with the broadest outlines of Jewish history as presented
in the Hebrew Bible, the phrase "the Chaldeans drove them out" in v 8
notwithstanding. Therefore, it is inconceivable that an author who knew well
his Jewish sacred history could be so poorly informed as to write such things
as Nebuchadnezzar was king of the Assyrians and ruled from his capital city
of Nineveh (1:1) or to put essentially *post*exilic elements (see NOTES on 4:3, 6,
8) into his *pre*exilic Palestine. In other words, the author's knowledge of
sacred Jewish history, as reflected here in Achior's speech and later on in
Judith's exhortation to the elders (8:24–27) and her prayer (9:2–4), argues, *a
priori,* that at least some of the more serious "deficiencies" or "errors" in the

author's knowledge of Jewish history were deliberate (see INTRODUCTION, pp. 48 and 79).

In Achior's speech, the author skillfully set up two antithetical views on the nature and origin of power. For Holofernes and his officers, strength and might were to be measured in material terms of size and numbers, of organization and armies (so vv 3, 23). For the Jews, strength and might were rooted in exclusive faithfulness to God (vv 7–9, 19) and righteous living (vv 17–18, 20–21). Thus, General Holofernes and the widow Judith will be ideal protagonists for their respective views.

Comment II

Achior was a wise man. But according to Cazelles (RSR 39 [1951]: 125–37, 324–27), Achior was also a wise man in the technical sense of that word. Cazelles maintains that behind the "Achior" of Judith actually stands "the profile figure of the celebrated Ahikar" (p. 129), a famous pagan wise man who was an advisor to the Assyrian kings Sennacherib and Esarhaddon and was the reputed author of a wisdom book containing a number of proverbs and fables. (For background information on him and his book, see S. Sandmel, "Ahikar," IDB, I, 68, and E. G. Kraeling, "Ahikar, Book of," IDB, I, 68–69.) While the details of the Ahikar-story vary in its Aramaic, Syriac, and Arabic versions, in all of them "he is, in principle, a good and just pagan who submits to the proven injustices on the part of the great of this world" (p. 132). Such a characterization well fits Judith's Achior. That the author of Judith was familiar with the Ahikar figure becomes more probable when one realizes that Tobit, a book whose composition many scholars date to the same general period as Judith, alludes to what was obviously a well-known story when Tobit on his deathbed instructed his son Tobias:

> Bury me properly, and your mother with me. And do not live in Nineveh any longer. See, my son, what Nadab did to Ahikar who had reared him, how he brought him from light into darkness, and with what he repaid him. But Ahikar was saved, and the other received repayment as he himself went down into the darkness. Ahikar gave alms and escaped the deathtrap which Nadab had set for him; but Nadab fell into the trap and perished. (Tob 14:10)

Here, the Assyrian Ahikar has been Judaized and become the nephew and benefactor of Tobit (Tob 1:21–22; 2:10). Thus, just as Holofernes in Judith represents a type of character rather than a historical figure, so, argues Cazelles, Achior is also a type, another ethnic transformation of Ahikar, the noble wise man who suffers and is ultimately vindicated and rewarded. Steinmann, however, while freely admitting that in Tob 11:20 the Vg renders the LXX's "Ahikar" as "Achior," insists that in Judith Achior's nationality (Ammonite), function (military general), and the particular character of his discourse in chap. 5 (i.e., not in the wisdom tradition) definitely preclude Achior from being a Judaized transformation of the famous Assyrian wise man (Steinmann, p. 56). It may well be that Cazelles is correct in seeing Achior as an Ammonite Ahikar, but it is certain that Achior serves to hold the two sections of Judith together (see INTRODUCTION, p. 59).

VI. Holofernes Rewards Achior for His Sound Advice
(5:22–6:21 [Vg 5:26–6:21])

5 ²² ᵃWhen Achior had finished saying all these things, all the people standing around the tent began muttering; and Holofernes' officers as well as those inhabiting the coastal region and Moab suggested thrashing him, ²³ saying, "We're not afraid of the Israelites! They're a weak people, unable to wage war. ²⁴ So let's go ahead, Lord Holofernes. Your army will eat them up!"

6 ¹ After the hubbub of the men outside the council had died down, Holofernes, the ranking commander of the Assyrian army, said to Achiorᵇ in front of all the assembled foreigners, ² "So who are you, Achior and you Ephraimiteᶜ mercenaries, that you play the prophet among us as you have done today, advising us not to make war against the people of Israel because their god will protect them? Who is god except Nebuchadnezzar? He will send his forces and wipe them off the face of the earth! Their god won't save them. ³ On the contrary, we, Nebuchadnezzar'sᵈ servants, will strike them down as if they were one man. They cannot withstand the strength of our cavalry. ⁴ With itᵉ we will destroy them. Their hills will be drunk with their blood, and their plains filled with their corpses. Not even their footsteps will survive! They will be completely wiped out! So says King Nebuchadnezzar, lord of the whole world. For he has spoken, and his commands will not be in vain.

⁵ "As for you, Achior, you Ammonite mercenary who has said these things in your day of insults, you shall not again see my face from this day until I take my revenge on this nation which came out of Egypt.

ᵃ Gk *kai egeneto.*
ᵇ LXXᴬᵈᵍᵐᵖˢᵘ add "and to all the Moabites," as does LXXᴮ in v 2.
ᶜ LXXᵇᵏᶠʳ OL, and Syr read "Ammonite"; Vg omits; see NOTE.
ᵈ LXX "his."
ᵉ LXX "them."

[6] When I[f] return, then the sword of my army and the spear[g] of my servants will run you through, and you shall fall among their wounded. [7] My servants will now 'deliver' you to the hill country and leave you at one of the towns in the passes. [8] You will not die—until you are destroyed with them! [9] And if in your heart you believe that they won't be taken, then don't look so depressed. I have spoken, and not one of my words will fail to come true." [10] Then Holofernes ordered those servants who waited on him in his tent to seize Achior and take him away to Bethulia and hand him over to the Israelites.

[11] So his servants seized him and took him out of the camp into the plain; and from the plain they went up into the hill country and came to the springs below Bethulia. [12] As soon as the men of the town[h] saw them, they grabbed their weapons and went out of the town to the top of the hill; and all the slingers were pelting them with stones to prevent them from coming up. [13] But ducking under the hill, 'Holofernes' men[i] tied Achior up, left him at the foot of the hill, and returned to their lord.

[14] When the Israelites came down from their town and found him, they untied him and took him back to Bethulia and brought him before the magistrates of their town, [15] who at the time were Uzziah son of Micah[j] from the tribe of Simeon, Chabris son of Gothoniel, and Charmis[k] son of Melchiel. [16] These called together all the elders of the town, and all their young men and their women[l] came hurrying to the assembly. They stood Achior in the center of all the people, and Uzziah questioned him about what had happened. [17] He answered by relating to them the decisions of Holofernes' war council, what [m]he himself[m] had said in the presence of the Assyrian leaders, and how Holofernes had boasted of what he would do to the House of Israel. [18] Then the people prostrated themselves in worship of God and cried out, [19] "Lord God of Heaven, consider their arrogance and pity the sorry plight of our nation. Look kindly this day on those consecrated to you." [20] They then reassured Achior and commended him highly.[n]

---

[f] LXX[B] "they."
[g] So OL, Vg, Syr; LXX *laos*, "people"; see NOTE.
[h] LXX[fk], OL, and Syr omit "on the top of the hill"; see NOTE.
[i] LXX "they."
[j] Gk *meicha*; LXX[A] *cheima*.
[k] Gk *Charmeis*; LXX[A] *chalmeis*.
[l] LXX[fk], Syr, and OL add "and their children."
[m] LXX[AN] and Eth "they."
[n] OL adds "saying, 'As it shall please God to do for us, so it shall be also for you.'"

21 Uzziah took him from the assembly to his own home and gave a banquet for the elders, and throughout that night they called upon the God of Israel for help.

Notes

5:24. Corresponding to this verse, the Vg has:

> That, therefore, Achior may know that he is deceiving us, let us go up into the mountains; and when their mighty men have been taken prisoners, then let him be stabbed with the sword, along with them: that every nation may know that Nebuchadnezzar is god of the earth, and besides him there is no other. (vv 28–29)

your army will eat them up! Lit. "they shall be food for all your army." The NEB's "your great army will swallow them whole," while a bit too paraphrastic, nicely captures the braggadocio of Holofernes' advisors.

6:2 *who are you?* An expression of rebuke here and in 8:12 (cf. also 12:14).

Ephraimite mercenaries [misthōtoi ephraim]. Cf. v 5. If the reading is correct, which is highly debatable (see textual notes *b* and *c*), the allusion is vague. It may be a term of contempt, possibly reflecting a Southern bias against the North (cf. 2 Chr 25:7–9, 15); or, less likely, *misthōtoi* may represent, as in the LXX of Isa 28:1, a misreading of *škwr*, "drunk," as *śkyr*, "mercenary" (so Ball, p. 295).

play the prophet. Unlike the reader, Holofernes never learned how ironic his words were. Cf. 1 Kgs 22:15–17. Achior is an Ammonite "Balaam," a Gentile who must speak only good about Israel (Num 22–24; see also R. F. Johnson, "Balaam," IDB, I, 341–42).

In fact, the Ammonite Achior may, quite literally, have been based upon Balaam son of Beor, a seer who, as we now know from the Deir Allah inscriptions, played an important role in the Ammonite literary traditions from at least 700 B.C. (see Hoftijzer and van der Kooij, *Aramaic Texts from Deir 'Allā;* see also Hoftijzer, BA 39 [1976]: 11–17). Located in southern Transjordan, Deir Allah is within the area that scholars have generally assigned to the Ammonites. These Aramaic texts, written in black (and occasionally red) ink on white plaster, are quite fragmentary and pose a number of problems (for further details, see P. Kyle McCarter, Jr., BASOR 239 [1980]: 49–60). Nonetheless, just as Balaam of Deir Allah brought to his people a communication from the gods, so later on another Ammonite, Achior, tried to enlighten his people about the nature and will of Israel's God.

Who is god except Nebuchadnezzar? This question is more than one more expression of Holofernes' characteristic bluster: it is *the* question posed by Judith itself, primarily because of the actions of such historical villains as Antiochus IV, Epiphanes.

Because she has been able to view the book of Judith as an entity rather than as an exciting tale (i.e., chaps. 8–16) preceded by "too long" an introduction (chaps. 1–7), Craven, far more than any other scholar, rightly perceived that "the question which subtly motivates the entire narrative [i.e., the entire book] is who is most powerful: Nebuchadnezzar or Yahweh" (SBLDS 70, p. 55). Again, it is Holofernes, not Nebuchadnezzar, who makes—and pays for—these blasphemous assertions (see COMMENT, p. 134). The GNB's "Nebuchadnezzar is our god, and that's all that matters" is quite dramatic but not at all true to the Greek text.

Their god won't save them. The assertion turns out to be as valid here as it was when made earlier by Sennacherib's envoys to Hezekiah (cf. Isa 36; 2 Kgs 18:32–35; 19:10–13).

4. *will destroy [katakausomen] them.* Lit. "will burn them up." Unhappy with the inappropriateness of this verb for describing an action accomplished by cavalry (but see 2 Sam 4:11, where it is used in the sense of "exterminate"), some scholars prefer one of the variant readings. For an ingenious explanation of how these variants might have arisen, see Zimmermann, JBL 57 (1938): 68–69.

Not even their footsteps will survive! Lit. "the trace of their feet will not stand before us." The idiom is unclear.

be completely wiped out! A Hebraism. Gk *apōleia apolountai* = Heb *'bd y'bdwn,* an infinitive absolute construction.

5. *you shall not again see my face . . . until I take my revenge.* Again, only the reader, not Holofernes, can appreciate the irony of these words. On the next occasion the two "meet," Achior will see only Holofernes' head (14:6).

this nation which came out of Egypt. Evidently, Holofernes chose to single out this particular phase of Jewish history because in Achior's summary the Israelites had been slaves only there (5:11–12).

6. *the spear of my servants.* The reading adopted here (see textual note *ᵍ*) assumes that *laos,* "people," is an error, possibly a corruption of *logchē,* "spear" (so Fritzsche).

and you shall fall among their wounded. I.e., Achior will be killed. The GNB's "You will be just another name on the casualty list" misses the point: Achior's certain death, not his anonymity, is being emphasized here.

7. *will now 'deliver' you.* Instead of seeing *apokatastēsousin,* lit. "they will bring back," as an expression of Holofernes' sarcasm, Ball regarded this word as the general's "covert insinuation that Achior had already been in the enemy camp" (p. 296). The truth is that Holofernes did not realize just how ironical his words here actually were.

9. *don't look so depressed.* Lit. "do not let your face fall." Cf. Gen 4:5, 6 (see Gruber, BAR 6 [1980]: 35–36). Holofernes could not resist giving Achior a final gibe.

12. *to [epi] the top of the hill.* While this identical Greek phrase occurs twice in this verse (see textual note *ʰ*), its first occurrence should be deleted, it best being regarded as a *homeoteleuton,* although Enslin would regard the second occurrence as the actual corruption, it being, he believed, a dittography.

13. *tied Achior up.* The Vg adds "to a tree by his hands and feet," which may reflect a reading in Jerome's Aramaic text.

15. *Uzziah . . . from the tribe of Simeon.* Ozeias is the Gk equivalent of Heb *'zyh,* "Yah(u)-is-my-strength." Given the attitude and performance of Uzziah later on (cf. 7:29–31; 8:9–17, 28–31), his name is most ironic. Weak and wavering, he is the perfect foil for the widow Judith and the Gentile Achior. Not only Uzziah and Judith (so 9:2) but presumably most of the inhabitants of Bethulia were Simeonites.

The designation of Uzziah, Judith, and her husband as "Simeonites" is curious. Like others of the so-called Twelve Tribes of Israel, Simeon's location changed drastically over the centuries. On the basis of such passages as Genesis 34, scholars generally understand the secular tribe of Simeon (along with Levi) to have once lived in central Palestine, in the general vicinity of Shechem. Moreover, the fact that Simeon's name heads the list of those standing on Mount Gerizim (near Shechem), blessing the Israelites as they passed between it and Mount Ebal (so Deut 27:12–13), seems to confirm that location. However, the Simeonites were evidently unable to maintain there either their power or their location. The tribe became so insignificant that it was mentioned in neither the Song of Deborah (Judges 5) nor the Blessing of Moses (Deuteronomy 33). Moreover, Judg 1:17 places the Simeonites to the south of Judah in Zephath/Hormah (mod. Tell es-Seba‘), about three miles east of Beersheba. Simeon's later history was that of Judah (see Judg 1:3); in fact, the list of Simeon's cities in Josh 19:1–8 is actually the towns of Judah in the days of King Josiah (see K. Elliger, "Simeon," IDB, IV, 356).

While the NT occasionally gives tribal designations to certain individuals (e.g., the prophetess Anna was from the tribe of Asher [Luke 2:36], Barnabas was out of Levi [Acts 4:36], and the Apostle Paul was a Benjaminite [Rom 11:1]), such designations represented the general area from which these people descended rather than their actual tribal or bloodlines. (For introductory remarks on the very complicated subject of the Twelve Tribes in general and of Simeon in particular, see K. Elliger, "Tribes, Territories of," IDB, IV, 701–10). Thus, although "Simeonites" would have lived in southern Palestine when Judith was composed, the author had in mind as the setting for his story the tribe's ancient patriarchal location. For in those days Shechem not only stood between Jerusalem and the army of Holofernes but it was also the site of an event which loomed large in the mind of Judith, namely, the rape of Dinah (see Jdt 9:2–4).

Chabris [chabris] . . . *Charmis.* So far as we know, the name "Chabris" is confined to the book of Judith. Regarding these two Jewish names as Hellenized Hebrew names (i.e., *ḥbry* and *krmy)* and the other four names in the verse as "unHellenized," Steinmann (p. 65) sees this as evidence of a mixed population in Samaritan Bethulia. However, Enslin is surely right in regarding the "correct" spelling of all the names in this verse as of minor importance—and some of them, we might add, of great uncertainty (see textual notes *ʲ* and *ᵏ)*—the names having been offered only to provide the story with a little color.

17. *the decisions.* The Gk *rēmata* undoubtedly represents here the Heb *dbrym,* "words/things." Achior would have not only repeated the words but conveyed also the feelings of the council.

the House [oikon] of Israel. This is but one of a variety of expressions in just this chapter which the author uses to designate the people of Israel: *genos* (v 19), *genos israēl* (v 2), *genos tōn ex aigyptou* (v 5), *uioi israēl* (v 14), and *laos* (v 18). A rich and varied vocabulary is one of the outstanding features of the Greek text of Judith.

20. Like the OL (see textual note *ⁿ),* the Vg has an expanded version of this verse:

They comforted Achior, saying, "The God of our fathers, whose power you have set forth, will make this return to you, that you shall see their destruction. And when the Lord our God shall give this liberty to his servants let God be with you also in the midst of us: that as it shall please you, so you with all yours may converse with us." (Vg 6:16c–18)

It seems unlikely that Jerome himself composed this passage rather than followed his Aramaic text.

21. *a banquet.* Because the Greek word used here, *potos,* is lit. "a drinking party" (= Heb *mšth),* Steinmann wrote: "The banquet which the 'mayor' of Bethulia offers to Achior resembles strikingly the last cigarette of a man condemned to death" (p. 60). More likely, however, it was simply a meal where, quite naturally, wine was served. In any event, this *potos* was actually the setting for an all-night prayer session.

Comment

The more we know about a story's villain, about his heroic qualities as well as his foibles and flaws, the more interesting his downfall is (see also pp. 84–85). For then it is a well-known individual that falls rather than a faceless Great Name. In this section the author continues to develop the character of Holofernes, showing him to be decisive and courageous but also blustering and braggadocious (6:3–4, 5–8). While loyalty to one's lord is certainly an admirable quality, Holofernes' loyalty to Nebuchadnezzar exceeds common sense (v 2).

Deeply offended by Achior's counsel, Holofernes would nonetheless be "merciful" to him by delivering him into the hands of the very people Achior had sided with—that later Achior might be killed along with them (vv 7–9)! Clearly, Holofernes had a sense of humor, albeit sarcastic and cruel (v 9). But if the reader can appreciate, if not approve of, Holofernes' sense of humor, the reader can also smile at Holofernes, who several times spoke more ironically than he knew (see NOTES on "play the prophet" [v 2]; "you shall not again see my face . . . until I take my revenge" [v 5]; and "will now 'deliver' you" [v 7]). In fact, the entire section is most ironic. For Holofernes would have said that by turning Achior over to the Israelites, he was "rewarding" Achior for his "sound" advice. The fact is, as the reader later finds out, Achior's advice *was* sound; and because his lot was cast with the Israelites, Achior survived.

VII. Holofernes Begins an Effective Siege Against Bethulia (7:1–32 [Vg 7:1–25])

7 ¹ The next day Holofernes ordered his entire army and all the people who had joined him as allies to break camp and move on Bethulia and to seize the passes up into the hill country and so make war against the Israelites. ² So every able-bodied man of them marched off that day, and the strength of their fighting force was a hundred and seventy thousand*a* infantrymen and twelve thousand*b* cavalry, not counting the baggage train and the men who managed it, an enormous number. ³ They encamped in the valley near Bethulia, beside the spring; and they deployed on a wide front from Dothan to Belbaim*c*, and in depth from Bethulia to Cyamon*d*, which faces Esdraelon. ⁴ When the Israelites saw this horde, they were quite alarmed and said to one another, "They will now strip clean the entire land. Neither high mountains nor valleys nor hills will bear their weight!" ⁵ After getting their weapons and lighting beacons on their towers, they stood on guard all that night.

⁶ On the second day Holofernes deployed his entire cavalry in full view of the Israelites who were in Bethulia. ⁷ He reconnoitered the approaches to their town; he found the water sources, seized them, and after posting detachments of soldiers over them, he returned to his main army.

⁸ All the rulers of the children of Esau, the leaders of the people of Moab, and the generals of the coastal region then came to him and said, ⁹ "If our master will listen to our advice, then his army will suffer no losses. ¹⁰ For this people, the Israelites, do not rely on their spears but on the height of the mountains where they live, since it is no easy task to get to the top of their mountains. ¹¹ So now, master, don't fight them in a pitched battle, and not a single man of your army will fall.

---

a LXXˢ "8,000"; Syr "172,000"; Vg and OLᶜ "120,000."
b Syr, OL, and Vg "22,000."
c So LXXᴮᴬ; LXXᴺ *belmaien;* LXXˢ *abelbaim;* Eth *belmaim;* Vg *belma.*
d LXX *kuamōnos;* OL *kelmōnos;* Vg *chelmon.*

¹² Remain in camp and keep all your men with you while your servants take possession of the spring which flows from the foot of the mountain ¹³ because it is from there all the people of Bethulia get their water. So thirst will destroy them, and they will surrender their town. Meanwhile, we and our people will go up onto the surrounding hilltops and camp there so as to prevent any man from leaving the town. ¹⁴ They and their women and children will starve, and before the sword touches them they will be lying in the streets outside their homes. ¹⁵ So you will make them pay dearly for rebelling against you and for not being conciliatory."

¹⁶ Because this advice was agreeable to Holofernes and his entire staff, he ordered it to be done just as they had recommended. ¹⁷ So a contingent of Ammonites*ᵉ*, along with five thousand Assyrians, moved forward; they encamped in the valley and secured the Israelites' water sources and springs. ¹⁸ Meanwhile the children of Esau and the Ammonites went up and encamped in the hill country opposite Dothan, and they sent some of their number to the southeast toward Egrebelᶠ, which is near Chousᵍ ʰon the Wadi Mochmurʰ. The rest of the Assyrian army encamped in the plain and covered every square inch of it; their tents and supplies formed an immense encampment, since they constituted such a very great number.

¹⁹ The Israelites then cried out to the Lord their God, for their courage had failed them because all their enemies had surrounded them, and there was no escape from them. ²⁰ The entire Assyrian army (the infantry, chariots, and cavalry) had blockaded them for thirty-fourⁱ days, and all the water reserves were depleted for all the inhabitants of Bethulia. ²¹ The cisterns were going dry, and no one could quench his thirst for even a day because the water had to be rationed. ²² ʲTheir children were listless, and the women and young men fainted from thirst and were collapsing in the town's streets and gateways, for they no longer had any strength.

²³ So all the people, including the young men, women and children, gathered around Uzziah and the town leaders and shouted in protest. And in the presence of all the elders they said, ²⁴ "May God judge

---

ᵉ OLˢ, Syr "Moabites."
ᶠ So LXXᴮᴺˢ; LXXᴬ *ekrebēl*.
ᵍ So LXXᴮᴺˢ; LXXᴬ *chousei*.
ʰ⁻ʰ LXXᴬ omits.
ⁱ "Twenty" in 7:11 of Vg.
ʲ Vg omits v.

between you and us! For you did us a great injustice by not making peace with the Assyrians. [25] We have no one to help us now. Rather, God has sold us into their hands, to sprawl before them in thirst and utter helplessness. [26] Contact them at once and hand over the whole town to be sacked by Holofernes' people and all his army, [27] for it is better for us to be sacked by them.[k] For although we shall become slaves, our lives will be spared; and we shall not witness with our own eyes the death of our little ones or our wives and children breathing their last. [28] We call to witness against you heaven and earth and our 'God, the Lord' of our ancestors, who punishes us for our sins and for the sins of our fathers, that "you do" what we have said, today."

[29] Then there arose a bitter and general lamentation throughout the assembly, and they cried loudly to the Lord God. [30] Uzziah then said to them, "Courage, my brothers! Let us hold out for five more days. By then the Lord our God will have pity on us, for he will not abandon us altogether. [31] But if these days go by and no help comes to us, then I will do as you say." [32] "He then dismissed the men° to their various stations (they went on the walls and towers of their town) and sent the women and children to their homes. But throughout the town they were very dejected.

---

[k] LXX[bcejlw] add "than to die by thirst."
[l-l] LXX[bdp] have *kñ ton thñ.*
[m-m] So LXX[lr] and verss.; LXX[BAS] "let him not do" (LXX[SN] omit "not"); see NOTE.
[n] Vg omits v.
[o] LXX "people."

Notes

7:2. *a hundred and seventy thousand.* If this figure is not corrupt (see textual note [q]), then Holofernes has evidently picked up from his allies an additional fifty thousand infantrymen (cf. 2:15). In the Greek Bible, errors in numbers are especially easy to make when some manuscripts, such as LXX[s] here, use alphabetic symbols for the number instead of spelling it out in full.

3. *Belbaim.* Almost every Greek manuscript and ancient version offers a different spelling for this town. Most scholars assume that it is the same town as the unknown one mentioned in 4:4.

Cyamon. Meaning "bean field" in Greek, the site is unknown, although many scholars identify it with Tell Kaimon (= Jokmeam in 1 Kgs 4:12), on the eastern slope of Mount Carmel, about fifteen miles northwest of Jezreel.

4. *Neither high mountains . . . nor hills will bear their weight!* Nor will the Israel-ites who live among them!

7. *to his main army.* Lit. "to his people." For this verse the Vg has an addition which can scarcely have been invented by Jerome:

Now Holofernes, in going about, found that the fountain which supplied them with water, ran through an aqueduct outside the city on the south side; and he commanded their aqueduct to be cut off. Nevertheless, there were springs not far from the walls, out of which they were seen secretly to draw water, to refresh themselves a little rather than to drink their fill. (Vg 7:6–7)

Suffice it to say, efforts to locate such an aqueduct in the presumed vicinity of Bethulia have been, thus far, in vain. (If the author or a later scribe believed that Bethulia was really Shechem [see NOTE in 4:6 on "Bethulia"], then the spring of the so-called Well of Jacob comes to mind.)

8. *children of Esau.* An archaic expression for the Edomites of Transjordan (cf. Gen 36:1), a people with whom Israel often had had hostile relations. The Idumeans, the postexilic occupants of Edom, were defeated by Judas Maccabeus in 164 B.C. (1 Macc 5:1–5) and ca. 120 B.C., according to Josephus, were forcibly converted to Judaism *(Ant.* 13.9.1; 15.7.9).

9. *will suffer no losses.* Lit. "there will be no fragment [Gk *thrausma]* in your army." Instead of *thrausma,* several manuscripts have *thrausis,* "a fragmentation"; both Greek words can go back to Heb *šbr,* "destruction." In any event, both the RSV ("lest his army be defeated") and the NEB ("and save your army from a crushing defeat") totally miss the point; for not only the Greek itself but also simple logic militates against such an interpretation. After all, these advisors to Holofernes had already seen what had happened to Achior for suggesting the possibility of an Assyr-ian defeat.

12. *take possession of the spring.* This advice is curious, especially in light of v 7, where we read that Holofernes had seized the springs in the vicinity.

13. *to prevent any man [andra] from leaving the town.* The plan was "successful" in that no *male* left the beleaguered town, but two women did, Judith and her maid. Did the ancient author intend this irony? Or, inasmuch as this Greek word is used some-times for "man" in the generic sense, is this double entendre only in the eye of the beholder?

17. The Vg here has "and he placed all around about a hundred men at every spring" (Vg 7:10).

18. *southeast toward Egrebel.* Lit. "to the south and east opposite Egrebel," i.e., hendiadys. Mentioned in the Bible only here, Egrebel is identified by most scholars with Acraba (mod. Akrabeh), a village some twenty-five miles north of Jerusalem and about ten miles southeast of Nablus. Josephus referred to it as "Akrabatta" *(Jewish Wars* 3.3.5).

Chous. Also mentioned only here in the Bible, Chous's location is unknown, al-though some scholars would identify it with the modern village of Quzeh, which is about six miles south of Nablus.

Wadi Mochmur. Possibly to be identified with Wadi Makhfurlyeh, south of Nablus (so Enslin and others), but identified by Avi-Yonah and Aharoni with Wadi Qana

(Macmillan Bible Atlas, Map 211), some fifteen miles from Egrebel, the site is best described as "unknown." With respect to the three places named in this verse, the words of Enslin are pertinent:

> Perhaps our author's geography in this district is less imaginative than in other areas, but it would appear that modern investigators tend to find rather more clues to identify than did the early translators who rival one another in variants for places they obviously had no slightest knowledge of. (p. 105)

All three of the place names in this LXX verse are missing in the Vg.

20. *for thirty-four days.* Lit. "four and thirty days"; this number is curiously specific. Craven (SBLDS 70, pp. 51–52) may very well be correct in seeing here the first part of a chiasm, in that later on Judith spends *four* days in the Assyrian camp (12:10) and the Israelites *thirty* days while they plundered it (15:11). But again, such equivalencies may be more in the eye of the beholder than part of the author's intent.

25. *God has sold us.* Although this phrase occurs also in Esth 7:4, it should be understood here in the sense of Isa 50:1 and 52:3, where God affirms that Israel was not sold for money; rather, "sold" is used here in the metaphorical sense of "go into servitude or exile" (cf. Lev 25:39; Rom 7:14).

27. *it is better for us to be sacked.* This argument of slavery or escape from death as "salvation" was subscribed to not only by many Jews in Egypt (Exod 14:10–12; 16:3; Gen 47:25) but also by Palestinian Jews in the days of Antiochus IV, Epiphanes (cf. 1 Macc 1:52f.).

28. *our God, the Lord [kurion] of our ancestors.* In the Bible, this expression occurs only here; elsewhere we have "the Lord, God of our Fathers," the Heb *yhwh* (= Gk *kurios)* being rightly understood as a proper name. If the accepted reading in this verse is, in fact, an error, then the transposed form could easily have arisen through the misreading of the common Greek abbreviations for "Lord" *(kñ)* and "God" *(thñ),* abbreviations recorded in three minuscules (see textual note ʰ).

who punishes us for our sins. Because the Bethulians believe that their God punishes sin and because they were suffering, they made the same incorrect inference that Job's three friends did, namely, suffering was itself proof of sin. Judith would have to provide them with an alternate explanation for their circumstances (see 8:18, 27).

that you do what we have said. As textual note ᵐ⁻ᵐ might suggest, the original reading is most uncertain, a fact confirmed by the wide range of interpretations of it in English translations. Difficulties arise not only from the omission of the negative by LXXˢ and several ancient versions, but also from uncertainty as to the subject of the verb *poiēsē* in LXXᴬᴮˢ: is it God or Holofernes? The reading adopted here sees *poiēsē* as 2d singular middle, i.e., "you," referring to Uzziah. Confirmation of this interpretation seems to be found in v 31.

29. Following its Aramaic original, the Vg has an addition influenced by Pss 106:6; 115:2; 2 Sam 24:14; and Joel 2:17:

> We have sinned with our fathers, we have done unjustly, we have committed iniquity. Have mercy on us, because you are good, or punish our iniquities by chastising us yourself, and do not deliver them that trust in thee to a people who do not know you. (Vg 7:19–20)

30. *hold out for five more days.* Uzziah was hoping for providential rains to fill the empty cisterns (so 8:31). Inasmuch as it was now well over a month (so 7:20) since the harvest (cf. 4:5; 2:27), the dry season had clearly set in, the rainy season in Israel usually lasting from October through March, with the summer months almost rainless. See also A. Momigliano's comments on p. 152.

As Alonso-Schökel has rightly pointed out (p. 6), this five-day limit had both a theological and a narrative function; for it "tempts" God by putting a time limit on him (so 8:12), and it sets a time limit within which Judith must carry out her plan, all of which increases the reader's interest and suspense. See COMMENT II, p. 154, for the view that this detail of fact (i.e., a limitation of only five days before surrendering to the enemy) was actually influenced by a Greek account of the Persian siege of Lindos.

32. *sent the women and children to their homes.* Ironically, in a sexist society where women belonged at home with the children while the men protected them, it will be two women who will leave the city and save it.

Comment

As the Assyrians settle down into a routine siege of Bethulia, the tempo of the narrative picks up, thanks in part to the author's skillful use of direct address. On three separate occasions in the chapter (i.e., one half of all the verses) people are quoted, each instance giving the reader a clearer insight into the character and feelings of the person/s in question (vv 4, 9–15, 24–28, 30–31). The Vg, presumably following its Aramaic text, has even more in the way of direct address (cf. NOTES on vv 7 and 29) but without improving the narrative's flow.

The situation in Bethulia was desperate. The town that had started out so bravely in its opposition to Holofernes has seen its courage, along with its water, dry up. The hopelessness of the people, which is prolonged but not really alleviated by Uzziah's compromise (vv 30–31), will be a perfect foil for Judith's radiant hope and faith as described in the next chapter.

VIII. Judith, a Pious Widow of Bethulia, Gets Permission to Carry Out Her Secret Plan (8:1–36 [Vg 8:1–34])

8 ¹ ªNews of what had just happened reachedª Judith daughter of Merari son of Oxᵇ, son of Joseph, son of Oziel, son of Elkiah, ᶜson of Ananias, son of Gideon, son of Raphainᵈ, son of ᵉAhitubᶜ, son of Elijah, son of Hilkiahᶠ, son of Eliabᵍ, son of Nathanael, son of Shelumielʰ, son of Zurishaddaiⁱ, son of Israel. ² Her husband Manasseh, who belonged to the same tribe and family, had died during the barley harvest. (³ He was supervising those binding the sheaves in the field when he suffered sunstroke. He took to his bed and died in his hometown of Bethulia, and was buried with his ancestors in the field between Dothan and Balamonʲ.) ⁴ Now Judith had been a widow in her home for three years and four months. ⁵ She had made a shelter for herself on the roof of her home and wore sackcloth around her waist and dressed in widow's clothing. ⁶ She fasted every day of her widowhood, except for sabbath eve, the sabbath itself, the eve of the new moon, the new moon itself, and the joyous feasts of the House of Israel. ⁷ She was also shapely and beautiful. Moreover, her husband Manassehᵏ had left her gold and silver, male and female servants, livestock, and fields; and she had remained on her estate. ⁸ Yet there was no one who spoke ill of her, so devoutly did she fear God.

⁹ In any event, she heard about the people's bitter attack against the magistrate because they had been demoralized by the lack of water. Judith had also heard about the response which Uzziah had made to

ªˉª LXX "And she heard in those days."
ᵇ LXX ōx; LXXᵇ, OLˢ, Syr ōz; OLᵐ ioas; Vg idox.
ᶜˉᶜ Only LXXᴮ omits.
ᵈ LXX raphaein; LXXᴬ raphain; Vg raphaim.
ᵉ LXX achitōb; LXXᴬ akithōn; LXXᴺ akinthōn.
ᶠ LXXᴬ and Eth omit; LXXᶠᵏ and OLˢ melchia; Syr melcia.
ᵍ LXXˢ and Copt "Enab."
ʰ LXXᴮᴺ salamiēl; LXXˢ samamiēl; LXXᴬ salamina.
ⁱ So LXXᴮˢ; LXX salasadai.
ʲ LXX balamōn; see NOTE.
ᵏ OLˢ adds Manasseh's genealogy, taken from v 1.

them, how[f] he had promised them to surrender the town to the Assyrians after five days. [10] So she sent the maid in charge of all her property to summon Uzziah[m], Chabris, and Charmis, the elders of her town.

[11] After they had arrived, she said to them, "Please hear me out, magistrates of the citizens of Bethulia. For the advice you offered the people today is not sound. And you confirmed this oath you made between God and yourselves, promising to surrender the town to our enemies unless the Lord comes to your aid within that time. [12] But now who are you to test God this day and to set yourselves above God among mortals? [13] You are putting the Omnipotent Lord to the test, but you will never learn anything! [14] If you cannot plumb the depths of a person's heart or understand the thoughts of his mind, then how can you fathom God, who made all these things, or read his mind or understand his reasoning? No, my brothers, do not provoke the anger of the Lord our God. [15] For if he does not choose to help us within those five days, he still has the power to protect us as long as he wants or even to destroy us in the presence of our enemies. [16] But as for you, do not impose conditions on the Lord our God; for God is not to be threatened as a man is or to be cajoled[n] as a mere mortal. [17] Rather, as we wait for his deliverance, let us call upon him to help us. He will listen to our voice, if he is so disposed.

[18] "For there has not been in our generation, nor is there among us today a tribe or family, a rural area or town that worships man-made gods, as was the case in former times. [19] That is why our ancestors were handed over to be slaughtered and sacked and so fell in a great catastrophe before our enemies. [20] But as for us, we recognize no other God than him; therefore we may hope that he will not[o] spurn us or any of our nation. [21] For if we are captured, then all Judea will be exposed[p], and our sanctuary will be looted; and we will answer with our blood for their desecration. [22] The slaughter of our brothers, the captivity of the land, the desolation of our heritage—[q]all this[q] he will bring upon our heads among the nations wherever we serve as slaves; we shall be

---

[f] So LXX *ōs;* LXX[B] *os,* "who."

[m] So LXX[N], most mins., and Syr; LXX[BAS] omit.

[n] Gk *diaitēthēnai;* LXX[N] *diartēthēnai,* "be indecisive."

[o] LXX[fkr] and OL add "remove his mercy and his salvation and will not."

[p] So LXX[BAS] *kathēsetai,* "will sit"; LXX[fk] and OL[sm] *lēphthēsetai,* "be taken away"; LXX[begs] *klithēsetai,* "lie prostrate."

[q-q] LXX omits.

an offense and a disgrace in the sight of our masters! ²³ For our servitude will not develop into favor; rather, the Lord our God will turn it into disgrace.

²⁴ "So then, my brothers, let us set an example for our countrymen. For their lives depend upon us; and the sanctuary, both the building and its altar, rests upon us. ²⁵ All this being so, let us give thanks to the Lord our God, who is putting us to the test, just as he did to our ancestors. ²⁶ Remember how he treated Abraham; how he tested Isaac; and 'what happened to' Jacob in Syrian Mesopotamia while he was working as a shepherd for Laban, his mother's brother? ²⁷ For he has not tested us, as he did them, to search their hearts; nor is he taking vengeance on us. Rather, the Lord scourges those who come near him so as to admonish them."

²⁸ Then Uzziah said to her, "All that you have said you have spoken with good intentions, and there is no one who can take issue with you. ²⁹ For today is not the first time that your wisdom has been evident; for from your earliest days all the people have recognized your good sense and sound judgment. ³⁰ But the people were terribly thirsty and so forced us to say^s what we told them and made us take an oath we cannot violate. ³¹ So now you' pray for us," for you are a devout' woman! Then God will send a downpour to fill our cisterns, and we will no longer be fainting from thirst."

³² "Listen to me," said Judith to them, "I am going to do something which will go down among the children of our people for endless generations. ³³ As for you, stand at the gate tonight, and I will leave with my maid. But within the period after which you promised to surrender the town to our enemies, the Lord will deliver Israel by my hand." ³⁴ But you must not inquire into the affair; for I will not tell you what I am going to do until it is accomplished."

³⁵ "Go to it!" said Uzziah and the magistrates to her, "May the Lord God go before you to take revenge on our enemies!" ³⁶ So they left her rooftop shelter and went to their posts.

~ LXX^N "how he tested."
' LXX "do."
' LXX^{Ncejlw} add the emphatic "you."
" LXX^{fk}, OL, and Syr add "and our God will promptly hear."
' Gk *eusebēs;* LXX^{fk} *theosebēs,* "religious"; Vg *sancta,* "holy."
* LXX^{fk}, OL, and Syr add "as I trust."

Notes

8:1. *Judith.* The Gk *ioudeith* represents the Heb *yhwdyt,* "Jewess," although since the Hittite wife of Esau also had the same name (Gen 26:34), it need not automatically be understood that way, especially since the male equivalent of the name was borne by a foreigner in Jer 36:14, namely, Jehudi. While the name may very well be allegorical, symbolizing the true type of the daughters of Israel or of even Israel itself (cf. 16:2), it was also borne by several persons, including a woman from the Persian period, Judith daughter of Dalluy (Aram *yhdt brt dlwy);* and Judith wife of Rabbi Hiyya, the latter a major figure in the late second or early third century A.D. *(b. Yebam.* 65; *Qidd.* 12). The absence of Greek personal names in Judith, the presence of such Persian names as "Holofernes" and "Bagoas," and the use of the name "Judith" in the Persian period— all this onomastic material suggests to M. Heltzer that Judith was the product of the Persian, not the Greek, period (ZAW 92 [1980]: 437).

daughter of Merari. The third son of Levi bore the same name (Gen 46:11).

son of Ox [ōx]. This non-Hebrew name may represent a corruption of "Uz" (see the LXX of Gen 22:21, where Heb *'ws,* "Uz," is rendered by the Gk *ōx);* or taking a clue from the ancient versions (see textual note *b),* we might regard *ōx* as a corruption of *oz,* as in *ozi* (= Heb *'zy,* "Uzzi"), a common enough Hebrew name (cf. 1 Chr 6:5–6; 7:2–3; Neh 11:22; 12:19, 42). For further discussion on the significance of all the names in v 1, see COMMENT II, pp. 187–88.

Craven makes, at least at first glance, the fascinating observation that Judith "is of a family two times seven generations removed from Jacob" (SBLDS 70, p. 85); but her finding is dependent upon her rather curious way of counting Judith's ancestors: "Judith is the daughter of Merari who is the son of the fourteenth generation of descendants of Jacob" (p. 84). At face value at least, it would seem that 8:1 lists sixteen ancestors for Judith, not fourteen.

Ananias. This is the Hellenistic equivalent of "Hananiah" (Heb *ḥnnyh,* "Yahweh is gracious"); cf. Tob 5:12; Acts 5:1; 9:10; 23:2.

Raphain. If the form is not corrupt (see textual note *d),* then the name occurs nowhere else in the Bible. However, some scholars, following the Vg, emend to "Raphaim," while others, such as Grintz, read "Rephayah."

Elijah [ēliou]. Or possibly "Elihu," since *ēliou* is used in the LXX for rendering both "Elijah" (2 Kgs 1:3) and "Elihu" (1 Sam 1:1).

Shelumiel [salamiēl]. Despite the variants (see textual note *h),* it is clear that the Greek name represents Shelumiel son of Zurishaddai, a leader of Simeon, who assisted Moses in a variety of ways (cf. Num 1:6; 2:12; 7:36, 41; 10:19).

Zurishaddai. Immediately after this name a number of texts (i.e., LXX^Nbfkr, OL, Syr, and Vg) preserve what must have been in the text originally, namely, "son of Simeon" (see NOTE above). Inasmuch as Simeon is so highly praised by Judith later on (see NOTE on 9:2), the absence of his name here can only be regarded as accidental (see COMMENT II, pp. 187–88). There is some merit to Deprez's suggestion *(Évangile* 47

[1962]: 33) that Judith, like such pseudepigraphical works as Jubilees 30 and the Testament of Levi, tends to rehabilitate the tribe of Simeon (cf. Jdt 8:2; 9:2).

Israel. I.e., Jacob son of Isaac (Gen 32:28).

2. *Manasseh . . . belonged to the same tribe and family.* While marrying within one's family or clan was regarded as praiseworthy (so Numbers 36 and Tob 1:9), it being a method for preventing a woman's wealth from being too dispersed, a certain amount of irony may have also been intended here. After all, in the Hebrew Bible it is ordinarily the husband, rather than his wife, who boasts of a genealogical line; but here Manasseh sits in the shadow of his wife's family tree!

had died during the barley harvest. I.e., in April or May, before the wheat harvest (see NOTE on 2:27). While some scholars have noted certain similarities between the death of Manasseh and that of the son of the Shumanite woman (2 Kgs 4:8–20), those similarities are, as Craven rightly notes (SBLDS 70, pp. 85f., n. 41), quite superficial.

3. *between Dothan and Balamon.* Both places are presumably in the vicinity of Bethulia (see "Dothan" in 4:6). This is the only mention in the Bible of Balamon, unless this is a variant of "Belmain" (4:4) or "Belbaim" (7:3), which may well be the case.

4. *a widow.* Proceeding from the assumption that the story is not historical, scholars have often raised the question of why Judith was depicted as a widow. While the lot of a Jewish widow was often a difficult one, remarriage even of a nonlevirate nature was sometimes a possibility, especially if the woman were, like Judith, beautiful and/or wealthy (cf. Abigail in 1 Sam 25:39, 42; Bathsheba in 2 Sam 11:27; and Ruth).

Enslin (pp. 180–81) sees the celebration of Judith's widowhood as the author's way of honoring the Hasmonean queen Salome Alexandra (76–67 B.C.), widow of Alexander Janneus and sister of the great Pharisee leader Simeon ben Shetaḥ. More likely, the widowhood of Judith actually served for the storyteller a variety of literary and theological purposes. For the plot itself, either a virgin, a prostitute, or a widow could have dared to undertake the "seduction" of Holofernes but certainly not a *good* Jewish wife! Or, as Enslin himself so drolly put it: "Perhaps the presence of a husband would have been an awkward hurdle for our storyteller" (pp. 180–81). Whatever Judith, as a widow, lacked in virginal appeal she could more than make up for with the knowledge and experience of a once married woman. Then too, as Alonso-Schökel has pointed out (p. 14), Judith's self-chosen role of continuing as a widow also qualified her to make special appeal to the God who is "the protector of widows" (Ps 68:5; Sir 35:15), even to the point of making her widowhood the basis of her prayer (Jdt 9:4–9). The more than three years of Judith's widowhood provided her an opportunity to establish in her community the full extent of her piety (so Shumaker, in Alonso-Schökel, p. 32). Then too, the image of the widow as a representation of suffering Israel was a well-established one (Isa 54:4; Lam 1:1; 5:3–4). Finally, there is real merit in the observation of Montague:

> Most unusual in the context of her times, Judith appears childless. Had she had children, the narrator would certainly have mentioned them, for the glory of a woman by the standards of those days was to be a wife and mother, and to be childless was a disgrace. The author therefore seems to be suggesting, at least in the case of Judith, that a woman's glory can consist in something else. Widowed Judith does not think of the right she has by Levirate law to marry a near relative; she

simply gives a part of her heritage to the family of her late husband Manasseh (Judith 16, 24). She retires to a life of prayer, remaining faithful to the love of her youth. Her example breaks with contemporary womanhood and points toward the beginnings of a consecrated religious life, of which there were examples in the first century in the Dead Sea community at Qumran and in the New Testament (see Anna, the prophetess, in Luke 2, 36–37). *(Books of Esther and Judith,* p. 11)

three years and four months. I.e., forty months. However, it is probably coincidental that just as Judith was alone for forty months as a widow, Bethulia was alone under siege for forty days. Had the author wanted to have suggested such a comparison, he would, in all likelihood, have said "forty months."

5. *a shelter . . . on the roof.* The most private part of a home, the rooftop was an appropriate place for Judith's praying (Ps 102:7; Acts 10:9), her mourning (Isa 22:1; Jer 48:38; 2 Sam 18:33), and her private meeting with the magistrates (8:11–36).

wore sackcloth around her waist. Scholars disagree as to the size, shape, and "location" of sackcloth as it was used throughout the Bible (see W. L. Reed, "Sackcloth," IDB, IV, 147). Here, for instance, it is unclear whether Judith's sackcloth was visible to others, for in 9:1 she "uncovered the sackcloth," thereby suggesting that it was next to her skin and so invisible to others. Yet, in 10:3, "she removed the sackcloth . . . and took off her widow's dress," which suggests that the sackcloth was worn on the outside of her dress. Conceivably, Judith was so religious that she wore a sackcloth in both places. More likely, this is one more instance in Judith where the author or a later editor could not keep all his details consistent with one another.

6. *She fasted every day . . . except.* See NOTE on 4:9. Judith's very strenuous fasting practices, which the author obviously approved of, are most in keeping with the beliefs of the Pharisees.

the joyous feasts. Lit. "feasts and joyfulness"; hendiadys. The author evidently had in mind such feasts as Passover and Tabernacles.

7. *shapely and beautiful.* Just like Rachel (Gen 29:17, where the Greek is almost identical), Sara (Gen 12:11), and Esther (Esth 2:7).

remained on her estate. She maintained the property as the proverbial good wife should (Prov 31:10–31). Struck by the ill-fortune of young widowhood, Judith had not just survived: she had prevailed!

8. *so devoutly did she fear God.* "Judith's fear of the Lord," says Craven, "is so profound that she fears no one or thing other than Yahweh" (SBLDS 70, p. 117), neither the magistrates of her town (8:12–17) nor rough Assyrian soldiers late at night in the middle of nowhere (10:11–13) nor even Holofernes himself, filled with wine and desire.

9. *In any event* [lit. "and"]. This verse resumes the story whose flow had been interrupted by the long aside in vv 2–8.

bitter attack. Lit. "wicked words."

10. *the maid [abran].* Although a slave (so 16:23), this unnamed woman exercised considerable authority over Judith's estate, even as the slave Eliezer had over Abraham's property (Gen 15:2; 24:2), and Joseph over Potiphar's (Gen 39:4). More important, she risked her life for her mistress (see Jdt 10:10 and 13:10).

That Judith had a female rather than a male in charge of her estate is one more reason why she was so highly respected in the community (8:8), that is, with no man around there could be no ugly rumors about any improper conduct on her part. Judith would, however, have had a few peasants or hired hands to do some of the heavy manual work. But such men would have occasioned no ugly gossip.

Uzziah. Inasmuch as Uzziah himself responds to Judith's chiding (v 28), he too must have been summoned, as the textual evidence suggests (see textual note ᵐ).

12. Vv 12–14 of the Vg are quite different from the Greek:

This is not a word that may draw down mercy, but rather that may stir up wrath, and enkindle indignation. You have set a time for the mercy of the Lord, and you have appointed him a day, according to your pleasure. But forasmuch as the Lord is patient, let us be penitent for this same thing, and with many tears let us beg his pardon.

to test God. I.e., God must either come to Bethulia's aid within the time period, or the citizens themselves will take drastic action. Cf. Deut 6:16. For an analogous situation, see 1 Sam 11.

14. *the depths of a person's [anthrōpou] heart.* This phrase, along with other "similarities" between this verse and 1 Cor 2:10, persuaded Rendel Harris (but evidently no one else) that the Apostle Paul had read the book of Judith and that 1 Cor 2:10, at least, had been influenced by it (ExpTim 27 [1915–16]: 13–15). But see Job 11:7 and Jer 17:9.

Although modern English translations regularly use here the word "man" (presumably in the generic sense), any sexist overtones are eliminated and the true meaning of the passage is clarified by the use of the word "person." Holofernes is a splendid case in point: clever though he was, he certainly could not read Judith's mind.

16. *do not impose conditions on.* Lit. "do not take the plans for a pledge." Cf. Job 24:3.

to be cajoled. Although the translation is uncertain (see textual note ʳ), it is clear that the author was influenced by the LXX of Num 23:19: "God is not indecisive as a man is, nor to be threatened as a mere mortal is."

18. Vv 18–20 are, perhaps, the chief lesson of Judith. The Vg here is quite different:

For we have not followed the sins of our fathers, who forsook their God, and worshipped strange gods. For which crime they were given up to their enemies, to the sword, and to pillage, and to confusion; but we know no other God but him. Let us humbly wait for his consolation, and the Lord our God will require our blood of the afflictions of our enemies, and he will humble all the nations that shall rise up against us, and bring them to disgrace.

there has not been in our generation [geneais]. Judith's claim that there has been no idolatry of any kind in her own day is further evidence of a postexilic origin for the Judith-story.

19. *a great catastrophe.* I.e., Nebuchadnezzar's destruction of Judah in 586 B.C.

20. *therefore . . . he will not spurn us.* So important is this idea that Israel cannot be defeated unless she sins against her God (vv 18–20) that the author makes the same point on three separate occasions: once by Achior before Holofernes (5:20–21), here, and by Judith before Holofernes (11:10). Of course, the author was not so naive as to think that because Israel was true to her God she could not lose any battles: she could

lose battles, but not the war. For instance, Israel lost many important battles against the Philistines; but the Philistines no longer exist, while the Jewish people still do.

21. *will be exposed.* Lit. "will sit." Frank Zimmermann (JBL 57 [1938]: 72) has suggested that the variant readings (see textual note *ᵖ*) go back to a confusion of the two Heb roots *yšb*, "to sit," and *šbh*, "to carry off." Probably some word like Heb *bdd*, "alone," has dropped out of the Hebrew text.

23. While too paraphrastic, the NEB does express the point quite clearly: "There will be no happy ending to our servitude, no return to favour; the Lord our God will use it to dishonour us." Possibly the author had in mind such happy endings as those of Joseph and Daniel.

24. *lives [psuchē].* Lit. "life," although *psuchē* is used sometimes for Heb *lb/lbb*, "heart," "courage" (Isa 7:2, 4; 13:7).

25. *thanks to . . . God . . . putting us to the test.* The benevolent intent and the salutary effects of God's discipline are to be found in both canonical (cf. Deut 8:5; Ps 94:12; Prov 3:11–12; Heb 12:5–6) and deuterocanonical books (Sir 2:1–6; Wis 3:4–6; Tob 4:20–23).

26. *Remember how he treated Abraham.* Commenting on this allusion to the patriarch, Montague has written: "The use to which the author puts historical names gives us some insight into his literary techniques. Not only is his work a collage of names and places ripped from an original context, it also reveals a studied artistry in what is called the anthological style." *(Books of Esther and Judith,* p. 8) He goes on to find a number of parallels between Judith's story and Abraham's campaign against the kings of the East (Genesis 14), including their very similar general situations and outcomes. While Montague's claim that Achior's release by the Bethulians was influenced, consciously or unconsciously, by Abraham's rescue of Lot strikes the present writer as strained and improbable (compare Exod 14:16 and Jdt 6:14), Montague is probably correct in suggesting that Uzziah's blessing of Judith ("My daughter, more blessed are you by God Most High than all other women on earth! Blessed also is the Lord God, who created the heavens and the earth, who guided you in crushing the head of the leader of our enemies!" [Jdt 13:18]) was influenced, consciously or unconsciously, by Gen 14:19–20: "Blessed be Abram by God Most High, maker of heaven and earth; and blessed be God Most High, who has delivered your enemies into your hand!"

how he tested Isaac. Exactly what event/s the author had in mind is unclear. Isaac's "testing" may have been his silent acquiescence to Abraham's intention to offer him as a human sacrifice (Gen 22:9–15). Then again, as one reads the story of Isaac (Gen 21–28), one might argue that Isaac's entire life was just one big test, consisting, as it did, of one trial after another. The least impressive of the patriarchs, Isaac spent most of his life under the psychological domination of someone else—his father Abraham, his wife Rebekah, Abimelech (Gen 26:1–16), his sons Jacob and Esau, and even his daughter-in-law Judith, who was married to Esau (Gen 26:34–35). Isaac's burdens were many and surely tested him: his wife's barrenness for twenty years (cf. Gen 25:21a, 26b); his blindness (Gen 27:1); and the day-in-day-out tension and hostility between Jacob and Esau, which culminated in Jacob's lying and deceiving his father and, with Rebekah's help, stealing his brother's blessing (Genesis 27). Clearly, Isaac did not have an easy life!

Jacob in Syrian Mesopotamia. I.e., Paddan-aram (Gen 28:2; 31:18), the Syrian Plain and the desert west of the Euphrates in what today is south-central Turkey. In this verse, the Vg adds the name "Moses" (Vg 8:23).

27. *he has not tested [epurōsen].* Lit. "he has not made pass through the fire." Although arguing that *epurōsen* probably means here simply "tested" (as in Ps 66:12 and Isa 43:2), Aage Bentzen (BiblOr 9 [1952]: 174–75) went on to observe that the Greek translator might have been aware of the legend of Abraham in the fiery furnace, a rabbinic tradition traced back to the early second century B.C. V 27 is quoted by Clement of Alexandria in his *Stromata* 2.447. The theodicy of v 27 would probably have been acceptable to the author of Heb 12:7–11.

28. Alonso-Schökel (p. 10) has rightly observed that vv 28–29 are the author's way of forewarning his readers to be alert for subsequent cleverness and subtlety on Judith's part (see especially her double entendres in chap. 11, NOTES *passim).*

with good intentions. Lit. "with a good heart."

29. *and sound judgment.* Lit. "how good is the image of your heart," this Greek phrase occurs only here in the LXX; it may, however, reflect the opposite of that Hebrew idiom found in Gen 8:21: *yṣr lb rʿ,* "the image of the heart is evil."

30. *But the people . . . forced us.* Such a lame excuse by "leaders" is not new to the Bible (cf. Aaron's plea in Exod 32:22, and Saul's excuse in 1 Sam 15:20–24).

an oath we cannot violate. Though made under duress, a promise is a promise. In ancient Israel, no matter how rash (cf. Lev 5:1–4; Judg 11:35) or self-injurious (Ps 15:4) an oath might be, it was still to be regarded as inviolate, even if that oath had been made in good faith under false assumptions (cf. Isaac's blessing of Jacob [Gen 27:34–38]). For more details on the subject, see M. H. Pope, "Oaths," IDB, III, 575–77.

31. *for you are a devout [eusebēs] woman!* Cf. 11:17. In the LXX, *eusebēs* is used to render Heb *ṣdyq,* "just" (Isa 24:16; 26:7), and *yrʾh,* "fear" of the Lord, i.e., reverence (Isa 11:2; 33:6). In any event, Uzziah was speaking to Judith with polite but ironic condescension (so Steinmann, p. 79). Uzziah was saying, in effect, "All *our* prayers have been to no effect, but *yours* God will listen to—and grant!" Evidently the elders allowed Judith to pursue her secret strategy (vv 32–36) not because they had such great confidence in her but because they had nothing to lose.

Then too, as D. N. Freedman has rightly observed:

> The elders may have been quite willing to let Judith go and be lost. Pious and virtuous as she was, she may have been a pain in the neck to the leadership. This is too cynical, but it is very difficult to see how responsible town leaders could allow a lone woman (or two of them) to go off on an adventure like this without more scrutiny and inquiry. . . . Obviously, the author doesn't want to have to divulge anything at this point, so he doesn't bother to resolve the problem. After all, he can do what he pleases in moving his characters along. (private correspondence with this writer)

Freedman's last sentence is especially pertinent; for too often scholars criticize a biblical narrator for not solving a "problem" when, in fact, the narrator's overriding concern was to tell a good story. In other words, effective storytellers know that a reader is, ordinarily, more interested in movement and action than in logical consistency or completeness of detail.

32. *Listen to me.* Not "Hear what I am about to say" but rather "Would you please

listen to what I *have been* saying to you." Judith had been arguing for a radical change in the thinking of the magistrates (vv 12–17, 26–27). But they had not really heard her: all Uzziah could think of was getting an extension of time through a providential rain (v 31).

I am going to do something. Unlike Esther (Esth 4:4–17), Judith acts rather than reacts. Being a woman with neither husband nor foreman to depend upon (cf. 8:10), Judith had learned during her widowhood to depend upon herself.

for endless generations. Lit. "to generations of generations." The author skillfully foreshadows for his readers Judith's subsequent success by emphasizing here her certainty of success and, at the same time, he increases the reader's suspense by not indicating how she will accomplish her mission (vv 33–34).

Once again, the Vg has something quite different here by having Judith say to them:

> As you know that what I have been able to say is of God: so that which I intend to do prove you if it be of God, and pray that God may strengthen my design. (Vg 8:30–31)

34. *the affair [tēn praxin].* As Craven has rightly noted (in "Artistry and Faith in the Book of Judith"), there may very well be a pun intended here; for the Greek word means not only "doing, transaction, business," but also "retribution" *and* "sexual intercourse" (see LSJ, p. 1459).

35. *Go to it!* Lit. "Go in peace." While the Hebrew expression may conjure up in the reader's mind strange but pleasant images of long-gone biblical days, here the idiom represents an enthusiastic "yes," with strong overtones of best wishes for success (cf. Judg 18:6; 1 Sam 1:17; Luke 7:50; 8:48).

May the Lord God go before you. Cf. the LXX of Judg 4:14.

36. *So they left her rooftop shelter.* Cf. v 5. The use here of a participial phrase, while perfectly good Greek, is a relatively rare phenomenon in Judith, the Greek translator usually preferring the literal paratactic succession of Greek verbs joined by *kai,* "and," in imitation of the Hebrew *waw* consecutive. It is curious that the translator was so prosaic and literalistic in his grammatical constructions and yet so prolific and effusive in his Greek vocabulary (see INTRODUCTION).

Comment I

Enter the heroine. At last! Although it has taken the author seven whole chapters (146 verses!) to set the stage for Judith's appearance, now that she is on the scene he quickly and deftly introduces her, beginning with what is most important to him: her Jewish lineage (v 1), and her religious character and practice (vv 2, 4–6). Only after that does the author note that Judith is also beautiful, shapely, and wealthy (v 7). After all, while it will be Judith's physical assets that will enable her to entice Holofernes, it is her piety and faith in God that really qualify her for the task—and assure her of success.

In spite of Judith's beauty and wealth, no one spoke ill of her (v 8). A further measure of Judith's stature in the community was the fact that, although a female *and* a widow, she could still summon the town magistrates to her home for a private meeting. Moreover, despite an initial deference to them ("Please hear me out" [v 11]), Judith proceeded to address them not as a peer but as their superior, rebuking them for their faithless and presumptuous act of putting God to the test (vv 11–17).[127] Rightly regarding the people's interpretation of their circumstances as a counsel of despair (see 7:23–28), Judith insisted on a different theological explanation for the siege: instead of God's abandoning his people (as the elders had argued in 7:30) or punishing them for their sins (as the people had maintained in 7:28), God was actually testing them, just as he had their ancestors (8:18–27). With some justification, one might describe Judith as the sole female theologian in the OT.

But Judith did more than explain the crisis: she acted on it. Instead of waiting for God to do something for them, the people themselves, she argued, should act, calling upon God to help them help themselves (v 17). And so when Uzziah continued to remain passive in a wait-and-see attitude, justifying his position on the grounds that he could not violate the promise he had made earlier to the people (vv 28–31), Judith again took the initiative, promising to do something with her own hands that would make her name immortal among her people (vv 32–34). It is the final measure of Judith's stature and of the magistrates' passivity that they immediately approved her proposal and allowed two defenseless women to go out and brave the Assyrian army. God, they assured her, would be going with her (v 35). (But none of the men of Bethulia would.) The magistrates, in their passivity and lack of faith, serve well as foils for the assertive, believing Judith.[128]

---

[127] Craven rightly characterizes the entire scene with the elders as comic: "That the three officials drop everything and come to the house of this pious widow for a sound upbraiding is a marvelously incongruous occurrence in a story as thoroughly male dominated as is the story of the Book of Judith" (SBLDS 70, pp. 86–87). An appreciation for the humor in Judith sometimes prompts amusing, if idle, speculations by modern commentators; for example, Enslin's fascinating observation: "Judith herself may be a bit too good to be true, and the reader may be inclined to wonder if her husband Manasseh did not find life with her at times as trying as presumably Xantippe *[sic]* had with Socrates. But these wonderings come as we reflect on the story, not while we are reading it." (p. 42)

Reacting to the preceding quotation, D. N. Freedman was prompted to observe: "We know very little about Judith before her widowhood, so it is hard to tell what kind of wife she was: no doubt she was the model of rectitude, and no doubt such people can be hard to live with. . . . The fact that she is able to play the part of a vamp and seductress (even if it is done very chastely) implies a more flexible personality." (private correspondence with this writer)

[128] To be sure, as D. N. Freedman has observed to this writer: "For obvious reasons the author didn't want any men along. That would make the ruse and the plan much more difficult. Only women make it possible and feasible. There is an analogy in the story of Abraham and Sarah in Genesis 12; Sarah must do the job herself, and thus save Abraham's life. The theme of attractive women using their physical attributes to save their men is not unknown, but in the biblical cases the women must also preserve their virtue. That is what gives the stories their unusual appeal, and makes them safe for the Bible." One can agree with Freedman's observations, but the fact

Comment II

Judith, with at least sixteen named ancestors, has the longest genealogy of any woman in the Bible. Apart from "Ox," which is probably a corruption, all are good Hebrew names. Nonetheless, only three names in the genealogy unquestionably represent the well-known historical personage bearing that name, namely, her three most-distant ancestors: Shelumiel, Zurishaddai, and Israel. This section of the genealogy is what Martin Noth has termed a "primary genealogy" (i.e., a genealogy that exists apart from the narrative in which it is presently found), in contrast to a "secondary genealogy," which has no existence apart from the narrative in question (Noth, *History of Pentateuchal Traditions*).

Inasmuch as Judith's covers a time span of well over a thousand years, the list, if genuine, is obviously incomplete; for not only are important names like "Simeon" omitted, but there is an interval of several hundred years between the time of Zurishaddai and Israel/Jacob.

Considerable new light on the forms and functions of OT genealogies has been cast by Robert R. Wilson, who has drawn extensively upon anthropological studies of present-day "primitive" peoples (JBL 94 [1975]: 169–89). Wilson has shown that genealogies in the OT as well as Sumerian and Akkadian king lists serve a wide variety of functions, including political, social, geographic, and religious purposes (or, to use Wilson's categories, the domestic, the politico-jural, and the religious spheres). Because function can influence form and form, in turn, can impose restrictions on function, the historiographic worth of OT genealogies, argues Wilson, must be determined in each individual case, for "in dealing with the issue of the historiographic value of genealogy, no generalizations are possible" (p. 189). In short, genealogical lists can tell the historian a lot, but not much about actual bloodlines and descent.

It may very well be that Judith's genealogy is totally fictitious, designed solely to provide historical coloring (so Ball); but if so, it is "strangely elaborate" (Cowley, p. 256). E. J. Bruns (CBQ 16 [1954]: 14) thinks that the genealogy's very length argues for its authenticity. Perhaps more persuasive is Steinmann's theory that the author, after looting certain genealogical lists from Numbers and Nehemiah, made up his genealogy in order "to mock the aristocrats of his time [i.e., in the days of Demetrius I, Soter] who fabricated their genealogies for themselves whenever genuine pedigree were lacking to them" (p. 74). If Steinmann is correct in this, then Judith's long genealogy is

---

remains that neither Abraham nor the men of Bethulia increase in stature because of the actions of a Sarah or Judith. In both situations, the stature of the men is diminished.

but one more example of the author's sense of humor. On the other hand, the genealogy may well have served another and more important purpose for the ancient reader: it confirmed for him the Jewish lineage of Judith by tracing her ancestry all the way back to Simeon and Jacob.

IX. Judith Prays God to Help Her
(9:1–14 [Vg 9:1–19])

9 ¹Then Judith prostrated herself, put ashes on her head,ᵃ and uncovered the sackcloth she had been wearing. And just as the evening's incense offering was being offered in the Temple at Jerusalem, Judith cried aloud to the Lord and said, ²"Lord, the God of my ancestor Simeon, into whose hand you put a sword to take revenge on the foreigners who had violated the virgin's womb, uncovering her thighs to her shame and polluting her womb to her dishonor. For you said, 'This shall not be done!' Yet they did it. ³So you handed over their leaders to slaughter and their bed, ᵇblushing for her deceivedᵇ, to bloodshed. You struck down the slaves with the princes and the princes upon their thrones. ⁴You handed over their wives for rape and their daughters for slavery and all their spoils for distribution among your beloved children, who had been so zealous for you and had been appalled at the pollution of their blood and had called upon you for help. God, my God, hear me also—a widow!

⁵"For you are responsible for all these things and for what preceded and what followed them. You designed the present and the future; and what you had in mind has happened. ⁶The things you have planned present themselves and say, 'Here we are!' For all your ways are prepared beforehand, and you judge with foreknowledge.

⁷"Here are the greatly reinforced Assyrians, boasting of their horses and riders, priding themselves in the strength of their infantry, trusting in shields and javelins, in bows and slings! They do not know that you are 'the Lord who crushes wars; ⁸the Lord is your name.' Dash their might by your powers;ᶜ in your anger bring down their strength! For they plan to desecrate your sanctuary, to defile the tabernacle, the resting place of your glorious name, to knock off the horns of your altar with the sword! ⁹Observe their arrogance and bring your fury on

---

ᵃ LXXᶠᵏ, OL, and Syr add "she took off her dress."

ᵇ⁻ᵇ So LXXᴬˢ and a number of mins.; LXXᴮ "ashamed *[ēdesato]* of the deceit they had practiced"; see NOTE.

ᶜ LXXᶠᵏ, OLˢ, and Syr add "Eternal, crush their number."

their heads: put into my hand—a widow's—the strength I need. [10] By the guile of my lips strike down the slave with the ruler and the ruler with his servant.[d] Break their pride by the hand of a female! [11] For your strength does not depend upon numbers nor your might[e] upon powerful men. Rather, you are the God of the humble; you are the ally of the insignificant, the champion of the weak, the protector of the despairing, the savior of those without hope.

[12] "Please, please, God of my father and God of Israel's heritage, ruler of heaven and earth, creator of the waters, king of all your creation, hear my prayer: [13] Grant me a beguiling tongue for wounding and bruising those who have terrible designs against your covenant and your sacred house, even against Mount Zion and the house your children possess. [14] Demonstrate to [f]every nation[f] and every tribe that you are God, [g]the God[g] of all power and might, and there is no one who protects the people of Israel but you."

[d] LXX[s] adds "Send your wrath upon their heads. Give into my hands, a widow's, what I need."

[e] LXX[fk], OL[s], and Syr add "nor share."

[f-f] So LXX[fk] and OL; the rest have "all your nation"; see NOTE.

[g-g] LXX[B] omits by haplography.

Notes

9:1 *Then [de].* This *de* is but one more reminder of the Hebraic cast of the translator's Greek; for, as Enslin has rightly pointed out (p. 121), instead of using *kai* for the Heb *wa,* "and," as the translator usually does, he employs here the mildly adversative *de;* yet only once does the translator use *de* in its classical sense as a follow-up for the Gk *men* (5:21).

the evening's incense offering. Burned in the morning and evening on the incense altar inside the Temple before the veil of the Holy of Holies (cf. Exod 30:7–8; 40:5; Lev 4:7; 1 Chr 28:18), the "pure" incense of Herodian times contained, according to Josephus *(Wars* 5.5.5), thirteen ingredients. While some of the ingredients were local, others were imported and more exotic (see Nigel Groom, *Frankincense and Myrrh: A Study of the Arabian Incense Trade,* as well as D. F. Graf's review of it in BA 45 [1982]: 63).

2. *Simeon, into whose hand you put a sword.* In spite of the fact that Gen 34:30 and 49:5–7 are quite critical of Simeon's taking revenge on the Shechemites for Hamor's rape of his sister Dinah (cf. Genesis 34), Judith spoke approvingly of Simeon's act, possibly because Judith found herself in a position analogous to Dinah's, i.e., she herself might end up being raped by the uncircumcised Holofernes. To say that Judith has some concern for being raped—what woman wouldn't?—is not to deny the truth of D. N. Freedman's observation: "Judith is going to emulate Simeon, not Dinah; I doubt whether she is much worried about being raped. She was much more concerned about killing Holofernes. In other words, she identifies with the avenger, Simeon, rather than with the victim, Dinah." (private correspondence with this writer) On Judith's revisionist position toward Simeon, see NOTE on "Zurishaddai" in 8:1.

Here, as in 9:9 (see NOTE there on "my hand"), the Greek word *cheir* (= Heb *yd)* must be translated literally as "hand," instead of figuratively as "power."

who had violated the virgin's womb. Lit. "who loosened the virgin's womb." Virtually all modern English translations ignore the unanimous witness of the Greek manuscripts which have *mētran,* "womb," preferring instead to accept Grotius's suggestion of long ago that *mitran,* "headdress," "girdle," or possibly "veil," was the original reading. While the unanimous agreement of Greek manuscripts is certainly not sufficient reason for automatically accepting a particular reading as original, neither is such unanimity to be lightly dismissed, especially if a reasonable case can be made for the reading's retention. Such is the case here. For while scholars such as Enslin are undoubtedly correct in insisting that the underlying Hebrew phrase here could not have been *pth rhm* "to loosen/open the womb," because such a Hebrew idiom would refer to God's ending a woman's barrenness (cf. Heb *sgr rhm* in 1 Sam 1:5; cf. also Gen 20:18) rather than to a man's raping a woman, there is no certainty as to what the underlying Hebrew word in Judith actually was. In any event, the Greek word used here, *luō,* "to loosen," can also mean "to break" or "to violate" (cf. LSJ, pp. 1068f.). Thus, instead of regarding the three Greek verbs in this verse as representing three successive stages in the rape, we are better advised to regard the first verb as a description of the offense and the next two verbs as specific stages in that violation, namely, the exposure and rape of the maiden's body. Such an interpretation justifies rendering the last two verbs as English participles.

3. *blushing [ēdesato] for her deceived.* This translation, along with those in modern versions, is most uncertain. It is unclear from the Greek evidence whether the personified bed is ashamed of Hamor's conduct (so LXX[B]) or is embarrassed about the virgin's plight (so LXX[AS]). In either case, however, it would seem that such a "sympathetic bed" did not deserve being further stained by blood; yet it was. The JB would attempt to avoid all these difficulties by translating *ēdesato* as "defiled": "For this you handed their leaders over to slaughter, their bed defiled by their deceit, to blood."

and the princes upon their thrones. There is no manuscript support in the Greek for JB's "and the chiefs with their servants," although, admittedly, the phrase makes an attractive chiasmus to the preceding one, "You struck the slaves down with the chiefs." The chiasmus of v 10 notwithstanding, the Greek text does not justify such an emendation.

4. *their wives for rape [eis pronomen].* Cf. the second NOTE on 4:12, where the same expression occurs. Although Gen 34:2–31 does not explicitly state that any of the sons of Jacob raped any women of Shechem, certainly that can be assumed. (The preceding statement presupposes the popular view that "Simeon" and "Levi" in Genesis 34 are eponymous names, representing members of those two clans and not just two individuals.) If there had been no raping during the taking of Shechem, the situation would

have been rare in the annals of man, i.e., a violent, bloody attack against a city for its sexual insult, with slaughter, looting—but no raping—as part of that retaliation.

a widow! This is a nice touch by the author. At least defenseless Dinah had brothers to help her. Judith has no one.

5. *you are responsible [epoiēsas].* Lit. "you made/did."

You designed [dienoēthēs] . . . the future. Lit. "you intended the things now and the things that are coming." Although the Greek of v 5 is rather clumsy, the author is giving clear enough expression to an idea frequently found in Deutero-Isaiah, namely, the foreknowledge of God (cf. Isa 41:22–23; 42:9; 43:9; 44:7; 46:9f.). While the term "foreknowledge" does not occur in the OT, the concept itself is clearly present there (for details, see B. W. Anderson, "Foreknow, Foreknowledge," IDB, II, 311–14).

6. *Here we are!* This response of historical events, which are personified here, is reminiscent of that of the lightning in Job 38:35 and of the stars in Bar 3:34.

you judge with foreknowledge [prognōsei]. Lit. "your judgment [is] with foreknowledge." In the LXX, this term occurs only here and in 11:19, although it does occur also in Acts 2:23 and 1 Pet 1:2.

7. *greatly reinforced [eplēthunthēsan en dunamei].* Lit. "they are increased in power." See NOTE on 7:2.

horses and riders. Here begins an allusion to the Song of the Sea (cf. Exod 15:1).

7–8. *the Lord who crushes wars; the Lord is your name.* (Cf. also Jdt 16:2.) Judith is quoting here Exod 15:3 as found in the LXX, a rendering which differs somewhat from the MT's "The Lord is a man of war; the Lord is his name." (Because Judith is praying to God, she, understandably, has recast the quotation into the second person rather than leaving it in the third.) Failure to recognize this passage in Judith as a biblical quotation resulted in SG's offering a translation which, while grammatically possible, is clearly semantically incorrect: ". . . that you are a lord that crushes wars. The Lord is your name." God's very name, "Lord" (Gk *kurios),* is the expression of his supremacy over all the world.

The corresponding verse in the Vg is considerably different and clearly has Exodus 15 in mind:

> Look upon the camp of the Assyrians now, as you were pleased to look upon the camp of the Egyptians, when they pursued armed after your servants, trusting in their chariots, and in their horsemen, and in a multitude of warriors. But you looked over their camp, and darkness wearied them. The deep held their feet, and the waters overwhelmed them. (Vg 9:6–7)

9. *bring* ["send"] *your fury.* Evidently another phrase taken from the Song of the Sea (Exod 15:7).

my hand. As Patrick Skehan has rightly pointed out (CBQ 25 [1963]: 94–110), the word "hand" (Gk *cheir* = Heb *yd)* looms large in Judith once the heroine appears, it being mentioned only once prior to her appearance (2:12) and nine times after chap. 7. Where "hand" designates "a meaningful instrument," it should, according to Skehan, be translated literally (so in 8:33; 9:2, 9; 13:14; 15:10); in the remaining instances it should be translated figuratively (so in 9:10; 12:4; 13:15; 16:5). Skehan insists that just as in the Exodus story God's hand (Exod 3:19, 20; 13:9; 14:31) was Moses' (cf. Exod 4:2; 10:21–22; 14:21, 26–27), so, he argues, in Judith God uses the weakest of hands, a widow's. This theme of God using the hand of the weak and lowly, Skehan notes, is also developed in the *War Scroll* from Qumran (1QM xi and xiii, 13–14).

10. The verse contains a striking example of chiasmus:

strike down the slave with the ruler
and the ruler with his servant

and the ruler with his servant. I.e., everyone; a good example of merismus. Judith is again alluding to "the Shechem incident" (Genesis 34).

by the hand of a female! Inasmuch as *thēleia* is used here rather than *gunē* (the latter the most common Greek word for "woman"), modern versions have weakened Judith's point by rendering *thēleia* here as "woman"; for *thēleia* (= Heb *nqbh)* is the less honorific of the two, it not being a term restricted to humans. Nonetheless, for a man to be killed by a woman was regarded as a disgrace (Judg 9:52–54).

One familiar with the OT can scarcely read the phrase "by the hand of a female" without thinking of Jael, who made Sisera's defeat ignominious as well as total by driving a tent pin through his skull (Judg 4–5). Possessing the beauty and brains of Queen Esther, Judith had also the audacity and physicality of Jael. Neither Jael nor Judith could be said to be the least bit squeamish.

In the Vg, the verses corresponding to 9:9–10 of the LXX are quite different:

> Bring to pass, O Lord, that his pride may be cut off with his own sword. Let him be caught in the net of his own eyes in my regard, and strike him by the gracious words of my lips. Give me constancy in my mind, that I may despise him, and fortitude that I may overthrow him. For this will be a glorious monument for your name, when he shall fall by the hand of a woman. (Vg 9:12–15)

11. *your strength does not depend upon numbers nor your might upon powerful men.* A common enough view in the OT, this idea was also voiced by David to Goliath (2 Sam 17:45–47), by Hananai to King Asa (2 Chr 16:8–9), and by God himself to Gideon (Judg 7:2).

As in the preceding verse, we have here a chiasmus:

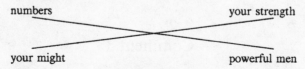

ally . . . protector . . . savior.* While such ideas and terms can be found scattered throughout the Bible, the influence of the Song of the Sea here is indisputable, for these Greek words in Judith *(boēthos, skepastēs,* and *sōtēr,* respectively) even occur in the same order as in the LXX of Exod 15:2. Yet vv 11b–12 are more than just a faint echo of Exod 15:2; for as Craven has so astutely noted, they constitute a litany composed of ten titles for God, five on either side of the words "Please, please." (AFBJ, p. 91) Brian McNeil *(The Downside Review* 96 [1978], 199–207) views this verse as "the basic meaning" of the entire book of Judith (p. 200).

ally of the insignificant. Lit. "helper of the smaller."

12. *my father. Patros mou* may refer to Simeon, in which case it should be translated "ancestor/forefather" (so Ball and NEB); but more likely, the author had in mind Judith's own father, inasmuch as the five appellations go from the specific ("God

of my father") through the more general ("God of Israel's . . . waters") to the all-inclusive ("king of all your creation"). Several of these expressions, at least in their Greek form, occur nowhere else in the LXX, namely, "God of Israel's heritage," "ruler of heaven and earth," and "creator of the waters" (so Ball, p. 324). Nonetheless, they sound Semitic and seem quite compatible with the religious sentiments of the day.

13. *Grant me a beguiling tongue.* Lit. "Give me a word *[logon]* and a deceit *[apatēn],*" which is hendiadys. Instead of *logon,* the Syriac has *dolon,* "cunning," which clearly represents an inner-Greek corruption, *lambda, delta,* and *gamma* being on occasion easily confused with one another (cf. the LXX of 2 Sam 14:20; Ps 138:4).

The theme of deceit *[apatē]* figures prominently in Judith's prayer, some form of it being mentioned also in vv 3 (twice) and 10.

As Craven has rightly observed: "The Book of Judith calls for a radical reorientation of religious sensibilities. Were Job to say to Judith as he said to Zophar, 'Will you speak falsely for God, speak deceitfully for him?' (Job 13:7), Judith might respond that in certain circumstances such unexpected behavior might be justified." (SBLDS 70, p. 114)

who have terrible designs. Lit. "who intended harsh things." This is Judith's justification for asking God for that which a good Yahwist would ordinarily abhor, a beguiling tongue. Compare Add Esth C 24, where Esther prays for "persuasive speech." (For other comparisons between the prayers of Judith and Esther, see COMMENT II, p. 197).

14. *to every nation and every tribe.* I.e., to all the world, not just to Jews. In spite of the fact that this interpretation reflects a distinctly minority reading (see textual note *ʳ⁾*), it is probably correct; otherwise, we should have to understand that Israel did not already know that God alone protected it. And that would seem to contradict Judith's own earlier assessment of Israel's faith (cf. 8:18, 20).

Comment I

A woman of habitual prayer, Judith quite naturally prayed to God immediately before undertaking her dangerous mission. While she does not indicate to the reader exactly what strategy she has in mind, it is clear from the prayer that Judith herself knew. The author does give his reader some intimation of it by having Judith cite as the justification for her dangerous and deceitful task the precedent set by her ancestor Simeon. Some scholars argue that Judith prayed for the success of her mission (i.e., that her enemies be destroyed) but, to her credit, did not pray for her own physical survival or honor.

Judith's religious views, while neither felicitously nor memorably expressed, are nonetheless quite clear, namely, retributive justice (vv 2–3),

God's omnipotence and omniscience (vv 5–6), the true basis of might and power (vv 7–8, 11), the central importance of Jerusalem and its Temple (vv 8, 13), and God's universality (vv 12, 14). As Craven has so rightly observed: "Hers is the creator/redeemer God known in history. Judith proposed nothing that the psalmists had not already prescribed:

> Let the high praises of God be in their throats
> and two-edged swords in their hands,
> to wreak vengeance on the nations and chastisements
> on the peoples. (Ps. 149:7–8)." (SBLDS 70, p. 114)

But if most, or at least many, of the important ideas of Judaism exist in Judith, that is all they really do, that is, they do not seem alive and vibrant. In short, this is not one of the great prayers of the Apocrypha.[129]

Comment II

The religious and literary strengths and "weaknesses" of Judith's prayer are brought into higher relief when it is compared with the LXX's Prayer of Queen Esther (Add Esth C 12–30), the latter prayer, *a priori*, being the one one might most expect to resemble Judith's.

Although the Hebrew account of Esther does not explicitly say that Esther prayed to God before she dared present herself to the king unannounced (cf. Esth 4:10–17), the author of that book certainly intimates to his readers that she will pray when he has Esther say to Mordecai:

> "Go and gather all the Jews now in Susa and fast for me. Don't eat or drink for three days, either day or night; and I, with my maids, will fast as you do. In this condition I'll go to the king, even though it's against the law." (Esth 4:16)

Here Esther was certainly asking, in effect, for the Jewish community to pray for her; but in keeping with the author's practice elsewhere in the book of Esther, he studiously avoided clear references to things *obviously* religious, like the words "God," "prayer," "intervene," "intercede." (For details on the absence of religious elements in Esther as well as on "fasting" as a code word for praying, see AB 7B, pp. xxxii–iv and 51f., respectively.)

But what can, at best, only be inferred from the Hebrew account of Esther is explicitly stated in its Greek version: Esther prayed a long prayer before going to the king unannounced. (For a discussion of the religious elements in the Greek version of Esther, see AB 44, pp. 158–59.) Esther's prayer, re-

---

[129] While none of the prayers in Judith rank with the great prayers of the Apocrypha, let alone of the OT, they do contain the basic tenets of Judaism (for details, see references *passim* in Johnson, *Prayer in the Apocrypha*, especially pp. 67–77).

corded in what is conventionally called an Addition (or Add), is found in Add Esth C 12–30 (= Vg 14:1–19):

C   12 Queen Esther was terrified and sought refuge in the Lord. 13 She took off her stately robes and put on clothes appropriate for distress and mourning, and instead of extravagant perfumes she covered her head with ashes and dung. She debased her body completely, and she covered with her disheveled hair those parts which she ordinarily loved to adorn. 14 Then she prayed to the Lord God of Israel and said,

"My Lord, only you are our king! Help me who am alone and have no helper except you, 15 for I am risking my life. 16 All my life I have heard in my family's tribe that you, Lord, chose Israel from all the nations, and our fathers from all their predecessors, for a perpetual inheritance; and you treated them just as you had promised.

17 "But now we have sinned against you, and you have handed us over to our enemies 18 because we extolled their gods. You were in the right, Lord. 19 Nevertheless, they are not satisfied that we are in galling slavery; but they have made an agreement with their gods 20 to nullify the promise you made, to blot out your inheritance, to silence the lips of those who praise you, to quench the glory of your house and altar, 21 to open the mouths of the pagans for the praise of idols, and to idolize for ever a mere mortal king. 22 Do not relinquish your scepter, Lord, to nonexistent gods. And do not let them laugh at our downfall. Frustrate their plot and make an example of him who started it all! 23 Remember, Lord, reveal yourself in this time of our afflictions! Give me courage, King of the gods and Lord of all governments!

24 "Make me persuasive before the lion and dispose him to hate the one who fights against us so that there may be an end of him and of those agreeing with him. 25 Rescue us by your hand and help me who am alone and have no one except you, Lord.

"You know everything 26 so you know that I hate the pomp of the wicked, and I loathe the bed of the uncircumcised—and of any foreigner. 27 You know my 'duty': that I loathe that symbol of my exalted position which is upon my head. When I appear at court—I loathe it like a menstruous rag—I do not wear it when I am not at court. 28 Your maid servant has not dined at Haman's table, nor have I extolled a royal party nor drunk the wine of libations. 29 From the day I arrived here until now, your maid servant has not delighted in anything except you, Lord, the God of Abraham. 30 God, whose might prevails over all, hear the voice of the despairing, and save us from the hands of the wicked! And Lord, protect me from my fears!"

For a detailed analysis of this translation, which is the present writer's, see AB 44, pp. 208–14.

Esther's prayer, like Judith's, is quite appropriate for her particular circumstances. Recognizing the dangers confronting herself personally (vv 14b–15, 25) and her people in general (vv 19–23a) and their cult and Temple in Jerusalem (v 20), Esther asked for courage and persuasiveness in dealing with the king (vv 23b–24, 30c). Convinced that the present exile of the Jews was deserved punishment for their sins (vv 17–18), Esther was nonetheless mindful of God's ancient promises to his people (vv 16, 20). For her, God was both a personal reality (v 29) who responds to the prayers of the despairing (v 30) and yet is transcendent, being both omnipotent (vv 23, 30) and omniscient (vv 25, 27). And lest the fact that she served as Persian queen be interpreted as proof that she had been compromised by the uncircumcised Gentiles, Esther stressed both her anti-Gentile position and her great concern for kašrût, i.e., laws concerning ceremonial, ritual, or dietary "cleanness" (vv 26–29). For the author of this particular addition[130] Esther's prayer provided him the opportunity to express his own theological concerns. While a number of those concerns are not present in the MT of Esther, or at least they are not explicitly mentioned, one of his views needs special comment, namely, the author's anti-Gentile attitude (vv 26, 28). Unlike the MT, where the author of Esther evidences a somewhat sympathetic attitude toward the Gentile king, the LXX Esther is very anti-Gentile, i.e., what in the MT had been essentially a court intrigue became in the Greek version an eternal, cosmic conflict between Jew and Gentile (see in AB 44 the NOTES on Add Esth A 6; F 5, 8; see there also p. 249).

When the prayers of Esther and Judith are compared, both their similarities and differences are quite evident. Both prayers well express the particular yet similar needs of the heroines: courage and persuasiveness for Esther (Add Esth C 23–24, 30); strength and guile for Judith (Jdt 9:9–10, 13). Both prayers became vehicles for expressing the respective author's religious views. Both women prayed more for the success of their cause than for their personal safety (but see Add Esth C 15). If Judith's prayer seems more self-assured and violent than Esther's, that, too, is understandable; for the one woman was accustomed to the dependencies and niceties of harem life; the other experienced life as a widow, albeit a rich one. Then too, while Esther fully accomplished her mission through the exercise of "feminine wiles" (cf. Esth 5:1–8; 7:1–10), without literally staining her hands, Judith had to resort to "masculine brutality" by beheading Holofernes (13:7–9).

While a reasonably convincing case can be made for saying that the Greek literary style of Esther's prayer is "better" than that of Judith's, the question of which prayer is *ethically* better is more open to debate. This presents somewhat of a dilemma; for while Judith is pious (Jdt 8:4–8, 31) but deceitful and personally violent (9:9–10, 13), the Greek Esther is pious but strongly anti-Gentile (Add Esth C 26, 28). But then again, neither saints nor great leaders are ever perfect; otherwise their people would not understand them or follow them.

---

[130] There are six Additions in the LXX Esther, and they had more than one author. For details on the Additions in general, see AB 44, pp. 153–55 and 165–67.

X. After Prettying Herself Up, Judith Goes to the Camp of the Enemy (10:1–17 [Vg 10:1–16])

10 [1] When[a] Judith had stopped calling on the God of Israel and had finished saying all these things, [2] she arose from her prostrate position, summoned her maid, and went down into the house where she spent her sabbaths and feasts. [3] She removed the sackcloth she had been wearing and took off her widow's dress. Then she bathed all over with water, anointed herself with rich perfume, fixed[b] her hair, put a tiara on it, and dressed herself in the clothes she used to wear on the joyous occasions when her husband Manasseh was alive. [4] Then she slipped sandals on her feet and put on her anklets and bracelets, her rings and earrings, and all her jewelry. (She had made herself very fetching so as 'to catch the attention of the men' who would see her.) [5] She then handed her maid a skin of wine and a jug of oil, filled a bag with roasted grain, dried fig cakes, and pure bread;[d] then she packed all her dishes and 'had her maid carry them'.

[6] They then went toward the town gate of Bethulia and found Uzziah standing there with the other town elders, Chabris and Charmis. [7] And when they saw her (for her face was so transformed and her clothes so different), they were much struck by her beauty. They said to her, [8] "May the God of our ancestors grant you favor and fulfill your plans so that the Israelites may glory and Jerusalem exult!" She[f] bowed ᵍto themᵍ [9] and said to them, "Order the town gate to be opened for me, and I will go out and accomplish the things you have just mentioned to me." So they ordered the young men to open up for her,

---

ᵃ Gk *kai egeneto.*
ᵇ LXX "arranged"; LXXᵇᵇ, OL "combed"; OLᶜ and Vg "plaited"; Syr "anointed"; see NOTE.
ᶜ˗ LXX *eis apantēsin,* "for meeting [LXXᴺˢ, Eth *apatēsin,* "enticing"; LXXᶠᵏ, OLˢᵐ, Syr *arpagēn,* "ravaging"] of men's eyes."
ᵈ LXXᵇᶠᵏ, OL, Syr, and Vg add "and cheese."
ᵉ˗ Gk "she put [them] on her."
ᶠ LXXᴺ and many mins. "they."
ᵍ˗ᵍ LXX and verss. all read "to God"; see NOTE.

just as she^ had asked, ^10 and they did so. When Judith went out, accompanied by her maid, the men of the town kept staring after her until she had gone down the hill and crossed the valley, where they lost sight of her.

^11 As the women^i were going straight on through the valley, an Assyrian patrol came upon her, ^12 took her into custody, and demanded, "What is your nationality? Where are you coming from? And where are you going?" "I am a daughter of the Hebrews," she replied, "and I am running away from them because you are about to eat them up! ^13 So I am on my way to Holofernes himself, the general in command of your army, with reliable information, and only in his presence will I indicate a way by which he can go and conquer all the hill country without risking life or limb of his men."

^14 As the men listened to her explanation and studied her face, they were much struck by her beauty, so they said to her, ^15 "By hurrying down to our lord's presence you have saved your life. So now proceed to his headquarters, and some of us will escort you and deliver you into his hands. ^16 And when you are standing before him, don't be afraid. Tell him what you have just told us, and he will treat you well^j." ^17 They then detailed from their number a hundred men to conduct her and her attendant, and these led them to Holofernes' quarters.

^h So LXX^ANS and most mins. and verss.; LXX^Bℵ "they."
^i LXX "they."
^j Gk eu; LXX^A euthē, "fairly."

Notes

10:1. This verse, which in Greek seems, stylistically speaking, needlessly repetitious as well as too literalist a rendering of the Hebrew (see textual note ^a), well illustrates the problems and temptations confronting an English translator. At the one extreme is the slavishly literal KJ ("And it came to pass, when she had ceased . . . all these words"); at the other is the NEB ("When Judith had ended her prayer"), which is far too paraphrastic. While the modern reader may well prefer the brevity of the NEB's conciseness, that "conciseness" is not so much a translation of the Greek as a rewriting of the story in English. Like Odysseus, who had to steer between Scylla and the equally destructive Charybdis, the conscientious translator of the Bible has to steer a middle course between the rocks of literalism and the whirlpool of paraphrase. Although Odysseus successfully avoided both dangers, biblical translators regularly find themselves caught on one or the other.

3. *removed the sackcloth . . . and . . . her widow's dress. . . . dressed herself in the clothes . . . [of] joyous occasions.* Just as a soldier facing battle takes much care preparing himself and his arms, so our Female Warrior dressed herself with much deliberateness. Any similarities here between the preparations of our Female Warrior and those of Ishtar in the *Hedammu* myth, rightly says Bentzen, are purely coincidental *(Archiv Orientâlní* 18 [1950]: 1–2). Had she appealed to Holofernes in drab clothes and without first prettying herself up, Judith would have had a more difficult time gaining a hearing or establishing credibility (so Lamparter, p. 169). Alonso-Schökel has perceived a more literary and subliminal reason for all this: "If the mourning of Judith was also a lament for the destitution of her people, so her festive attire anticipates their solution . . . [as in] Isa 52:1–2 . . . Baruch 5:1–2 . . . Judith's recovered beauty is almost a 'symbolic action' of salvation" (p. 7). Both explanations are correct, the same words or images in good writing often having more than one level of meaning or truth.

bathed all over. Lit. "washed her body." In the LXX, *periekluzō* occurs only here and Tob 6:2.

fixed her hair. Cf. 16:8. Exactly what Judith did to her hair is unclear. She could even have braided it (so SG), as we know from braided human hair found at Masada, dating to A.D. 73. Zimmermann (JBL 57 [1938]: 69) would explain all the variant readings (see textual note *ᵇ)* not as uncertainties as to the precise meaning of the Aramaic or Greek term but rather as the corruption of the original Hebrew term itself, namely, Heb *wtsk,* "she anointed," > *wtsdr,* "she arranged," > *wtsrq,* "she combed."

anointed herself with rich [lit. "thick"] *perfume.* Not "dabbed herself," as modern women often do, putting here and there a drop of perfume. In the Ancient Near East, some women went so far as to saturate or "fumigate" their bodies (see W. F. Albright, "Lachish Cosmetic Burner," pp. 25–32).

3–4. *She removed . . . took off. . . . bathed . . . anointed . . . fixed . . . put . . . dressed. . . . slipped . . . put on.* Depending upon how one counts these verbs (i.e., "removed" along with "took off" and "bathed" along with "anointed" may be counted either as the four original verbs or as two verbs and their glosses), one might say that the author described Judith's preparation in terms of seven stages. "Sequenced physical descriptions are known," writes Craven, "by the genre designation *wasf.* Notable parallels appear in a seven-fold description of the beauty of the beloved in the Song of Songs (4:1–7) and in an eleven-fold description of Sarai's beauty in the Genesis Apocryphon (20:2–6)." (SBLDS 70, p. 92, n. 52)

4. *anklets.* Lit. "chains"; probably anklets, although some scholars think that *chlidōnas* (= Heb *ṣ'dh)* can mean a "step-chain," i.e., a delicate chain which shortens a woman's stride, thereby making her walk more mincingly and "ladylike" (cf. Isa 3:16).

earrings [enōtia], and all her jewelry. Inasmuch as *enōtia* is used in the LXX for Heb *nzm,* which can mean either "earring" (Gen 35:4) or "nose ring" (Gen 24:47), "nose ring" may very well be the more accurate translation here because the verse seems influenced by Isa 3:18–23, where "nose ring" occurs. That virtually all English translations prefer here in Judith "earrings" to "nose rings" may more reflect unconscious Western preferences in female jewelry and decoration than rigorous, scientific translation. As for "all her jewelry," Isa 3:18–23 provides the reader with the broad range of possibilities and, according to Dubarle (VT 8 [1958]: 350), is the immediate model for the verse.

to catch the attention of the men. Lest his readers infer that Judith was acting out of vanity or repressed lasciviousness, St. Jerome (or, more likely, his Aramaic source) "reassured" his readers by adding:

> And the Lord also gave her more beauty, because all this dressing up did not proceed from sensuality but from virtue; and, therefore, the Lord increased her beauty so that she appeared to all men's eyes incomparably lovely.

5. *wine . . . roasted grain . . . bread.* Abigail had provided David and his men with the same items but in much greater quantities (cf. 1 Sam 25:18).

pure [katharōn] bread. It is unclear whether the author meant that the bread was kosher (so GNB: "bread baked according to Jewish food laws" [cf. Ezek 4:14–15]) or that it was pure in quality (so NEB). However, Dubarle *(Judith,* p. 166) argues that *artōn katharōn,* "pure bread," represents a corruption of *artōn kai turou,* "bread and cheese" (see textual note *ᵈ).* Dubarle's explanation is both ingenious and possible, for cheese was one of the basic staples of Israelite diet (cf. 1 Sam 17:18; 2 Sam 17:29).

packed [periediplōse] all her dishes. The verb is a *hapax legomenon.* Like Daniel (cf. Dan 1:8–16), Judith's scrupulousness with regard to *kašrût* is far greater than that of Esther, who evidently ate delicacies from the king's cuisine (so Esth 2:9), although LXX's Esther is, by contrast, quite scrupulous about her diet (Add Esth C 28). Judith's attitude toward food has some relevance for determining the date of the book's composition.

7. *they were much struck* ["amazed"] *by her beauty.* Judith's great beauty, breathtaking and thought-depriving for every man who would now see her, is a *Leitmotif* for the rest of the chapter. Bethulia's sentries (v 10), the Assyrian outpost (v 14), the entire Assyrian camp (10:18), including its highest officers and general (10:23)—all are struck by Judith's beauty. Dancy (p. 106) thinks there is a touch of the storyteller's humor in all this: "strong" men, young and old, significant and insignificant, they all fall immediately victim to the "defenseless" widow.

As with the Hebrew account of Esther (cf. Esth 2:17; 5:2–3), there is nothing here to suggest that there was anything miraculous about the heroine's captivating beauty. By contrast, however, LXX's Esther has a beauty which is enhanced by God's miraculous power: "Raising his face, flushed with color [the king] looked at [Esther] in fiercest anger. . . . But God changed the king's spirit to gentleness." (Add Esth D 7a, 8; see NOTE on verse in AB 44, p. 218) In other words, while LXX's Judith, devout though she was, accomplished her mission without God miraculously intervening, in the Greek Esther it was God's power, not Esther's courage or beauty or even male weakness, that saved the day.

8. *She bowed to them.* I.e., she acknowledged their good wishes. This reading proposed long ago by Movers, while lacking manuscript support, assumes that the original Hebrew was *wtšthw 'lyhm,* "she bowed down to them," and that it was misread by either a Hebrew copyist or the Greek translator as *wtšlhw(h) l'lhym,* "she bowed down

to God," i.e., Judith worshiped God. The conjectured reading makes good sense; LXX reading does not, as it interrupts the rapid flow of events in vv 8–9.

9. *as she had asked.* The variant reading (see textual note *ʰ)* would mean "as they had promised," referring to the elders' tacit promise in 8:35.

10. *where they lost sight of her.* The author was not concerned with the question of how the women could have been seen at night and so clearly for such a distance (cf. 8:33; 11:3); rather he was concerned with making a very skillful transition of scenes, shifting from that of Bethulia to the Assyrian outpost (v 11). With some justice, Alonso-Schökel has characterized this rather sophisticated literary technique as "cinematographic" (p. 7), since the movies have so marvelously perfected it.

12. *a daughter of the Hebrews.* Judith's response here is somewhat surprising. One might have expected her to have identified herself as "a daughter of Israel" (so OLᵐ), which would have been consistent with her people's usual name throughout Judith, namely, "Israelites" (lit. "sons of Israel"). To be sure, in Judith (2:11; 14:18) as well as elsewhere in the MT, "Hebrew" is sometimes the foreigner's term for an Israelite, the latter word being the name the Israelites preferred to call themselves. But since even in the book of Judith foreigners sometimes identified the Israelites by that same name (5:23; 6:2; 7:10), the question remains: Why on this particular occasion did Judith choose to identify herself as a Hebrew?

The answer may be that the author simply wanted to provide his readers a little variety in vocabulary, which his Greek translator was also interested in doing (see INTRODUCTION, p. 93).

Taking his clue from the NT, D. N. Freedman maintains that Judith could not have called herself a Jew:

> After all, why does Paul call himself a Hebrew of the Hebrews [Phil 3:5]? Probably because he could not very well call himself a Jew (i.e., Judahite), since he was in fact of the tribe of Benjamin. The same with Judith: strictly speaking she was a Simeonite, and could call herself that, or an Israelite, or a Hebrew, but hardly a Jew, except in some off-hand way. It was not until much later I guess that these people lost all sense of tribal affiliations. Most were Jews in the strict sense, but by no means all. (private correspondence with this writer)

More likely, however, Judith chose to use the word "Hebrew" on this occasion because of the pleasant connotations the term had for Assyrian captors, that word being in most frequent use during the period of Israel's enslavement in Egypt (cf. Gen 40:15; Exod 1:15; 2:6; 3:18). This line of argument becomes somewhat more persuasive when one remembers that in 6:5 Holofernes derogatorily refers to the Israelites not by that name but as "this nation out of Egypt," choosing to identify the Jewish people by singling out from their long history the *one* period when they were slaves, i.e., during their stay in Egypt. Cf. also Jdt 14:18a. Lest it be argued that the author would not have expected his readers to draw such a sophisticated or subtle inference from Judith's choice of words here, one should remember that a great story is like a great painting, which is the product of thousands of small strokes and colors and hues, all of which contribute to the painting's general effect and yet may go individually undetected by the untrained or casual observer. On the other hand, not every effective aspect of a work of art must be the result of the deliberate and conscious intent of the artist; for as Eliseo Vivas has so rightly written,

> The genuine work of art comes from the unknown depths of the soul, where its growth is even more mysterious than the development of a foetus. The artist, moved by forces over which he exercises only limited conscious control, does not know clearly what he wants to say till the labor of the file is finished and he can discover his intention in his composition. *(Creation and Discovery,* p. 104)

running away from them. Lit. "running away from their face *[prosōpou autōn]."* Occurring sixty-eight times in Judith (so Enslin, p. 131), the Gk *prosōpon* is regularly used, as here, where one would expect the Hebrew text to have used *pnh* ("face," in its idiomatic sense). Thus, the ubiquitous *prosōpon* serves the reader as a constant reminder that LXX's Judith is a translation from Hebrew.

you are about to eat them up! Lit. "they are about to be given to you for fodder [Gk *katabrōma]."* Judith's explanation here would have had the ring of truth for the Assyrian soldiers, whose own leaders had made such a prediction earlier (5:24).

13. *reliable information.* Lit. "words of truth."

a way. Here the reader is given a foretaste of Judith's way with words, a skill which will be so evident and amusing in chap. 11. Her word "way" (Gk *odos* = Heb *drk)* is clever and deliberately ambiguous here; for to the soldiers it could be taken either as a secret route or a secret strategy. But in either case, it was not for them to decide but rather to make sure that Holofernes himself could by their bringing Judith to him quickly and unharmed.

without risking life or limb of his men. Lit. "not one body or life of his men will be missing." What better prospect could be offered to soldiers than the promise of success without death or even injury!

14. *they were much struck by her beauty.* Cf. v 7. Judith's disarming beauty has just claimed its first victims among the enemy. Now the Assyrians are only captivated by Judith; later they will be killed by her (chap. 15).

15. *and deliver you into his hands.* With this verse, the irony in Judith has begun in earnest. The sentries say Judith has saved her life by being delivered into Holofernes' hands, when, in actual fact, she will save her life by taking Holofernes into *her* hands. Unfortunately, the irony of this passage is considerably reduced in such translations as the SG's "until they deliver you into his charge."

Comment

Scholars agree that it has taken considerable time and space for the storyteller to have Judith get the elders' permission to undertake her secret plan (chap. 8) and to prepare herself spiritually for carrying it out (chap. 9). But once those fifty verses are behind the reader, the rest of Judith moves with great speed, primarily because the author has his heroine always moving quickly and decisively. Here in chap. 10, for instance, Judith promptly makes herself as beautiful as possible, sees to it that she can continue to observe her dietary laws in the Assyrian camp, says good-bye to the elders, leaves Bethulia, and falls into the hands of the enemy—all this in just the first eleven verses!

To fantasize in the safety of one's home about how one will deal with the enemy is one thing; to have to deal with the enemy face to face is quite another. In Judith's first encounter with the Assyrians, the author shows his readers that she is up to the task. The brevity and shrewdness of her immediate response to her captors proves that Judith was not intimidated by her frightful predicament, i.e., two helpless young women caught in the middle of nowhere, in the dead of night, by rough Assyrian soldiers. Nor was Judith the least bit unnerved by their rapid-fire interrogation (v 12a). In order that she not be detained or abused by them, Judith immediately made the soldiers an offer they could not refuse, namely, she assured them that she had reliable, inside information which assured risk-free success for the Assyrians, and that only their general should hear it (vv 12–13). What soldier in his right mind would have delayed, let alone abused, such a messenger!

By her beauty and intelligence Judith gained more than just the soldiers' permission to go on to Holofernes: she had so won their trust and good will that they offered her helpful advice on how to succeed with Holofernes (vv 14–17). Thus the irony in Judith continues: captive Judith captured her captors.

XI. Judith Goes to Holofernes Himself
and Presents "Inside" Information
(10:18–11:23 [Vg 10:17–11:21])

10 ¹⁸ There was a general stir throughout the camp as word of her arrival spread from tent to tent. And they came and crowded around her as she stood outside Holofernes' tent until they told him about her. ¹⁹ They were struck by her beauty;*ᵃ* and judging by her, they speculated on the Israelites, saying to one another, "Who can despise these people when they have such women among them? It is not wise to let a single male of theirs survive; for if they are let go, they will be able to beguile the whole world!"

²⁰ Then Holofernes' bodyguard and all his personal servants came out and led her into the tent. ²¹ Holofernes was resting on his bed under a canopy, which was woven of purple, gold, emeralds, and other precious stones. ²² When they had announced her, he came out into the front part of the tent, preceded by *ᵇ*silver lamps.*ᵇ* ²³ When Judith came before him and his attendants, all were struck by her beautiful face.

When she had prostrated herself and done obeisance to him, his servants helped her to her feet. 11 ¹ Then Holofernes said to her, "Courage, woman! Don't be afraid. For I have never hurt anyone who chose to serve Nebuchadnezzar, king of the whole world. ² But as for your people who occupy the hill country, if they had not insulted me, I would not have raised my spear against them. They brought this upon themselves! ³ In any event,*ᶜ* tell me, why did you run away from them and come to us? You are safe now. Don't worry; you will live through this night and for a long while to come, ⁴ for no one is going to hurt you. Rather, you will be well treated, just like all the servants of my lord, King Nebuchadnezzar."

⁵ "Accept the words of your servant," said Judith to him; "permit

---

ᵃ LXXᵏ, OL, and Syr add "and they accepted her words because they were good."

ᵇ⁻ᵇ LXXʳᵏ, OLˢ, Syr "very many silver lamps, and they brought her to him."

ᶜ LXX "And now."

your maidservant to speak to you, and I will say nothing false to my lord this night. [6] And if you follow the advice of your maidservant, God will accomplish something through you, and my lord will not fail to achieve his ends. [7] For I swear by Nebuchadnezzar, king of all the earth, and by the might of him who has sent you to correct every person, that because of you not only do human beings serve him, but so also the beasts of the field, the cattle, and the birds of the heavens. *Thanks to you,[d]* Nebuchadnezzar and all his house shall prosper. [8] For we have heard of your wisdom and your adroitness. The whole world knows that you, above all others in the kingdom, are brave, experienced, and dazzling in the arts of war.

[9] "We have also heard Achior's account of the advice he offered in your war council; for the men of Bethulia rescued him, and he told them everything he had said to you. [10] Don't ignore his advice, my lord and master, but take it to heart. For it is true: our nation cannot be punished nor can the sword subdue them, unless they sin against their God. [11] But as it is, my lord need not be exposed or unsuccessful, and death will fall upon them. Sin has them in its power; and they are about to enrage their God when they commit a sacrilege. [12] Because their food supply is exhausted and their water almost gone, they have resolved to kill their cattle.[e] Moreover, they have decided to consume all that God in his laws has forbidden them to eat. [13] They have decided to eat the firstfruits of the grain and the tithes of wine and oil which they had consecrated and reserved for the priests who officiate in the presence of our God at Jerusalem, even though it is not lawful for any of the laity[f] so much as to touch these things with their hands. [14] They have sent men to Jerusalem to get[g] permission from the Council, because even there the people have been doing the same things. [15] The result will be that when *they get permission[h]* and they act upon it, on that day they will be given to you to be destroyed.

[16] "Knowing all this, I, your servant, made my escape from their presence. God has sent me to accomplish with you things which will astonish the whole world whenever people hear about them. [17] For your servant is devout and serves the God of Heaven night and day. So I will remain with you now, my lord; and every night your servant will

---

[d-d] LXX "through your strength."

[e] OL, Vg, and midrashim add "and to drink their blood"; see NOTE.

[f] LXX "the people."

[g] So LXX (Gk *metakomisantas*), Eth, and Syr; *metoikisantas* of LXX^AB makes no sense here.

[h-h] LXX "it is announced to them."

go out into the valley and pray to God, and he will tell me when they have perpetrated their offenses. [18] I will then come and report it to you; and you shall march out with your whole army, and there won't be a single one of them to resist you. [19] I will guide you through the heart of Judea until you reach Jerusalem; and I will set your throne[i] right in the middle of her. You will lead them like sheep that have no shepherd! Nor will a dog so much as growl at you! I have been given foreknowledge of this; it was announced to me, and I was sent to tell you."

[20] Her words delighted Holofernes and all his attendants. They were struck by her wisdom and exclaimed, [21] "In terms of beauty and brains, there is not another woman like this from one end of the earth to the other!" [22] Then Holofernes said to her, "God did well to send you before the people to give strength to our hands and destruction to those who insulted my lord. [23] You are both beautiful and eloquent. If you do as you have promised, your god shall be my god; and you shall live in King Nebuchadnezzar's palace and be famous throughout the world."

[i] LXX *diphon*, "chariot seat," which LXX[Ndgmrs] regard as figurative for "throne" *(thronon)*.

Notes

10:18. *a general stir.* Lit. "a running together" (Gk *sundromē*). This is one of the many rare words in Judith, occurring in the LXX only here and in 3 Macc 3:8.

word of her arrival. The importance of the event and the impression it had upon the soldiers in the camp is underscored by the Greek translator's choice of the word *parousia,* a term regularly used for the arrival of a distinguished personage such as a god or king (see LSJ, p. 1343; also H. K. McArthur, "Parousia," IDB, III, 658–61).

19. *they speculated on.* Lit. "they wondered at" *(ethaumazon).*

It is not wise [kalon, "good"]. Like the skilled magician who gets his audience to look where he wants them to look rather than where they should, the author, ironically enough, has the soldiers turn their attention to the threat posed by Israelite males when, in point of fact, it was a female of the species that bore watching. To be sure, because Judith was so beautiful, we may assume that the Assyrians continued to study her throughout her stay in camp, but beguiled *(katasophisasthai,* "outwitted") by her beauty, they did not see what she was really about.

20. *bodyguard.* Lit. "those who sleep beside," which could also refer to Holofernes' most trusted companions (so RSV) or his ministers (so Syr).

21. *a canopy [kōnōpiō].* Invented in Egypt for protection against gnats (Gk *kōnōps)* and other insects, such netting was regarded by the author as a prized possession (cf. 13:15; 16:19) and, possibly, as a symbol of self-indulgence and decadence. At least that is the way the Latin poet Horace regarded such netting *(Epodes* 9.16; see also Herodotus, *Hist.* 2.95). While the net now protected Holofernes' entire body, later it would protect only his decapitated head (cf. 13:9–10, 15).

22. *the front part of the tent.* Befitting such an important general, the tent had several sections, or "rooms" (cf. 13:1–3; 14:14–15; Isa 54:2).

preceded by silver lamps. Because it was night, Holofernes needed light, of course; but the mention of *silver* lamps is the author's way of subtly emphasizing Holofernes' wealth and power.

23. Some of the midrashim delight in expounding at this point on Holofernes' thoughts and feelings on seeing Judith for the first time. For details, see Dubarle, *Judith: Formes et sens,* I, 80–84; II, 98–177.

11:1. *Courage, woman! Don't be afraid.* These words notwithstanding, Judith, in sharp contrast to Queen Esther of the LXX, does not appear particularly distressed or afraid at the beginning of her fateful audience (see COMMENT II, pp. 212–13).

I have never hurt anyone who chose to serve Nebuchadnezzar. Holofernes' protestations of his innocence and fair dealings might have come as a surprise to certain peoples who had already tasted his "just" treatment (2:10; 3:7–8).

2. *not have raised my spear against.* I.e., would not have punished. Enslin's suggestion (pp. 134–35) that this is the idiom which occurs in 2 Sam 23:18 and Jer 43:10 (= 50:10 of LXX, where "canopy" is replaced by "weapons") seems incorrect.

3. *You are safe now.* Lit. "you have come for safety." The phrase may mean "you have saved your life" (so NEB); but see 10:15, where a different Hebrew verb seems to have been used.

Don't worry. Lit. "be brave/confident."

and for a long while to come [kai eis to loipon]. Lit. "and for the rest"; cf. 2 Macc 11:19. Judith's safety, Holofernes was assuring her, was not to be short-lived. Judith *is* safe: Holofernes is the one who is in danger now!

4. *you will be well treated.* As Alonso-Schökel has so well observed, Holofernes

begins his speech in a protective tone and ends with a display of magnanimity (iv 1–4, 23). Judith nourishes his sensuality and vanity as two allies, as a fifth column within the fortress; in her presence something within the general is violently stirred and agitated. (p. 9)

5. *I will say nothing false to my lord.* With her opening words, Judith deliberately used the ambiguous term "lord," which can be interpreted as referring to the general (and so Holofernes obviously understood it) or to God, inasmuch as Judith would not lie to the Lord. Judith used this ambiguous word several times in her first interview with Holofernes. To say that she preferred to equivocate rather than deliberately to lie is to miss the point. Humor, not moral compunctions, dictated the author's choice of words here; for Judith had no compunctions against lying to Holofernes (see her petition in 9:13 for "a beguiling tongue"). Rather, the author delighted in the irony of it all; here, for instance, so powerful and confident is Holofernes that it never occurred to him to look behind the face of this beautiful woman. Samuel almost made the same

mistake of judging a person's capability by his outward appearance (see 1 Sam 16:1–13).

Commenting on this particular verse, Dancy observed: "If it is legitimate to kill in war, it can hardly be wrong to lie" (p. 109). Moreover, while it is clear that many biblical writers had no difficulty in accepting the view that "the end justifies the means" (cf. Judg 3:20–21; 4:18–21; 1 Sam 21:13–15; 27:5–11), Ball's lament of nearly a century ago seems, after two world wars, even more valid today: "Even the modern world has been slow in attaining to the conviction that not everything is fair in war" (p. 332). For more on the morality or ethical standards of the author, see COMMENT I, p. 212.

6. *God will accomplish.* What greater assistance could Judith offer Holofernes than that: divine help!

my lord will not fail. Once again the correct interpretation of Judith's promise is dependent upon the proper identification of the ambiguous word "lord." Here again Holofernes quite naturally understood the term as referring to himself, while, in point of fact, Judith really meant that, thanks to Holofernes, her God would accomplish a marvelous thing for her people. The classicist is immediately reminded here of that famous incident in Herodotus where King Croesus of Lydia, upon learning from the Delphian Oracle "If you cross the Halys River a mighty empire will fall," did so, thinking that the empire referred to was Persia, only to realize just before he was killed that the empire in question was his own *(Hist.* 1.53.71.86).

As in 11:5, this double entendre is the result of literary (i.e., its humorous effect) rather than moral considerations; for Judith promptly concocted a bold-faced lie to explain why she had come to Holofernes' camp (11:12–16). Double entendres are but one of the many aspects of irony, a subject discussed briefly in the INTRODUCTION, pp. 78–85, and in great detail by Good, *Irony in the Old Testament.*

7. *I swear by Nebuchadnezzar . . . and [his] might.* Lit. "as Nebuchadnezzar lives . . . and his might lives." Cf. Jdt 2:12; 12:4; 13:16. For similar asseverations, see Judg 8:19; 1 Sam 14:45; 25:26; 28:10; 2 Sam 11:11; and Ezek 17:16. Judith gains Holofernes' trust by solemnly swearing by what was most sacred to him, namely, his lord Nebuchadnezzar and his might, all of which Judith regards as having no authority for herself. What a masterful stroke of irony!

to correct every person [psuchēs]. Evidently the allusion here is to Nebuchadnezzar's charge to Holofernes to bring into line the disobedient and rebellious nations of the West (cf. 2:6–7, 10).

not only do human beings [anthrōpoi] serve him. While virtually all English translations render *anthrōpoi* here as "men" without any sexist intent, i.e., in the generic sense of "mankind," the true meaning of the Greek word is best expressed here by such terms as "humans," "human beings," or "people."

but also the beasts of the field, the cattle, and the birds of the heavens [serve him]. Judith, with a perfectly straight face, is mocking Holofernes, the possible influence of Dan 2:37–38 and Jer 27:4–7 on this passage notwithstanding.

Nebuchadnezzar . . . shall prosper [lit. "shall live"]. Here the Gk verb *zaō* = Heb *ḥyh,* "prosper" (cf. 2 Sam 16:16; 1 Kgs 1:25).

8. *you, above all others* [lit. "you alone"] . . . *are brave, experienced, and dazzling.*

Here Judith's flattery, which at first glance might seem excessive or too sweeping to be effective, was evidently proportionate to Holofernes' vanity (so Soubigou, p. 551).

10. *Don't ignore his* [i.e., Achior's] *advice.* As D. R. Dumm has so aptly observed, "an ironic situation in which the victim encourages the executioner" *(Jerome Biblical Commentary,* p. 627).

nor can the sword subdue them, unless they sin. This is a major conviction in Judith. For the author, "sinning" can be either moral or ritual in character.

11. *a sacrilege [atopian].* Modern English translations fail to capture both the seriousness and the specificity of Judith's charge with their bland renderings of the Gk *atopia* (RSV: "what is wrong"; NEB: "They do wrong"; SG: "when they shall do what they should not"). A *hapax legomenon* in the LXX and NT, *atopia,* lit. "being out of the way," is defined by Judith in vv 12–15 in terms of stealing or desecrating sacred things, i.e., sacrilege (cf. also LSJ, p. 272). A serious charge in any religion in any time or place, sacrilege by the Israelites has not been previously mentioned in Judith and so is presumably a bold-faced lie on Judith's part, albeit a clever one.

12. *to kill their cattle.* While a Jewish reader might have understood this phrase to have included eating the fat and drinking the blood of the cattle, both of which were strictly forbidden to the Jew (see Lev 3:16–17; 17:10–14; 1 Sam 14:31–34), it is unlikely that a Gentile like Holofernes would have been aware of this particular taboo without having it explained as such. While that may be the reason for the Latin versions' having the explanatory addition ("and to drink their blood"), the Latin variant may actually be a survival of the original rather than a gloss inasmuch as the midrash (and presumably also Jerome's Aramaic text) had the same reading.

Commenting on this verse, Alonso-Schökel wrote of Judith: "She enters into a disquisition on the sacred and the profane in Jewish religion, leading [Holofernes] into a world where he is weak and confused, a world where she can play the irreplaceable counselor. At a deeper level the author may be denouncing the collaborationist party." (pp. 9f.)

13. *firstfruits . . . and the tithes . . . reserved for the priests.* Cf. Num 18.

not lawful . . . to touch . . . with their hands. If this be the expression of an actual Pharisaic prohibition (so Barucq, p. 56), there is, according to Dancy (p. 110), no record of such even in late rabbinic tradition. Like some other practices mentioned in Judith (cf. 4:12), it is most likely an expression of so-called "Oriental exaggeration."

Holofernes need not have believed or even understood Judith's religious views. It was enough for him that *she* believed them, to the extent that she was willing to betray her people.

14. *to get permission from the Council.* Although also arriving at the same conclusion that physical survival took precedence over unquestioning observance of the Law, Mattathias and his followers did not ask the Council for its permission but assumed full responsibility for their decision (see 1 Macc 2:31–41). That the road from Bethulia to Jerusalem was open is another indication that Holofernes was attacking from the north.

even there the people . . . doing the same things. Judging from the content of the rest of Judith, we may safely conclude that this was an outright lie. Moreover, Judith's ancient readers would have understood its function in the story and so would not have been offended by it. Dancy's view (p. 71) that this assertion was resented by the

Pharisees and so contributed to the book's exclusion from the Jewish canon seems improbable (see INTRODUCTION, pp. 86–87).

15. *The result will be.* Lit. "it shall be." As Enslin (p. 140) rightly pointed out, the Greek is not a simple future tense but expresses the sure and certain fulfillment of the divine intent, equivalent to "Thus says the Lord."

16. *to accomplish with you things.* The phrase "with you [Gk *meta sou*]" is deliberately ambiguous. Holofernes naturally understood it in the positive sense of "through you/by your efforts," whereas, Judith was actually using the phrase in the sense of "against you." As in 11:6 (see NOTES), the author was introducing some humor into the scene rather than trying to protect Judith from the moralistic charge that she had deliberately lied to Holofernes.

17. *devout [theosebēs].* Cf. 8:31; also Job 1:1, 8 of the LXX.

I will . . . go out . . . and pray. Judith makes no mention here of her nightly bath (12:7), the latter a "detail of fact" which looms large in certain later Jewish accounts (see INTRODUCTION, pp. 103–4 and 105–6).

God . . . will tell [Gk erei] me. Judith does not specify in exactly what form her information will come. Not surprisingly, a later Jewish version makes her "a daughter of the prophets" (see INTRODUCTION, p. 106).

19. *sheep that have no shepherd!* For Babylonians and Assyrians, as well as for Israelites, "shepherd" was used sometimes to refer to kings or leaders (cf. Num 27:17; 1 Kgs 22:17; Ezek 34:1–10; ANET², p. 89; and G. E. Wright, BA 2 [1939]: 44–48). It will be Holofernes' people, not Judith's, that will be "sheep without a shepherd"!

Nor will a dog so much as growl at you! Lit. "a dog will not speak against you with its tongue," i.e., you will meet no resistance (cf. Exod 11:7 and Josh 10:21).

I have been given foreknowledge of this . . . and I was sent. While only hinting here of the possession of a prophetic gift, Judith actually makes such explicit claims in the midrash: "All this was told me in the visions of God."

21. *beauty and brains.* Lit. "loveliness of face and wisdom of words."

22. *before [emprosthen] the people.* The meaning of this is most unclear. While the phrase "the people" probably refers to the inhabitants of Bethulia (so OLˢ, the JB's "ahead of your people," and the NEB's "out from your people"), the phrase can also be interpreted as referring to Holofernes and those assembled with him. In either case, Holofernes' claim in v 22 is ironic; for Judith's arrival actually begins the destruction of Holofernes and the deliverance of Israel.

23. *your god shall be my god.* Cf. Ruth 1:16. Filled with high spirits and amorous intentions, Holofernes will say anything to please Judith (cf. 6:2). Knowing that once hostile Gentiles sometimes were reputed to have accepted Yahweh as God (e.g., Naaman in 2 Kgs 5:17; and Heliodorus in 2 Macc 3), some scholars have debated whether Holofernes was being sincere here (so Lamparter, p. 170) or just polite (Soubigou, p. 554).

In keeping with the ironic character of the book of Judith, D. N. Freedman offers a curious interpretation: "Maybe Holofernes really means the reverse of what he says, namely, that her coming over to the Assyrian side means that she has abandoned her God and accepted his [i.e., Nebuchadnezzar]. The two would have the same god." (private correspondence with this writer) However, if the story is ultimately fictitious, then such debate is fruitless. Besides, the main point of v 23 is not the possible

conversion of Holofernes but the certainty of his downfall, he being completely under
Judith's spell. And "spell" is the correct word here, for as Montague has so rightly
observed: "Her beauty is hypnotic. . . . The general is mesmerized both by Judith's
beauty and by her promise of aid." *(Books of Esther and Judith,* pp. 18–19)

   you shall . . . be famous throughout the world. Holofernes never knew how truly
he spoke!

Comment I

Any reservations the first-time reader might have had about Judith's ability
to deal with Holofernes were certainly dispelled by the preceding section. For
in the presence of a man who had life-and-death power over her, Judith
conducted herself most masterfully. From Holofernes' point of view, this
beautiful woman had shown herself to be appropriately respectful and impressed with him (see 10:18–11:1, 5, 7–8), yet not so awed as to be unduly
timid or indirect in advising him: "Accept the words of your servant" (11:5);
"Don't ignore [Achior's] advice . . . but take it to heart. For it is true"
(v 10); "I have been given foreknowledge of this . . . I was sent to tell you"
(v 19). Finally, Judith not only promised Holofernes success with the Israelites (11:6, 18–19)—but maybe even with herself (cf. 12:12, 16)!

   But if Holofernes saw the scene in that way, the reader is given a far
different picture. To the reader, Judith showed herself to be almost the exact
opposite of what Holofernes had envisioned. Actually, Judith was not only
sarcastic (11:7–8) and equivocal (vv 5, 6, 16) but also dishonest. In fact, of the
fifteen verses of her speech, *only one* of them contains unequivocal truth,
namely, 11:9: "We have also heard Achior's account of the advice he offered
in your war council; for the men of Bethulia rescued him, and he told them
everything he had said to you." Certainly it is Judith's cleverness rather than
her beauty which strikes the reader. Unfortunately for Holofernes, he was the
victim of both!

Comment II

Regardless of what fears or anxieties Judith might have had earlier (see 9:2, 4,
9–10, 12), in her audience with Holofernes she appears to have been in complete control of the situation, the reassuring words of Holofernes in 11:1 and
4 notwithstanding. In this respect, she is reminiscent of Queen Esther, who in
the MT also evidenced little or no outward signs of stress during her fateful
appearance before the king:

So it was that on the third day Esther put on her royal robes and stopped in the inner court of the palace, opposite the royal apartment. The king was seated on his throne in the throne room, facing the building's entrance. Finally, when the king noticed Queen Esther standing in the court, she won his favor; and the king extended to Esther the gold scepter that he was holding. Then Esther came up and touched the tip of the scepter. The king then said to her, "What do you want, Queen Esther? What is your petition? Even if it be half my kingdom, you may have it."

"If it please the king," said Esther, "let the king come with Haman today to a dinner that I have prepared for him." (Esth 5:1–4)

However, according to Add Esth D 1–15 of the LXX version of Esther, the situation was quite different:

[1] On the third day, when she had finished praying, she took off the clothing of a suppliant and dressed herself in splendid attire. [2] After she had called upon the all-seeing God and savior, she, looking absolutely radiant, took two maids, [3] leaning daintily on the one, [4] while the other followed carrying her train. [5] She was radiant, in the prime of her beauty, and her face was assured as one who knows she is loved, *but her heart was pounding with fear.*

[6] When she had passed through all the doors, she stood before the king. He was seated on his royal throne, arrayed in all his splendid attire, all covered with gold and precious stones—a most formidable sight! [7] Raising his face, flushed with color, he looked at her in fiercest anger. *The queen stumbled, turned pale and fainted, keeling over on the maid who went before her.*

[8] But God changed the king's spirit to gentleness. The king leaped down from his throne in alarm and took her up in his arms *until she revived.* He comforted her with reassuring words, [9] saying to her, "What's the matter, Esther? I'm your brother. Relax. [10] You're not going to die! This practice applies only to our subjects. [11] Come here!" [12] Then he raised his gold scepter and tapped her neck; he hugged her and said, "Talk to me!"

[13] "My lord," she said, "I saw you like an angel of God, and I was upset by your awesome appearance. [14] For you are wonderful, my lord, and your face is full of graciousness."

[15] And as she spoke, *she sagged with relief.* The king was upset, and all his court tried to reassure her. (italics added)

As with other sections of Judith and Esther, there are some striking parallels between the two accounts, especially between Judith and the LXX version of Esther, namely:

Both women undertook their fateful audiences with their male benefactors only after praying to God (Jdt 9; Add Esth C 12–30; D 1–2).

Each woman was accompanied by a trusted female attendant (Gk *abra*). (In the Greek version, Esther had two maids with her when she appeared before the king [Add Esth D 2], while in the MT she appeared alone.)

In both Judith and the LXX account of Esther, the male protagonists felt con-
strained to speak reassuring words to our heroines (Jdt 11:1–4; Add Esth D 8–12,
16).

In both accounts, the heroines resorted to shameless flattery (Jdt 11:7–8, 16; Add
Esth D 13–14).

The most striking similarity between Judith and the Greek Esther is that
both women were ultimately relying upon the Lord God. (In the MT, God is
nowhere mentioned in the book of Esther; but Esther's reliance upon him is
nonetheless implicit [see AB 7B, p. 52].)

Given these parallels between Judith and the Greek Esther, a few scholars
have speculated on the possible influence of one upon the other. Unfortunately, there has been no detailed analysis of the issue, or at least the present
writer is unaware of such. Crucial to an analysis would be a prior decision as
to the nature and date of the Additions to Esther in general, and of Addition
D in particular.

The six extended passages of the Greek version of Esther (107 verses),
which have no counterpart in the Hebrew text, are commonly called the
Additions (or Adds).[131] Both the external and internal evidence indisputably
indicate that these six Additions were not originally a part of the Esther-story
but were added later, and at different times. Included in the external evidence, for instance, is the absence of these Additions in such ancient Semitic
translations as the Talmud, Targums, and the Syr.[132] As for the internal
evidence, while the narrative in the MT is an intelligible and consistent
whole, the Greek Additions contradict the MT at a number of points (for
details, see AB 44, NOTES and COMMENTS, *passim*).

But if scholars are almost unanimous in believing that the Additions are
secondary, there is still considerable debate as to the Additions' authorship,
date, and original language/s of composition. That Additions B and E (i.e.,
the texts of the two royal edicts) were originally composed in Greek is almost
universally accepted, while the view that Additions A, C, D, and F are Greek
translations of Semitic texts—the position taken by the present writer—is still
a matter of some dispute. (For details on this as well as many other matters
relating to the Additions to Esther, see AB 44, pp. 150–252.)

---

[131] While the textual designations for these Additions have varied over the years among scholarly editions and texts, they are frequently referred to as follows: Add A (= Vg 11:2–12:6):
Mordecai's dream (vv 1–11) and his discovery of a plot against the king (vv 12–17); Add B (=
Vg 13:1–7): the text of the royal edict against the Jews (vv 1–7); Add C (= Vg 13:8–14:19): the
prayers of Mordecai (vv 1–11) and of Esther (vv 12–30); Add D (= Vg 15:4–19): Esther's
unannounced appearance before the king (vv 1–16); Add E (= Vg 16:1–24): the text of the
second royal edict (vv 1–24); Add F 1–10 (= Vg 10:4–13): the interpretation of Mordecai's
dream; Add F 11 (= Vg 11:1): the colophon to the Greek version of Esther.

[132] A Hebrew version of some of these Additions does exist, but it was made in the Middle
Ages (see AB 44, p. 154, n. 3).

Unlike Additions B and E, Addition D is so simple and straightforward that, *a priori*, it could quite easily be a Greek translation of a Semitic text. More important, as Torrey has pointed out (HTR 37 [1944]: 8), *charitōn meston*, "full of graciousness," in D 14 presupposes Aram *ml' r't'*, inasmuch as the corresponding passage in the AT of Esther has *metron idrōtos*, "a measure of perspiration."[133] Undoubtedly the best reason for believing that Addition D had a Semitic *Vorlage* is the work of R. A. Martin, who, on the basis of syntax criticism, has shown that such was the case (JBL 94 [1975]: 65–72). As for when the Semitic form of Addition D was first written, on the one hand, it (like the other Additions) was obviously composed after the Hebrew Esther; on the other hand, it was certainly part of the Esther-story by no later than A.D. 93, that being the date for the appearance of Josephus's *Jewish Antiquities*, where Addition D is paraphrased.

The existence of a Semitic *Vorlage* for Addition D is important for establishing any possible relationship between Judith and the LXX Esther because the Greek vocabulary and style of Judith and the LXX Esther are sufficiently dissimilar so that the question of whether one was inspired by the other does not cogently arise. Or, to put the matter somewhat differently, if there was any influence of the one story or scene upon the other, then it would have been during their Semitic stage, not their Greek. Such a conclusion is a mixed blessing. For, on the one hand, the possible influence of one account on the other remains a real possibility in spite of the fact that their Greek style and vocabulary do not justify such a view; on the other hand, since we lack the original Semitic texts for Judith and the Additions to Esther, the question of possible influence of one Semitic text upon the other seems insolvable.

Nonetheless, the present writer is disposed to speculate that *if* there was any influence in the Semitic stage, it seems more likely that, in the case of Addition D at least, Judith inspired Addition D rather than vice versa. The principal reason for his saying this is that virtually every verse in Judith's audience with Holofernes is integral ("indispensable" might be a better word) to the plot, whereas Addition D, in comparison to Esth 5:1–4 of the MT, "only" increases the scene's dramatic interest and underlines the religious motif. However, if Addition D was inspired by Judith, that inspiration was most fateful because Addition D is, unquestionably, the dramatic climax of the Greek Esther (especially God's miraculous transformation of the king's mood in D 8), whereas in the Hebrew account the establishment of Purim (chap. 9) is the main consideration. Finally, the sharp contrast between

---

[133] Since Codex Vaticanus (or LXX^B) is usually regarded as the best extant text of the LXX of Esther, the LXX version of Esther is often referred to by scholars as the "B-text," in distinction to the "A-text" of Esther, which is generally regarded as the "Lucianic recension" of the LXX. In point of fact, however, the A-text of Esther (in contrast to the A-text of other biblical books) is not part of the Lucianic recension but a separate translation of the Hebrew (for details, see AB 44, pp. 162–65). But see also Emanuel Tov, *Textus* 10 (1982): 1–25.

Judith's inner feelings and outward conduct and those of Esther has a logical basis: Esther had to rely more on the capricious king's goodwill and affection, while Judith was appealing more to Holofernes' intelligence and self-interest. Consequently, Judith more than Esther had to project for her male protagonist a confident and self-assured image.

XII. Judith as a Guest of Holofernes
(12:1-9 [Vg 12:1-9])

12 [1] He then ordered them to bring her into where his silver dinnerware was set out and to serve her from his own delicacies and wine. [2] But Judith said, "I will eat none of that lest it be an offense to God. Besides, I have enough with what I brought with me." [3] But Holofernes said to her, "But if you run out of what you have, how can we get you more of the same? For there is no one of your nationality[a] here among us."[b] [4] Judith replied, "As sure as you live, my lord, your servant will not exhaust her supplies before ᶜthe Lord Godᶜ accomplishes by my hand what he had planned."

[5] Holofernes' attendants then brought her into the tent, whereᵈ she slept until midnight. ᵉToward the morning watchᵉ she got up [6] and sent word to Holofernes, saying, "Let my lord please give orders for your servant to be allowed to go out and pray." [7] Holofernes then ordered his guards to let her pass. So she stayed in the camp three days, and each night she would go out into the valley of Bethulia and at the spring would bathe herself ᶠfrom the uncleannessᶠ. [8] When she had finished bathing, she would pray to the Lord, the God of Israel, to guide her in her plan to deliver the children of herᵍ people. [9] Having made herself ritually pure, she would go back and stay in the tent until her meal was brought to her in the evening.

ᵃ So LXXᴮ *ethnous;* LXXᴬᴺ *genous;* LXXᶠᵏ, OLˢ *laou.*
ᵇ LXXᶠᵏ, OL, and Syr "who has such things."
ᶜ⁻ᶜ All texts and verss., except LXXᴮ, have either "the Lord," "God," or both.
ᵈ LXX "and."
ᵉ⁻ᵉ OL "before light."
ᶠ⁻ᶠ LXX and most verss. have "in the camp"; LXXᵐ, OL, and Syr omit; see NOTE.
ᵍ So LXXᴬ, most mins., Eth, and Syr; "his" in LXXᴮᴺˢ.

Notes

12:1. *delicacies [opsopoiēmatōn].* The noun is a *hapax legomenon* in the LXX. The author would have his readers understand that Holofernes' cuisine was appropriate for his silver service—and for a man of self-indulgent appetite. Judith, by contrast, ate simply and sparingly (see v 9).

2. *lest it be an offense [skandalon] to God.* Lit. "that it not be an offense." A "simple" and unsophisticated woman, Judith was, in effect, acknowledging to Holofernes that she did not know what his fancy foods were and whether they were prohibited to the Israelites. So, to "play it safe," she would not eat or drink any of it (cf. 12:19).

Here, most scholars miss a major reason for Judith's taking the position she did. Either, like Ball (p. 337), they devote space to commenting on Judith's ethical priorities or "strange scruples" (i.e., she would not eat unkosher food, yet lied and equivocated without conscience); or scholars take the position that such "details of fact" are justifiable on strictly literary or dramatic grounds (e.g., "The [biblical] authors are storytellers, trying to tell a story effectively, not careful historians or professors of ethics arranging lists of ethical demands in the exact order of importance" [Enslin, p. 144]). While Enslin is certainly correct, Judith's position here nonetheless fulfills a very specific purpose, namely, by scrupulously avoiding any prohibited foods, Judith was confirming for Holofernes the sincerity of her offer. In other words, Holofernes would now believe that Judith felt so strongly about obeying dietary laws that she could actually betray her own people if they ignored such prohibitions (11:12–13). To accept his explanation for Judith's not eating any of Holofernes' food in no way denies the importance of *kašrût* for the author, a view shared by other writers of the first and second centuries B.C. and A.D. (see Add Esth C 28 [Vg 14:17]; Dan 1:8; Tob 1:10–11; 1 Macc 1:62–63; 2 Macc 5:27; 6:18–7:2).

4. *As sure as you live [zē ē psuchē sou].* Cf. 2:12; 11:7. Although a mild asseveration in the OT (cf. 2 Sam 11:11; Hos 4:15; Amos 8:14), the expression is obviously ironic for anyone who already knows the Judith-story.

accomplishes by my hand [poiēsē en cheiri mou]. The rendering of this phrase by the JB ("will have used me to accomplish") and the NEB ("accomplishes through me") deprives the first-time reader of the story of a subtle foreshadowing of events, i.e., something will be done by Judith's *hand!*

5. *Toward the morning [eōthinēn] watch.* Cf. Exod 14:24. Here the author gives us, perhaps, a slight clue for dating the narrative. He subscribes here to the OT's three-watch system for dividing the night (see Judg 7:19), which was used by Palestinian Jews until it was superseded in the Christian Era by the Greco-Roman four-watch system, as in Mark 13:35 ("Watch therefore—for you do not know when the master of the house will come, in the evening *[opse],* or at midnight *[mesonuktion],* or at cockcrow *[alektorophōnias],* or in the morning *[prōi]*").

6. *be allowed to go out and pray.* Such predawn praying is nowhere prescribed in the OT; three times a day, with the first prayer being offered after dawn, was sufficient for such Jews as the distraught author of Psalm 55 and the pious Daniel (see Ps 55:17; Dan 6:10). Although Judith had earlier told Holofernes that she would be going out nightly into the valley to pray (11:17), either Holofernes had forgotten her request or had simply neglected to instruct his sentries about it. In the Vg, Judith's request is made much earlier in the evening (Vg 12:4–6), rather than right before dawn. In any event, Judith's going out to pray while it was still dark not only provided her with additional strength and courage for carrying out her daring plan (see also 13:7), but by so doing Judith was also establishing a pattern, or escape route, for when she would need it (see 13:10).

It should be noted that Judith made no mention here of the need for bathing or ablutions (but see vv 7 and 9), although in a Hebrew midrash reminiscent of the Judith-story, the heroine's bathing represented her ritual cleansing at the end of her menstruation period, thereby making sexual intercourse possible (see INTRODUCTION, p. 104).

7. *would bathe herself [ebaptizeto]*. Evidently Judith immersed herself in the water (so also v 8) rather than just sponged off. If so, Enslin regards this as one of the very few instances where *baptizein* refers to a purification bath, dipping being the normal means of purification (see Exod 30:17–21).

from the uncleanness. The reading in the LXX and most ancient versions (i.e., "in the camp") makes no sense. The place where Judith prayed each night had to be outside the camp proper, otherwise how could she have fled to Bethulia (cf. 13:11)? Therefore, the NEB (see also textual note *ʲ*) omits the phrase, evidently regarding it as a dittography of an identical phrase earlier in the verse, while the JB paraphrases the Greek (i.e., "Where the picket had been posted"), in accordance with 7:3, where the spring was near but still outside the camp proper.

The reading adopted here follows that of Movers, who conjectured that the LXX's *en parembolē*, "in the camp," was a misreading of Heb *mhndh*, "from the uncleanness," as *bmḥnh*, "in the camp." In keeping with this reading, Judith would have been cleansing herself from either menstruation (see Lev 15:19–30) or defilement by Gentiles (see Acts 10:28; see also Gedalyahu Alon, "Levitical Uncleanness," pp. 146–89). Dancy believes that the earliest version of the folktale had the heroine cleansing herself from menstruation: "If the Jews can hold out for five more days, Judith can hold Holofernes off for that period, a day at a time" (p. 115). However, in the present form of the narrative, her bathing represented the ablutions prior to prayer.

8. *When she had finished bathing*. Lit. "and she came up," i.e., out of the water where she had immersed herself (v 7).

9. *her meal . . . in the evening*. By eating only one meal a day, Judith is more reminiscent here of David (see 2 Sam 3:35) than of Esther (cf. Esth 4:16).

Comment

Brief though this section is, it serves as a skillful transition between Judith's first and final encounters with Holofernes (11:1–23 and 12:10–13:10, respectively). The contrasting characters of the two antagonists are subtly indicated by their respective attitudes toward food: Holofernes, the hedonist, dined on delicacies with expensive silver service (v 1), while the pious Judith ate only simple food (see 10:5; 12:2–4), and then only once a day (v 9).

Just as in a chess game, where the moving of a piece may have several possible purposes, all legitimate, so Judith's going outside the camp for nightly prayer had several meanings, all integral to the story. For Holofernes, her nightly pilgrimages were the necessary preliminaries to Judith's finding out for him when he might attack Bethulia without incurring loss of life or limb (see 10:13; 11:17–18). For the first-time reader—and even for the reader who already knows the entire story—Judith's praying in a remote place at night represented her understandable quest for courage and divine help. Finally, while certainly regarding prayer as providing support and wisdom (see v 8), Judith, who alone at this point in the story knows what she intends to do by her own hand (v 4), also considered her nightly visits outside the camp as establishing her means of escape later on (see NOTE on v 6).

XIII. Filled with Lust and Wine, Holofernes
Loses His Head to Judith
(12:10–13:10 [Vg 12:10–13:12])

12 [10] *a*"On the fourth day Holofernes gave a party for his retinue*b* only and invited none of his commanders. [11] He said to Bagoas*c*, the eunuch in charge of his personal affairs, "Go 'persuade' the Hebrew woman who is in your care to join us, and to eat and drink with us. [12] For we will be disgraced if we let such a woman go without having her, because if we do not make her, she will laugh at us."

[13] Bagoas then withdrew from Holofernes' presence and went to Judith and said, "May this lovely maid not hesitate to come before my lord to be honored in his presence and to enjoy drinking wine with us and act today like one of the Assyrian women who serve in Nebuchadnezzar's palace."

[14] "Who am I," responded Judith, "that I should refuse my lord? I will do whatever he desires right away, and it will be something to boast of until my dying day."

[15] So she proceeded to put on her dress and all her accessories. Her servant preceded her and spread on the ground opposite Holofernes the lambskins which Bagoas had provided for her daily use to recline on while eating.

[16] When Judith entered and lay down, Holofernes was beside himself with desire, and his brain was reeling; and he was very eager to have relations with her. (From the day he had first seen her he had been watching for an opportunity to seduce*d* her.) [17] So Holofernes said to her, "Do have a drink. Enjoy yourself with us!"

[18] "I will indeed drink, my lord," said Judith, "for today is the greatest day of my whole life."

[19] Then she took what her servant had prepared, and ate and drank in his presence. [20] Holofernes was so delighted with her that he drank

a LXX *kai egeneto.*
b LXX *doulois,* "servants."
c Vg *vagao.*
d LXX*n*, OL, Syr "meet"; see NOTE.

a great deal of wine, much more than he had ever drunk on a single day since he was born. **13** [1] It grew late, and his retinue[e] hurried away. Then Bagoas closed the tent from outside and dismissed those attending his lord, and they went to bed; for they were all very tired, since the party had lasted so long.

[2] So Judith was left alone in the tent with Holofernes sprawled on his bed, [f]dead drunk.[f] [3] (Now Judith had instructed her servant to stand outside her bedroom and wait for her to come out as usual; for she had said she would be going out for her prayers. She had also said the same thing to Bagoas.) [4] So all had left them[g], and no one, either important or insignificant, was left in the bedroom.

Then Judith, standing beside his bed[h], prayed silently, "Lord, God of all power, look in this hour upon the work of my hands for the [i]greater glory[i] of Jerusalem, [5] for now is the opportunity to come to the aid of your inheritance, and to carry out my plan for the destruction[j] of the enemies who have risen up against us." [6] She went up to the bedpost by Holofernes' head, and took down from it his sword; [7] and approaching the bed, she grabbed the hair of his head and said, "Lord[k] God of Israel, give me the strength, now!" [8] Then she struck at his neck twice with all her might, and chopped off his head. [9] Next, she rolled his body off the bed[l] and yanked the canopy from the poles. A moment later she went out and gave Holofernes' head to her servant, [10] who put it in her food sack.

The two of them then went out, as they always did, "to pray." They passed through the camp, bypassed that valley, and climbed up the slope to Bethulia and approached its gates.

[e] See [b] above.
[f-f] OL "drunk with wine"; see NOTE.
[g] "From his [LXX^dgmps, OL^p; LXX^fk "Holofernes' "; LXX^AN, most mins., and Eth "her"] presence."
[h] "Head" in LXX^k, Eth, OL; Vg adds "praying in tears."
[i-i] Gk upsōma, "elevation."
[j] So LXX^B (thrauma); LXX^AN and many mins. thrausma, "crushing."
[k] Only LXX^BNbfh omit.
[l] Eth and OL^m add "on to the floor."

Notes

12:10. *gave a party*. Lit. "made a drinking party." Compare 6:21, where the same Greek word, *potos*, is used. The truth of the old German saying *Man ist, was man isst*, "One is what one eats," is well illustrated by the way the author has his characters use wine. For the *potos* of the men of Bethulia led to all-night prayer (6:21); Holofernes' *potos* led to drunkenness and death (12:20; 13:2, 8).

invited none of his commanders. Cf. 1 Macc 10:37. Inasmuch as the purpose of the evening's affair was the seduction of Judith (cf. 12:12), the smaller the number of people present, the better. Besides, surrounded by only his personal servants, Holofernes knew that he would appear more impressive than if his dashing fellow officers were also present.

11. *Bagoas*. The name is Persian, but its meaning is uncertain. Some scholars would derive it from Old Pers *baga*, "god," while others think it means "eunuch." In any case, several Persians of that name are known to us, including a general of Artaxerxes II, Mnemon (404–358 B.C.), who later became governor of Jerusalem (Josephus, *Ant. Jud.* 11.7.1); and an influential advisor of Artaxerxes III, Ochus (358–338 B.C.), in the latter's campaign against Phoenicia and Egypt who later became a king-maker (Diodorus Siculus, *Hist.* 31.19.2–3; 16.47.4). However, according to Pliny *(Natural History* 13.41), eunuchs were regularly called "Bagoas." In any event, there is no reason to think that either of these Persian leaders was intended here (but see INTRODUCTION, p. 55).

12. *without having [ouch omilēsantes] her*. I.e., without sexual intercourse. The GNB is reasonably faithful to both the spirit and the words with its "It would be a shame to pass up an opportunity to make love to a woman like that. If I don't try to seduce her, she will laugh at me." Such bowdlerized translations as "without enjoying ["having" in GS] her company" (so RSV, NEB, and SG) are true neither to the character and personality of Holofernes nor to the Greek itself. The verb *omileō* occurs also in Sus v 54, where it can refer only to sexual intercourse. After all, Susanna was being tried for adultery, not for indiscreet conduct. (For the various Greek terms for sexual intercourse in Susanna, see NOTE on "So let us have you" in AB 44, p. 98.)

if we do not make [mē epispasōmetha] her. I.e., have sexual intercourse with her. Doubtless this translation will strike some readers as needlessly coarse or too colloquial. If so, then the reader might prefer one of the following:

"if we do not draw her to us" (SG)
"If we do not embrace her" (RSV)
"without knowing her better" (JB)
"if we do not win her favours" (NEB)

However, the advantage to the proposed translation is twofold. First, the English verb "to make," in its colloquial sense of "to have sexual relations," combines both meanings of the Gk verb *epispaō*, "to allure," "to force." In other words, while *epispaō* can be used for sexual seduction, it can also include rape. Both kinds of sexual behavior are subsumed under the colloquial expression "to make." Second, the use of a collo-quial term, one especially filled with "healthy" realism and directness, is completely in keeping with the character and personality of Holofernes as developed by the author. After all, as was already seen in 6:2–5, Holofernes was a man of direct and blunt speech, given to braggadocio. Too often biblical translators bowdlerize and "genteelize" biblical words and phrases which are quite explicit in the original Hebrew or Greek. Where, for instance, but in a modern English translation of the Bible would an English reader encounter the word "harlot"? Anywhere else—in newspapers, mag-azines, or TV—the word "prostitute" or "whore" would be used. Biblical stories have survived, in part, because, quite rightly, they have been perceived as being honest and true to life, a perception which has not always been conveyed by sanitized translations of the Greek or Hebrew.

13. *May this lovely maid.* The word "maid" *(paidiskē)* is deliberately chosen here because of its ambiguous meaning in English, signifying as it does either a "maiden," a flattering and honorific term, or a "servant," a term indicating a subordinate relation-ship. *Paidiskē* not only includes both meanings but can also be applied to a prostitute (see LSJ, p. 1287)! Hence, Bagoas's request is, at least in the Greek, a very polite but subtle "request" for Judith to serve Holofernes *as fully as* Nebuchadnezzar's palace women serve their king. Bagoas's addressing Judith in the third person is an effective way of softening her command performance. All of this is lost in the NEB by recasting Bagoas's request in the second person: "Bagoas . . . said, 'Now, my beauty, do not be bashful; come along to my master and give yourself the honour of his company. Drink with us and enjoy yourself, and behave today like one of the Assyrian women in attendance at Nebuchadnezzar's palace.' " Such paraphrasing as this almost amounts to an editing of Judith rather than a translating of it.

14. *Who am I . . . to refuse my lord.* Here, as in 11:5–6, "my lord" is ironic, being understood by Bagoas as referring to Holofernes, while the informed reader realizes that Judith was only affirming her obedience to God, not promising herself to Holofer-nes. As with other ambiguous and ironic statements by Judith, this is an expression of the author's sense of humor, not his attempt to keep Judith from telling an outright lie.

whatever he desires. Lit. "whatever is pleasing in his eyes" (= Heb *kl ḥṭwb bʿynyw*). This is another clever touch by the author; for both Holofernes and God *desire,* but in quite different ways!

something to boast of [lit. "be my source of joy"] *until my dying day.* Judith was speaking quite frankly, except that whereas Bagoas thought she was speaking of what she would do *for* Holofernes, Judith had in mind what she would do *to* him!

15. *the lambskins . . . to recline on.* Whether Judith's use of this fleece was one more means of escaping ceremonial defilement (so Deprez, *Évangile* 47 [1962]: 51, n. 2) or a prop for Judith's appearing more sexually alluring (so Alonso-Schökel, p. 48) or just "one more of the colorful details in this lush picture" (Enslin, p. 149) is unclear. Certainly the opening sentence in the verse suggests that Judith was primarily concerned with making herself look as attractive as possible.

To recline while eating was a later Jewish practice (possibly under Babylonian influence [see Ezek 23:41], but certainly by the Greco-Roman period), sitting at a table being the earlier Israelite practice (see 1 Sam 20:24; Prov 23:1; Esth 7:8).

16. *Holofernes was beside himself with desire.* Lit. "Holofernes' heart was driven crazy *[exestē]* over her."

have relations [suggenesthai] with her. Cf. Sus v 39, where the same rather neutral term for sexual intercourse is also used.

he had been watching [etērei] . . . *to seduce [apatēsai] her.* As Zimmermann (JBL 57 [1938]: 70) has rightly noted, the variant of LXX[fk], OL, and Syr *(exētei* . . . *apantēsai,* "he sought . . . to meet her") presupposes Heb *wybqš l'dth,* "he sought to meet her," while the LXX presupposes *wybqš ld'th,* "he sought to know her," i.e., to have sexual relations with her.

His prey in sight, General Holofernes was filled with desire. As Enslin has rightly noted: "The picture of the lusting Holofernes, frantic in his desire to seduce Judith, tends to quiet the reader's scruples as to Judith's coldly planned act" (p. 150). Craven has described the entire situation quite accurately:

> Throughout [10:11–13:10a] he is biding his time, awaiting the moment when he can "deceive" her *(apatēnsai,* 12:16). Thus Judith and Holofernes are playing at the same game; she is there to "deceive" the Assyrians and bring about their demise; he is waiting for the day when he can "deceive" her and bring about her disgrace. She praises his "wisdom" *(sophian,* 11:8); he marvels at her "wisdom" *(sophia,* 11:20). In the end, Judith proves the more skillful. Her wisdom is indeed a marvel, and her deceit a complete success. (SBLDS 70, p. 96)

17. *Enjoy yourself with us!* Lit. "and be with us for joy." Holofernes' greeting was undoubtedly a subtle invitation for Judith to enjoy herself sexually. For the same Greek expression "be with us" *(genēthēti meth ēmōn)* is also what the lecherous elders used in Sus vv 20–21, when they caught Susanna, naked and alone in her garden, and propositioned her: " 'Look!' they said, 'the garden gates are shut, and nobody can see us; and we desire you. So let us have you [lit. "so assent and be with us" *(kai genou meth ēmōn)].* If not, we will testify against you saying that a young man was with you *[ēn meta sou]* and that is why you had dismissed your maids.' " The same phrase, "be with us," occurs in the LXX version of Gen 39:10 and Tob 3:8, both verses also referring to the sex act.

18. *I will . . . drink, . . . today is the greatest day of my whole life.* Compare v 20, where many of the same Greek words are used for describing Holofernes' conduct: "he drank . . . more than he had ever drunk on a single day since he was born." By constructing this chiasmus, the narrator emphasized the importance of this "fourth day" (cf. v 10; so Craven, in "Artistry and Faith in the Book of Judith," p. 87). Moreover, the chiasmus also points up more sharply the character differences of the two antagonists: Judith herself drank moderately and succeeded in her goals, while the exact opposite was true of Holofernes.

19. *what her servant had prepared.* I.e., Judith's usual one meal of the day. "If worst comes to worst, she may be defiled, but not through eating unclean food" (Enslin, p. 150). Judith's overriding concern for dietary laws and ritual purity even in a time of great personal crisis is somewhat reminiscent of Ezekiel's attitude in Ezekiel 4, where

having to act out symbolically the terrible fate of Israel did not seem to upset Ezekiel as much as the prospect of personal ritual defilement (see Ezek 4:12–14)!

20. *Holofernes was . . . delighted with her.* Montague is at pains to show that Holofernes' downfall was more attributable to weaknesses within himself than to any deceit on Judith's part. She, in Montague's judgment, was much more virtuous than most deceitful people in the OT:

> Her recourse to deception has many parallels in the previous sacred literature, and the author's intentional comparison of Judith with her predecessors in this regard highlights her greater virtue. Rebecca deceived her own blind husband (Genesis 27); Simeon and Levi by ruse massacred the men of Shechem for the sin of a single man, quite to the disapproval of Jacob (Genesis 34); Tamar obtained the descendence to which she had a right, but at the cost of incest (Genesis 38); Jael slew Sisera in her tent despite the previous good relationship between her clan and his (Judges 4–5); even Ruth's winning over of Boaz issues in her own self-fulfillment rather than in an act of national heroism. It is precisely Judith's magnanimity, courage, purity, and lack of self-interest which these allusions highlight. Judith does not attempt to seduce Holofernes; she is reserved and simply uses the occasion of his own lust and gluttony to undo the whole Assyrian army. *(Books of Esther and Judith,* p. 10)

much more than he had ever drunk. Hoping to master Judith, Holofernes was mastered by his wine, both his drinking and Judith getting out of hand. Or as Alonso-Schökel put it: "Holofernes, inebriated with passion and wine, abdicates his power and surrenders to Judith while thinking that it is she who has surrendered to him" (p. 12).

13:1 *his retinue hurried away.* By tactfully withdrawing and leaving him alone, Holofernes' staff was "giving him his head." As D. N. Freedman has noted:

> The irony is very evident here. The withdrawal of the attendants and the non-invitation of the military leaders, no doubt all part of the strategy of Holofernes and Bagoas, play into Judith's hands, who could not have planned it better if she had given the orders herself. Also, her own planning must have been based on just this expectation, which is no doubt why she advertised her physical attractions and did everything possible to make Holofernes believe that his expectations were to be fulfilled. Very clever plotting on the part of the writer. (private correspondence with this writer)

2. *Judith was left alone . . . with Holofernes.* She used her "solitude" to good effect: while he slept, she prayed twice (vv 4–5 and 7) and chopped off his head (v 8)— all within six verses!

dead drunk. Lit. "for the wine had drenched him"; see textual note ʰ.

4. *either important or insignificant.* Lit. "from small to great." Another example of merismus. Cf. Esth 1:20.

prayed silently. Lit. "she prayed in her heart."

5. Some scholars, including Barucq and Steinmann, make much of the fact that in her prayer Judith gives no expression here to personal hatred or revenge but is concerned only with protecting Israel in general (v 5), and Jerusalem in particular (v 4).

Moreover, it should be noted that the same emphases are also to be found in her earlier prayer (9:8, 13).

However, it cannot be denied that by killing Holofernes Judith was also disposing of his personal threat to her. Even though she may have been willing, from the start, to seduce Holofernes if necessary, Judith, like any woman, did not relish the idea of being sexually abused. In fact, the first part of her prayer in chap. 9 reflects Judith's strong concern for the sexual violation of the female (see 9:2–4). Thus, in killing Holofernes Judith had protected Israel *and* her honor (see 13:16).

Craven, however, views Judith's praying in a radically different light: "Judith's pausing to pray before chopping off his head [is one of the] acts which satirize standard behavior in such settings" (SBLDS 70, pp. 115–16).

6. *the bedpost.* Lit. "the bar/rod *(kanoni)* of the bed"; this rod was evidently vertical, possibly helping to hold up the canopy.

sword. A Persian loan word, the *akinakēs* was a short, straight sword (Herodotus, *Hist.* 3.118) and not, as is usually translated here, a scimitar. Dundes is correct in saying: "In terms of irony, it is essential that it be Holofernes' own sword which is used to cut off his head" (Dundes, in Alonso-Schökel, p. 28). However, Dundes does not underscore the real irony of this act. It is not so much that Judith used Holofernes' own sword; after all, hacking off an enemy's head with his own weapon was not particularly uncommon (see below). What *is* ironic here is that Judith had entered Holofernes' camp unarmed, otherwise she would not have been admitted: the only weapon available to her was that of Holofernes.

7. *now!* Lit. "this day," which *may* have been intended by the author to have included everything, i.e., her successful escape as well as Holofernes' assassination; but her most pressing need would seem to have been sheer, physical strength. In this, her crucial moment, she is unflinchingly brave.

8. *chopped off his head.* Lit. "took his head from him." Like Jael, who bashed in the head of General Sisera in the plain of Esdraelon (Judg 5:26), and like David, who stunned the mighty Goliath and decapitated him with his own sword (1 Sam 17:51), Judith by a comparable act gained immortal fame among her people.

It is precisely this act that, for better or worse, has immortalized Judith. Clearly John Ruskin thought it was for the worse, for he wrote:

Do you happen to know anything about Judith yourself, except that she cut off Holofernes' head; and has been made the high light of about a million vile pictures ever since, in which the painters thought they could surely attract the public to the double show of an execution, and a pretty woman, especially with the added pleasure of hinting at previously ignoble sin? *(Mornings in Florence,* p. 53.)

9. *rolled his body off the bed.* Now Holofernes has fallen at Judith's feet, figuratively and literally.

yanked the canopy. Cf. 16:19. By not explaining why Judith took the canopy, the author increases reader interest. She took it "as a trophy" (Cowley, p. 263); "if proof were to be needed" (Dancy, p. 116; and Lamparter); "this piece of finery . . . attracted her woman's eye" (Ball, p. 343); she was "adding insult to injury" (Enslin, p. 153). Sometimes, as here, more pleasure is provided the reader by leaving some details out than by explaining them in full.

10. *"to pray."* When the story is told aloud, then the speaker's voice inflection can indicate the irony, i.e., that their going out for prayer was the ostensible but not the real reason for their departure. Quotation marks serve the same function in a printed text.

Comment

This section, which represents the climax to the book of Judith, is a masterful blend of directness, brevity, and subtle irony. There is the drama and immediacy of direct address, nine of the twenty-one verses being in that form, with Bagoas being quoted once (12:13), Holofernes twice (12:11–12, 17), and Judith four times (12:14, 18; 13:4–5, 7). The author pulls no punches in describing Holofernes' intentions toward Judith:

". . . we will be disgraced if we let such a woman go without having her, because if we do not make her, she will laugh at us." (12:12)

. . . Holofernes was beside himself with desire, . . . and he was very eager to have relations with her. (12:16a)

. . . he had been watching for an opportunity to seduce her. (12:16b)

Judith's actions are described even more simply—and brutally:[134]

. . . she . . . put on her dress and all her accessories. (12:15)

. . . approaching the bed, she grabbed the hair of his head. . . . (13:7)

. . . she struck at his neck twice with all her might, and chopped off his head. (13:8)

. . . she rolled his body off the bed and yanked the canopy from the poles. (13:9)

. . . she . . . gave Holofernes' head to her servant, who put it in her food sack. (13:9b–10a)

Various forms of irony, so characteristic of the book of Judith elsewhere, are also abundantly present in this section:

"May this lovely maid not hesitate to come before my lord . . . and act today like one of the Assyrian women who serve in Nebuchadnezzar's palace." (12:13)

"Who am I," responded Judith, "that I should refuse my lord? I will do whatever he desires . . . and it will be something to boast of. . . ." (12:14)

---

[134] In the Vg, she is perhaps a bit more tenderhearted (or perhaps only more fearful): "And Judith stood before the bed praying with tears" (Vg 13:6a).

> "Do have a drink. Enjoy yourself with us!" (12:17)
> The two of them then went out . . . "to pray." (13:10)

But as noted earlier, the greatest irony is that Holofernes was mastered by the very person he thought he had mastered—and with his own sword.

The subtleties noted above have as their natural foil a number of hyperboles and all-inclusive assertions:

> "I will do whatever he desires right away, and it will be something to boast of until my dying day." (12:14)
> From the day he had first seen her he had been watching . . . to seduce her. (12:16)
> ". . . today is the greatest day of my whole life." (12:18)
> . . . he drank . . . much more than he had ever drunk on a single day since he was born. (12:20)
> . . . Judith was left alone in the tent with Holofernes sprawled on his bed, dead drunk. (13:2)
> . . . all had left them, and no one, either important or insignificant, was left in the bedroom. (13:4)

An indication of just how clear and concise the section is may be found, perhaps, in the fact that the various uncials, minuscules, and ancient versions offer, comparatively speaking, very few variants. For instance, these forty-two lines of printed Greek require one hundred and thirty-eight lines for the variants in the *apparatus criticus* of the Larger Cambridge Septuagint, while the forty-two lines of Greek text preceding 12:10 require two hundred lines for the variants, and the forty-two lines of Greek text after 13:10 require one hundred and fifty-three lines for the *apparatus criticus.*

XIV. After Recounting Her Night's Work, Judith Reveals Her Plans for the Next Day's Battle (13:11–14:10 [Vg 13:13–14:6])

13 [11] While still some distance away, Judith called out to the sentries at the gates, "Open! Open the gate! God our God is with us, still displaying his strength in Israel and his might against our enemies, as he has today!" [12] *When her townsmen heard her voice, they hurried down to the city gate, and called the elders of the town. [13] So everyone, *regardless of status*, came running (for they were surprised she had returned); they opened the gate and welcomed them; they lit a fire to give some light and crowded around them.

[14] Then she raised her voice and said, "Praise God! Praise him! Praise God, who has not withdrawn his mercy from the House of Israel, but has shattered our enemies by my hand this very night!" [15] She then produced the head from the sack. And holding it up, she said to them, "Here's the head of Holofernes, the general in command of the Assyrian army! And here's the canopy under which he lay in his drunken stupor! The Lord has struck him down by the hand of a female! [16] Yet I swear by the Lord, who protected me in the course I took so that my face tricked him and brought his downfall, Holofernes* committed no sin with me to defile me or to disgrace me." [17] The people were all quite amazed. And bowing down and worshiping God, they said, "Blessed are you, our God, who this day has mortified the enemies of your people!"

[18] Uzziah then said to her, "My daughter, more blessed are you by God Most High than all other women on earth! Blessed also is the Lord God, who created the heavens and the earth, who guided you in crushing the head of the leader of our enemies! [19] People will never forget *to praise you* when they remember the power of God. [20] May

---

* Gk *kai egeneto*.
- "From young to old" in LXX^{fk}; merismus.
* LXX "he."
- LXX^{fk}, OL, Syr, Eth "our praise"; LXX "your hope"; see NOTE.

God make ʿyour deedᵉ redound to your everlasting honor, and grant you every blessing! For you risked your own life when our nation was brought to its knees. You went out boldly to meet the disaster that threatened us, walking a straight line before our God." Then all the people said, "Amen! Amen!"ᶠ

14 ¹ Then Judith said to them, "Please hear me out, my brothers. Take this head and hang it from the battlements of our wall. ² And as soon as day breaks and the sun comes out over the land, each of you take up your weapons, and let every able-bodied man leave the town. Appoint a commander forᵍ them as if you were about to descend upon the plain against the Assyrian outpost. Only you must not descend! ³ Then ʰthe Assyrian outpostʰ will grab their weapons and make for camp. They will rouse the officers of the Assyrian army and then rush into Holofernes' tent, and not find him! Then they will panic and retreat at your advance; ⁴ and you and all who live within Israel's borders will pursue them and cut them down in their tracks. ⁵ But before doing all this, bring Achior the Ammonite to me so that he may see and recognize the one who despised the House of Israel and sent him to us as if to his death."

⁶ So they summoned Achior from Uzziah's house. But when he arrived and saw Holofernes' head held by one of the men in the assembly of the people, he collapsed; and his breathing was faint. ⁷ But when ᶦthey picked him upᶦ, he threw himself at Judith's feet and did obeisance to her, saying, "Blessed are you in every tent of Judah! In every nation those who hear your name will be in dread. ⁸ Now tell me all that you have done these past few days."

So Judith related to him in the people's presence everything she had done from the day she left up to the moment she was speaking to them. ⁹ When she had finished speaking, the people shouted at the top of their lungs and made the town ring with their cheers. ¹⁰ When Achior saw all that the God of Israel had done, he believed in God completely. So he was circumcised and was admitted to the community of Israel, as are his descendants to the present day.

ᵉ⁻ᵉ LXX "them."
ᶠ Vg puts Judith's interview with Achior here.
ᵍ So LXXᴮᴬᶠᵏᵘ; "against" in LXXᴺᵈᵍʰˡᵖˢ, Eth, Copt, and Syr.
ʰ⁻ʰ LXX "these."
ᶦ⁻ᶦ So LXX; "he recovered himself" in LXXᴬᴺᵇʰᵘ, Copt, and OL.

Notes

13:11 *Open! Open the gate!* Instead of saying something to the effect that the two women were relieved and happy to be back home again, their terrible ordeal behind them and safety in front of them, the author conveyed it all with Judith's triumphant cry: "Open! Open the gate!"

God . . . displaying his strength . . . his might . . . as he has today! With the humility befitting a saint, Judith gave God the full credit for the night's work (so also v 15).

13. *regardless of status.* Lit. "from small to great" (see 13:4). Here the term includes those differing in age, size, and social status (see textual note ᵇ⁻ᵇ).

14. The Vg has here an addition which may well have been in Jerome's Aramaic text, namely, "And she went up to a higher place, and commanded silence to be made. And when all were quiet, Judith said . . ." (Vg 13:16b–17a)

15. *produced* ["pulled out"] *the head from the sack.* Like the magician who surprises his audience by pulling out of his hat or bag something unexpected or "impossible," Judith produced from her sack something quite unexpected; and her audience, too, was surprised (so v 17).

The Lord has struck him down by . . . a female [thēleias]! Judith not only gave all the credit to God, but instead of referring to herself as "a woman," she further depreciated herself by referring to herself as a *thēleia* (= Heb *nqbh),* a term applied to animals as well as people (see Gen 7:2 of LXX).

16. *I swear by the Lord.* Lit. "as the Lord lives." Although this idiom is the same as that in 2:12 and 12:4, here (as in 11:7) it must be expressed more strongly.

the Lord, who protected me. Evidently St. Jerome's Aramaic text was quite different here, for in the Vg Judith mentions an angel:

"But as the same Lord liveth, his angel has been my keeper both going out and staying there and returning from there here; and the Lord has not allowed me his handmaid to be defiled, but has brought me back to you without the pollution of sin, rejoicing for his victory, for my escape, and for your deliverance. All of you give glory to him because he is good, because his mercy endures for ever." (Vg 13:20–21)

no sin . . . to defile me or to disgrace me. I.e., her honor was still intact. It was Judith's face, not her body, which had tricked *[ēpatēxen]* Holofernes. Not surprisingly, this verse and the Vg are utilized in the Office of St. Joan of Arc (so Barucq, p. 62).

17. *Blessed [eulogētos] are you, our God.* The verb *eulogeō* occurs seven times in Judith (13:17, 18 [twice]; 14:7; 15:9, 10, 12). Whether such a number of appearances is purely coincidental is impossible to say.

18. *daughter.* Regarding Uzziah's use of this word as "strange"(!), Steinmann speculated as to whether its use here was just an expression of Uzziah's paternalism as the

town's chief magistrate or a "reminder" that the original heroine was a young girl, not a woman (p. 113). Nowhere in Judith is there any clue as to how old Judith was when she wed Manasseh or how long they were married before he died. Inasmuch as women in the Near East were usually married shortly after their menarche (say between twelve and fourteen years of age) and since Judith was childless and there was neither a confession nor charge of barrenness, it is likely that she had been married only a couple of years when her husband died. Thus, if she had been wed at age thirteen and widowed a couple of years later, then three years after Manasseh's death (so 8:4) Judith would have been about eighteen years of age.[135] In short, it would have been most natural for Uzziah to have addressed her as "my daughter."

more blessed are you. . . . blessed also is the Lord . . . who guided you. A comparison of this and the LXX of Gen 14:19–20 shows that Uzziah's blessing was modeled closely after Melchizedek's blessing of Abram. The clause "more blessed are you" is reminiscent of Judg 5:24a. This verse in Judith, along with 15:10, was often applied to the Virgin Mary in the liturgy of the Roman Catholic Church.

Since Vatican II, however, the situation has evidently changed, for McNeil has observed:

The book of the Bible least employed in the liturgy of the Church today is the Book of Judith. It is never read in the sequences of *lectio continua* in the Mass lectionary or the one-year lectionary of the Office of Readings in the Roman Breviary. Its use in the Mass is confined to one reading (8, 2–8) for Masses of widowed saints and one alternative responsorial psalm (13, 18–20) for Masses on feasts of our Lady for which no proper psalm is provided; in the Office it provides one canticle (parts of the hymn of Judith in 16, 2ff.), one scripture reading (8, 21b–23, on Monday of Week 4), and one alternative *Benedictus* antiphon (15, 9) for the Saturday *memoria* of our Lady. If the comparison be not irreverent, one may perhaps be reminded of the Cheshire cat which vanished, leaving only a smile behind it; for in the older lectionary a part of Judith, the praises of Uzziah and Joakim, was read on the feast of the Assumption each year. *(The Downside Review* 96 [1978]: 199)

19. *People will never forget.* Lit. "hope will never leave the heart of people *[anthrōpōn]*", i.e., they will not forget. According to ancient Hebrew anatomy and psychology, memory resided in the heart (so Prov 3:3; Luke 1:66), that organ being, among other things, an instrument of thought (see Gen 6:5; 1 Chr 29:18; Prov 16:9). For details on the biblical understanding of this organ, see R. C. Dentan, "Heart," IDB, IV, 549–50.

to praise you. Zimmermann (p. 71) has ended all debate on the LXX's ambiguous reading by showing that the LXX's *ē elpis sou,* "your hope" (= Heb *t(w)hltk),* represents a misreading of Heb *thltk,* "your praise," a reading attested by a number of ancient texts (see textual note *d-d).*

20. *For you risked . . . brought to its knees.* Lit. "you did not spare your own life because of the humiliation of our nation." The JB's "our nation was brought to its knees," while quite paraphrastic, is a most appropriate figurative expression for "because of the humiliation of our nation."

---

[135] Joan of Arc, whose sainthood is celebrated in the Roman Catholic liturgy by the use of the book of Judith, was only nineteen when she was martyred.

walking a straight line before our God. Like their heroine, the people had no misgivings about such an ethical problem as whether a good end could be justified by an immoral means. Ball evidently did have such misgivings; for he lamented that "the highest moral excellence is thus attributed to this deed of Judith" (p. 345).

14:1. *Take this head and hang it.* The cutting off and display of an enemy's head had a long history in the Bible (so Goliath's head in 1 Sam 17:54; Saul's at Beth-shan in 1 Sam 31:9–10; Ahab's relatives' in 2 Kgs 10:7–8; John the Baptist's in Matt 14:8). The present incident, however, is strikingly reminiscent of that in 1 Macc 7:47, where Judas's men "seized the spoils and the plunder, and they cut off Nicanor's head and the right hand which he had so arrogantly stretched out, and brought them and displayed them just outside Jerusalem." See also 2 Macc 15:35: "And he [Judas] hung Nicanor's head from the citadel" (see INTRODUCTION, p. 50).

2. *Only you must not descend!* Because of the inequality of military forces present, Judith regarded some such ruse as this feigned attack on the outpost as necessary. No longer just an assassin, Judith was now acting as military leader and chief strategist. In her own person, then, Judith combined the roles of both Deborah, the strategist, and Jael, the assassin.

3. *they will panic and retreat.* Steinmann's contention that the Assyrians were "the prey of a supernatural panic" (p. 105) is unjustified, or at least unjustified on the basis of the Greek version. Steinmann's view may have been influenced either by the Vg, where the intervention of an angel is mentioned (Vg 13:20–21), or possibly also by the similarity of this event to Nicanor's defeat by Judas Maccabeus:

Then Judas prayed and said, "When the messengers from the king spoke blasphemy, thy angel went forth and struck down one hundred and eighty-five thousand of the Assyrians. So also crush this army before us today. . . ." . . . The army of Nicanor was crushed, and he himself was the first to fall in the battle. When his army saw that Nicanor had fallen, they threw down their arms and fled. (1 Macc 7:40b–42a; 43b–44)

However, to recognize the influence of the Nicanor-story on the Holofernes-story does not mean that *all* aspects of the former are necessarily represented in the latter. The Vg is far more graphic and gruesome here: "And when their captains shall run to the tent of Holofernes, and shall find him without his head wallowing in his blood, fear shall fall upon them" (Vg 14:4).

4. *in their tracks.* So NEB. Lit. "in their ways"; see 15:2.

5. *bring Achior . . . to me.* Flushed with success, Judith was, "to say the least, a little dictatorial" (Bissell, p. 193). More important, Judith's interview here with Achior (14:5–10) seems somewhat out of place, especially since she had to go through the whole story for him *again* (so v 8). Not surprisingly, taking their clue from the Vg, which places Judith's encounter with Achior between what would be 13:20 and 14:1 of the LXX (i.e., Judith interviewed Achior *before* she outlined the battle strategy for the next day [14:1–4]), some scholars believe that 14:5–10 is intrusive and that the Aramaic text which Jerome presumably followed here had the preferred sequence, that is, Achior appeared before Judith prior to her announcing the next day's battle plans.

that he may see [idōn] and recognize [epignoi]. I.e., that Achior, the one person among the inhabitants of Bethulia who actually knew Holofernes, could testify that the head was really the general's.

6. *he collapsed* [lit. "he fell on his face"; a Hebraism]; *and his breathing [pneuma] was faint.* Utilizing here a good storytelling technique, the author simply reported what happened, leaving it to his reader's imagination to understand why Achior had fainted. Achior may have fainted from shock, the result of a combined sense of surprise and relief, his own life now no longer threatened by Holofernes (so Fritzsche). But even more important, by fainting, Achior not only confirmed for all that the head was indeed that of Holofernes, but his fainting emphasized again Judith's courage and toughness. For here was the courageous and outspoken Ammonite commander who earlier had braved the anger of Holofernes (chap. 5) *fainting* at the sight of a head which Judith had cut off with her own hands! In terms of stereotyped sex roles, the author has completely reversed the sex roles of the male Achior and the female Judith (see INTRODUCTION, pp. 65–66). But whatever the reason for it, Achior's passing out greatly increases the scene's dramatic effect.

7. *Blessed are you in every tent of Judah!* The clause is reminiscent of Judg 5:24, where an earlier female assassin is praised: "Most blessed of women be Jael, the wife of Heber the Kenite, of tent-dwelling women most blessed."

In every nation [ethnei]. Both the JB and the NEB read this phrase with the preceding clause (e.g., "Your praises will be sung in every camp in Judah and among all nations" [NEB]), the "nations" evidently being all those who had suffered at the hands of Holofernes. Such an interpretation, however, does not immediately suggest itself from the Greek. Rather, "every nation" would appear to refer to any pagan nation that would consider being hostile toward the Israelites.

9. *shouted at the top of their lungs.* Lit. "shouted in a loud voice."

made the town ring with their cheers. So NEB. Lit. "made a sound of joy in their town." While admittedly paraphrastic, the NEB's translation better conveys Bethulia's sense of joy than the RSV's rather literal "made a joyful noise in their city."

10. *he was circumcised and was admitted.* This would appear to be in direct contradiction to Deut 23:3: "No Ammonite or Moabite shall enter the assembly of the Lord; even to the tenth generation none belonging to them shall enter the assembly of the Lord forever." Possibly we should understand here that Achior was given a special dispensation (so Soubigou); after all, Ruth, the Moabitess and grandmother of King David, was admitted to the Jewish community. According to Zeitlin (JQR 40 [1949–50]: 237–38), during the Second Jewish Commonwealth some rabbis felt the prohibition applied to males but not females (so *Yebam.* 76b); others thought that even males could be accepted *(Yad.* 4:4); but still other rabbis insisted that there were to be no exceptions (see *Yebam.* 8:3). Craven, without herself seriously subscribing to it, offers the ingenious possibility that "since Judith is more than ten generations removed from Jacob (8:1), it could be argued that Achior is more than ten generations away from the Ammonites and Moabites who mistreated the Israelites" (SBLDS 70, p. 103, n. 68). Or perhaps the storyteller was giving expression here to that universalism and benevolence of late Judaism so eloquently expressed in the book of Jonah (so Deprez, *Évangile* 47 [1962]: 58); but if so, such tender and compassionate feelings toward non-Jews is observable nowhere else in Judith. There is some merit to D. N. Freedman's observation:

I don't think the conversion of Achior and his acceptance into Israel reflects a different point of view in Judith (here and nowhere else), but rather the plain truth that there are always exceptions even to the most Draconian rules. Achior was like Balaam; and just as Balaam was regarded as a prophet of Yahweh in spite of being a foreigner, so Achior clearly was regarded as a true friend of Israel and a righteous Gentile. (private correspondence with this writer)

Orlinsky finds in this verse the principal reason for Judith's not being canonized by the Jews when it had none of the "faults" of Esther, namely, no mention was made here of Achior being baptized, baptism being an indispensable step in conversion to Judaism according to the Rabbis who established the Jewish canon *(Essays in Biblical Culture,* p. 281). See also INTRODUCTION, pp. 86–87.

as are his descendants to the present day. Lit. "until this day." Unless one assumes here that Achior was still alive when Judith was written, a view which virtually no scholar subscribes to today, then the Greek makes no sense. The Vg is probably correct in having the phrase refer to Achior's descendants (so Vg 14:6; and the midrash).

Comment

Rather than simply state for his readers the significance of Judith's act, the author had the various characters in his tale do that. (Of the twenty verses in the section, fifteen of them [or 75 percent] contain direct address.) In keeping with her reputed modesty and piety (so 8:28–31), Judith gave all the credit for the night's victory to God, saying:

"God our God is with us, still displaying his strength in Israel and his might against our enemies, as he has today!" (13:11)

"Praise God! Praise him! Praise God, who has not withdrawn his mercy from the House of Israel, but has shattered our enemies by my hand this night!" (13:14)

"The Lord has struck him down by the hand of a female!" (13:15)

"Yet I swear by the Lord, who protected me in the course I took. . . ." (13:16a)

It remained for others in the narrative to point out Judith's accomplishments. While her people certainly did give God the primary credit ("Blessed are you, our God, who this day has mortified the enemies of your people!" [13:17]), as did Uzziah ("Blessed also is the Lord God . . . who guided you in crushing the head" [13:18b]), recognition of Judith's personal contribution was clearly recognized:

Uzziah then said to her, "My daughter, more blessed are you by God Most High than all other women on earth! . . . People will never forget to praise you. . . . For you risked your own life when our nation was brought to its knees. You went out boldly to meet the disaster that threatened us. . . ." (13:18–20)

[Achior said to her,] "Blessed are you in every tent of Judah! In every nation those who hear your name will be in dread." (14:7b)

One of the reasons why the second "half" of Judith (i.e., chaps. 8–16) is more interesting to most readers than the first "half" is the author's greater use of direct address in chaps. 8–16. For instance, in chaps. 1–4, which many readers probably find the least interesting portion of Judith, only 12 of the 69 verses are in direct address, i.e., 17 percent. In chaps. 5–7, where the tempo of the story increases with Achior's history of the Israelites (chap. 5) and the ultimatum of Bethulia's citizens to their magistrates (chap. 7), 58 percent of the verses are in direct address, i.e., 45 out of 77 verses. Whereas the first seven chapters have approximately 36 percent of their verses in direct address, the last nine chapters have 59 percent, i.e., 115 verses out of 193. In the second half, only chap. 15 has little direct address (2 verses out of 14); but then that chapter concerns itself with describing the rout of the Assyrian army, a subject which does not readily lend itself to dialogue. In sum, one of the reasons why the second half of Judith is more interesting than the first is its much greater use of direct address, giving as it does a directness and an immediacy to the action.

XV. On Learning of Holofernes' Death, the Assyrians Panic and Are Decisively Defeated (14:11–15:7 [Vg 14:7–15:8])

14 ¹¹ When dawn came, they hung Holofernes' head from the wall. Then every man ªof Israelª picked up his weapons, and they went out by groups to the mountain's passes. ¹² When the Assyrians saw them, they sent word to their superiors, who reported to their generals, their commanders of thousands, and all their other officers. ¹³ They arrived at Holofernes' tent and said to the one in charge of all his affairs, "Please rouse our lord, for ᵇthese slavesᵇ have dared to come down and fight against us so that they may be wiped out to a man!"

¹⁴ So Bagoas went in and shook the curtain partitioning the tent (for he had supposed that he was sleeping with Judith). ¹⁵ When no one answered, he drew aside the curtain and went into the bedroom and found him on top of the bedstool—a discarded corpse, with his head missing! ¹⁶ He let out a yell; and with wailing, groaning, and shouting ripped his clothes. ¹⁷ He then went into the tent which Judith had occupied; and when he did not find her, he rushed out to the people, shouting,ᶜ ¹⁸ "The slaves have duped us! A single, Hebrew woman has brought shame on the House of King Nebuchadnezzar. Look! Holofernes is lying on the ground! And his head is missing!"

¹⁹ When the officers of the Assyrian army heard this, they tore their clothes in consternation; and their cries and shouting were very loud throughout the camp. 15 ¹ And when those who were in their tents heard, they were appalled at what had happened. ² Then, quivering with fear, no man stood firm with his comrade, but with common impulse they tried to escape along every path in the plain and the hill country. ³ Those who were encamped in the hills around Bethulia were fleeing, too. Then the Israelites, every fighting man among them, sal-

ᵃ⁻ᵃ So LXXᴮᶜ; LXX omits.
ᵇ⁻ᵇ Vg "the mice coming out of their holes"; see NOTE.
ᶜ So LXXᴮ.

lied out after them. ⁴Uzziah dispatched men to Bethomasthaim*ᵈ*, Chobai*ᵉ*, Chola*ᶠ*, and all the territory of Israel to tell them what had been accomplished and to urge them all to rush upon the enemy and annihilate them. ⁵As soon as the Israelites heard the news, then as one man they fell upon them and cut them to pieces as far as Choba. Those in Jerusalem and all the hill country also rallied, for they had been told what had happened in the enemy camp. The men in Gilead and those in Galilee outflanked them, causing heavy losses until they were past Damascus and its borders. ⁶Meanwhile, the rest, who had stayed in Bethulia, fell upon the Assyrian camp and looted it, making themselves very rich. ⁷When the Israelites returned from the slaughter, they seized what was left. Even the villages and hamlets*ᵍ* in the hill country and the plain got a lot of booty, for there was a tremendous amount of it.

ᵈ LXXᴮ *baitomasthaim;* LXXᴺ *betomasthaim;* LXXˢ *baitomasthen.* LXXᴬʲʳᵘ and Eth add *kai bēbai,* with many mins. offering a variant of it; see NOTE.
ᵉ LXXᴮᴬ *chōbai;* LXXᴺ *chōba;* LXXˢ *abelbaim.*
ᶠ LXXᴮ *chōla;* LXXᴬᴺ *kōla.*
ᵍ So LXXᴮʰᵖ *epauleis;* "cities" (Gk *poleis)* in LXXᴬᴺˢ, Eth, and Syr.

Notes

14:11. *by groups [kata speiras].* Like so many other words in Judith, *speira,* "a group of soldiers," is a relatively rare term in the LXX, occurring only here and in 2 Macc 8:23 and 12:20, the latter two passages concerning Judas Maccabeus's battles with Nicanor, a campaign which obviously influenced the author (see INTRODUCTION, p. 50).

12. *superiors [ēgoumenous]* . . . *generals [stragēgous]* . . . *commanders [chiliarchous]* . . . *officers [archonta].* While in keeping with the book's possession of an extensive vocabulary, especially in military matters, these terms, whose meaning is rather imprecise in this context, nonetheless convey a distinct impression, namely, *all officers,* from the highest to the lowest, were alerted to the danger.

At this point, the Vg has an addition, whose very length suggests that it was part of the Aramaic text:

And they that were in the tent came and made a noise before the door of the chamber to awake him, endeavouring by art to break his rest, that Holofernes might awake, not by their calling him but by their noise. For no man dare knock, or open and go into the chamber of the general of the Assyrians. (Vg 14:9–10)

13. *these slaves [oi douloi* = Heb *h'bdym]*. Although "slaves" is a perfectly legiti-mate term for the Assyrians to use here for those enemies they held in special con-tempt (cf. 6:5; 14:18), some scholars, following Movers, emend "slaves" to "Hebrews" (= Heb *h'brym)*, the Heb *resh*, they argue, having been misread as a *daleth*. That there may have been some confusion by an early copyist is suggested by the Vg, which has "the mice [= Heb *h'kbrym]*," instead of "the slaves," a reading the Vg shares with the "ancient" Hebrew texts (but see INTRODUCTION, pp. 101–2).

may be wiped out to a man! Lit. "may be destroyed to the end." The Assyrians regarded the Israelite attack as deliberate suicide. The GNB nicely captures the Assyr-ian view: "they are just asking to be destroyed."

14. *shook the curtain.* I.e., the one inside the tent (cf. 10:20–22; 13:2–4). Recogniz-ing the difficulty of "knocking" on a tent curtain, the editors of JB, following the Vg, have here "clapped his hands in front of the curtain."

15. *on top the bedstool [chelōnidos*, lit. "tortoiseshell"]. So Enslin, p. 161. The trans-lation, however, is uncertain. Evidently, the object in question was either made of tortoiseshell or shaped like one. "Threshold" (so KJ and JB) seems most improbable; and "step" (SG) or "platform" (RSV) is but slightly better.

his head missing! And so was the army's! The Vg adds the colorful phrase "welter-ing in his blood" (Vg 14:14). Some scholars would attach great Freudian significance to the fact that Judith cut off Holofernes' head rather than just stabbed him to death, the latter task being much easier to do (see INTRODUCTION, pp. 72–73). However, D. N. Freedman rightly maintains that there is no need here for Freudian "analysis": "There are many cases where the head is required for identification. . . . In view of the extraordinary if not preposterous circumstances (two unarmed women invading a heavily armed enemy camp), anything less than the head would probably have been met with skepticism if not derision. . . . Incidentally, it also made sure that the enemy would be aware as well since with the head in the possession of the Israelites, there was no way the Assyrians could pretend that nothing was amiss and that noth-ing had happened." (private correspondence with this writer)

18. *have duped us [ēthetēsan]!* I.e., all Judith's promises in 11:18–19 were lies, a story solely designed to gain the confidence of Holofernes. It is no coincidence that the same Greek word *(atheteō* = Heb *bgd)* was used earlier in v 23 of Judges 9, a chapter where the duped Abimelech also perished ignominiously at the hands of a woman, his head being crushed by a millstone (Judg 9:53).

19. *in consternation.* Lit. "their soul was much troubled." The grief and the mount-ing fear and confusion in the camp stand in sharp contrast to the joy and confidence among the Israelites (see 14:9).

15:2. *quivering with fear.* Lit. "trembling *(tromos)* and fear *(phobos)* fell upon them." Compare Exod 15:16, where the same two words also appear, but there in the sense of immobilizing fear rather than as here, i.e., as panic flight.

no man stood firm with his comrade [lit. "the neighbor"]. There was complete "pandemonium . . . with all vestiges of military order vanished" (Enslin, p. 163). That this contagious fear was sweeping through an army of almost two hundred thousand men (so 7:2) clearly shows that the Assyrian army had, in both a literal and figurative sense, lost its head.

3. *Those . . . encamped in the hills.* I.e., the Idumeans and the Ammonites (see 7:18).

4. *Bethomasthaim.* Presumably this is a variant spelling of that site mentioned in 4:6. The town of Bebai, mentioned here after Bethomasthaim among the uncials only by LXXᴬ (see textual note *ᵈ*), is otherwise unknown. Its historicity, according to Jozef T. Milik (RB [1955]: 253–54), is not confirmed by the mention of a Bebayou in line 1 of an Aramaic contract, for that town was in southern Palestine.

Chobai. This place is also unknown. Possibly it represents a variant spelling (see textual note *ᵉ*) of that town mentioned in 4:4, Choba.

Chola. This unknown site is sometimes identified with Holon (Heb *ḥln*, in Josh 15:51; 21:15).

rush upon. Epekcheō, "to pour out upon" (the verb used here), and *ekcheō,* "to pour out," (in 15:2, 3), both well illustrate the Greek translator's propensity for using a word not hitherto used in his story and then in the next verse or so using a related word, i.e., one having the same root but a different prefix.

5. *Choba [chōba].* Whether this town is to be identified with the Choba of 4:4 (see NOTE) or with another town of the same name or with Chobai of 15:4 (see the NOTE there) is impossible to say.

all the hill country. I.e., Judah (cf. Jdt 5:3, 15; 7:10).

6. *the rest . . . in Bethulia.* These would have been the noncombatants: women, children, and old men.

and looted it. The contrast here between Esther and Judith is quite striking. Whereas the author of Esther delighted in the massacre of his enemies but eschewed any plundering of them (see Esth 9:5–10, 13–16), the reverse was true for the author of Judith, where looting but not killing *per se* is emphasized (see Jdt 15:6–7, 11), the assassination of Holofernes notwithstanding. The circumstances in the two stories were quite different (on possible reasons for the Jews in Esther refraining from plundering their enemies, see the NOTE in Esth 9:10 on "not . . . lay a hand on," in AB 7B, pp. 87–88). The despoiling of one's enemies, the practice subscribed to in Judith, is unquestionably the natural, normal response of victorious nations, both ancient and modern: "To the victor belong the spoils."

Comment

Presumptuous Holofernes, not the mighty Assyrian army, is the hated enemy in Judith. The ancient author lavished loving care on his description of Holofernes' death and its discovery (13:1–10 and 14:11–18, respectively), but here he gave scant attention to the defeat of the Assyrians themselves, in fact, only eight verses (14:19–15:7). Although the author certainly reveled in the gory details of Holofernes' death (13:6–9), when it came to the defeat of the Assyrian army, he was much more interested in Israel's looting of it than in the killing *per se* (see final NOTE on 15:6). Thus, there is some justification for the view, offered more frequently by Roman Catholic than Protestant scholars, that Holofernes is an archetypal figure, a symbol of evil (see INTRODUCTION, pp. 73–75). Such an interpretation would be compatible with the rampant apocalyptic and eschatological emphases of Jewish thought at that time, i.e., sometime between ca. 200 B.C. and A.D. 90.

XVI. The Israelites Celebrate Their Victory, and Judith Offers Her Hymn of Praise (15:8–16:20 [Vg 15:9–16:24])

15 ⁸ Joakim the high priest and the Israelite Council who lived in Jerusalem came to see for themselves the wonderful things the Lord had done for Israel, and to see Judith and to wish her well. ⁹ When they came to her, they blessed her with one voice and said, "You are the glory of Jerusalem! You are the great pride of Israel! You are the great boast of our nation! ¹⁰ For by your own hand you have accomplished all this. You have done well by Israel; God is well pleased with it. May the Omnipotent Lord bless you in all the days to come." And all the people said, "Amen!"

¹¹ It took the people a month*ᵃ* to loot the camp. They gave to Judith Holofernes' tent, with all his silver dinnerware, beds, bowls, and gear. She took them and loaded her mule; then she hitched up her carts and piled the things on them. ¹² All the women of Israel flocked to see her and sang her praises; *ᵇ*some of them performed a dance*ᵇ* in her honor. She took branches in her hands and distributed them to the women who accompanied her. ¹³ She and those who accompanied her crowned themselves with olive leaves. Then, at the head of all the people, she led all the women in their dancing while all the men of Israel, armed and garlanded, followed, with songs of praise on their lips. ¹⁴ In the presence of all Israel Judith began this thanksgiving, and all the people *ᶜ*lustily sang*ᶜ* this hymn of praise. 16 ¹ And Judith sang,

Begin a song to my God with tambourines.
Praise the Lord with cymbals.
Raise to him a *ᵈ*psalm of praise*ᵈ*.
Extol him and invoke his name.

ᵃ Lit. "thirty days."
ᵇ⁻ᵇ Syr "they chose from themselves groups of singers"; see NOTE.
ᶜ⁻ᶜ *Uperephōnei;* LXX^Ndprs *upephōnei.* "echoed."
ᵈ⁻ᵈ So LXX; "new song" *(psalmon kainon)* in LXX^ANdgpsu, OL^s, and Syr.

² For the Lord is a God who crushes wars;
   ^eBringing me^e into his camp among his people,
   He delivered me from the power of my pursuers.
³ Assyria came from out of the mountains of the north;
   He came with myriads of his warriors.
   Their numbers blocked up the wadis;
   And their cavalry covered the hills.
⁴ He boasted that he would set fire to my territory,^f
   Kill my young men with the sword,
   Dash my infants to the ground,
   Seize my children as spoil,
   And would carry off my maidens.

⁵ The Omnipotent Lord has foiled them
   By the hand of a female.^g
⁶ For their champion did not fall at the hands of young men;
   Nor did the sons of Titans strike him down,
   Nor did towering giants set upon him;
   But Judith daughter of Merari
   Undid him by the beauty of her face.
^{7h} For she took off her widow's dress
   To rally the distressed in Israel.
   She anointed her face with perfume
⁸ And fixed her hair with a tiara
   And put on a linen gown to beguile him.
⁹ Her sandal ravished his eyes;
   Her beauty captivated his mind.
   And the sword slashed through his neck!
¹⁰ The Persians shuddered at her audacity,
   And the Medes ⁱwere dauntedⁱ by her daring.
¹¹ When my oppressed ones raised their war cry
   And my weak ones ^jshouted^j,
   ^k The enemy^k ^lcowered in fear^l,

---

^{e-e} So OL and Syr; LXX omits; see NOTE.
^f *Oria*; LXX^B *orē*, "mountains."
^g LXX^{bfk}, OL, and Syr add "and brought them to shame."
^h LXX^k omits vv 7–9 and 11–12.
ⁱ⁻ⁱ So LXX^{AN} (*etarachthēsan*) and Eth; "shivered" (*errachthēsan*) in LXX^{BS}; OL and Vg omit.
^{j-j} So LXX^N and many mins. (*eboēsan*), OL^s, and Syr; *ephobēthēsan*, "they were afraid," in LXX^{BASuv}.
^{k-k} LXX and verss. "they."
^{l-l} Gk *eptoēthēsan*; LXX^{Nbhr} *ēttēthēsan*, "they were defeated."

Screamed and ran.
¹² Mere boys ran them through
And wounded them like deserters' children.
They were destroyed by the army of my Lord!

¹³ I will sing to my God a new song:
Lord, you are great and glorious,
Marvelous in strength, invincible.
¹⁴ Let all your creation serve you!
For you spoke, and they were created;
You sent forth your spirit, and ^mit formed them^m.
And there is none who can resist your voice.
¹⁵ For the mountains will be moved from their foundations ⁿlike
    waterⁿ;
The rocks will melt before you like wax.
Yet to those who fear you
You will show mercy.
¹⁶ For any sacrifice for its pleasant smell is a little thing,
And any fat for a whole burnt offering is to you insignificant;
But he who fears the Lord is always great.
¹⁷ Woe to the nations which rise against my people!
The Omnipotent Lord will take vengeance on them on the day
    of judgment;
He will consign their flesh to fire and worms,
And they will wail with pain forever.

¹⁸ When they arrived at Jerusalem, they worshiped God. As soon as the people were purified, they offered their burnt offerings and their votive offerings and their gifts. ¹⁹ Judith dedicated all the possessions of Holofernes, which the people had presented her. The canopy which she had taken for herself from his bedroom she also gave to God as a votive offering. ²⁰ For three months the people continued their celebrations in Jerusalem in front of the sanctuary; and Judith stayed with them.

^{m-m} ōkodomēsen; LXX^{Sr}, OL, and Eth "they were formed."
ⁿ⁻ⁿ LXX and verss. "with waters"; see NOTE.

Notes

15:8. *Joakim . . . and the Israelite Council.* See NOTES on 4:6 and 8, respectively.

the wonderful things [lit. "good things"] *the Lord had done.* The author never confuses his priorities: the victory was God's, Judith's hand being but God's means. By contrast, in the Song (notably 16:5–10) Judith is given full credit for her accomplishment, 15:8 notwithstanding.

to wish her well. So NEB. Lit. "to speak peace with her." For this common Hebrew expression, see especially Jer 9:8 and Ps 85:8 [85:9, in MT].

9. *they came to her [eisēlthon pros autēn].* The LXX was "corrected" by one scribe to *exēlthe pros autous,* "she went out to them" (so LXX^{bfk}, OL, and Syr), evidently in a pious attempt to preserve the dignity of the Israelite officials. In the liturgy of the Roman Catholic Church, the entire verse is used in praise of the Virgin Mary and of Joan of Arc.

10. For this verse the Vg has something quite different:

> For you have acted manfully, and your heart has been strengthened, because you have loved chastity, and after your husband you have not known any other: therefore also the hand of the Lord has strengthened you, and therefore you shall be blessed for ever. (Vg 15:11)

all of which would have had special appeal to Jerome and his celibate colleagues.

11. *a month to loot the camp.* So vast and thoroughgoing was their task!

mule Being the hybrid offspring of a male ass and a female horse, the mule (Gk *ēminos,* lit. "half-ass") was evidently far less common among the Jews than either of the other two animals (cf. Ezra 2:66–67), probably because of the breeding restriction in Lev 19:19 (for later Jewish conventions concerning mules, see *Kil.* 1.6; 8.4–5).

12. *performed* [lit. "made"] *a dance [choron].* Cf. 3 Macc 6:32, 35; and 7:16. See also Exod 15:20, where Miriam and the Israelite women danced after they had been delivered from their enemies. Possibly under the influence of the Syr (see textual note^{b-b}) and the OL^s, which translates Gk *choron* with the Latin *choros,* "choruses," the JB renders this as "they formed choirs of dancers." However, Zimmermann (p. 71) has plausibly suggested that the Syr reading results from a misreading of Heb *mḥlwt,* "dances," as *mhllwt,* "singers of praise."

took branches [thursous]. Judith's spontaneous conduct here finds some precedence in what is prescribed for the Feast of Booths: "And you shall take on the first day the fruit of goodly trees, branches of palm trees, and boughs of leafy trees, and willows of the brook; and you shall rejoice before the Lord your God seven days" (Lev 23:40). The NEB's "garlanded wands," however, reflects a very literal translation of *thursos,* which, properly speaking, is a *"wand wreathed in ivy and vine leaves with a pinecone at the top,* carried by the devotees of Dionysus [italics added]" (LSJ, p. 812). In any event, the occurrence of the word only here and in 2 Macc 10:7 is one more indication of the relatively late date of our narrative.

13. *crowned themselves with olive leaves* [lit. "with the olive"]. Although in the OT the olive symbolized various concepts, including life, peace, and thanksgiving (see J. C. Trever, "Olive Tree," IDB, III, 596), the wearing of an olive wreath was a Greek custom, not a Jewish one. Thus, the mention of this particular activity is another indication that the narrative received its final form in the Greek period.

led all the women in their dancing. I.e., like Miriam in Exod 15:20f., the triumphal celebration after which the present incident is modeled.

14. *this thanksgiving.* Although the Gk *exomologēsis* literally means "a confession," it is sometimes used in the LXX to translate the Heb *twdh,* "thanksgiving" (see Ps 147 [146]:7).

lustily sang [uperephōnei]. Both this word and its variant (see textual note `ᶜ⁻ᶜ`) are *hapax legomena* in the LXX.

16:1. The poetic character of this song is indicated by the obvious parallelisms in the very first verse:

> Begin a song to my God with tambourines.
> Praise the Lord with cymbals.
> Raise to him a psalm of praise.
> Extol him and invoke his name.

tambourines [tympanois]. The reference is evidently to a popular membranophone (Heb *tp),* carried by women and struck by hand; apparently it was not used in the Temple itself (see Gen 31:27; 2 Sam 6:5; 1 Chr 13:8; Ps 68:25 [26]).

cymbals. The OT speaks of several types of cymbals, the *mṣltym* being reserved exclusively for the use of the priests. Thus, the type referred to here would have been the Heb *ṣlṣlym,* which were of two kinds, those held vertically and those held horizontally. (For illustrations of both kinds, see IDB, III, 471, figs. 79 and 80.)

psalm of praise [psalmon kai ainon]. Lit. "psalm and praise," which is hendiadys. The variant reading (see textual note `ᵈ⁻ᵈ)` is less likely to be the original LXX reading.

2. *the Lord . . . crushes wars [suntribōn polemous].* Cf. 9:7. Although the translation is reasonably certain, this clause has prompted considerable debate, primarily because Jerome's Vg version of Judith (which is based upon his Aramaic text rather than upon the Greek [see INTRODUCTION, pp. 95–97]) seems to follow here the Greek. More specifically, the Vg has here *dominus conterens bella; dominus nomen est illi,* "The Lord puts an end to wars; the Lord is his name," which agrees more with the LXX version of Exod 15:3 *(kurios suntribōn polemous, kurios onoma autō,* "The Lord crushes wars; the Lord is his name") than with its presumed Hebrew *Vorlage* as preserved in the MT *(yhwh 'yš mlḥmh yhwh šmw,* "Yahweh is a man of war; Yahweh is his name"). This close agreement between the Latin and Greek versions of Jdt 16:2 becomes even more significant when one realizes that in Exod 15:3 the Vg translated the Hebrew rather faithfully (i.e., *dominus quasi vir pugnator, omnipotens nomen eius),* that is, the Vg's rendering of Exod 15:3 was not used for the Vg rendering of Jdt 16:2 but rather a fresh Latin translation was made of the latter. Thus, inasmuch as Jdt 16:2 seems to reflect the LXX version of Exod 15:3, and assuming that in Jdt 16:2 Jerome was faithfully translating his Aramaic text, then we are justified in concluding that Jerome's Aramaic version must have been based upon the LXX (unless one argues

that the LXX translation of Exod 15:3 accurately reflects a Hebrew *Vorlage* differing from that of the MT, a possibility which cannot be entirely dismissed). But, as in any ancient text, later scribal contamination by other ancient versions is always possible.

Bringing me . . . among his people. The translation is most uncertain, the Greek clearly being corrupt (see textual note *^c*). Not without merit is Cowley's suggestion (p. 265) that, originally, a Heb *'l bḥnwhw btwk h'm,* "God, when he encamped among the people," was misread as *'l-mḥnwtyn btwk h'm,* "to the camps among the people." Thus, the JB, following also the OL, renders this as "he [i.e., God] has pitched his camp in the middle of his people."

delivered [katadiōkontōn] me. Although Judith herself was speaking here (so v 1), the "me" may refer to all the people of Israel, not just to Judith. For as Skehan has rightly pointed out (CBQ 25 [1963]: 97), in Exodus 14 (which is the prose account of Israel's miraculous deliverance from Egypt and the chapter immediately preceding Exodus 15, the chapter after which Judith's hymn is patterned) the verb *katadiōkō* is used four times to describe the Egyptian pursuit of *Israel* (vv 4, 8, 9, 23).

3. *his warriors [dunameōn]. . . . their cavalry [ē ippos autōn].* Lit. "his armies. . . . their horse." Cf. the LXX of Exod 15:4: "Pharaoh's chariots *[armata]* and his host *[dunamin]* he cast into the sea." As befitting poetry, the Greek of the hymn is more compact and less precise than in a prose account, all of which provides a translator with greater latitude in carrying out his task. For example, *ippos autōn* is variously translated: "their horses" (JB); "their horsemen" (RSV and Enslin); and "their cavalry" (RSV, SG; "his," NEB).

4. *He boasted.* Lit. "he said"; cf. Exod 15:9 and 2 Kgs 19:23. Such terrible boasting was not idle but frequently carried out in the biblical world (see 2 Kgs 8:12; Ps 137:9; Hos 13:16; Judg 5:30).

my territory . . . my young men . . . my infants . . . my children . . . my maidens. Thanks to this succession of possessive pronouns, the verse underscores that childless Judith, like any good mother, holds in highest value people, not possessions.

5. *By the hand of a female [thēleias].* See NOTE on *thēleia* in 13:15.

6. *their champion [dunatos].* I.e., Holofernes; yet nowhere in the Song does the author dignify him by referring to him by name. The same Greek term is applied to Goliath in 1 Sam 17:4 and 51.

sons of Titans. Inasmuch as this expression properly applies in Greek mythology to the divine children of Uranus (the heavens) and Ge (earth), it seems quite out of place on the lips of Judith. However, in the LXX, *titanes* is used in 2 Kgs 5:18, 22 to translate Heb *rp'ym,* which evidently refers to mortals.

giants [gigantes]. In the LXX, *gigantes* is used to translate several different Hebrew words for "giants," namely, "Anakim," "Rephaim," "Nephaim," and "Nephilim." There are evidently two basic types of giants mentioned in the Hebrew Bible: very tall mortals (e.g., Deut 2:11, 20; 3:11; 2 Sam 21:16–22) and semidivine creatures called "Nephilim," who were the offspring of divine beings and mortal women (see Gen 6:1–4; for introductory remarks on this obscure term, see H. F. Beck, "Nephilim," IDB, III, 536).

Judith. Although singing about herself, the heroine refers to herself in the third person rather than the first (see COMMENT II, p. 253; see also Judg 5:7, 12, and 15, where Deborah, also singing about herself, uses the second person).

7. *perfume [murismō].* Lit. "an anointing"; another *hapax legomenon* in the LXX.

8. *linen gown [stolēn linēn].* Made from the very thin stalk fibers of flax, linen was a luxury item. Egyptian linen, which was the most prized, has fibers "so finely woven that they cannot be distinguished from silk without the use of a magnifying glass" (J. M. Myers, "Linen," IDB, III, 134–35).

9. *Her sandal ravished . . . Her beauty captivated.* Brief though the Song is, the irony continues; for Holofernes had intended to violate Judith!

And the sword slashed through his neck! This clause is a masterpiece of description and brevity. Just as in Judg 5:26b, where the striking repetition of an idea matches Jael's pounding of the tent peg:

> She struck Sisera a blow,
> she crushed his head,
> she shattered and pierced his temple

so in the present clause the description of the murderous act is as quick and clean as the flashing blade itself: "And the sword slashed through his neck!" The clause also stands in brief and brutal contrast to the description of Judith's *toilette* (vv 7–9b).

10. *Persians . . . Medes.* Cf. 1:7. Given the prose account of Judith, a reader might be surprised here by the mention of these two peoples, especially since according to Judith, the Medes had been destroyed the year prior to Holofernes' present invasion of Palestine (see Jdt 1:13–2:1). Therefore, do these two terms refer to those Persians and Medes who were now serving as auxiliaries in Holofernes' army? Or are they intended only to represent "types of strong and warlike peoples; or as the most remote of nations" (Ball, p. 355)? Or do these two terms represent a momentary memory lapse on the part of the author, i.e., the events actually had occurred in the Persian period but were moved back by the author to an earlier period (so Cowley, Bissell, and Dancy)? Or is this just one more illustration of the influence of the Song of the Sea as a prototype for the Song, i.e., where people to the east are cited: "The peoples have heard, they tremble; pangs have seized on the inhabitants of Philistia" (Exod 15:14)? None of these suggestions seems particularly persuasive.

However, D. N. Freedman argues, with considerable merit, that the allusion was part of the story's Persian setting and that for reasons unknown to us, the story was pushed back into the Assyro-Babylonian era; in any event: "Mentioning Medes and Persians probably did not bother the author or editor since in a vague way he would know that they were around during both periods" (private correspondence with this writer).

In any event, as the phrase currently stands, giving top billing to the Persians, it is anachronistic; for in the assumed setting of Judith (i.e., the days of Nebuchadnezzar), the Medes were the dominant power and the Persians only a petty state and ally of the Median confederacy (for further details, see David F. Graf, *Medism;* also his forthcoming "Medism: The Origin and Significance of the Term").

11. *my weak ones shouted.* So reads the variant to the LXX; the LXX reading (see textual note ʰ⁾) is not an appropriate parallel to its preceding clause (i.e., "When my oppressed ones raised their war cry").

cowered in fear. As Zimmermann (p. 70) has shown, *ptoeō* of the LXX and its variant, *ēttaō* (see textual note ʰ⁾), are both legitimate translations of the same Hebrew verb, *ḥtt.* The real difficulty in translating this verse lies in the fact that while there is definitely a change of subject (i.e., from the Israelites to the enemies), there is no clear indication of exactly where that change takes place, all the verbs being in the third person plural.

12. *Mere boys [uioi korasiōn].* Lit. "the sons of young women." Because *korasion* is often used in the LXX for a female slave, some translators regard this phrase as adding insult to injury, i.e., the sons of servant girls(!) stabbed the Assyrians (so SG, RSV, and NEB). Cf. 14:13, where the soon to be defeated Assyrians contemptuously referred to the Israelites as "these slaves."

like deserters' [automolountōn] children. This is a most powerful simile. For not only would the children of deserters have often been especially vulnerable and without protection, but sometimes they must have borne the brunt of a besieged people's anger and frustration, especially that of fellow children ("mere boys"), who, as most adults regretfully acknowledge, can be quite cruel.

13. *a new song.* Cf. Ps 144:9. While Craven (SBLDS 70, p. 110) would regard chap. 16 as a two-part psalm, consisting of the reasons for the singing (vv 1–12) and the new song itself (vv 13–17), vv 13–17 do, in fact, constitute a new poem. For, on the one hand, clear references to the Judith-story are lacking here, and, on the other hand, the psalm consists of snippets from other songs, notably, from Psalms, Judges 5, and Isaiah. (For details, see COMMENT II, pp. 254–57.)

Lord . . . strength. The Greek is similar to the LXX version of Pss 86:10 and 147:5.

invincible [anuperblētos]. Another *hapax legomenon* in the LXX.

14. *and it formed them [kai ōkodomēsen].* I.e., God's spirit served as the creative agent, as in Ps 33:6 and 9:

> By the word of the Lord the heavens were made,
> And all their host by the breath [Heb *rwḥ*] of his mouth.
> For he spoke,
> And it came to be;
> He commanded,
> And it stood forth.

and as in Ps 104:30a:

> When thou sendest forth thy Spirit [Heb *rwḥ*],
> They are created.

The capitalization of the word "Spirit" in Ps 104:30 (and in Gen 1:2) of the RSV is unfortunate, in that some Christian readers might conclude that the ancient Hebrew text (where all the letters were in capitals) was alluding to the Holy Spirit, i.e., the Third Person of the Trinity.

Concluding that *ōkodomēsen* is awkward, Zimmermann (p. 73) has suggested that an original Heb *wtbnm*, "it formed them," was misread as *wtbynm*, "it gave them understanding." However, given the fact that the idea of God's word and spirit as creative agents is so well established in the Bible, Zimmermann's emendation seems unwarranted.

none . . . resist your voice. According to ancient Hebrew psychology, once a word was spoken, it had a separate and independent existence (for example, once made, an oath could not be retracted [see NOTE on 8:30]). If that was true of *man's* spoken word, then how much more so of God's commands! So Isa 55:11: "So shall my word be that goes forth from my mouth; it shall not return to me empty, but it shall accomplish that which I purpose, and prosper in the thing for which I sent it."

15. *like water.* The LXX's *sun udasin,* "with waters," is awkward. Paul Joüon *(Biblica* 3 [1923]: 112) was probably correct in suggesting that an original Heb *kmym,* "like water/s," which would nicely parallel "like wax," was misread as *bmym,* "with water/s."

rocks will melt. Compare Ps 97:5a: "The mountains melt like wax before the Lord." See also Mic 1:4.

16. Although the entire verse is but a faint echo of the theology of great passages such as Ps 51:16–17 and Isa 40:16, it at least attests to the fact that the original psalmist (who may very well not have been the author of Judith [see COMMENT II, p. 253]) believed that ritual *per se* was not enough and that reverence for the Lord was even more important, a view shared by Ben Sirach (cf. Sir 1:11–14).

"God," insists Craven, who believes the author of Judith also composed the psalm, "is not a God to be manipulated with acts of piety. . . . I read these lines not as a prophetic-like disparagement of cultic practices, but as a reminder that excessive piety cannot be used to manipulate Yahweh." (SBLDS 70, pp. 109ff.)

17. Although the psalmist was clearly influenced by the concluding verse of the Song of Deborah ("So perish all thine enemies, O Lord" [Judg 5:31a]) and even more by the last verse in Isaiah ("And they shall go forth and look on the dead bodies of the men that have rebelled against me; for their worm shall not die, their fire shall not be quenched, and they shall be an abhorrence to all flesh" [Isa 66:24]), it is debatable whether the storyteller really goes beyond them by promising punishment for the wicked *after death.* While Goodspeed saw in this verse "more than a hint of future punishment" (p. 50), a view which both Cowley (p. 267) and Ball (p. 358) expressed in even stronger terms, Enslin regards the phrase *eōs aiōnos,* "forever," in the verse as only "a rhetorical flourish" (p. 175). In support of Enslin's view, it should be noted that nowhere else in Judith is there any evidence of a belief in life after death, not even in Judith's prayer (chap. 9) or her earlier conference with the magistrates (8:11–27), where it might reasonably be expected. On the other hand, if the psalmist did believe in a judgment after death, then that would be another indication of Judith's relatively late date of composition (see Dan 12:2; Sir 7:17; Enoch 103:8; 90:26, where punishment after death *is* affirmed).

day of judgment. Steinmann may be correct when he observed that with this phrase we have left "abruptly the domain of history and the milieu of politics" for eschatology (p. 117); but given the nonmiraculous character of the rest of Judith, we are probably better advised to view this expression in naturalistic terms, i.e., referring to judgment in this world rather than the next.

fire and worms. Cf. Sir 7:17: "Humble yourself greatly, for the punishment of the ungodly is fire and worms." See also Mark 9:48. According to 2 Macc 9:9, the body of Antiochus IV, Epiphanes, Israel's arch-villain, "swarmed with worms" even while he

was still alive, all of which *may* have been an example of the type of punishment
included in the phrase "day of judgment" (see above).

18. *the people were purified.* While killing solely in self-defense did not incur blood-
guilt (see Exod 22:2), fighting which resulted in contact with the dead *did* defile a
person (so Num 19:11–13; 31:19). Moreover, even those women and children who had
touched no dead bodies but had looted the Assyrian camp were also unclean (see Num
19:14–22).

they offered . . . burnt offerings . . . votive . . . gifts. Cf. 4:14. Steinmann's comment here that "the human sacrifice of Holofernes shall be celebrated by the ritual
sacrifices at Jerusalem" (p. 97) seems somewhat snide; for every nation and religion,
regardless of its moral and ethical views, naturally rejoices at the defeat of those who
would have destroyed them.

19. *canopy . . . as a votive offering [eis anathēma].* I.e., a devoted thing (Heb *ḥrm),*
as in Lev 27:28. Goliath's sword and Saul's armor had been given similar treatment
(see 1 Sam 21:9; 31:10).

20. *the sanctuary.* Lit. "the holy ones," i.e., all the buildings of the temple complex.
Cf. 4:12.

Comment I

There are several possible clues in this section for helping to date the book of
Judith, namely, "She took branches" (see NOTE on 15:12); Judith and the
women "crowned themselves with olive leaves" (NOTE on 15:13); and, possibly, the "eschatological" character of 16:17. All of these suggest a date no
earlier than the Greek period and probably later, possibly during the Hasmonean period. On the other hand, Judith is probably not later, either. For as
Grintz has quite correctly observed: "It [i.e., the Song] reveals no traces of
sectarianism, as do the works written in the post-Hasmonean period"
(p. 452).

Comment II

The nature of Judith's Song and its relationship to the rest of Judith are
among the most important but difficult problems confronting students of
Judith. Few assertions can be made with any certainty, and most observations
about the Song or its component parts can be made only with varying degrees
of confidence.

However, virtually all scholars rightly agree that vv 5–10 unquestionably
reflect the Judith-story (their sole difficulty is the very puzzling reference to
the Persians and Medes in v 10):

⁵ The Omnipotent Lord has foiled them
  By the hand of a female.

⁶ For their champion did not fall at the hands of young men;
  Nor did the sons of Titans strike him down,
  Nor did towering giants set upon him;
  But Judith daughter of Merari
  Undid him by the beauty of her face.

⁷ For she took off her widow's dress
  To rally the distressed in Israel.
  She anointed her face with perfume

⁸ And fixed her hair with a tiara
  And put on a linen gown to beguile him.

⁹ Her sandal ravished his eyes;
  Her beauty captivated his mind.
  And the sword slashed through his neck!

¹⁰ The Persians shuddered at her audacity,
  And the Medes were daunted by her daring.

From a purely literary point of view, this particular passage is *the* most effective part of the Song, it being the most vivid (vv 6 and 10), detailed (vv 7–8), and ironical (vv 5, 6, and 9). There can be no doubt about its appropriateness for Judith. (However, as we shall see later, the same cannot be said for the rest of the Song.)

But did the author of Judith actually compose this section, or did someone else? Some authors, such as Jansen *(Acta Orientalia* 15 [1936]: 63–71) and Dancy, argue that just as the poetic Song of Deborah (Judg 5:1–31) antedated and inspired its prose account in Judg 4:4–24, so what is now Jdt 16:5–10 antedated and inspired the prose account of Judith. In support of this theory, Dancy (p. 68) rightly points out that only in vv 5–10 of Judith's Song is she *spoken about* (i.e., she is referred to there only in the third person singular), whereas in vv 2–4 and 11–17 the first person singular is used instead (i.e., "I," "me"). On the other hand, this alternation of speaker could be simply a reflection of the Song's antiphonal character.

If we had the original Hebrew Judith, then scholars could make a study of the Hebrew vocabulary in the prose and poetic sections and so determine, perhaps, whether the same or different authors probably were involved. But as it is, to compare the Greek of the two sections is not very helpful. However, because the irony and vividness of vv 5–10 are consistent with the irony and high literary character of Judith (especially of 11:1–13:10), it would seem more reasonable to conclude that the author of Judith was himself responsible for vv 5–10 rather than that he adopted them from elsewhere. Craven, while freely conceding that she cannot resolve the problem, also suspects that the entire "song was included in the original composition of the story" (SBLDS 70, p. 105).

Certain other parts of the Song are also applicable to the Judith-story, but not exclusively so; for instance, vv 3–4:

> [3] Assyria came from out of the mountains of the north;
> He came with myriads of his warriors.
> Their numbers blocked up the wadis;
> And their cavalry covered the hills.

> [4] He boasted that he would set fire to my territory,
> Kill my young men with the sword,
> Dash my infants to the ground,
> Seize my children as spoil,
> And would carry off my maidens.

and vv 11–12:

> [11] When my oppressed ones raised their war cry
> And my weak ones shouted,
> The enemy cowered in fear,
> Screamed and ran.

> [12] Mere boys ran them through
> And wounded them like deserters' children.
> They were destroyed by the army of my Lord!

While applicable to the Judith-story, neither of the above passages is necessarily so. That is, one can just as easily imagine such descriptions as originally being applied to other wars and other times. For instance, Assyria's advance and ruthless boasting in vv 3–4 were, unfortunately, characteristic of that cruel nation throughout its millennia-long history; then too, the very name "Assyria" personifies all those nations that had attacked Israel throughout her long history (so Deprez, *Évangile* 47 [1962]: 62). And the "my," occurring eight times in vv 4, 11, and 12, could well be Israel speaking at any number of points in her checkered history.

Not surprisingly then, a number of scholars, including Jansen, Deprez, and Dancy, have suggested that the Song of Judith originally had nothing to do with Judith herself. Rather, it was simply an already existing hymn of community thanksgiving, possibly used in a local synagogue, that was adopted and adapted by the author of Judith.

According to H. Ludin Jansen in his detailed analysis of the Song *(Acta Orientalia* 15 [1936]: 63–71), the author of Judith adopted and adapted an ancient psalm, consisting basically of the following:

1. A hymn of thanksgiving to be used by the worshiping community. With slight variations, this portion of that psalm survives in 16:1–4.
2. A detailed account of a divine intervention, which was to be recited by the king. While the storyteller replaced this section with an already existing poetic legend about Judith (i.e., the present vv 6–10), remnants of that displaced account still survive in v 5 (slightly reworked so as to refer to a woman instead of God) and vv 11–12, which contain the troublesome allusion to the Persians and Medes.
3. A concluding hymn of thanksgiving, which may have been revised by the storyteller himself, is still basically present in vv 13–17.

Jansen thought that although the original psalm may have had in it some older elements, the Song in its present form dates to "later than the middle of the second century B.C." *(Acta Orientalia* 15 [1936]: 71), the "eschatological" character of v 17 being, he believed, clear proof of that.

The idea that the Song may not have been composed *de novo* by the author of Judith becomes even more persuasive when one realizes how very different vv 13–17 (which are introduced in v 13 as "a new song") are from the rest of Judith. First, vv 13–17 are a less than eloquent pastiche of older biblical ideas and phrases (see NOTES *passim).*[136] Then too, whereas in the prose section of Judith the great event Judith brought about was in no way miraculous or supernatural, in the Song what *might* be termed "apocalyptic" or "eschatological" elements are suddenly stressed: "mountains will be moved from their foundations . . . ;/The rocks will melt before you" (v 15); "The Omnipotent Lord will take vengeance on them on the day of judgment;/He will consign their flesh to fire and worms,/And they will wail with pain forever" (v 17). Most surprising of all—and in sharp contrast to the rest of Judith, where matters of *kašrût* and the punctilious observance of the Law loom so large— the Song now insists that ritual and sacrifice are distinctly subordinate to a person's having the right attitude: "For any sacrifice for its pleasant smell is a little thing,/And any fat for a whole burnt offering is to you insignificant;/But he who fears the Lord is always great" (v 16). This theological view, while perhaps meritorious in itself, is very infelicitously stated in the Greek. The passage is quite inferior in its literary style to vv 3–4 or 5–10. In short, the literary and theological differences between vv 13–17 and what has preceded them raises the distinct possibility that vv 13–17 are a later interpolation (see INTRODUCTION, pp. 75–76).

In all fairness, it should be noted that this writer's low assessment of vv 13–17 is not shared by all scholars. Craven, for instance, has said of vv 14–16:

---

[136] In this respect, there are, as D. N. Freedman has rightly noted, "something like the Thanksgiving Hymns [i.e., the *Hôdāyôt,* or 1QH] of the Dead Sea Scrolls, which likewise are pastiches of biblical poetry strung together without much regard for form or structure."

Here Yahweh is hailed in cosmic terms that recall the language of Judith's requests in her first prayer that God be known as "ruler of the heaven and the earth, creator of the waters, king of all creation" (9:12). In a real way, the sentiment of this passage expresses a resolution to the story of the Book of Judith. Now the people know that Yahweh, not Nebuchadnezzar, is the true "king of all the earth." (SBLDS 70, p. 109)

Whether vv 13–17 were originally a part of an old synagogal psalm or were added later, why would the storyteller have even considered adopting and adapting such a psalm in the first place? The most obvious answer is that the synagogal hymn was already patterned after the Song of the Sea (Exodus 15), a hymn which was not only *the* song of triumph *par excellence* but which also had a motif especially appropriate to the Judith-story, namely, the hand of the Lord. The following parallels between Exodus 15 and Judith 16 are rather instructive:

Exodus 15	*Judith 16*
3 The Lord is a man of war. . . . (LXX: "The Lord crushes wars.")	2 For the Lord is a God who crushes wars. . . .
4 Pharaoh's chariots and his host he cast into the sea. . . .	3 Their numbers blocked up the wadis; And their cavalry covered the hills.
9 The enemy said, "I will pursue, I will overtake, I will divide the spoil, my desire shall have its fill of them. I will draw my sword, my hand shall destroy them."	4 He boasted that he would set fire to my territory, Kill my young men with the sword, Dash my infants to the ground, Seize my children as spoil, And would carry off my maidens.
14 The peoples have heard, they tremble; Pangs have seized on the inhabitants of Philistia.	10 The Persians shuddered at her audacity, And the Medes were daunted by her daring.

Admittedly, only Jdt 16:2 shows indisputable influence of the Song of the Sea; but perhaps that was all that was really necessary to attract the storyteller's eye to what we have posited as "a synagogal hymn." As noted earlier, the Song of the Sea is not only the premier song of triumph in the OT; but as Skehan has pointed out, it has a motif especially appropriate for Judith: the hand of the Lord. "In Exodus, the Almighty hand of God (Exod 3:19, 20; 13:9; 14:31) uses the hand of Moses (Exod 4:2; 10:21–22; 14:21, 26–27) as his instrument; in Judith, the hand of a woman" (CBQ 25 [1963]: 108).[137] More specifically, in the Song of the Sea, "the hand of the Lord" is a dominant image:

[137] Skehan (pp. 109–10) notes that this theme of God's using the hand of the weak and lowly for the salvation of his people is also found in the Dead Sea *War Scroll* of Qumran *(Wars of the Sons of Light and the Sons of Darkness,* 1QM xi and xiii, 12–14).

Thy right hand, O Lord, glorious in power,
Thy right hand, O Lord, shatters the enemy. (Exod 15:6).

Thou didst stretch out thy right hand,
The earth swallowed them. (Exod 15:12)

Such a motif would, quite naturally, have appealed to the storyteller. "There is no doubt," writes Skehan, "as to what is the poetic prototype for the canticle of Judith: it is the canticle of the Exodus (Exod 15:1–19), connected with the name of Miriam. The festive participation of all Israel, including the women, is the same in both. . . . The speaker on both occasions is Israel, or the Israelites simply and in chorus." (CBQ 25 [1963]: 96). Whether the author composed Judith's Song, as Skehan thinks, or adapted it from a synagogal hymn (which seems more likely), the influence of Exodus 15 on it is undeniable.

XVII. Epilogue
(16:21-25 [Vg 16:25-31])

16 ²¹ After that*ᵃ* everyone went back home*ᵇ*. So Judith returned to Bethulia and lived on her own estate. In her time she was famous throughout the whole country. ²² Many men wanted her, but for the rest of her life (from the day Manasseh her husband died and was gathered to his people) no man had relations with her. ²³ *ᶜ*Her fame continued to increase*ᶜ*, and she lived in her husband's house until she was a hundred and five years old. *ᵈ*She emancipated her trusted servant.*ᵈ* And when she died in Bethulia, she was buried in the same cave as her husband Manasseh; ²⁴ and the House of Israel mourned her for seven days. (Before she died she had distributed her property among *ᵉ*those most closely related to her husband Manasseh and to*ᵉ* her own nearest relatives.) ²⁵ Not again did anyone threaten the Israelites during Judith's lifetime, or for a long time after her death.*ᶠ*

ᵃ LXX "these days."
ᵇ LXX "to his inheritance"; LXXᶠᵏ, OLˢ, and Syr "tents."
ᶜ⁻ᶜ So Latin; see NOTE.
ᵈ⁻ᵈ LXXᵏ, OL, Syr, and Vg put after v 24.
ᵉ⁻ᵉ LXXˢ omits by haplography.
ᶠ LXXᴮᵇ add "Amen."

Notes

16:21. *went back home.* Lit. "hitched up for his inheritance *[klēromian]*." Cf. Josh 1:15.

22. *Many men wanted [epethumēsan] her, but . . . no man had relations with [egnō, "knew"] her.* According to Montague: "Judith resisted many offers of marriage, viewing them as obstacles to her total dedication to God. As dedication to a holy war led to abstention from sexual relations in a more ancient Israel [see, for example, 1 Sam 21:4-5], so Judith's singleness of purpose and her dedication to her people's destiny make her their fitting type." *(Books of Esther and Judith, p. 21).*

Given the earlier erotic and murderous conduct of Judith toward Holofernes, one might well question whether all male intentions toward her were quite as honorable and formal as some modern translations suggest:

> Many desired to marry her, but she remained a widow all the days of her life. (RSV)

> She had many suitors; but she remained unmarried all her life. (NEB)

While the JB is somewhat better ("She had many suitors, but . . . she never gave herself to another man"), one cannot help visualizing what the word "suitors" implies, i.e., formal wooers for her hand in marriage. Inasmuch as Judith has so fired the hearts and imagination of Western artists, especially in the Renaissance, translators are justified in assuming that the same would have been true of Judith's own male contemporaries, be they rich or poor, "honorable" or not. In sum, the modern translator is not justified in rendering the earlier parts of the Judith-story in an accurate and forthright manner (especially chaps. 12–13) only to bowdlerize the epilogue, where Judith is even more honored than before. Besides, the parenthetical phrase in the verse serves as the author's final and emphatic assurance to his readers that Holofernes had not had sexual relations with Judith. And Holofernes could hardly be described as a "suitor"!

Jerome's Vg has "And chastity was joined to her virtue, so that she knew no man all the days of her life, after the death of Manasseh her husband" (Vg 16:26). Celibate Church Fathers, like Jerome, certainly would have approved of Judith's conduct. Consider, for example, his unsolicited advice to Salvina, a recently widowed and wealthy Roman aristocrat whom he had never met:

> Let those who feed on flesh serve the flesh, whose bodies boil with desire, who are tied to their husbands and who set their hearts on having offspring. Let those whose wombs are burdened cram their stomachs with flesh. But you have buried every indulgence in your husband's tomb. . . . Let paleness and squalor be henceforth your jewels. Do not pamper your youthful limbs with bed of down or kindle your young blood with hot baths. . . . Take no well-curled steward to walk with you, no effeminate actor, no devilish singer of poisoned sweetness, no spruce and well-shorn youth. . . . Keep with you bands of widows and virgins. . . . Let the divine Scriptures be always in your hands and give yourself frequently to prayer that such shafts of evil thoughts as ever assail the young may find thereby a shield to repel them. (Epistle 79.7–9)

23. *Her fame continued to increase.* Lit. "she advanced (*ēn probainousa*) very greatly." Although the verb *probainō* is regularly used in antiquity for growing older, the Latin versions are probably correct in seeing the reference to Judith's increasing reputation (see textual note ⁓), unless, of course, we should understand the next clause ("she lived . . . a hundred and five years") as a gloss, which is possible.

a hundred and five years old. Whether by ancient or modern standards, this was a ripe old age. Ben Sirach was correct when he wrote: "The number of a man's days is great if he reaches a hundred years" (Sir 18:9). Enslin, however, would see more here than just the OT view that long life was a sign of divine favor (see Job 42:16; Prov 16:31; 20:29). Inasmuch as the Maccabean period was one hundred and five years long (168–63 B.C.), so Judith's identical length of days represented, argued Enslin, "the prayerful hope, later to be expressed as the concluding word of some of the midrashic versions of Judith and of the Megillath Antiochus: 'May God in his mercy work signs and wonders in this time and at this hour as he has done in the days of our fathers' " (p. 181). Certainly one objection to Enslin's interpretation is that it makes the date of the book's composition too late (see INTRODUCTION, pp. 67–70). However, if "the detail of fact" on Judith's age be a gloss (see above), then Enslin's explanation may be correct.

She emancipated her trusted servant. Though unnamed, this faithful slave was not forgotten. This particular detail, while underscoring Judith's generosity, is also one more example of the author's concern for balance: "Just as Judith's first act was to send her to summon Uzziah, Chabris, and Charmis, now her last act is to free her" (Craven, SBLDS 70, p. 112).

buried in the same cave as . . . Manasseh. Another archaism harking back to the patriarchal period (see Gen 23:19; 49:29–32).

24. *for seven days.* The OT does not prescribe a specific length of time for mourning. However, Ben Sirach (early second century B.C.) matter-of-factly reports: "Mourning for the dead lasts seven days" (Sir 22:12).

distributed her property. While little is known about a Hebrew woman's inheritance rights in general (but see Num 27:6–11), let alone details on how the possessions of a childless widow should be distributed, the author evidently regarded Judith's conduct in this matter as exemplary.

25. *for a long time.* Lit. "for many days," which the Vg rightly translates as "for many years." Frustratingly imprecise, this Hebrew expression can mean at least a couple of decades (so 1 Sam 7:2). Thus, if Judith were, say, eighteen years old when her great exploit occurred (see NOTE on 13:18) and then lived on for another seventy or eighty years (i.e., a very long life), then, counting "the many days" after her death, we may say that the *Pax Iudith* might have lasted for as long as a century. Such a protracted period of "peace" would best fit in either the second half of the Persian period or in the Maccabean period, especially after the death of Nicanor ca. 161 B.C. In any event, Judith's success was twice that of Jael's, the latter bringing her people forty years of peace (Judg 5:31c).

According to the ancient author, Judith not only did something for her people but also something *to* them; for as Craven so perceptively observed:

> The people find in Judith a model of freedom and courage. . . . after her death no one spread terror among the people. . . . The real change in the story actually happens in the hearts of the members of the community. In the time sequence of the story, Judith appears publically but briefly—four days in the Assyrian camp and a month plundering and celebrating the victory. Then she withdraws back to her roof-top solitude where she lives until her death at one hundred five years old. . . . The community find in her not a permanent leader but a way to acquire permanent freedom. She appears at a time when her people are between times, so to speak. . . . She is a sign of the ancient truth that by vocation they are a freed people, that they choose life and freedom if they rely wholly upon their God. (SBLDS 70, p. 115)

Immediately after the words "for a long time" the Vg has an addition, namely,

> But the day of the festivity of this victory is received by the Hebrews in the number of holy days, and is religiously observed by the Jews from that time until this day. (Vg 16:31)

Mentioned in none of the ancient versions of Judith, this "detail of fact" is a gloss, possibly inspired by the analogy of the festivals mentioned in Esther (i.e., "Purim" of Esth 9:27–28) and Maccabees (i.e., "Nicanor's Day" in 2 Macc 15:36 [cf. 1 Macc 7:49]). The authenticity of the verse is also questionable, due to the fact that, ordinarily, the author of Judith uses the word "Israelites" (not "Hebrews" or "Jews") to identify his people. (It is the Gentiles in Judith who think of the Israelites as "the Hebrews" [cf. 10:12; 12:11; 14:18].) If there is any justification for the gloss, it lies, suggests Zeitlin (pp. 26, 37), in the probability that the Judith-story, along with *Megillath Antiochus,* was used by Jews in their synagogues at the feast of Hanukkah. (For a Hanukkah lamp featuring Judith, see Plate 7.)

Comment

Like the epilogues of Job (42:7–17) and Esther (Esth 10:1–3), the epilogue of Judith is, in comparison with the rest of the book, very brief. Nevertheless, the epilogue reassures its readers on several very important points. For her services to God and country, Judith was well rewarded with fame and long life (vv 21b and 23). From the day of her husband's death until the day of her own, her "honor" remained intact (v 22). In her relations with others, including her trusted servant and the closest relatives on both sides of her family (vv 23–24), Judith continued to act in an exemplary manner. Most important of all, thanks to Judith's efforts, her people went for a very long while without being threatened by enemies (v 25). What more could be said about the saint who murdered for her people!

APPENDICES

APPENDIX I: LIST OF KINGS

Neo-Assyrian

B.C.

935–913	Asshur-dan II	727–722	Shalmaneser V
913–892	Adad-nirari II	722–705	Sargon II
884–860	Ashurnasirpal II	705–681	Sennacherib
860–825	Shalmaneser III	681–669	Esarhaddon
825–812	Shamshi-adad V	669–627	Ashurbanipal
812–784	Adad-nirari III	629–612	Sinsharishkun
784–744	(Period of great weakness)	612	Fall of Nineveh
744–727	Tiglath-pileser III	612–609	Ashur-uballit II

Neo-Babylonian

B.C.

626–605	Nabopolassar	560–556	Neriglissar
605/4–562	Nebuchadnezzar II	556–539	Nabonidus
562–560	Amel-marduk	539	Fall of Babylon

Achaemenian

B.C.

550–530	Cyrus the Great	423–404	Darius II, Nothus
530–522	Cambyses	404–358	Artaxerxes II, Mnemon
522–486	Darius I, Hystaspes	358–338	Artaxerxes III, Ochus
486–465	Xerxes I, the Great	338–336	Arses
465–424	Artaxerxes I, Longimanus	336–330	Darius III, Codomannus
423	Xerxes II	336–323	Conquests by Alexander the Great

Seleucid

B.C.

312–280   Seleucus I, Nicator

Ptolemaic

B.C.

323–285   Ptolemy I, Lagi

280–261	Antiochus I, Soter	285–246	Ptolemy II, Philadelphus
261–246	Antiochus II, Theos		
246–226	Seleucus II, Callinicus	246–221	Ptolemy III, Euergetes
226–223	Seleucus III, Soter		
223–187	Antiochus III, the Great	221–203	Ptolemy IV, Philopator
		203–181	Ptolemy V, Theos Epiphanes
187–175	Seleucus IV, Philopator	181–145	Ptolemy VI, Philometer
175–163	Antiochus IV, Epiphanes		
163–162	Antiochus V, Eupator		
162–150	Demetrius I, Soter		
150–146	Alexander Balas		
146–142	Antiochus VI, Theos	145–117	Ptolemy VII, Euergetes II
142–138	Trypho		
138–129	Antiochus VII, Sidetes		
125–96	Antiochus VIII, Grypus	117–108	Ptolemy VIII, Soter II
116–95	Antiochus IX, Philopator	116–107	Ptolemy IX, Lathyrus

Maccabean

B.C.

167–161	Judas
161–143	Jonathan
143–135	Simon

Hasmonean

B.C.

135–104	John Hyrcanus I	76–67	Salome Alexandra
104–103	Judas Aristobulus I	67 B.C.	John Hyrcanus II
103–76	Alexander Janneus	67–63	Aristobulus II
		63	Rome conquers Judea

APPENDIX II:
DATES OF CLASSICAL AND PATRISTIC WRITERS

Ambrose of Milan (339?–397)
Amphilochius of Iconium (339?–?394)
Athanasius of Alexandria (293?–373)
Augustine (354–430)
Cassiodorus (485?–?585)
Clement of Alexandria (150?–?215)
Clement I, of Rome (30?–?99)

Cyril of Jerusalem (315?–386)
Diodorus Siculus (fl. first cent. B.C.)
Epiphanius, bishop of Constantia (315?–403)
Gregory of Nazianzus (330?–?389)
Herodotus (484?–?425 B.C.)
Hilary of Poitiers (315?–?367)
Innocent I (reigned 401–417)
Isidorus of Miletus (560–636)
Jerome (340?–420)
John of Damascus (645?–?749)
Josephus (37?–?100)
Julius Africanus (180?–?250)
Junilius (fl. ca. 542)
Leontius of Byzantium (485?–?543)
Melito of Sardis (fl. ca. 167)
Methodius of Tyre (d. ca. 311)
Nicephorus of Constantinople (758?–829)
Origen (185?–?254)
Polybius (201?–?120 B.C.)
Pseudo-Athanasius (fl. fourth cent. A.D.)
Ptolemy (fl. second cent. A.D.)
Rhabanus Maurus (780?–856)
Scylax (fl. sixth cent. B.C.)
Strabo (64 B.C.?–?A.D. 24)
Sulpicius Severus (363?–?420)
Tertullian of Carthage (160?–?230)

For brief introductions to the above, the reader may consult *The Oxford Classical Dictionary,* edited by N. G. L. Hammond and H. H. Scullard, 2d ed, Oxford: Clarendon Press, 1970. For more detailed introductions to the Church Fathers, see Berthold Altaner, *Patrology,* translated by H. C. Graef, Edinburgh and London: Nelson, 1960.

INDICES

I. AUTHORS

II. TOPICS

III. SCRIPTURAL AND OTHER REFERENCES

(Jdt)

3:14–15 of Vg   141, 143
4   47
4–16   54, 55, 70
4:1   79, 93, 142
4:1b   153
4:1–4   208
4:1–15   58
4:2   39, 57, 60 (2x), 153
4:3   39, 46, 50, 60, 161
4:4   39, 44 (3x), 51 (2x), 69, 100 n. 94,
    151, 180, 241
4:5   102, 133, 175
4:6   39, 44, 45, 47 (2x), 50 (3x),
    51 (2x), 55, 60, 61, 69, 93, 94, 101,
    102, 143, 150 (3x), 161, 173, 180, 241,
    246
4:7   44, 45, 47, 92, 101, 102, 153, 154
4:8   50, 55, 102, 149, 150, 161, 246
4:9   181
4:9–15   56
4:10   153
4:11   60, 102, 153
4:11–13   45
4:12   60, 128, 147, 153, 191, 210, 252
4:12–14   95, 99
4:13   39, 60, 63
4:14   60, 102, 149, 153
4:14–15   60
4:15   50, 94, 153
4:23   208
5   47, 57, 59, 79, 83, 163
5–6   59
5–7   237
5:1–6:11   58
5:2   50, 128, 141
5:3   162, 241
5:5   39, 59 (2x), 166
5:6–9   60, 93
5:6–19   48, 147
5:7   39
5:7–9   162
5:8   39, 48, 50, 60, 161
5:9   48
5:10   39
5:11–12   167
5:11–16   99
5:12–15 of Vg   159
5:15   241
5:15–19   95
5:16   39, 51
5:17   161
5:17–18   48 n. 7, 54, 60, 162
5:18   161
5:18–19   46, 53 n. 17
5:19   67 (2x), 162
5:20   67, 93, 96

(Jdt)

5:20–21   48 n. 7, 60, 162, 182
5:21   93
5:22   67
5:23   57, 162, 202
5:24   203
5:28–29 of Vg   166
6:2   66, 74, 75, 81, 96 n. 92 (2x), 129,
    134, 168, 169, 202, 211
6:2–4   83
6:2–5   224
6:3   95
6:3–4   169
  6:4   67
6:5   82, 168, 169, 202, 240
6:5–8   169
6:6 of Vg   96 n. 92
6:7   101, 169
6:7–8   82
6:7–9   169
6:9   103 n. 101
6:9 of Vg   103 n. 101
6:10   101
6:11   101, 150
6:12–21   58
6:14   168, 183
6:15   39 (2x)
6:16–18   95
6:16c–18 of Vg   168f.
6:17   93
6:18   168
6:19   60, 159
6:20 of Vg   168f.
6:21   60, 95, 102, 223 (2x)
7   192
7:1   133
7:1–5   58
7:1–22   95
7:2   192, 240
7:2–3   44
7:3   44 (2x), 101 (2x), 102, 143, 148,
    180, 219
7:4   57, 175
7:6   101, 102
7:6–7 of Vg   173
7:6–32   58, 99
7:7   101, 175
7:7–10   99
7:8   44, 51, 128, 141 (2x), 158
7:9   66, 101, 160
7:9–15   175
7:10   67 (2x), 202, 241
7:11   67, 102
7:12–13   150
7:15   67
7:17   133, 161

KEY TO THE TEXT

Chapter	Verses	Section
1	1–16	I
2	1–13	II
2	14–28	III
3	1–10	III
4	1–15	IV
5	1–21	V
5	22–24	VI
6	1–21	VI
7	1–32	VII
8	1–36	VIII
9	1–14	IX
10	1–17	X
10	18–23	XI
11	1–23	XI
12	1–9	XII
12	10–20	XIII
13	1–10	XIII
13	11–20	XIV
14	1–10	XIV
14	11–19	XV
15	1–7	XV
15	8–14	XVI
16	1–20	XVI
16	21–25	XVII

AA28